THE PSYCHOANALYTIC FORUM

Volume Five

A forum for the open exchange of ideas and for the broadest range of discussion of all matters pertaining to psychoanalysis—and, therefore, to the challenge of the art of living.

THE PSYCHOANALYTIC FORUM

VOL. 5

EDITED BY *John A. Lindon*, M.D.

INTERNATIONAL UNIVERSITIES PRESS　　　New York

MANUFACTURED IN THE UNITED STATES OF AMERICA.

Library of Congress Catalog Card Number: 74–10226

ISBN: 0-8236-4425-1

Introduction

TRY BROWSING IN THIS BOOK. Possibly start with an Author's Response. Or pick any discussant you find interesting. Read what he has to say. See then if you wish to read how the author responds to the criticism. Then perhaps with quickened interest you will want to read the essay which is being discussed.

This is the experience with previous volumes which many readers, both scientists and laymen, have reported to us. Some of our colleagues have confessed that they never would have read some essay we published because "it represented thinking I just don't agree with." Rather, they confide, they had eagerly turned first to the discussion remarks of someone they knew shared their poor opinion of the author's ideas, and vicariously enjoyed his demolishment. Then they raced on to read the Author's Response "to see how the poor so-and-so would try to squirm his way out of that"; and to a mixture of dismay, admiration, disappointment, and intrigue, found that the author had dealt head-on with the apparently devastating criticisms, that there was not, after all, an unbridgeable chasm separating the ideas. Now, openmindedly, they turned to read the controversial thesis in question.

This pleased us beyond belief! It was as if our fantasies, spoken and secret, from the time of conception of *The Forum* were now coming true, for this has been our aim from the very beginning.

So—browse. Please!

For appetizers try these excerpts from some of the authors' responses in this, Volume 5 of *The Psychoanalytic Forum*:

> . . . I would suggest today that the therapist's anxiety lest the patient murder him is likely to be based . . . also upon some increment of an unconscious longing on the therapist's part to be murdered by the patient.

— v

. . . I experienced fear in response to each of the three patients described at length in this paper, and I reassert the importance of the therapist's projection upon the patient of [his] unconscious—and to me quite understandable, under the circumstances—murderous feeling.

. . . I agree that we need "systematic ways of observing and recording our observations." . . . we need also a deeper understanding of the complexity of systems. Thomas Park for ten years has raised two species of flour beetles in a closed, precisely monitored universe. According to the competitive exclusion principle one species will always win out and survive; this has invariably happened. *But* Park and his co-workers have not been able to specify which species! The interaction of flour beetles with their environment is so complex that it is, so far, not possible to specify the conditions which give a competitive advantage to one species over the other. Whenever I hear a case history these days, I can't get those damn flour beetles out of my mind!

. . . my hunches . . . come from such disparate and vulnerable sources as Shakespeare's *Coriolanus*, cigarette ads, and the study of female transsexuals, those most masculine of females. . . .

. . . I do not believe, for example, that the life history of patients is useful to work with—not because a patient's history isn't important; it is simply too complex and inaccessible to scientific observation. It's a simple and obvious fact that we are in no position to observe scientifically experiences of which we are not a part. Yet we gather our histories and recapitulate entire childhoods, deductively elaborating sweeping conclusions. The issue of history-taking brings to mind Marlowe's words:

> Thou hast committed—
> Fornication? but that was in another Country:
> And, besides, the Wench is dead.

. . . Were it not for the bad blood between psychoanalysts and academic learning theorists, we might more easily absorb their work—such as that on conditioning and imprinting—and weave it into our construction of personality development. Dr. Bowlby has been one of the greatest contributors to this advent; perhaps he will agree that psychoanalysis has been more sullen than graceful about considering the work of learning theorists.

. . . The example I gave of the group of analysts in a social setting who impulsively favored capital punishment for a particularly heinous crime was intended not to justify cruelty, but rather to emphasize that we must not deny the existence of what may be a universal impulse, the need for retribution.

. . . It is hard to accept Dr. Rosenbaum's claim that a majority (he suggests 95%) of criminals find prison life preferable to the harsh deprivations of reality outside. Other than O'Henry's derelict, who preferred the jail's Christmas dinner, I have not been aware of many people battering down the Bastille gates to be admitted. His statement leaves me at a loss to understand the intense efforts of those indicted to avoid prison.

. . . Judging from my experiences of self, family, analysands, community
—including the psychoanalytic community—I have little doubt that hate
and primitive fantasies are here to stay; whether psychoanalysis and cooperative alliances and ego psychology are, I am not prepared to say. . . .

May your appetite for learning never be satisfied.

JOHN A. LINDON, M.D.

Contents

CONTENTS

Contents

Lucia E. Tower, M.D.

Leo Stone, M.D.

Author's Response

Violence in Schizophrenia

HAROLD F. SEARLES, M.D.
JEAN M. BISCO, M.D.
GILLES COUTU, M.D.
and RICHARD C. SCIBETTA, M.D.

Dr. Searles has been a Supervising and Training Analyst in the Washington Psychoanalytic Institute since 1958, and was President of the Washington Psychoanalytic Society in 1969–71. He is a Clinical Professor of Psychiatry at Georgetown University School of Medicine in Washington, D.C. and a Consultant in Psychiatry at the National Institute of Mental Health in Bethesda, Maryland. From 1963–1970 he was Consultant in Psychotherapy at the Sheppard and Enoch Pratt Hospital in Towson, Maryland. Until 1964, Dr. Searles served for nearly 15 years on the staff of Chestnut Lodge Sanitarium in Rockville, Maryland, and as Senior Psychiatrist during the last several of those years. From 1964–1973 he was Lecturer in Psychiatry at the National Naval Medical Center in Bethesda, Maryland and at the College of Physicians and Surgeons, Columbia University, New York City.

Dr. Bisco received her residency training at the Sheppard and Enoch Pratt Hospital, Towson, Maryland. She is presently an Instructor in Adolescent Psychiatry at the Johns Hopkins Hospital in Baltimore, and is a Candidate in the Baltimore/District of Columbia Psychoanalytic Institute. She is in private practice in Baltimore.

Dr. Coutu received his residency training at the Sheppard and Enoch Pratt Hospital. He is currently a Lecturer in the Department of Psychiatry at McGill University in Montreal, Canada; a Staff Member at a children's hospital, Sainte-Justine de Montréal; and is a Candidate in the Canadian Psychoanalytic Institute.

Dr. Scibetta received his residency training at the Sheppard and Enoch Pratt Hospital. He is currently a Colonel in the Medical Corps of the U.S. Air Force, and is Chairman, Department of Mental Health Services, USAF Medical Center, Wright-Patterson Air Force Base, Ohio.

Discussants

JOHN N. ROSEN, M.D.

Formerly Clinical Professor of Psychiatry at Temple University Medical School, Dr. Rosen is now President of the Doylestown Foundation and Director of Training at the Direct Psychoanalytic Institute. He has written three textbooks and numerous papers on direct psychoanalysis, and his work in the treatment of schizophrenic patients is the subject of the best-selling novel, *Savage Sleep*. In 1971 he was presented with the American Academy of Psychotherapists' Award of the Year for having invented his method of treating schizophrenia.

MILLEN BRAND

In 1937 Mr. Brand published the important exploratory novel, *The Outward Room*, portraying an early stage of the psychoanalytic treatment of psychosis. In 1968 he published *Savage Sleep*, which gave an account of Dr. John N. Rosen's therapeutic technique, Direct Analysis. Co-author of the screenplay of *The Snake Pit*, Brand has worked as a psychiatric aide and as part of a treatment team in Dr. Rosen's organization. He has had wide access to mental institutions.

ARTHUR MALIN, M.D.

On the Senior Faculty of the Los Angeles Psychoanalytic Society and Institute, Dr. Malin is also Associate Clinical Professor of Psychiatry at the University of Southern California, and Guest Consultant in Psychiatry at the University of California and at Mount Sinai Hospital, Los Angeles, where he teaches the course, "Psychoanalysis and Psychotherapy of Schizophrenia." His deep involvement in teaching and education extends to his membership on the Board of Education in the Beverly Hills Unified School District.

MARGARET LITTLE, M.R.C.S., L.R.C.P., M.B.C.PSYCH.

Ms. Little is a Member of the British Psychoanalytic Society and on the staff at Tavistock Clinic. She is the author of "Early Mothering Care and Borderline Psychotic States," and many other publications.

GUSTAV BYCHOWSKI, M.D.†

Dr. Bychowski was Clinical Professor of Psychiatry and Training Analyst at the Downstate Medical Center, Brooklyn, New York, and Preceptor in the Department of Psychiatry at the Mount Sinai School of Medicine. His many contributions to the theory and practice of psychoanalysis include his book *Psychotherapy of Psychosis*, on the problems of schizophrenia, and his paper "Congealment and Fluidity: Two Basic Patterns of the Defective Ego Dealing with Introjects," in Volume 4 of *The Psychoanalytic Forum*.

MILTON WEXLER, PH.D.

A psychoanalyst in private practice in Los Angeles, California, Dr. Wexler has also been active in research on the problem of schizophrenia since 1948, when he first received a grant for such investigations at the Menninger Clinic. A number of his publications on this subject have appeared in various journals and books.

HERBERT A. ROSENFELD, M.D.

He has been a Training Analyst and Lecturer at the Institute of Psychoanalysis in London since 1949, and has treated many psychotic and borderline patients in his private psychoanalytic practice. He is the author of the book *Psychotic States* and of numerous papers on narcissistic, depressed, and schizophrenic patients whose analyses involve difficult technical problems.

ROBERT C. BAK, M.D.

Dr. Bak is Associate Clinical Professor of Psychiatry, New York University. He is Temporary Attending Psychiatrist at the Psychiatric Division, Montefiore Hospital, New York, and is on the Faculty of the New York Psychoanalytic Institute. He is the author of "The Schizophrenic Defense Against Aggression."

ALFRED FLARSHEIM, M.D.

Dr. Flarsheim is Clinical Assistant Professor of Psychiatry at the University of Illinois; Consultant Psychiatrist at a residential treatment center, the Sonia Shankman Orthogenic School of the University of Chicago; and Member of the Attending Staff, Fox River Hospital, Chicago, Illinois. Dr. Flarsheim has published several papers on the outpatient and inpatient treatment of severe personality disorders.

Violence in Schizophrenia

HAROLD F. SEARLES, M.D.
Washington, D.C.

JEAN M. BISCO, M.D.
Baltimore, Maryland

GILLES COUTU, M.D.
Montreal, Quebec

RICHARD C. SCIBETTA, M.D.
Wright-Patterson Air Force Base, Ohio

THE PRIMARY PURPOSE OF THIS PAPER is to highlight certain aspects of the etiology and the psychotherapeutic management of violence in schizophrenic patients. Its secondary purpose is to provide examples of a kind of interviewing technique developed by the senior author which seems to have proved, in several hundreds of teaching interviews over the past several years at the Sheppard and Enoch Pratt Hospital and at a variety of other institutions, reasonably effective for teaching, for evoking diagnostic data, and, not infrequently, for catalyzing the patients' psychotherapy.

This paper was written by the senior author, and the theoretical formulations it contains are his; he will write henceforth, therefore, in the first person singular. Bisco, Coutu, and Scibetta are listed as co-authors as my way of expressing my gratitude to them for their most kind permission to include data from my teaching interviews with patients who were in therapy with them—data which largely comprise this paper and are utterly indispensable to it.

Case 1

Mr. Raymond Delaney,[1] a 17-year-old freshman in a college near Baltimore, was admitted to the Sheppard and

---

[1] A pseudonym, as is each of the names of patients described here.

Enoch Pratt Hospital after his mother discovered that he had hidden an Italian revolver, with bullets carefully selected to fit it, under his mattress, in the frankly and dispassionately admitted determination to kill a male classmate who had been "bugging" him since their high school years together in the Washington area. Both parents, from past experience, firmly believed him capable of carrying out this intention. The youth revealed, during his consultation interview with the college psychiatrist, that throughout his upbringing he had felt isolated as the smallest boy in his class, repeatedly picked on by his larger classmates, recurrently drawn toward the notion of joining a gang and shooting someone to relieve his frustration, and had become increasingly convinced that he was a juvenile delinquent who belonged in prison among the tough men whom he openly admired. He made it clear that his mind was filled with violent thoughts, and he confirmed in a chillingly matter-of-fact way his determination to kill the particular classmate whom he had selected as "my target."

The female therapist who began working with him at Sheppard soon found reason, in his paranoid glares and delighted laughter while venting his preoccupation with bloodshed, to join the parents and the college psychiatric consultant in their fear of him. It was learned that when he had been seen briefly at a community clinic at age 16, he had been found to be preoccupied with homicidal fantasies, and had left that psychiatrist with the impression that there was considerable probability that he would act upon these. The psychological report following his admission to Sheppard stated:

> . . . Very strong aggression is indicated and although the aggression appears to be absorbed to a large extent in fantasy, the poor controls implied in his impulsiveness are likely to lead to acting-out behavior that might well include homicidal attempts. . . . The patient's self-image is that of a powerful, competent individual who is prepared to demolish any opposition he may encounter. However, it is interesting to note that on the Rorschach the most frequent percept that he repeated was that of a gnat. This most insignificant insect probably represents his secret fears of his own basic feelings of inadequacy. [The patient had revealed

to his therapist a long-standing fear lest he be "stomped" by a gang of fellow students.] . . . He appears to have adopted a vindictive, vengeful attitude toward the world and seems determined to act out against this threatening environment. This youth is seen as a dangerous person and the diagnostic impression is that of a schizophrenic reaction, paranoid type. If the patient does not respond to therapy in this hospital, a case might be made to have him declared a defective delinquent and transferred to the Patuxent Institution.[2]

When I went into the one-way-mirror interview room at Sheppard for a resident-teaching interview with this youth, I was shaking in my boots. Significantly, my fear was, and remained throughout the interview, future-oriented rather than present-oriented. I had little if any fear that he would harm me during the interview itself, but great fear lest he kill me at some indeterminate time in the future when he would be armed and on the loose again, and bent on revenge for my having "bugged" him in some manner. A tall, slender youth, neither markedly attractive nor unattractive physically, he had the demeanor of a frightened kid, which was interlarded with paranoid suspiciousness (especially of the mirror), angry glares, and recurrent verbal expressions of an arrogant murderousness that was both frightening and infuriating. Much of the (tape-recorded) interview went on in a vein of my harshly bugging him. Within the first few minutes he was saying,

Mr. Delaney: . . . I wouldn't mind being out of this—hospital.
Dr. Searles: You wouldn't?
Mr. Delaney: Uh-uh.
Dr. Searles: You mean in a prison? Or what are you—speaking of?
Mr. Delaney: Just *out*, ya know [suddenly].
Dr. Searles: That is an *absurd* thing to say, isn't it? What do you mean, out? [scornfully, exasperatedly]
Mr. Delaney: Out on the outside.
Dr. Searles: You mean *before* these murderous feelings of yours are— worked out? [incredulously]
Mr. Delaney: I won't—murder anybody [scoffingly].
Dr. Searles: That was just *talk?* [ironically]
Mr. Delaney: Yeah.
Dr. Searles: You were *lacking* something to talk about, were you? You just—it was like the latest movie, only you didn't have anything else to *talk* about? Huh?
Mr. Delaney: No—yeah, I guess *so*.

[2] A Maryland state institution for mentally ill young criminal offenders.

Dr. Searles: You *do* feel we are such *idiots*, huh?—as to turn you loose, huh?—until you—are no longer—uh—likely to kill somebody, huh? You think we are that *idiotic?* [scornfully]

Mr. Delaney: *I* have a—thought: If you want to straighten me out, this isn't the place to straighten me out [nastily].

Dr. Searles: In this room, huh?

Mr. Delaney: I mean anywhere in this hospital.

Dr. Searles: Oh. [20 second pause] Well, you feel you get your *pick*, is that the idea?

Mr. Delaney: How do you mean?

Dr. Searles: Where you get straightened out, huh?

Mr. Delaney: Well, yeah.

Dr. Searles: Ya do. [i.e., "Ya do feel so."]

Mr. Delaney: I don't think that I'm that—I am not the kind of kid that could come here and be straightened out.

Dr. Searles: You are not the kind of kid that could come here and be straightened out, huh?

Mr. Delaney: I think that this is for, you know, people with other kinds of problems. You know what I mean?

Dr. Searles: You mean more *minor* problems, or what? [ironically]

Mr. Delaney: Well, I really wouldn't call it *minor*; but, ya know, it's major problems for *them*.

Dr. Searles: "Major problems for them," huh?

Mr. Delaney: Uh-huh. [several seconds' pause] You know, like one guy talks to himself all the time. Another guy cries every 10 or 15 minutes, ya know. Stuff like that. I mean, it's—

Dr. Searles: Hard to feel any relation to people like that?

Mr. Delaney: Yeah. I think *they* should be—belong here.

Dr. Searles: Whereas you feel that somebody who's got more than his share—of *homicidal* impulses should be where? I am not clear where you feel such a person should be.

Mr. Delaney: Reform school.

Dr. Searles: Reform school. You know anybody who is in reform school?

Mr. Delaney: Plenty of them.

Dr. Searles: They all seem to like it, or what?

Mr. Delaney: Oh, no. They don't *like* it; but, you know, if I had a choice of a mental hospital or a training school, I'd take a training school.

Dr. Searles: You are quite disappointed in this place, I get the impression.

Mr. Delaney: Well, I'm not too happy in it.

Dr. Searles: It hasn't so far proved to be what you had—rather thought it would be, or what?

Mr. Delaney: Why, I didn't want to come here in the first place, when I found out it was a mental hospital. But—ya know, my parents said for me to give it a try—see how I like it.

Dr. Searles: See how you like it? [in amazement]

Mr. Delaney: Yeah.

Dr. Searles: They thought the idea was that you should *like* it? [incredulous tone] Really? *Jesus Christ*, it seems so *irrelevant!* I thought you

—7

had made clear that you were a *menace* to *society*, huh? And *any* place you could go that would help you to get over being a *menace* to *society*, there would be a *hell* of a lot of reason for *gratitude* about, huh? But *they* thought on top of *that* you were supposed to *like* it or something?

Mr. Delaney: Well, they thought it could straighten me out.

Dr. Searles: They thought it could straighten you out? Now, you have been here a month?—about a month?

Mr. Delaney: Yeah. A month last Saturday.

[A couple of minutes later in the dialogue—]

Dr. Searles: Are you curious at all why you got it in your mind to—*kill* a former classmate?

Mr. Delaney: I *know* why I'd kill him.

Dr. Searles: Why?

Mr. Delaney: 'Cause he bugged me a lot.

Dr. Searles: Bugged you?

Mr. Delaney: Him and a bunch of other kids, back in high school, bugged me a lot.

Dr. Searles: Well, so—your reasoning is—what?—that you would kill him, huh?

Mr. Delaney: That *was* my reasoning; but it's not that any more.

Dr. Searles: You've got other reasons now?

Mr. Delaney: No. I wouldn't kill him now. I wouldn't kill anybody now [unconvincingly].

[Later, in making some brief reference to his mother's reminiscing about Ireland, he looked full of grief and homesickness, which I took as a portrayal of her demeanor at such times.]

Dr. Searles: Have you ever cried? [gently] Let's see what comes to mind.

Mr. Delaney: Yeah. [pause of several seconds]

Dr. Searles: Now I've got to ask you *when*, or what? You know damned well I want you to say [exasperatedly, but not roughly].

Mr. Delaney: When I was 11 years old.

Dr. Searles: Eleven years old, huh? Let's hear what your thoughts are.

Mr. Delaney: I walked on the paint. My father just painted the door and I—walked on the—uh—the painted sill. I went downstairs and he followed me and hit me in the face a couple of times, hard.

Dr. Searles: . . . And you cried? Hum? [pause of several seconds] Had you and he been on pretty good terms before that?

Mr. Delaney: Yeah [softly].

. . .

Dr. Searles: Would you rather *shoot* a number of people than *cry*, huh?

Mr. Delaney: I wouldn't do neither.

Dr. Searles: They're equally bad? [pause of few seconds] Are they? Where the hell did you get that idea? [persistently]

Mr. Delaney: I just picked it up.

Dr. Searles: From your *father*? [surprised tone] Did he see you cry? After he hit you and you cried, did you—did he see you cry? [gently, persistently]

Mr. Delaney: [affirmative mumble]

Dr. Searles: Did he show any reaction to that?

Mr. Delaney: He told me he was sorry he hit me.

Dr. Searles: Said he was sorry he hit you?

Mr. Delaney: Uh-huh.

Dr. Searles: He said it immediately after having hit you, when you started to cry?

Mr. Delaney: No. About five minutes later. [silence of more than half a minute]

Dr. Searles: What's going on in your mind in the silence? What—what do you find yourself thinking?

Mr. Delaney: I don't know. Looking at the walls.

Dr. Searles: What's your thought about them.

Mr. Delaney: They're pretty walls [sincere tone].

Dr. Searles: Nice and solid looking?

Mr. Delaney: Yeah. [pause of nearly 30 seconds]

Dr. Searles: You like walls, huh?

Mr. Delaney: I don't know. [pause of several seconds]

Dr. Searles: It's as bad to *cry* as to *kill* somebody?—huh? [tone of awe and disbelief]

Mr. Delaney: Sometimes. I don't know. I guess *not*. [long pause]

. . .

As the interview progressed, I inquired into his relationship with his mother and, forewarned by the therapist, felt that I was venturing into particularly explosive ground. At the end of the session I shook hands with him and said, "Good luck to you," to which he said, "Thank you." Hardly had those words fallen from my lips when I felt as though I had just wished him "happy hunting," and the persons viewing the interview from behind the mirror all agreed that this had clearly sounded so to them, also.

I thought of this as in part a clue to my own unconscious murderousness, projected onto the patient and pressing toward vicarious fulfillment through his carrying out his plan to kill his classmate; and in part due to my fear of him, and to my wanting, therefore, to keep his murderousness safely directed toward someone other than myself. But in one who works with such patients, who commit few if any actual violent acts but who keep one under an intensely threatened suspense lest they do so, there is, I believe, an even more basic mechanism operating: it becomes deeply important to one that the patient commit some violent act in reality, so that one can thereby differentiate between one's own murderous fantasies and his murderous act.

Until that violent act occurs, one becomes increasingly enmeshed in guilt about and fear of one's own subjectively omnipotent murderous fantasies. The patient instills so much helpless fear into one that one intensely hates him, but because one feels so much in fear and at bay, the hatred is not freely accessible to awareness; one projects it onto the patient instead. One then reaches a state where one may be told, as I was told by a charge nurse unimpressed with the potential violence of a hebephrenic man I was treating, "If Tom *should* become assaultive, he would only be acting out *your* assaultiveness." In Mr. Delaney's case, his therapist became growingly concerned lest he commit violent acts but exasperated that "he doesn't *do* anything" to give reality to her increasing concern.

I saw the therapist in monthly, tape-recorded supervision of her work with Mr. Delaney. In my first session with her, she said, "Well, you remember the session when he was with you—sort of a scared little boy. . . . But the next session [following the mirror interview] was the one when I decided I couldn't see him in the office any more, because he came and he said he hated you. I tried to pinpoint why. It was because of the remarks you made about his mother" (my commenting—not disrespectfully, in actuality—upon her having emigrated from Ireland, and my having asked about what his classmates had said to him about this). The therapist went on:

> This was one of the times when I became very aware of what his hate was really like. I had not really seen it quite so clearly until this time. And he started saying that the boys said things about his mother. He was kind of hiding his face, as he said "dirty things." I said, "Do you mean sexy things, dirty sexy things?" and then he said, "I felt so bad in high school that I thought I'd die. I thought anybody who felt that bad just had to die. He just couldn't go on."
> Dr. Searles: "Felt that *bad*." Was this the connotation [i.e., bad = evil] that he made or—
> Therapist: No. No. He was just miserable. He felt so bad that he just had to die. And then he said that he would like to get a .38 and he would just like to push it in this kid's stomach and shoot him and just watch him squirm around on the ground in his blood and just scream. He said, "I want it slow. I don't want it fast."

10 —

When he was describing this, it was very vivid. . . . I know he was unaware that I was in the room at all. He wasn't looking at me and there was as if there was a kind of—if he was away. Well, it was as if he was away. I don't know how to describe this—as if he was in the fantasy, describing what was happening.

Dr. Searles: Isn't there, in retrospect, an implication that this was just how miserable he felt? [Therapist in the background: Yes.] Was that your impression at the time?

Therapist: Well—he described the feeling of misery as vividly as the other, and one went right into the other. Then I had the tremendous feeling of hate. A quite sort of overwhelming, all-encompassing hate.

Dr. Searles: You had a feeling of hate. Now you see, that doesn't make clear where the hate was located. *You* had the feeling of tremendous hate.

Therapist: Well, I didn't have the feeling that it had a locus. It was much more of a kind of general thing. And then I had the feeling that he thought this of the boy.

Dr. Searles: But is it conceivable to you that you were hating him intensely, or that the hate was something in which you were participating?

Therapist: I can't say. Because I was, I think, more stunned because I hadn't seen this.

In the course of the therapy, the patient revealed that his parents, especially his mother, had beaten him severely when he was younger. As the therapist described it in supervision, ". . . it was the spoke out of the picket fence—that she beat him with this. At this point he looked suddenly very cold and really quite frightening and he said, 'She nearly killed me and it didn't hurt her a bit. She beat me until I was as big as she was, and then she stopped. . . . She has no conscience; therefore neither do I. How can she wonder why I'm here?' " The parents explained to the therapist that it was "only a few hits on the back of his legs with a rod"; but the mother talked of this in some detail and went off into much laughter about her son's description of being beaten.

The mother, a wan, shabbily dressed woman, who is described as looking as though she had just stepped off a boatload of immigrants, would suddenly come alive in tirades about Americans, pouring out hatred and envy of those who had more material possessions than she. Also, in an interview with the therapist, she became carried away in a psychotic kind of excited laughter in describing how omnipresent her

—11

mother-in-law used to be during visits to the marital home. "She used to follow us all over the house . . . right up to the bed. About the only place we were ever alone was in bed, and his mother used to try to get in there, too."

She had worked as an aide in another psychiatric hospital, and was quick to relegate her son to the category of non-persons such as she considered mentally ill patients to be. When told that her son had come not to want the usual week-end visit from his parents, she immediately observed, "They are hopeless when they refuse to see their parents." At one point in giving the history to the therapist, she suddenly appeared threatened and said, "I'm not going to say any more. I already know from experience [at the sanitarium where she had worked years before] . . . that if they find out you talked about them, they really rip. They tear up the walls . . ." This latter comment, tying in with her son's comment about "the walls" during my interview with him, seemed to spring in part from her fear, and his, at an unconscious level, lest the wall between (meaning the distinction between) fantasy and reality be completely destroyed.

Also, he had said to me, in explanation of why his school-mates' jibes about his mother had so greatly infuriated him, "No one likes anybody to make fun of a person's mother." It was as though he felt his status as a person to be at stake—a *person* rather than something less than a person, as his mother seemed so ready to conclude.

As more came to light about the mother, it appeared that his own smiling and looking happy when he fell to talking about stabbing, shooting, and other forms of bloodshed was in part due to his feeling happily immersed in identification with his mother, who so often in his upbringing would go off unreachably into her private, apparently comparably violent, fantasies.

As the treatment relationship developed, one of his per-sistent reactions to the therapist consisted in his perceiving her as an obstacle to his having unlimited privileges, unlim-ited freedom. In this regard, it appeared that he was reacting to her much as his fantasy-ridden mother had reacted to him as an unwanted child, an obstacle the reality of which recurrently prevented her being freely and continually immersed in exciting, violent fantasies. He had much reason to feel that it was his own aliveness, his own existence, which accounted for his mother's more customary demeanor of depressed deadness. It was as though any sign of his own aliveness interrupted, did violence to, her immersion in her fantasy world; this world was suddenly destroyed each time she had to attend to him. By the same token, he was evidently given to feel that, in subsequent relationships, only if he were violent or threatening violence would he be, in the view of other persons, anything more than part of the woodwork—as if only by that means could he make the supposedly oblivious others become aware of his existence.

The excerpts from my interview with him suggest a poignant severing of his efforts to identify with his father as a male. In addition, the parents described with amusement how much it had upset him when the father, at home, would teasingly walk with the hip-swinging, mincing gait of a girl. In the words of the therapist, "If Raymond tried to tell him how much it bothered him, his father would say no, it didn't really bother him." Additional data suggested that when the patient attempted to find in the father a real person with whom to relate, such as the fantasy-ridden, depressed mother could not adequately provide, he was faced with the threat of becoming the rapist of the father, as the agent of the mother's phallic strivings.

These historical data about the father linked up with my reaction upon learning one morning, on my weekly visit to Sheppard a few weeks following my interview with this patient, at a time when I was prominent among the persons whom he was hating, that he had just escaped from the hospital. I had innumerable frightened fantasies that he would come to my private office or my home and shoot me. Other data, with which I need not burden the reader, inescapably made me see that, however much basis in reality there was for this fear, my own unconscious passive homosexual longings had been aroused by my interview with him; I could triangulate, although not actually feel, the desire to be sexually "shot" by him. I shall never forget the relief I felt, late that evening on my return home, to see on the table inside the front door a note from my wife, conveying a telephone message which had come from the Director of In-Patient Services while I was driving home: "Delaney is back home safe with his mother."

The subsequent course of Delaney's treatment gave little cause for amusement, however. He was brought back promptly to the hospital by his parents and subsequently committed. But despite much skillful work by his therapist, who provided a rare combination of strength, courage, and ability to perceive and relate to his dependent needs, Delaney's violence in action became sufficiently serious so that the staff were no longer divided between those who regarded this as a real and frightening problem and those who scoffed at it as being nothing but a cloak worn by a frightened boy. For example, he made a pre-planned and serious attack, from behind, on his male administrator one day when the administrator was walking down the corridor toward morning rounds. He hit the administrator hard, and it required two or three attendants to drag the patient back into the seclusion room. On another occasion, he made a similar attack upon a male patient, and four attendants were needed to get him back into the seclusion room. Incidentally, one evidence of his poor distinction between fantasy and reality was his way of raging to the therapist about the administrator. He would say to her, *"Look at Edwards* [the administrator] . . .", just as though Dr. Edwards were a tangible presence with them in the therapist's office.

As the months went by it became necessary for the therapist to see him in a cold wet-sheet pack. After two such sessions he again ran away, was found and taken by his parents to another sanitarium, and ran away from there and joined the Marines without divulging his psychiatric background. Our last bit of information about him was a telephone call to the therapist from an official at an Army prison, stating that this man had stabbed a fellow Marine three times,

14 —

that his victim was barely surviving, and that an investigation was under way to determine whether Delaney was mentally competent to stand trial. The therapist and I agreed that he had finally committed the violent act which we both had known he eventually would. Again I want to emphasize the aspect of relief, of certainty, which this clearly afforded me and, I felt, the therapist also. It was as though the distinction between the patient's actualized murderousness and our own murderous fantasies and feelings was now clear beyond anyone's questioning it.

The experience with this patient highlights a number of psychodynamic aspects of violence in schizophrenia. His non-differentiation between the human and non-human, animate and inanimate ingredients of his perceptual world, this non-differentiation being an unconscious defense against otherwise unbearably ambivalent feelings of hatred and love, is recurrently in evidence. He expresses chillingly dispassionate murderousness toward "my target," as if his classmate were an inanimate thing, comparable with the views his mother expresses of psychiatric patients and the view she presumably had of him in his childhood. The psychologist finds in the Rorschach evidence that the patient has an unconscious self-percept as a gnat; and the therapist finds that he reacts to her, in part, as an essentially non-human obstacle to his having unlimited privileges.

His appreciation of the useful limit-setting, differentiating, function of my confrontation of his murderousness is expressed, in a displaced fashion, by his sincere appreciation of the "pretty walls" of the room. Such walls between fantasy and reality, and between herself and him, his mother evidently feared he would destroy ("They tear up the walls").

Both the therapist and I, in relating to him, evidently had mobilized in ourselves such intensely conflicting feelings of love and of murderous hatred that a regressive de-differentiation occurred in our respective ego-functioning, such that we attributed to the patient our own murderous hatred, and unconsciously hoped that he would give vicarious expression to our own violence, so as to restore the wall between him and

—15

us. More broadly put, such a patient evokes in one such intensely conflicting feelings that, at an unconscious level, one's ego-functioning undergoes a pervasive de-differentiation: one loses the ability deeply to distinguish between one's self and the patient, and between the whole realms of fantasy and reality. Thus the patient's committing of a violent act serves not only to distinguish between one's own "fantasied" violence and his "real" violence but, more generally, serves to restore, in one, the distinction between the whole realms of fantasy and outer reality.

Case 2

Mr. Leonard Myers, a 25-year-old salesman, had been hospitalized repeatedly in a series of institutions, over the preceding eight years, for chronic paranoid schizophrenia. He had been fired from various jobs because of his belligerence. At home he had become increasingly abusive verbally, and increasingly slovenly, lying about naked. His father had threatened repeatedly to throw him out of the house, but his overprotective mother each time had intervened. She herself had required psychiatric hospitalization at one period, and both she and her son had received electroshock treatment, at different times, from the same psychiatrist.

The patient had come to spend several days and nights consecutively in pool rooms, and in his grandiose belligerence had gotten himself beaten up there. He had begun driving recklessly during the preceding year: "I closed my eyes—I was going about 80 miles per hour—I closed my eyes and counted to ten. And I opened them and was kind of surprised when nothing happened."

His first psychotic episode had occurred at age 17. Two years later he married a girl during her second pregnancy by him. (For her first pregnancy they had· obtained an illegal abortion.) This pregnancy went to term and a daughter was born. While the daughter was still in infancy, he became violently angry at her and attacked her, slamming her against her pillow several times and causing serious neurological injury which subsequently required more than one brain operation and which left a permanent strabismus in the child, now six years of age. His wife meanwhile separated from him, and retained custody of the daughter.

It was evident that his parents had allowed him, figuratively, to get away with murder. He idealized his father as a great family man, a strong and good provider, in contrast to his own sorry record as a father, but said that "he gives in too much to my mother, who coddles me." He said that, for example, he had just heard from his mother that she had prevailed upon the father to buy him a new car when he left Sheppard. It was evident that the overprotective mother, whose covert malevolence the patient had particular resistance to discovering in the course of his therapy, had never permitted him to find firm limits in his father. In this family setting, which so hindered the development of firm object relationships and thus the achievement of individuation on his part, it was evident that just as his parents did not exist as firm external objects for him, neither did he for them. Poignantly, he once recalled to his therapist that the only time either of his parents had ever turned to him for his opinion about some family matter was when his father consulted him as to whether the mother should receive electroshock treatment.

The report of the diagnostic conference on his admission to Sheppard states:

> . . . He instantly revealed disorganized thought and speech, and during the entire interview remained rather restless, apprehensive, impulsive, aggressive, obviously trying to conceal murderous rage. His paranoid trend . . . was obvious, although not systematized. Inasmuch as this interview seemed to induce great fear in the patient, it was discontinued after a few minutes.

Seven months after Mr. Myers's admission, at the staff conference in which the therapist presented his history prior to my interview with him, I felt an atmosphere of unusually electric tension; it was as if all of us present were acutely aware that this was an unusually frightening, formidably ill patient. I myself felt quite afraid of going into the one-way mirror viewing room for my interview with him. When he came in he proved to be a burly, highly volatile-looking man who spoke in an impulsive, staccato fashion, with many liquidly restless physical movements. His eyes were narrow, shifty, and blinking rapidly; he seldom looked at me.

I had felt much ambivalence as to whether to shake hands, at the outset, with this man who had come so near to killing his infant daughter, but I did so, with little or no warmth, when he walked in. Throughout the interview I was unaware, as I realized later, of any rage, condemnation, or contempt toward him, and instead sat passively in my armchair.

Now, to present some passages beginning about one-third of the way through the interview:

> Dr. Searles: How did your parents react to this incident of your—injuring your daughter—
> Mr. Myers [quickly interjects]: They didn't know about it.
> Dr. Searles: —damned near killing your daughter?
> Mr. Myers [again quickly]: They didn't know about it.
> Dr. Searles: They didn't know about it?
> Mr. Myers: I told my father and he said, "It is not true. You didn't do it." He doesn't want me to think I did and I know I did.
> Dr. Searles: He would rather you would be crazy, huh, on that score, and not know reality?
> Mr. Myers: He would rather me feel that I didn't—Yeah—that I didn't know reality that it happened, and I *know* it happened. I'm *sure* it happened [tone of healthy self-assertiveness].
> Dr. Searles: Well, but it's—what?—as though *he* can't bear to think that it happened?
> Mr. Myers: Maybe that's it. I am not sure. It could be that.
> Dr. Searles: Have you noticed that in him?
> Mr. Myers: This was a couple of years ago. I don't really remember. He loved my—my daughter.
> Dr. Searles: You are putting that in the past tense.
> Mr. Myers: Yes, because he said he gave her up because she is not my baby anymore.
> Dr. Searles: Not yours, or his?
> Mr. Myers: His. That's just—the way he talks. He knows it is not [embarrassed, brief laugh]. What I mean is—when the marriage broke up—uh, we used to go over there—*before* the marriage broke up we used to go over there twice a month on Sundays. He was very fond of my *daughter*. And after the marriage broke up we weren't going over there and—my father asked to see her one time, and take her out and buy her some clothes. And my daughter—and my wife said no, so he just gave up trying to see her, said, "She's not my baby any more."
> ... [Then, a minute or so later—]

Dr. Searles: Your mother—did she show any reaction to being told of it by you, or whatever? What did she say? About your daughter—

Mr. Myers: I don't think I told her. Just my father.

Dr. Searles: Why didn't you tell your mother?

Mr. Meyers: I don't know. I didn't tell *anybody*—I mean, it was such a serious thing. One day—I was living in my parents' house for six months without working or doing anything and I just felt guilty and I decided to tell my father what happened. He wouldn't believe it and wouldn't let me try—to make me not believe it, that it happened. But I know it did. I think my wife knows it—that it did, too.

Dr. Searles: You think she does?

Mr. Myers: I think she knows but I never told her. I think the doctor might have told her because she was beaten about the head and there were bruises. This is just an assumption; I don't know—whether she —whether she knows *I* did it or not. . . . It didn't show up in convulsions and spitting up of the milk until two months later. . . . She was about two months old when I picked her up by the neck and banged her head on the pillow.

Dr. Searles: You say it as though it *still* in a way feels kind of *good*. Do you feel you *would* like to do that with *some*body?

Mr. Myers: No—yes, *some*body.

Dr. Searles: Well, anybody come to mind?

Mr. Myers: Yes, one person. Corbin [another patient on his ward]. . . . I feel hostile towards him. . . . I have had the desire to—to—to, uh, hit him in the mouth. I never have. I can control my anger lately much better than I used to.

Dr. Searles: You haven't noticed the slightest irritated feeling toward *me* so far?

Mr. Myers: Yes, I have; a little bit.

Dr. Searles: How does it—make itself felt? What are your thoughts or feelings?

Mr. Myers: There *are* no thoughts right now. I am just trying to get as much in as we can. I don't think it is important whether I like you or dislike you. I don't even know you.

Dr. Searles: You don't? How long does it take you—

Mr. Myers [interrupting]: I'll probably never see you again.

Dr. Searles: Probably so [agreeing]—and—I must—I will be as candid as I *can* be: frankly, I *hope so*. To be quite honest with you, you kind of frighten me. . . . You strike me as an extremely impatient guy. Do you feel you are?

Mr. Myers: Yes.

[A minute or so later, after further conversation—]

Dr. Searles: You didn't feel hurt when I said frankly I hope I don't see you again?

Mr. Myers: I was a little surprised [tone of covert disapproval].

Dr. Searles: Doesn't sound like a very big person—for me to say that?

Mr. Myers: No.

Dr. Searles: Doesn't? Is either of your parents afraid of you?

Mr. Myers: I don't think so [confident tone].

— 19

Dr. Searles: The idea has never occurred to you, though, has it?

Mr. Myers: Probably has.

Dr. Searles: You sound as though it hasn't crossed your mind.

Mr. Myers: I say it probably has occurred to me. I don't think it's a big problem [offhand tone]. I'm not the kind of person who goes around hurting other people. I did it once, and uh—I think the reason was I was afraid—afraid to face responsibility. I wanted to get rid of what [n.b. as though referring to something inanimate] was making me feel obligated to work every week—to be up tight about everything. [There was much evidence, from other portions of this interview and elsewhere, that throughout the patient's life the father had been a highly compulsive worker; it appears here as though the patient found intolerable the only kind of father-identity which he had known.] [Then, after a minute or so of further dialogue—]

Mr. Myers: . . . I *am* curious why you said you hoped you would never see me again. You said you were afraid of me. I can't see why you would be afraid of me. I don't understand it.

Dr. Searles: It happened *once* that you wanted to kill your daughter. It seems like a completely isolated instance, huh?

Mr. Myers: Yes, it does. Because I haven't done anything since then—violent, physical. This was—five years ago.

Dr. Searles: . . . Well, you come in—with somewhat of a—of a bully look about you. You look in better physical shape than *I* feel; you look, uh—you are certainly younger. I think I would have a difficult time with you in a physical tussle—see? You're *impatient* as all hell. You strike—you strike me as very *volatile*—impatient and volatile. These are *some* of the things about you. Then I may be *projecting* onto you some of my *own* problems because I was very afraid I would kill [a member of my parental family] . . . so that I may be afraid of *myself* still, more than I thought, and I may be taking it out on you. . . .

By the end of the interview, some ten minutes later, each of us had come to feel so close to the other that we mutually expressed the hope that we *would* see one another again. I found myself feeling deeply moved at the end of the interview.

In the conference-discussion period following the interview, the therapist reported that he had felt jolted by my telling Mr. Myers that hoped I would not see him again because I was afraid of him. This set the therapist to wondering why he himself had never felt afraid to be in a room with the patient, and he went on to wonder whether he had promoted unwittingly a dependent relationship on the patient's part such as the overprotective, subtly malevolent mother had with him, as a protection against the patient's violence.

20 —

This interview proved, in retrospect, one of the most memorable teaching interviews I have ever had, in being utilized by both patient and therapist in a highly effective way during the subsequent course of their work together. Two subsequent interviews at yearly intervals, as well as occasional informal reports to me from the therapist in the interim, substantiated this. The patient is now living outside the hospital, while continuing to work with the same therapist.

The interview which I have detailed seemed to have helped appreciably to undermine the therapist's unconscious denial of his fear of the patient, and thus to enable the continuing fact of the patient's violent urges, and his own fear of them, to be explored in the psychotherapy. Listening to the tape of my interview with Mr. Myers I was amused at my own uncharacteristically patient and soothing manner. I have found over and over again, in my own and in my colleagues' work with such patients, that one's fear is for a long time largely dissociated, but that this dissociated and deepening fear causes an increasing, subtle, and unrecognized constriction of one's freedom to speak and to feel. One's own unconscious murderous rage at the patient for thus throttling one's freedom becomes projected upon him. One then tends to feel only that one is afraid of him, not of one's own quite unavailable murderous rage toward him. Thus one inevitably comes to behave toward him over a prolonged period as did his subtly malevolent mother.

One can surmise that it was just such a malevolently constricting, infantilizing, and infantile mother whom the infant daughter had represented to the patient in his nearly fatal attack upon her. Further, this act, stigmatizing him as so terribly bad a father, enabled him to preserve some little portion of his own long-cherished image of his father as being relatively at least a good father, rather than seeing him as a father with his own problems of unconscious destructiveness. Surely it was not coincidental that this father's successful and steady work-functioning had gone on in a context of either the mother's or the son's having to be hospitalized repeatedly for mental breakdowns.

Case 3

The following brief report is presented in order to highlight two psychodynamic points which I consider to be of general validity among schizophrenic patients: first, the degree to which rigid superego standards preclude subjective aliveness; and second, the function of violence in providing the patient with a subjective realization of his own aliveness, as a relief from the superego-enforced subjective deadness which customarily grips him.

Today at —— Clinic I saw an ambulatory schizophrenic young man who had had two hospitalizations, the most recent of them ending only about two months ago. He described his having been shot at, while over at —— University, and said that he had a mark on his thigh to prove it. I regard this experience as having been clearly delusional, nonetheless. He said that because his life was being threatened, he had pretended to be violently drunk in order to get placed within the refuge of a hospital. He had succeeded, as he described it, in getting himself taken to D. C. General Hospital, but upon admission there had been "jumped" by five male attendants, after they had had him take his clothes off. He evidently still has the delusion that they were bent on raping him. He knows karate, and this proved to be one of the most tense interviews I have ever had before a group of residents. There were a number of times during the interview when I felt it essential to be very casual lest he jump me, and it was evident that he was an extremely threatened person, by reason of his projection of both his murderous and homosexual feelings.

To this man violence evidently means throwing off a subjective feeling of deadness. He said of his mother, "She is alive," and there was momentarily a tremendous aliveness in his tone as he said that. It was clear that his view of her is in marked contrast to his own experience of himself. He is an extremely rigid person with tremendously rigid superego standards. His therapist's father died very recently,[3] and in terms of this patient's superego, he feels that any person must feel shock and grief at the death of his father—although it is very evident that, if anything, he himself tended to feel only vengeful satisfaction at the death of his own hated father two years ago. Secondly, according to his superego standards, a "mature man" would not reveal outwardly anything of his grief under these circumstances; thus, he expressed the conviction that when he does see his therapist next, his therapist will be feeling grief but will not be showing any of it. These are but two examples of many which

[3] The patient had already been informed of this. The therapist, one of the residents, was therefore out of town at this point, and I was exploring with the patient his feeling about the death of his therapist's father, the consequent absence of the therapist now, and the prospect of his seeing the therapist upon the latter's return.

pointed up the tremendous rigidity of this man's superego, which precludes any real aliveness. It was apparent that he experienced a submerged kind of excitement when talking about the various things (a mixture of reality and delusion) that have happened to him; at one level, these apparently had the quality of a lively, exciting playfulness.

He was an extremely well-dressed young man of perhaps 30 who, when I first saw him, I immediately assumed to be an obsessive-compulsive individual. Rather soon, however, it became evident that I was dealing with a schizophrenic person. The look on his face combined grief, of a locked-in sort typical of schizophrenic patients, locked in with a great deal of repressed rage, vindictive satisfaction (as for example over his father's death), and intense contempt toward people, whom he seemed clearly to equate with insects or germs.

As an example of his apparent absence of conscious emotion, he seemed genuinely unaware of feeling, or of having ever felt, any *fear*, except for once—he had been afraid when the police had come to his apartment to investigate his pretended drunkenness, for they were armed. But it was evident throughout the interview that he is filled with dissociated fear and, in fact, terror.[4] He stated that he had had infectious hepatitis prior to his first psychiatric hospitalization, "and the sheets were yellow," he added, as though by way of emphasizing how severe the jaundice had been. In essence, he is a man who is so convinced that to feel any fear is by definition cowardice—figuratively speaking, yellowness—that he has been unaware of any but the tiniest bit of the tremendous fear that clearly fills him, and instead, with hallucinatory exaggeration, may have perceived the sheets as being literally[5] and completely yellow.

Case 4

Mrs. Joan Glaser, a 25-year-old mother of two living children (a daughter of five and a half and a son of three years), had been admitted to the hospital five months previously after having drowned, two days before, her third child, an infant daughter two months of age. Mrs. Glaser herself was the younger of two siblings, with a brother about three years older than herself. After the births of each of the two older children she had had a postpartum depression lasting a few months. This third child had not been wanted by either her or her husband. Immediately upon her return home following

[4] It appears that a schizophrenic individual may experience the *outer* world as being intensely *threatening* without feeling that he possesses *fear within* himself. As so frequently happens in schizophrenic experience, the disturbance is perceived as being entirely *outside* him.

[5] I do not doubt that there was a nucleus of literal reality in his perception of the sheets, but his tone and manner in describing them conveyed an hallucinatory exaggeration as well.

the delivery, she had started voicing such thoughts as, "It seems that I have no more energy left for that child. . . . It is too much. I am tied down. I had forgotten how bad it was to have a baby. I cannot cope. Let's put the baby away for a while. I love the baby but I cannot take care of her." She tried to persuade a neighbor to take the baby, explaining that she wanted to give her away for good. Also, she would say, "I cannot raise her. I love all children. I cannot harm her; I love her." Once in a while she would go into the baby's room and stare at her for a long time without moving or speaking. She was also seen staring into space at times. Her mother-in-law, who had been called into the home by the husband to help take care of the children and the home at the time of the delivery, remained there.

On returning from work one evening, the husband got the impression, from the way his agitated wife was behaving, that she had smothered the baby with a pillow. She had not; but he was now sufficiently concerned to have her hospitalized. She was then hospitalized, elsewhere; but to his surprise, he received word after only three days that she was now all right, and she was discharged to her home. Not long thereafter, while giving the infant a bath, the patient "blacked out," and when she came to, the infant had drowned in the tub.

At the time of this interview, the patient was persistently expressing to her therapist her conviction that she was now well and able to return to her husband and her two living little children, and it was my impression that all concerned, husband and hospital staff alike, were more or less inclined to leave hands off and let it go at that. I sensed in myself, and surmised to be present in my colleagues at the residents' teaching conference, the primitive fear and awe which, I felt, are aroused in anyone by a mother who has killed her own child; I had never interviewed such a person before.

Her diagnosis at the time of her admission was schizophrenic reaction, schizo-affective type. I found her to be a woman of average size, not openly psychotic now but with a relatively impassive, detached, and somewhat childlike, sheltered de-

meanor. I shall now give some of the exchanges which occurred during our half-hour recorded interview before a one-
way viewing mirror:

> Mrs. Glaser: . . . my father is still living. He is quite old—in fact, he is
> 80 years old. He is an inspiration to me.
> Dr. Searles: To live long?—an inspiration to live long?
> Mrs. Glaser: Well, it's amazing how long he *has* lived and stayed in such
> good health. Before the baby was born—I assume [said as an aside, in
> the dispassionate tone of an autopsy report] you know I'm here partially
> due to the death of the infant.
> Dr. Searles: Yeah—I would say *primarily;* that was my thought. Yeah.
> Before then, what?—before the birth of the baby—?
> Mrs. Glaser: Yes, my father had a stroke and this was quite a blow to me.
> Dr. Searles: He'd always been so well?
> Mrs. Glaser: Yes. He'd always been well. He'd never been sick, and of
> course it was—I couldn't go to him because the baby was due to be
> born too—you know, too soon for me to go to him. I—I know the
> mistakes I made now. I—after the—baby was born I had the post-
> partum blues again, and—we learned we were going to be moved and
> somehow it was too much for me, I guess, and I—relied on my mother-
> in-law and leaned on everybody too much. I think I was—almost
> making them sick by being so—un—able to—control myself and my
> emotions.
> Dr. Searles: When you said you relied on your mother-in-law I kinda
> got some impression that perhaps you feel she let you down?
> Mrs. Glaser [quickly and protectively]: No, not at all. She helped as
> much as she possibly could.
> Dr. Searles: Well, she didn't keep you from murdering your baby, you
> know [bluntly, and by way of reminder]. I don't know whether you
> feel she let you down in *that* sense, huh?
> Mrs. Glaser: Why did you use the word "murder" my baby? [tone of
> surprise, but much softer, more personal, than when she had spoken
> of "the death of the infant"]
> Dr. Searles: Because I understood this is what happened—that you
> drowned your infant, huh? [in tone of stating the obvious] I mean,
> maybe there's some more euphemistic way of putting it; but isn't this
> the fact?
> Mrs. Glaser [subdued tone]: Yes.
> Dr. Searles: Well, this is why I used it. Why do you ask why I used it?
> [in tone of vigorously consolidating this newly won territory]
> Mrs. Glaser: The word just—
> Dr. Searles: "Murder?" You prefer not to think in those terms?
> Mrs. Glaser: I can never forget it [weeping].
> Dr. Searles: Well, do you feel that your mother-in-law let you down in
> that sense, perhaps?—she didn't prevent you from doing it?
> Mrs. Glaser: Well, I asked her to take the other children for a while,
> and I should have taken the walk with them instead.

Dr. Searles: Then *she* would have murdered the baby, or—?

Mrs. Glaser: No, no; I hardly think so.

Dr. Searles: It wouldn't be like her to do that?

Mrs. Glaser: No.

Dr. Searles: She's a very kind person.

Mrs. Glaser [quickly]: Very kind—she's a very kind person and my husband is a very kind person [tone of subdued resentment and bitterness].

Dr. Searles: Sort of infuriatingly kind, or what?

Mrs. Glaser: No.

Dr. Searles: Have you wondered, for example, why your husband hasn't killed *you?*

Mrs. Glaser: Regardless of what happened he still loves me very much [as though reciting something].

Dr. Searles: How does *that* make you feel?—have ya any idea?

Mrs. Glaser: Well, it makes me feel good to know that under the circumstances he still loves me [still as though reciting].

Dr. Searles: Does it cause any other feelings, besides feeling good?

Mrs. Glaser: Well, it—it helps to know that somebody still cares [weeping].

Dr. Searles: He seems to be the only one who still does?

Mrs. Glaser: No, my mother-in-law still cares—my two children still care.

Dr. Searles: How do you know? You say you haven't seen them?

Mrs. Glaser: I talked with them on the phone.

Dr. Searles: They are aware that you killed their—?

Mrs. Glaser: No, I'm quite sure they—don't know that—I don't know what they think.

Dr. Searles: You don't know what your husband or mother-in-law has told them? You have a daughter and son, right?—the older one is the daughter.

Mrs. Glaser: Yes.

Dr. Searles: Your son is about three and a half?

Mrs. Glaser: Yes. My oldest daughter was six Friday.

Dr. Searles: I notice this constellation—of a daughter, and then a son, and then an infant daughter you had. This infant daughter then had a brother three years older than she?

Mrs. Glaser: Yes.

Dr. Searles: And you have a brother five years older—is that right?

Mrs. Glaser: No; my brother is about three and a half years older than I am.

Dr. Searles: Three and a half? Ya see, I was wondering about the repeating of history thing—whether this infant daughter of yours represented something of yourself in terms of births: girl baby born into a home where this brother—huh?

Mrs. Glaser: No. I just didn't want to admit to myself that I was as sick as I was.

Dr. Searles: And nobody else perceived it?—nobody else perceived that you were?

Mrs. Glaser: Yes, they did, but—uh—and my husband—

Dr. Searles [interrupts with intensity]: I wonder how in *God's* name, then, they let you stay at home?

Mrs. Glaser: I don't know.

Dr. Searles: Have you ever *wondered?*—have you ever *wondered* why?

Mrs. Glaser: Well, I guess they didn't realize I was quite as sick as I was.

Dr. Searles: You think they still realize it, or that they still fail to realize it?

Mrs. Glaser: I don't know if it is possible to get 100% well again. I feel like I'm well again [pleading but unconvincing tone].

Dr. Searles: You feel you *understand* why you killed your daughter, is that right? I mean, to *me* at least, this would be the primary thing—the test, really, of whether you're *well*, you see, and not to be "back-out-with-your-family" [as though to say just for the sake of being so, as a matter of form]. Have you thought in those terms?—have you thought that that would be a criterion of whether you are well, whether it's safe for you to be at home?

Mrs. Glaser: Yes [small, unconvincing voice].

Dr. Searles: You have thought in those terms? So, you feel you are well [ironically]. What's your explanation?—how do you account for your having killed your infant daughter? [persistently]

Mrs. Glaser: I don't know how I could have done such a thing [in a voice once again broken by weeping].

Dr. Searles: Um, you aren't *well*, isn't it?—isn't that the fact?

Mrs. Glaser: I *wasn't* at the time, no.

Dr. Searles: You don't know how you could have done such a thing.

Mrs. Glaser: I think about her *constantly*; I think about her *constantly*.

Dr. Searles: Think about her living, or dead, or—how do you think of her?

Mrs. Glaser: I think of her as—as—something that was very lovely that I couldn't see at the time [voice very broken with weeping].

Dr. Searles: "*Some thing*"—you think of her as something?

Mrs. Glaser: As a little—

Dr. Searles: [interrupts]—that was lovely.

Mrs. Glaser: [weeping] I'm sorry, Doctor [apologetically].

Dr. Searles: Do you feel it is an *offense* to a psychiatrist to *weep* in his presence about these matters, or what? Why do you say you are sorry? I don't get that [exasperatedly]. Do you want some of this stuff, huh? [holding out some Kleenex to her]

Mrs. Glaser: No; that's all right. I am very sorry.

Dr. Searles: You say "something," ya see, and I wondered if *that* has some significance: it was hard for you to grasp or to feel that she was a living person, a living creature, a living creature. Do you suppose if you felt she was a *thing*—

Mrs. Glaser [interrupts]: Oh me, I didn't mean *something*. I meant she's—she was a little doll—she was a very pretty baby.

Dr. Searles: "She was a little doll." A doll is a thing, is it not?

Mrs. Glaser: That's right.

Dr. Searles: Is there perhaps no significance in the words you use, or *is* there maybe something that you and I can both—learn, you see—from the way it comes out—"something beautiful"—"beautiful doll"?

—huh? [persistently; then, turning away from this effort—] When you were a child, did you have a doll, or—?

Mrs. Glaser: Yes, I did [comfortable, unpressured tone now].

Dr. Searles: Do you have any memories of playing with your doll?

Mrs. Glaser: Yes, I do.

Dr. Searles: Could I hear—let's hear whatever comes to your mind.

Mrs. Glaser: Well, I can remember—playing with a doll like you would a real baby—and bathing the doll and—although I usually—didn't use water; I just—used a washcloth or something like a sponge bath.

Dr. Searles: Usually didn't use water, huh? Any idea why not?

Mrs. Glaser: Well, when I was little the dolls weren't made of the same material as they are now and you couldn't really put them in water. [pause of several seconds; then, in slightly broken voice—] I guess I should feel very fortunate that I have the second chance to go back home.

Dr. Searles: Had that thought not occurred to you before? [gentle tone]

Mrs. Glaser: Well, I guess I—feel like maybe I don't *deserve* to go back [crying heartbrokenly now; this is the one point in the interview when, in playing back the tape, I felt like weeping in compassion for her; I do not recall whether I felt so during the interview itself].

[A minute or two later on in the dialogue—]

Dr. Searles: . . . Let's see, . . . you mentioned your mother died—she died in '57—do you remember *her* as being a kind person, much like your—mother-in-law?

Mrs. Glaser: Yes, she was very kind—they both were alike in some respects,—that they were—uh—very much interested in the house, it had to be just so all of the time.

Dr. Searles: "They both were"—you mean your mother and father?

Mrs. Glaser: Uh-huh. My father was a building contractor. He was very good—he was a perfectionist on how he built his homes. [A few minutes later in the interview—] You see, after she [i.e., the now-dead daughter] was born I went to—uh, I was doing fine and then—I started this postpartum blues again, and my husband had talked with my—doctor who had delivered the baby and—uh, they prescribed some medicine for me—but it was—too powerful and when it wore off I would be twice as nervous as before,—so I stopped taking the medicine—I still had bad thoughts towards the baby or myself—either one.

Dr. Searles: "Still had bad thoughts"—you hadn't mentioned to me that you had found yourself having what you call "bad thoughts" toward the baby?

Mrs. Glaser: Yes.

Dr. Searles: —and toward yourself?

Mrs. Glaser: Yes.

Dr. Searles: When—uh, prior to the baby's birth—or—?

Mrs. Glaser: No. Afterwards.

Dr. Searles: "Bad thoughts"—what do you refer to?—"bad thoughts?"

Mrs. Glaser: Well, just the fact we had another baby and I found out we were going to be moving—leaving the area, and it was a question of leaving—leaving our friends behind—

Dr. Searles: Are those bad thoughts?

Mrs. Glaser: No, *that* isn't bad thoughts; but I felt life would be much simpler without the baby.

Dr. Searles: Well, was that a bad thought? [disbelievingly]

Mrs. Glaser: *Yes*, I think it *was*—a very *sick* thought [emphatically].

Dr. Searles: Realistic in a way, wasn't it?

Mrs. Glaser: My husband put me in a hospital and I—*thought* I was all right and I *left*—that was the mistake I made.

Dr. Searles: Now wait a minute—your husband—you would doubt that your *husband* would ever permit *him*self to have such a thought at that time, for instance,—how much simpler life would have been had this baby not been born?

Mrs. Glaser: No; he didn't have thoughts like that [emphatically, and clearly resenting my question].

Dr. Searles: How do you know? [persistently]

Mrs. Glaser: I know he loved her very much.

Dr. Searles: You can read his mind?

Mrs. Glaser: No; but he *told* me he did, and I *know* he did [insistently, vehemently, and pleadingly, as though I were trying to convince her that her own father did not really love her as a child].

Dr. Searles: Well, I *still* question—

Mrs. Glaser [interrupts]: He wanted to take care of her and he liked to see her.

Dr. Searles: I still question whether you *know* what is in a person's *thoughts*, from what they *say* or the way they *behave*. You see, you have been speaking to me today about what you call bad thoughts, huh? But you—feel confident your husband would never have such—such a thought, huh?

Mrs. Glaser: No [confirmatively].

Dr. Searles: Hard to imagine that he would ever have a thought about how much simpler life would be, if he didn't have you or any of the children?

Mrs. Glaser: Well, of course nobody could *prove* that [loud, argumentative tone]; but most people are able to control their thoughts and emotions.

Dr. Searles: *You* didn't accept the *thoughts*, did you?—I mean, you thought they were bad just because you had such *thoughts*, huh?

Mrs. Glaser: I should have stayed in the hospital in New Orleans longer. [A couple of minutes later in the interview—]

Dr. Searles: You would—uh—doubt that *your* mother ever had occasion for any such feelings at *all* about *any*thing?

Mrs. Glaser: I don't know. She could have had feelings I don't know about.

Dr. Searles: Was it very hard to know *what* she was feeling or thinking?

Mrs. Glaser: She was very dedicated to the family [helplessly, as though her mother had been completely unreachable]—the same way my

—29

mother-in-law is—they do everything they can for their children and their husbands [sniffing].

[A couple of minutes later—]

Dr. Searles: Let's see, now—your growing up—your mother was very dedicated to—the family, huh?—was she aware of *individuals in* the family? Or do you think she saw the *family* as a unit?

Mrs. Glaser: I think more as a unit—I was not very close to my mother —I was much closer to my father.

Dr. Searles: You say you were not very close to your mother—would you put it among other things—you *hated* her considerably or—

Mrs. Glaser: *No, no;* I didn't [unconvincing protest].

Dr. Searles: Was there hate there?

Mrs. Glaser: No.

Dr. Searles: You feared her?

Mrs. Glaser: Fear her? Yes, fear would be a better word [as though relieved to be off the spot].

Dr. Searles: You *did* fear her; I see [accepting this]. What comes to mind there, as to what you feared in her; let's see what comes up.

Mrs. Glaser: Well, when I went to school I had to come home right away after school, and if I didn't get home right away she would ask where had I been and all this type of thing. I wasn't free to stop in for a Coke or something like that [in tone of feeling sure of father-Dr. Searles's sympathy].

Dr. Searles: I was thinking there of how your infant daughter made you so unfree also, huh?—wouldn't you guess?

Mrs. Glaser: Yes [very soft, subdued tone].

Dr. Searles: You weren't free to stop in as a child growing up—stop in for a Coke the way the other kids did? 'Cause if you did, then she would wonder where you'd been and you'd never hear the end of it— is that the idea?

Mrs. Glaser: Yes. If I just left the room she would ask where I was going [in a tone, again, of confidence in her having father-Dr. Searles's sympathy].

Dr. Searles: I'm conscious, in our session today [said in a tone as though I were her therapist, and as though we would have subsequent sessions], of *interrogating* you—uh, to a degree I interrogate everybody whom I interview here, but I'm more conscious of it with you. Now, I gather *she* used to *interrogate* you a great deal—huh? [pause of a few seconds; no audible reply from her] I'm still a *little* puzzled as to what was to be feared—it was such a maddening thing?—she'd keep interrogating endlessly, would she?

Mrs. Glaser: Well, I can remember when I was even—after I went to college, even when I was *in* college, if I left the room she would ask, "Where are you going?" I might just be going to the bathroom.

Dr. Searles: Did she seem very anxious for you to be out of her sight, for a few minutes, a few seconds?

Mrs. Glaser: It seemed—I think she was overprotective, and I don't want to be that way with my children—if I ever get the chance to be a mother to them again [sniffing].

[A couple of minutes later—]

Mrs. Glaser: . . . No matter how I—*try* I can't go back to that day and change what happened—that's what my mind wants to do. What I did was very very wrong and very sick [crying].

Dr. Searles: Well, you put it still, there, as though you were a very naughty girl. When you were a child did—did your mother *treat* you as being a naughty girl?

Mrs. Glaser: Not exactly; I guess I've stopped thinking about my child-hood. [pause of a few seconds] I guess I think this is costing an awful lot of money and can it—is it—can *I* get well do you think? [demanding tone; loud sniff]

Dr. Searles: I don't know, frankly I don't know [humbly]. But you wonder if you can, huh?

Mrs. Glaser: I *feel* that I am well again—I certainly don't have any bad thoughts again—the ang—any anger I have is all gone [unconvincing tone].

Dr. Searles: I'm very sorry to hear that. You never feel angry at anybody or anything? That to you is *well?* [incredulous tone]

Mrs. Glaser: No, possibly not. But somehow because of what happened I just don't have any anger left in me.

Dr. Searles: Well, maybe that *served* to *express* a very great deal of anger.

Mrs. Glaser: It certainly did, didn't it.

Dr. Searles: At whom—would you say—everybody, or somebody in par-ticular, or—? [pause of several seconds] Any—anyone come to mind?

Mrs. Glaser: No. I certainly didn't *gain* anything by what I did; I *lost* everything [protesting tone].

Dr. Searles: Well, but the thought comes to mind, though; the thought comes to mind. You say you certainly didn't *gain* anything by it and yet the *idea* that possibly one might have gained something by that, that *does* seem to come to mind. You—you say no, that you didn't, but is there any thought about what one conceivably might gain from such an experience?

Mrs. Glaser [tired sigh]: Well, I think I've learned to—if nothing else, to be a lot more loving and kind towards people.

Dr. Searles: You didn't used to feel that you were a loving, kind person?

Mrs. Glaser: No, not all the time—no.

Dr. Searles: Jesus! I find that rather staggering [sigh]. You've learned now to be a loving and kind person *all the time*, huh? Doesn't seem like somewhat of a strain?

Mrs. Glaser: Yes, it is ['small voice].

Dr. Searles: Well—are you—well, this the way your husband and mother-in-law are—they're loving and kind all the time, are they?

Mrs. Glaser: Not all the time, I'm sure. My mother-in-law [quavering, resentful tone] seems to be all the time.

Dr. Searles: Your voice quavers when you say that. Does she kind of frighten you?

Mrs. Glaser: No.

Dr. Searles: What do *you* guess—

> Mrs. Glaser [interrupting loudly]: I'm very thankful we *have* her. But the only trouble is—
>
> Dr. Searles: [interrupting] You wouldn't want *her* dead, huh?
>
> Mrs. Glaser: No.
>
> Dr. Searles: You've never thought life would be a helluva sight simpler if she would expire?
>
> Mrs. Glaser: No.
>
> Dr. Searles: Never did? [pause of a few seconds] You've heard of people often feeling that their mothers-in-law are intrusions?—you've heard of that.
>
> Mrs. Glaser: I know; but I've never felt that—in fact, I wanted her to come *live* with us.
>
> Dr. Searles: Against your husband's objections—or what?
>
> Mrs. Glaser: No, my *husband* didn't object to it—he wanted her to, too; but she didn't want to.
>
> Dr. Searles: Why not?—is she bashful or something?
>
> Mrs. Glaser: She likes her home and—where she grew up. You can't ask somebody else to give up something if they don't want to. [several seconds' pause] And it shows that I needed her very much.
>
> Dr. Searles: "It shows," huh?, about the—uh—having killed the—baby —shows that, huh?—Is that what showed?
>
> Mrs. Glaser: Partially I think [sniffs]. I certainly don't want anything to happen to my *other* two children.
>
> Dr. Searles: Thought wouldn't even *occur* to you [ironically].
>
> Mrs. Glaser [quickly]: No.

The interview ended a few minutes later. During the subsequent discussion it quickly became clear that there had been a shocked reaction, among the approximately 20 staff members who had been watching the interview, at my having confronted her so directly with the fact of her having murdered her infant daughter. As the therapist himself expressed it, "I was awfully angry with you at first. . . . I was extremely moved during that interview; at first when you talked about the 'murder' I got so furious. . . . Then I realized more and more how much I hated that woman—I could not communicate with her—I was seeing her but I had to deny all those feelings. . . . Then I had the feeling how much I would like to work with her. . . ." (Incidentally, to dispel any lingering doubt in the reader's mind, I should emphasize that the therapist indicated that in the course of the psychotherapy it had become clear that Mrs. Glaser had indeed actively drowned her infant during her "blackout.")

I had occasion to serve as a supervisor to the therapist during the patient's several subsequent months in the hospital, before she returned home, and it was my impression that this interview had helped to foster a deep and useful feeling-involvement between patient and therapist, in the course of which her murderousness became more fully explored and resolved than it had been prior to the interview.

In the psychodynamics of this woman's murderous act, as suggested by what occurred during the interview, a number of elements can be discerned:

1. In murdering her daughter she not only was acting out her own largely denied hostility toward the infant, but also was acting out vicariously the also vigorously denied murderousness toward the infant on the part of her husband and mother-in-law, to whom she had telegraphed so clearly her brooding murderousness toward the little girl.

2. The current denial, by not only her husband but also the hospital staff, of the reality of her murderous action was serving to keep under repression much of their fear, awe, and murderously condemnatory feelings toward her. In this regard I noticed in myself, during the first few minutes of the interview, urges to kill her in condemnation for her having murdered her own child; but as the interview continued these intensely negative feelings became unavailable to me—not, I believe, because they had been genuinely resolved, but rather because they had become repressed as being too threatening to me in that situation.

3. She was clearly struggling to preserve idealized images of both her parents, her husband, and her mother-in-law, and to repair an idealized image of herself. It was as though she lived in a world of such images, and, in fact, their preservation had taken priority over the life of her flesh-and-blood infant.

4. There is some reason to presume, from the repeating-of-history sequence of the birth of the little girl with the brother about three years older, that the infant was unconsciously perceived by the patient as her own infant self, and that she, the mother, gave undisguised expression to the murderousness

implicit in her own mother's overprotectiveness toward her in her childhood.

5. Presumably the confining infant daughter was also perceived unconsciously by the patient as being equivalent to the patient's own confiningly overprotective and unconsciously hated mother. It is notable that the birth of this daughter had kept the patient from visiting her beloved father following his stroke; and one may assume that her mother's overprotectiveness during her own childhood had inhibited her access to the father. Recurrently throughout the interview it was clear from the quality of her tearfulness in speaking of her father that her most genuine love was for him. Her cherishing of the love he had felt for her was indirectly revealed in her vigorous defense of her husband as really loving his little daughter.

6. She evidently had not clearly discerned, at an unconscious level, her alive infant daughter as being essentially different from an inanimate doll. Presumably this phenomenon is traceable to her having projected upon the infant a repressed self-image of a doll rather than a living person. Her own mother's overprotectiveness would seem to have fostered a sheltered, doll-like concept of herself, rather than one of being robustly alive.

An overprotective mother such as this woman had had tends to give her child a feeling that the child's own aliveness is dangerous—is equivalent to murderousness. The patient made it clear that her mother had behaved as though it were somehow unsafe to let her function on her own. When later, in adult life, the patient murdered her infant upon being left on her own at home by the mother-in-law who had gone out of the house, it was as though the patient were thus confirming her own mother's view of her alive, autonomous self as being a murderous self.

For a number of years I served as a co-therapist with Dr. Lyman C. Wynne in the psychotherapy of a family which included a father suffering from borderline or ambulatory paranoid schizophrenia, a chronically depressed mother, a hebephrenic teenage daughter, and an eight-year-old son who spent most of the time in autistic silence. Violence of various kinds by the various family members was a way of life to them. Of interest here is the abundance of data from the family interviews indicating that the son was led—particularly by his father and his sister—to construe as inherently violent any self-initiated signs of aliveness on his own part. The father and sister would frequently goad him into various forms of violently disruptive behavior during the sessions, then ostensibly chide him while appearing privately delighted with his vicarious expression of their own urges. But at the infrequent moments when he would start to express signs of life of his own, unprompted by them, their response became entirely different. No matter how slight nor how inherently sensible and healthily constructive and unviolent his signs of aliveness—his physical movements or his vocalization—were, his father or sister, or both, would react with savage and threatened reprimands, as though his coming alive were an intolerable intrusion into their state of being. In one session, for example, they repeatedly and sharply reprimanded him whenever he tried to speak or move, and while he was quietly playing with a doll which had a detachable head, arms, and legs, the father leapt over, in a frighteningly violent and urgently threatened manner, to seize and immobilize him. It seemed little wonder that, on the rare occasions when the boy was able to verbalize at length, he revealed that he lived in a world permeated with unpredictable and unmasterable violence and entertained many fantasies of himself as innately and omnipotently violent.

Incidentally, an interesting paper by Leo Rangell (1952), entitled "The Analysis of a Doll Phobia," complements without duplicating some of my comments here. Rangell formulates the material in classical psychoanalytic terms, delineating various of the intrapsychic determinants of the patient's doll phobia, with relatively little emphasis upon the family etiology. He mentions that at the beginning of his work with the neurotic 38-year-old male patient, who had suffered from the phobia since at least the age of five:

> The more lifelike a figure was, the worse it was; and it was particularly the moment of a figure "coming to life" or simulating movement which

was the most frightening. . . . To look at the doll was bad enough; to
touch or be touched by it was frightening to conceive; to have it rub
against his arm, even in thought, was enough to cause sweating and
near-panic.

7. It is evident that the patient's murderousness toward her
infant daughter had enabled her to force her mother-in-law,
who theretofore had been as inaccessibly devoted to the house
as the patient's own mother had been, to turn and attend,
instead, to the patient's own needs.

8. Lastly, one senses that this woman had unconsciously
hated her baby because she had unconsciously feared it as the
personification of her own unfulfilled infantile need for her
mother—not for the relatively emotionally accessible but
inescapably male father who evidently had fulfilled, and perhaps even largely usurped, the mothering role toward her, but
for her own biological mother, who had been so unreachably
devoted to "the house" and "the family." This basic meaning
of the act is best discerned in her saying of it, "It showed I
needed her," referring to the mother-figure mother-in-law. To
see the patient's murderousness as having been in the service
of repressing, and at the same time revealing, a legitimate
emotional need with which one can empathize enables one
genuinely to feel forgiving of her for her horrifying act. Just
as it is necessary to become aware of one's intensely negative
feelings toward such a patient in order to work with her, it is
also necessary to become able to feel, at a much deeper than
merely intellectual level, genuinely forgiving toward her.

Discussion

In earlier papers (Searles, 1965) I have elaborated upon
various other aspects of violence in schizophrenia, such as the
patient's equating individuation with murder of the mother
(= therapist), and have noted that his struggle to differentiate
between metaphorical and concrete thinking may appear, to
both the therapist and the patient himself, as murderously
violent behavior. I have described the violence which is done
to the therapist's cherished image of himself as a lovingly
dedicated physician (Searles, 1967), and wish to add here the

recurrent impression I have had in recent years, that those patients who tend most violently to damage one's image of oneself—those patients who most successfully make one feel malevolent and subhuman—have no need to resort to physical violence toward one.

As regards an additional covertly positive meaning of violent behavior, and related to the last-mentioned point above, I have seen that the urge to physical violence can express an effort to bridge a gulf of emotional unrelatedness. Thus, for example, in the course of my work with a male patient who for months made me feel threatened that he would physically assault me, I came to discover that I had been trying unconsciously to bring about this very event so that I would then have license to come to grips with him physically as—so I now came to see—a relief from the long-underlying, weird, and terrible unrelatedness which revealed itself as much more disturbing than any threat of physical—and therefore tangible and relatively human—violence.

We begin to see here, I believe, how inextricably intertwined are love and hate, how intense and ceaseless is the conflict between one's strivings toward oneness with the other person and one's strivings for individuation from him, and how at one moment a violent urge may express a striving to be free and at the next a desire to relate and be at one.

Before concluding this paper I wish to place more emphasis than the above-described clinical material (mostly drawn from single consultation interviews) has provided upon the role of repressed grief as one of the major affective components against which the patient's violence has been serving as an unconscious defense. In previous papers (1965) I described vengefulness as a defense against grief and separation anxiety, and assaultive behavior, among hebephrenic patients, as representing in part a distorted expression of the fierce grief which has been for so long pent up within them. In the latter connection, for example, when one hebephrenic woman's assaultive behavior, which she had many times manifested in our sessions together, was prevented by my finally and exasperatedly having her placed into a cold wet-sheet pack, she instantly began pouring out grief of an entirely unexpected and truly awesome intensity.

When five years ago I left Chestnut Lodge, one of the patients whom I had to leave was a 51-year-old hebephrenic man with whom I had been working, four hours per week, for eleven years. We had long since come to care for one another so violently that the sessions were often spent in an atmosphere of electric tension much like that prevailing the second before the gunfight at the O.K. Corral. Prior to his continual hospitalization, which had begun some 25 years previously, his chosen forms of sexual activity had included a highly promiscuous and sadomasochistic form of homosexuality in which he and his partner of the night would beat one another; and so sensational a display of transvestitism that he had succeeded in getting himself prohibited by the metropolitan police forces of several of the largest cities in the United States from again setting foot upon any of their respective domains.

Six months before I turned over his psychotherapy to another therapist, I told him this would occur. In those final six months of our sessions together it became evident that our nearly overmastering urges to tear each other physically to pieces was serving, for both of us, as a defense against the prospective loss of one another, which threatened to rend us helplessly into pieces, since we had so long since become so much a part of one another. For example, my notes concerning an hour five weeks from the end of our sessions together say:

> Early in this hour, we were so furious at one another that it occurred to me that maybe there should be safeguards—aides, or both of us in cold wet-sheet packs—against our tearing one another to pieces in the closing weeks of our work together. For the past few months, since I told him I'll not be going on with him, I've been as verbally furious and contemptuous at him as he has been for years at me.
>
> But later in the same hour I felt clearly that it is our loss of one another which threatens to tear us to pieces in these final weeks.
>
> He has been looking very grief stricken indeed of late . . . He still says, angrily and contemptuously and with infuriating defiance, "I don't know you!" But it is very evident indeed that he *cares* intensely, and that he is deeply convinced that he is the only one of us who cares.

I told him during this same hour, "I'll miss you terribly," and began to burst into tears as I said it, though I caught myself. He responded in a warmly understanding way to this—not that he said anything in particular."

[Concerning a session two days later—] His feelings about our coming separation are more explicit than ever. He said today, "I knew you'd leave me sooner or later," looking grieved and suffering. I responded, however, harshly and sarcastically, "Yeah—I've been the height of inconstancy, eh?—only worked with you for eleven years!"

. . . Whereas a week ago his main emphasis was on "I hate your rotten ass," now it's predominantly and explicitly grief. . . .

In the loneliness of my largely private-analytic-practice existence since I left the Lodge, I find that I not uncommonly talk to myself between sessions with patients. And more often than not I utter at myself, with fond nostalgia, the vitriolic curses which for so many years he poured upon me. My ambivalent regard for him ranks in intensity with that for my long-deceased father, to whom violence was the hallmark of masculinity. Both these men, though long mourned, continue to live—at times disturbingly—within me.

Summary

In this paper I have attempted to highlight the concepts that in schizophrenic patients (1) the tyrannically rigid superego makes for a subjective world of idealized—or, at the opposite extreme, diabolized—objects, a world in which any basic human aliveness is reacted to as innately violent, therefore to be kept under repression; and (2) the violent acts which are so typically latent among schizophrenic patients, and not rarely are actually committed by them, are in part referable to the patient's poor differentiation between the living and non-living, human and non-human ingredients of the world in which he lives. Thus the violent act can be thought of as made possible by the patient's failure to distinguish, for example, between a living baby and an inanimate doll, and at the same time as expressing his effort to achieve such a differentiation, as part of his undying struggle to establish more mature ego functioning and a better relationship with reality.

I have attempted here, further, to emphasize how difficult but essential it is for the therapist to spare neither the patient nor himself from his own awareness of feelings which, however uncomfortable and alien to traditional concepts of the compassionate physician, are crucial to the patient's grasping the reality of the latter's own violent urges and actions. I refer here to such feelings in the therapist as fear and murderous condemnation.

In closing, I emphasize that I regard the psychodynamics discussed here as not peculiar to schizophrenic persons, but rather in some degree characteristic of all human beings. I recommend as relevant reading a refreshing little book entitled *Human Aggression*, by a British psychoanalyst, Anthony Storr (1968). The tenor of that book is suggested by the following quotes from it:

> . . . there is so far no convincing evidence that the aggressive response is, at a physiological level, any less instinctive than the sexual response; and, provided that the term aggression is not restricted to actual fighting, aggressive expression may be as necessary a part of being a human being as sexual expression [p. 19].
>
> . . . if man were not aggressive, he would not be man at all [p. 26].
> . . . it is only when intense aggressiveness exists between two individuals that love can arise [p. 36].

Discussion

JOHN N. ROSEN, M.D.

Doylestown, Pennsylvania

Dr. Searles and his associates have rendered a distinct service to the psychodynamic exploration of violence in their study of four patients who were capable of murderous acts. Murder and suicide (self-murder) are the most terrifying human acts with which we are confronted in the gamut of violent behavior, which extends from wars and genocide—where murder is rampant, universal, and even condoned—to the criminal murder that we read about constantly in the newspapers. Although we are all familiar with this kind of human behavior, the dynamics of it are as yet poorly understood. Dr. Searles has attempted to evaluate the nature of these acts through a verbatim presentation of clinical material.

The patients described, although they were unquestionably psychotic at the time of their acting out, do not seem to me to fit into the classical categories of schizophrenia. Perhaps this form of psychosis requires a separate clinical category altogether; I myself find it difficult to know where to place them on the psychotic scale. They have been designated as paranoid schizophrenic, but I do not see in them the organized and systematized delusion which would be necessary for this designation. It is my feeling that the difficulty in accurate diagnosis stems from the lack of study of these kinds of patients.

Dr. Searles's study, which includes verbatim material, seems to me to be the kind of approach necessary to the understanding of the etiology of violent disorders. Unfortunately, it is a little difficult to experience the emotional impact implicit in the material presented and in his reaction to it without having actually been present during the therapeutic dialogue, as were his students. I also think—and this

—41

has always been my position—that psychotherapy should be taught by live demonstration before students. It has been my experience in many decades of treating schizophrenics in this way that they do not object to it and as a matter of fact are very often impressed by it and benefit from it. It is a significant therapeutic gain when a patient has enough ego to ask to be treated privately.

On the subject of the therapist's reaction to the patient's expressions of violence, Dr. Searles reports experiencing murderous feelings toward these patients. I myself have found, from the several cases that I have personally treated that were or could have been murderers, that my reaction was not one of violence. I did not feel like killing them. In one instance I recall distinctly that my reaction was great fear; I refer to the patient R.Z., whom I described in one of my earliest papers. He came into my office and opened up a razor, saying that "they" told him he had to cut my throat. I did not feel that I wanted to kill him, but I did feel terrified at the prospect of his cutting my throat. Fortunately for me, I managed to talk him out of it and get possession of the razor. It has been said about my own work, as Eisenbud has pointed out, that I don't seem to become disturbed at being confronted by a patient's unconscious, but I don't think that this is so. I have found that a patient's violent behavior can be very disturbing to me.

I imagine that there are two possible ways of responding to demonstrations of violence: either according to the talionic principle that a murderer should be murdered, or with a more civilized and humane reaction. It is interesting that the Supreme Court of the United States recently decided against capital punishment, or retributive murder by the State. This humane decision by the majority of the Supreme Court would illustrate that the talionic principle of an eye for an eye is not an inevitable human response.

Let me say in closing that Dr. Searles is to be complimented not only for the dynamic material presented in this paper, but also for confronting these violent patients with the reality of their acts. I'm especially impressed that Dr. Searles is willing to deal with patients in this way, knowing that the attitude at Chestnut Lodge when Frieda Fromm-Reichman was there was one of great concern about disturbing the exquisite sensitiveness of the schizophrenic patient. More clinical material of the kind that Dr. Searles and his associates have given us is necessary before we can come to any true understanding of the etiology of violence.

MILLEN BRAND

New York, New York

The main purpose of the case interviews recorded in Dr. Searles's and his co-authors' paper is to initiate therapy, to draw out some reality factors of the case and some of its emotional tone, and to prepare the patient for rapport with the doctor to whom he or she will be assigned. With that understood, there is no need to be critical of the interviews as therapy sessions.

In my novel *Savage Sleep* (1969), based on the work of Dr. John N. Rosen (and written in close association with him), I showed that the psychotic patient was in many respects in an opposite condition from the neurotic and required an opposite technique of treatment, one in which passivity gave way to active and even aggressive concern, and in which transference was encouraged and there was no fear of interpretation. Dr. Searles partly follows this path by not being afraid to express his own aggression and fear and by gaining the confidence of the patient with his honesty. But the patient in each instance is in complete verbal contact and not at the hallucinatory extreme where he is unaware of the role of the doctor as doctor or where the doctor needs to enter the psychosis to try to lead his patient out.

It may be for this reason that Dr. Searles does not assume a role of omnipotence, of the powerful parent able to bring his child up all over again, this time under loving and beneficent auspices.

Dr. Thomas Szasz and others have made much of democracy, of equality in the exchanges between patient and doctor. This is acceptable, even admirable, in cases like those presented here, but it breaks down in situations where, for example, the therapist has to take the patient to the bathroom and instruct him in the elements of hygiene.

Psychosis is, in its beginnings and in its depths, an oral problem. The first hint of paranoia usually is fear of poisoning, the danger of eating or drinking. In Case 4, Mrs. Glaser reported that as a child she "wasn't free to stop in for a Coke or something like that" on her way home from school. She was therefore "unfree," unfree to eat outside the home, where it would have been safer. If you have seen a patient late at night preparing his own meals and refusing anything prepared by his mother, you have some idea of the source of paranoid fears.

But everywhere is also the desperate need for mother's milk and love, without which the patient dies. Even a five percent love will be seen as salvation and fought for. In Case 4 the patient desperately denies that she hated her mother and, by implication, that her mother hated her. But her mother did hate her, and the hate was passed down, culminating in the patient killing her own baby. The patient's mother was "overprotective," meaning, "Would that you would die, my child." I myself interviewed a case at Brooklyn State Hospital where a mother had "protected" her newborn baby for about ten days by not letting anybody come near it, at which point it was discovered that the baby was starving to death. The mother then blanked out and thought she had been hospitalized "for a little alcoholism, I guess."

But it would be interesting in a paper like Dr. Searles's, even if he is not dealing with patients who are massively regressed, to trace out still more clearly the implications of the interviews for the oral phase and the first year of life, for here lie the origins of pathology and secretly or not they cry out.

Aggression in a parent may be healthy; it may have nothing to do with violence. Conversely, the overprotective parent may be quiet and seemingly loving. A baby who can scream and get red in the face may be a well baby; he may be confident that he is going to get what he wants and needs. But there remains a fine line between anger and fear, and this paper's dialogues can give therapists a useful indication of where that line should be drawn.

ARTHUR MALIN, M.D.

Beverly Hills, California

Once again we have a most revealing paper from Dr. Searles and his co-workers. The revelation is not only in understanding the schizophrenic patient, but also in recognition of the deep inner impulses and feelings stirred up in the therapist. Dr. Searles, through his years of writing, has repeatedly described his own inner turmoil and eventual growth from the "symbiotic relatedness" that he allows the patient to achieve with him.

I believe that it is extremely difficult for most psychoanalysts to allow their feelings to be expressed in the therapeutic relationship on the level that Dr. Searles suggests is natural for him. Most analysts would find it very difficult to bring these feelings into consciousness and to consider them as valid material for the therapeutic relationship; they would tend to regard them as countertransference phenomena best handled in self-analysis, or perhaps in a supervisory situation. There are usually some transient emotional phenomena occurring in the analyst that serve as important clues to his understanding of the patient, but to incorporate these feelings directly into the therapeutic process would be very unusual.

How does the patient experience the development and expression of such strong feelings on the part of the therapist? Dr. Searles and his co-workers point out that this can be an extremely therapeutic experience for the patient, since the resulting symbiotic relatedness provides a means by which the patient can re-experience his inner psychic turmoil of the past for the later development of a more mature and integrated ego. In other papers Dr. Searles has talked about the development of symbiosis from the ambivalent to the pre-ambivalent that he believes is necessary in the therapy of schizophrenic patients. In our paper "Projective Identification in the Therapeutic Process" (1966), Dr. Grotstein and I suggested that it is the way in which a therapist responds to the patient's projections that allows modification of these projections to occur. The patient's introjection and identification of his previous projections, now modified by the response of the therapist, can be re-experienced for a higher level of integration and functioning. Dr. Searles evidently believes that his open response to the patient would fit in with the workings of such a concept. Perhaps another way of looking at it is that the patient recognizes that the therapist is willing to become disturbed and upset in his actions and statements and can still maintain the further identity of a relatively stable individual. The therapist is open to the resulting symbiotic relatedness and is not destroyed by it, but can contain and handle the patient's projections. This can be the modification that takes place and is reintrojected back into the schizophrenic patient.

I do not agree that Searles's particular approach to the schizophrenic patient is always very helpful. In my experience there are a number of schizophrenic patients who will become very frightened by what would appear to them as a loss of control on the part of the therapist. They would experience the therapist expressing himself and his feelings in such a strong manner as Dr. Searles describes as terribly threatening. Such a patient might feel that if the therapist cannot maintain himself, how in the world is he going to help with such a chaotic inner life as the patient presents? The patient may also see this response as proof of his own inner destructiveness. I am suggesting that the problem of the way the therapist responds is a double-edged sword, and that Dr. Searles's approach is probably, at least in my experience, not applicable to all schizophrenic patients.

I want to re-emphasize, however, that when a therapist honestly expresses his feelings a patient can often feel, as Dr.

Searles describes, a very strong sense of gratitude that the therapist is willing to be a "real" person in the relationship.

The specific question of violence in the schizophrenic is complicated by the intensity of the feelings aroused in the analyst. The paper makes the important suggestion that the therapist can actually encourage the violence on an unconscious level as a way of dealing with his own anxiety. An interesting statement is made: that it is within this strong, angry, destructive part of one's self that we also find a kernel of love and gratitude in a relationship.

The idea that the "urge to physical violence can express an effort to bridge a gulf of emotional unrelatedness" is a significant recognition of the tremendous defensive struggles going on within the schizophrenic patient.

Dr. Searles's paper also raises the question of the negative therapeutic reaction. The angry, violent attitude that is demonstrated by the violent schizophrenic patient and projected into the therapist can be a way in which the schizophrenic patient is hanging on to the only internal object situation he can handle: the relationship to the primary objects, the breast-mother. Are we perhaps dealing with the situation in which any attempt at growth and development means to the patient that this breast-mother must be relinquished, which he perceives as a fragmentation of all inner psychic contents and a disappearance of the self? The reaction of anger and violence may be the patient's way of demonstrating the futility of achieving maturity or any significant human relationship. Better to maintain that inner relationship with the breast-mother rather than give it up in favor of a never-to-be, hopelessly futile attempt at maturity. It is in the responses of the analyst that the projection of the patient can be modified. Dr. Searles describes how he uses his awareness of the strong feelings stirred up in him by the violent patient as a way of gaining understanding of the schizophrenic.

MARGARET LITTLE, M.R.C.S., L.R.C.P., M.R.C.PSYCH.

Kent, England

I have been struggling to put together some reasoned and coherent discussion of this prodigious paper, and have finally had to put aside the idea of anything but broadly "associating" to it.

Two contradictory strands seem to run through the paper: one, the intensity and totality of the undifferentiated state shown in the various patients described; and the other, Searles's insistence on the rigidity and vindictiveness of the superego in each case—a phenomenon which argues at least some degree of differentiation.

The paradox of this seems to me the crux of the matter. Tenderness is vitally necessary somewhere (whether in therapist, relative, or patient), yet it is simultaneously life-destroying, violence (murder) being the equally essential alternative, as vitally necessary in the therapist as it is in the patient himself.

This has to do with the problem of containing the violence. The strength of the container must be at least equal to that which is to be contained.

The patients described show this in quite markedly different degrees—Mr. Delaney's violence being to all intents and purposes uncontainable; Mrs. Glaser's being containable in the measure that it could be first repressed, or dissociated, then that the repression or dissociation could be undone. In my view, this is of both diagnostic and prognostic significance. I have come across a number of people, in treatment situations and elsewhere, where schizophrenia was masked by a defensive use of psychopathy: when the psychopath broke down under stress a schizophrenic appeared. I would regard Mr. Delaney as an example of this, whereas Mrs. Glaser could almost be considered a "major hysteric."

Outside of psychiatry, a beautiful picture of this is shown in Ibsen's *Peer Gynt*. At the start of the play Peer is portrayed as a psychopath, consistently hostile to his mother, Åase. When she dies and he is driven out from the community, what reality sense he had is lost, and throughout the rest of his life he alternates between psychopathy and schizophrenia in response to varying external pressures.

I agree entirely with Searles that the reactions brought about in the therapist are of prime importance. The ability to allow his ego boundaries to dissolve temporarily—to let himself become merged with the patient, and to permit reality and delusional or hallucinatory experience to become indistinguishable—is the only route by which real contact, understanding, and ability to share in an experience can develop. But equally important are the ways in which the boundaries can be re-established and the speed and progression of the re-synthesis, when it is appropriate.

The method or technique described by Searles again is confirmed by my own experience, especially in terminating analyses of very sick patients which have been long and deeply felt on both sides.

Searles and his pupils have, on occasion, had recourse to wet packs or actual restraint. I have found it valuable when dealing with a paranoid patient to have some other person available, and known to the patient to be available even if not called upon, to relieve not only my own anxiety but also the patient's. I have, in fact, had very little experience of seriously threatened violence, for I have had little experience in treating schizophrenic patients.

Finally, this paper, which follows in the direct line of Searles's previous work, links up with a very great deal of which there is growing awareness generally, e.g., the "battered baby syndrome" and the widening fields of "protest" of all kinds, attended by widespread confusion, irrationality, and violence, which appear perhaps to be replacing "world wars" at the moment.

I think two papers of Winnicott's are particularly relevant here: one on the need for confrontation in adolescent disturbance, and the other on the use of an object, in which he describes the subject's need to "destroy" the object, and yet have it survive, in order that he may come into being as a person in his own right. (This is what the patient is doing when he induces de-differentiation in his therapist.)

This really subsumes the universality of violence (which, intellectually, we all recognize). Everything that exists in psychopathology exists also in normality, but the acceptance and acknowledgment of his own violence by the containing therapist are valid as assertion and demonstration both of his normality and of his growing freedom from superego dominance.

GUSTAV BYCHOWSKI, M.D.†

New York, New York

Every new publication of Dr. Searles must arouse the greatest interest in all of us who are deeply involved in the psychoanalytic treatment of psychosis. The particular topic which he and his co-authors discuss in this paper commands, of course, our special attention. One is not disappointed in one's expectations. The paper offers original observations and fascinating examples of Dr. Searles's penetrating interview technique. In his incisive and sometimes strikingly intuitive interpretations, he is able time and again to get to the core of the patient's unconscious conflicts. Sometimes I feel that his interpretations are perhaps too rapid or even shocking—in this respect somewhat reminiscent of John Rosen's "active" analysis. However, in many instances the interpretation strikes one as illuminating. One might argue as to the timing, but then we have to keep in mind that some of the interviews are really first interviews and that they serve a didactic purpose.

As I go over the cases presented, my principal disagreement is with Dr. Searles's by now well-known countertransference interpretations. I must admit that in his former publications I had been struck by his most unusual identification with his psychotic patients. In the present paper he intersperses his excellent interpretations of the patient's dynamics with his "countertransference" interpretations which, I must confess, seem to me arbitrary and farfetched.

He has, for instance, excellent insight into the dynamics and violent acting out of his first patient, even though I would consider it a rather wild interpretation to say that Mr. Delaney "was faced with the threat of becoming the rapist of the father, as the agent of the mother's phallic strivings."

But I cannot accept Dr. Searles's interpretations of his own feelings. Instead of simply noticing his obvious and understandable fear of this violent patient, he comments on his own "unconscious passive homosexual longings" which had been aroused by his interview with him: "I could triangulate, although not actually feel, the desire to be sexually 'shot' by him."

After the patient has assaulted a fellow marine, Dr. Searles comments that this violent act gave him (Searles) the relief of certainty, since "it was as though the distinction between the patient's actualized murderousness and our own murderous fantasies and feelings was now clear beyond any question."

To read Dr. Searles's further exposition of his and supposedly the other therapists' murderous impulses—apparently his entourage is also filled with all sorts of violent feelings toward the patients—is to be subjected to further shocks. One cannot help asking oneself: How can one help a patient if one identifies with him to such an extent, and how can one recognize one's own feelings if one is so ready to distort them by uncritical counteridentification? And, indeed, the speculations which Dr. Searles develops in further analyzing this situation acquire more and more the characteristics of fantasies. No wonder then that Dr. Searles confesses that "such a patient evokes in one such intensely conflicting feelings that on an unconscious level one's ego-functioning undergoes a pervasive de-differentiation: one loses the ability at this depth to distinguish between one's self and the patient . . . and between the whole realms of fantasy and reality."

Since our purpose is not just to study the patient and our own unconscious but also to help the patient, I fail to see how any help is possible when one is unable to distinguish between the patient's violence and one's own. Indeed, one wonders about the usefulness of this procedure as applied to a patient so manifestly dangerous. One has to ask whether some other therapeutic method, such as conditioning or retraining, based, of course, on the dynamic insights, might not be more appropriate.

Similar reservations apply to other case histories. At times Dr. Searles admits some of his countertransference feelings (or speculations?) to the patient. I don't see anything useful in telling the patient: "Then I may be *projecting* onto you some of my own problems because I was very afraid I would kill [a member of my parental family] . . . so that I may be afraid of *myself* still more than I thought, and I may be taking it out on you."

Some of the interviews presented are particularly moving, such as the one with the infanticide mother. But even here, as in many other instances, one feels that Dr. Searles makes too much of a patient's expression and interprets it according to his own theories. For example, when the infanticide mother speaks of her little drowned daughter as "something very lovely," Dr. Searles interprets it as her inability to see the child as a living creature.

There are many passages in the paper which strike me as unwarranted and too widely speculative. Dr. Searles's exaggerated ideas about the import of counteridentification lead to speculative interpretations which cannot, of course, be proved or disproved. It seems, for instance, gratuitous to assert that the infanticide mother "was not only acting out her own largely denied hostility toward the infant, but also was acting out vicariously the also vigorously denied murderousness toward the infant on the part of her husband and mother-in-law, to whom she had telegraphed so clearly her brooding murderousness toward the little girl." Dr. Searles admits that during the first few minutes of the interview with this mother he noticed in himself "urges to kill her in condemnation for her having murdered her own child."

It is not surprising that in view of his very special tendencies toward counteridentification, Dr. Searles develops most unusual relationships with his patients. One admires his ability to withstand the stresses of these relationships. However—to repeat—one wonders what is the value of identifying for eleven years, and even for many years after the end of treatment, with a highly disturbed, perverse schizophrenic. It was clear that in this extraordinary relationship the pychiatrist was taking over his patient's violent and perverse wishes; but the reader can judge for himself. It is in this case history that the psychiatrist admits to the patient that he will miss him terribly and begins to burst into tears.

In conclusion, I feel that the excellent and profound insights which Dr. Searles manifests in this as in his many other publications are vitiated by his ill-founded speculations and the hypertrophy of his counteridentification. It is to be regretted that he was unable to cope, as he confesses, with his introjects. He admits himself that the above-mentioned schizophrenic patient and his own long-deceased and violent father continue to live within him. I must sympathize with this situation, which I would find extremely disturbing in myself.

MILTON WEXLER, PH.D.

Beverly Hills, California

Searles and his colleagues have not only written on "Violence in Schizophrenia," but have managed to incorporate into the very structure and quality of their presentation some of the essential elements they wish to explain. The paper is filled with a violent honesty, an urgency to make direct contact with the mind and feelings of the reader, and a host of dark fears that need to be shared. From this viewpoint alone it is a remarkable document. It confesses, pleads, speculates, asserts, details, argues, exposes helplessness and insight, and jumps hey-diddle-diddle from the most concrete to the most abstract, from the most objective to the most personal.

Dr. Searles's interviews with patients deserve special mention. He is mainly reality-oriented, blunt, and guided as much by his inner feelings as by external facts, yet he is sensitive to the nuances of what is expressed and unexpressed by his subjects. He makes no pretence to special power, special understanding, or the Christian virtues of kindness, charity, forgiveness, and love. He is what he is: sometimes fearful, sometimes angry, always curious and open, and responsive both to the surface and to what may lie beneath it. In this psychoanalytic age it is refreshing to encounter an analyst who is not altogether dazzled by his own presumed mastery of primitive unconscious mechanisms.

Obviously no single formulation serves to explain the violence of the schizophrenic patient. The paranoid projections which lead to a sense of persecution and a violent defense against the persecutor represent one type. This is more nearly neurotic in structure, is based on inner unconscious conflict, and is resolved by an act of violence against the alleged persecutor. This paper deals with deeper, more regressive mechanisms, in which the threatened loss of the object, the "gulf of emotional unrelatedness," leads to violence as an act of reconstitution, reconstruction, restitution. While it may express some striving to be free, it may equally express an urgency to re-contact the object and be at one with it. In that sense we learn once again how very close love and hate can be. I personally do not fully accept the notion of "vengefulness as a defense against grief and separation anxiety"; I prefer to think of such angry retaliation as an effort at restoration, as reparative in nature. The term "defense" is not altogether inappropriate, but might suggest, for instance, that we eat in order to defend against hunger. The use of "defense" in this sense tends to stretch its meaning beyond useful boundaries.

It is a commonplace that schizophrenics inflict pain on themselves in order to feel alive. They scratch, tear, cut, burn, or injure their flesh to achieve the smallest sense of being real within the vacuum of their psychic lives. This goes even beyond the savagery of their superego demands and expectations. What Dr. Searles's paper presents with such clarity and in such depth is a valid corollary: schizophrenics can salvage a sense of being alive, being related, being in contact by inflicting pain and suffering on others, by a violence which for a moment may resurrect a sense that the world is not devoid of objects. What they often cannot tolerate is the feeling of living in a void.

Dr. Searles knows these things both objectively and subjectively. To his credit he has delved deeply enough in his own feelings to know his own rage at the dead, the lost, the absent objects. Therefore, he can understand schizophrenic violence, can properly fear it, and even, at moments, forgive it.

HERBERT A. ROSENFELD, M.D.

London, England

This paper is mainly a contribution to the psychotherapeutic management of violent and murderous patients, and also illustrates Dr. Searles's interviewing technique, wherein he attempts in one consultation to assess the personality structure of the patient through his own countertransference reactions. In his summary Dr. Searles stresses that he has highlighted various concepts relating to the schizophrenic's superego and the poor differentiation between the human and non-human ingredients in the schizophrenic's world. These latter aspects, however important and interesting they may be, do not come through very convincingly in the interviews, but this is hardly surprising; the personality structure and confusions of the schizophrenic often need very detailed psychoanalytic investigation to be properly understood.

I myself have never treated anybody who actually committed a murder. However, several of my acutely schizophrenic patients were violent and some of them suffered from delusions of having committed murder. I also treated a young married woman doctor, more than 20 years ago, who suffered from a severe syphilophobia which at times was clearly delusional. She had violent murderous impulses against her infant, particularly for the first three months of the baby's life, and she came for treatment soon after her confinement because she was convinced that without treatment her child's life was in real danger. While the severe syphilophobia related to an act of unfaithfulness to her husband several years previously, the illness as a whole had to be regarded as a post-partum psychosis, and was related to an intense projective identification of herself with the newborn infant, whom she misidentified as her sick paranoid baby self which she had never been able to accept and which she regarded as *not human*. Her murderous hatred against this self was also projected into the analyst, representing the mother; she constantly feared that the analyst could not stand her and wanted to get rid of her (kill her). In working through her earliest infantile anxieties in the transference, the patient gradually came to feel accepted by the analyst-parent (mainly standing for the mother) and made a good recovery. In the countertransference I never felt that I was the murderous mother, but I was aware of an intense pressure coming from the patient to change me into a punishing, frightening superego which threatened her with death and accused her of not being human. It was interesting that after the infant had survived its first three months of life, the patient gradually felt relieved and could accept the baby as more human. She made it quite clear that this happened when she began to feel that the baby had become more able to see the mother as a whole person; she had perceived the very young infant as aggressive, rejecting the mother and the breast, and completely preoccupied with the *nipple* as an exciting part-object—an experience which was gradually related to the poisonous syphilophobia which had completely dominated the patient since the birth of the child.

This patient was quite ignorant of psychoanalytic theories about early infantile experiences, but she taught me a great deal about the terrifying anxieties which infants seem to go through. I would agree with Dr. Searles that the patient's murderousness toward her infant was related to an identification with or complete submission to an early archaic persecutory superego.

I have further clinical evidence that many violent schizophrenic patients are dominated by a very primitive persecuting superego, as I illustrated in my 1955 paper on the superego conflict in schizophrenia. At that time I had treated an almost mute, violent schizophrenic patient in a mental hospital. The only room available for his treatment was the anatomy theatre of this institution where, one day, the patient managed to dig out of a box of bones a lower jaw of a skeleton. He held it in front of his face like a mask and then behaved threateningly toward me to illustrate his identification with his own threatening deathly superego. Occasionally he was able to express with a few words his preoccupation with death and dying, after which he would become more depressed. In his regressive persecutory experiences he obviously felt threatened by me, and at times became violent and murderous when he confused me with his superego. It was, however, important that while the patient had the greatest difficulty in using words himself, he often understood verbal interpretations. I used only my analytic understanding and verbal interpretations, and these generally succeeded in diminishing both his terror of me and his murderous violence, which was of course quite frightening.

There is no question that actively murderous and violent patients are the most difficult ones to treat and that they make enormous demands on the therapist's understanding. I am in general agreement with Dr. Searles that the countertransference of the therapist is of enormous help in understanding the non-verbal communications and projections of our psychotic patients. I think, however, that it is essential that the analyst who makes extensive use of the countertransference should be quite clear about the implications of his countertransference experience. Originally, countertransference reactions were regarded simply as a neurotic reaction of the analyst who transfers object relations and fantasies of the past onto his patients, thereby confusing the issue. The analyst's pathological, neurotic countertransference requires self-analysis, or analysis of the analyst, and Dr. Searles quite openly often does so in investigating his own neurotic transference feelings, illustrating in this paper the importance of self-analysis in dealing with this problem. But he does not seem sufficiently to differentiate the neurotic countertransference from the countertransference described by Heimann, Bion and myself, and many others, which is based on two factors: first of all, there is the patient's unconscious nonverbal communication, in which he projects impulses, fantasies, and even parts of his self into the analyst; and secondly, there is the analyst's sensitivity and receptiveness to the patient's projections, which enable him, through this type of countertransference, to pick up very important information from the patient.

In violent and destructively psychotic patients, it is of course particularly important for the analyst to be able to recognize whether or not the murderous violence which the patient communicates is a real desire to kill, because this immediately calls for protective measures for the safety of the potential victims rather than for analysis. On the other hand, the patient who communicates his murderousness out of fear of being overwhelmed by it is asking for the analyst's help in order to save himself and his objects. Here the analyst has to understand that the patient wants *him* to cope with fear and aggression better than he himself can. This kind of situation often responds well to analytic therapy.

Preverbal communications through projection of anxieties relating to destructive impulses have their basis in the situation where the small infant projects his destructiveness and his fear of it into his mother. It is the mother's capacity to contain both the aggression and the fear of disintegration (Bion) which gradually leads to a lessening of the sense of danger and to a strengthening of the infantile ego in coping with the aggressive impulses.

ROBERT C. BAK, M.D.
New York, New York

Many schizophrenics move on the extreme ends of the scale between passivity and aggressiveness. Passivity can be the expression of instinctual aim, but may just as well function as defense against aggression; sudden acting out of murderous fantasies is characteristic of some schizophrenics in the course of their illness. It is not easy to decide whether the murderous acts represent a breakthrough of aggression with the aim of destroying a person, or whether they appear in the course of restitution, i.e., re-establishing lost contact with the world (objects).

In my view, the withdrawal of libidinal investments from object representations leaves the schizophrenic with magic omnipotent self-love (narcissism) and often exposes the objects outside and their intrapsychic representation to destruction. The further course of dedifferentiation is an archaic defense of the ego *against* the destruction of objects. That from this dedifferentiation, from the experiences of fusion and loss of individuality, the aggressive act may serve the purposes of reintegration is by no means a contradiction.

The lack of differentiation between animate and inanimate objects is not a cause of violence but in a way a consequence of it; I mean by this that the withdrawal of love is the prerequisite for experiencing persons as things. So much for theory.

Dr. Searles's consistent approach of analyzing countertransference, identification, and defenses in the therapist for the understanding of the patient and the therapeutic process is certainly a model to follow. However, one cannot help feeling that these subjective reactions of the therapist and supervisor are overdrawn. Instead of using them as *signals* for intellectual awareness, they may be *lived* for longer than necessary. Also, there is too much emphasis on subjective observation. Taking for granted the existence of many subjective elements, especially when one is confronted with cases that challenge the deepest prohibitions in one's own personality, there is still room for clinical judgment and prognostication, at least partly based on experience. Searles may give the impression, for example, that in judging the murderous potential of a patient we are almost entirely at the mercy of our own anxieties, identifications, and projections. However, the therapist's secondary reactions, elicited from the patient, are of the utmost importance, as Searles emphasizes throughout. He consistently follows the epigrammatic maxim of Bertram Lewin: Analysis is the analysis of countertransference. But it should be analyzed, not acted upon.

ALFRED FLARSHEIM, M.D.

Chicago, Illinois

Much of what is written about the psychoanalysis of psychotic patients is extrapolated from work with borderline patients who may show psychotic mechanisms but are able to manage their lives outside of a hospital. Searles is one of the very few who have written about long-term psychoanalytic treatment of severely disturbed hospitalized schizophrenic patients.

This paper is very rich in concrete assistance for anyone working with severely disturbed patients, in or out of a hospital setting. For example, Searles's way of handling his patient's demand to be released from the hospital is most helpful. The patient seeks freedom from environmental restraint, which can reflect internal restraint, and Searles presents a good example of the kind of inner restraint from which a patient may need release. His patient's inner restraint is derived from anxiety over infantile helplessness and from domination by an archaic maternal introject with which the patient was partially identified. In *The Ethics of Psychoanalysis*, Thomas Szasz (1965) points out that not only the paranoid patient but also society and the hospital administration regard the psychiatrist in a mental hospital as the opponent of the patient rather than his agent or advocate. Searles shows us how he handles this crucial issue. He accepts the patient's view of hospitalization as something imposed upon him by others for their own protection, while searching for an area in which he and the patient can work together toward a shared objective.

Searles has pioneered in the use of countertransference as a diagnostic and therapeutic instrument. Everyone talks and writes about the importance of self-knowledge, but Searles shows us what this can mean and how to use it.

I have had psychiatric residents misuse Searles's writings to justify burdening patients with their own emotional reactions, which are disruptive to the treatment. Interpretation of countertransference anxieties is fraught with dangers. This is particularly true when the patient feels accused of causing the therapist anxiety, and that therefore he must inhibit the expression of feelings that the therapist finds unpleasant. Carried to its extreme, inhibition of expression is suicide. As long as the countertransference can be used as a source of mutual understanding of the patient who contributes to its formation, and as long as we can communicate that we are enjoying being taught by the patient, we can safely interpret even the negative feelings the patient arouses in us.

I have asked myself what indications of potential violence are most anxiety-provoking in my own hospital practice. Many factors are of course important, such as a history of violent behavior in the past. But the patient's way of relating also has prognostic value.

Two patients come to mind. Both have frightened me, the hospital staff, and other patients. Both live largely in a subjective delusional world and both have been considered to be potentially dangerous if crossed, that is, if a collision cannot be avoided between the patient's subjective world and external reality. One patient has a well-developed capacity for playfulness and humor. This provides a softening of the boundaries between internal and external reality, a buffer zone between the two areas enabling him to avoid direct collison between his unrealistic subjective world and external reality and thereby avoid being provoked into dangerous destructive behavior. The other patient has a grim and humorless demeanor, and no capacity for playfulness, which implies a rigidity of the boundary between internal and external reality, with few links between them. The first patient evades conflict by lies, manipulation, and by being a playboy, acting out constant flight from responsibility. The second patient isolates himself in a darkened room and glares at anyone who interrupts his reveries; he lacks this buffer zone and is therefore the more dangerous of the two.

Another mechanism that I have observed in violent patients is the use of external reality as a defense against internal reality. There are limits to the patient's capacity for actual, in contrast to fantasied, destruction. The latter can be without limits, particularly in the presence of ego fragmentation which separates love and hate so that love cannot set limits to hateful destruction. Anxiety about fantasied destruction can be a helpful area to explore with some patients whose dream and fantasy life is impoverished and who act out destructively. Discussion of the fantasied consequences of a fantasied act can make the act itself unnecessary. In addition, interpretation of the meaning of a fantasied action in terms of genetic reconstruction or of symbolic meaning can show the patient that the fantasies are valuable in themselves, and that violent actions are not needed to communicate meaningfully.

With outpatients we are more often concerned about possible suicide than about externally directed violence, and Searles's formulations about the therapist's fear of the patient's violence can be applied to violence directed against the self. I will devote the remainder of my comment to this topic.

In "Aggression: Adaptive and Disruptive Aspects," Peter Giovacchini (1969) classifies violent behavior along a hierarchical continuum from the diffuse temper tantrum on the one hand to aggression organized toward a specific aim and object on the other. Personality disintegration to the level of an infantile temper-tantrum is a self-destructive event, and hostile aggression directed toward a separate object externalizes destructiveness, and can thus defend against suicide.

Searles points out that the therapist's fear of the patient can be a derivative of the therapist's unconscious destructive impulse. The therapist's impulse to attack the patient can be repressed or denied, leading to vicarious relief and enjoyment when the patient acts out aggressively toward the therapist or toward others, or it can be experienced and used in the service of the therapy. The therapist's unconscious destructiveness toward the patient can also take the form of an unconscious wish for the patient to commit suicide; this may first be experienced by the therapist as anxiety lest the patient commit suicide.

Experiencing something in the present reality of the transference can be the patient's way of remembering and regaining unintegrated ego segments. Stimulating the therapist to experience something in the countertransference can also be a way for the patient to deal with unintegrated ego segments, which originally may have belonged to the self, to an object, or to an archaic undifferentiated self-object. I have had a patient who *needed* to stimulate me to want her to kill herself before she could start to free herself from suicidal impulses that derived from her mother's death wishes toward her when she was a small infant. Another patient, a 14-year-old girl, compulsively starts dangerous fires. The fire-setting is "exciting" for her, and I am only just beginning to get some ideas about possible reasons for the choice of fire-setting as the preferred form of destructive activity. We have, however, found that destructiveness is directed toward a maternal imago with which she is partially identified. Not only is there a suicidal element in the fire-setting itself, but when for some reason or other she is unable to set fires, she resorts to manifestly self-destructive behavior such as slashing her abdomen. In effect, her fire-setting defends against more direct methods of suicide.

Searles stresses that violence can be an unconscious defense against repressed grief. I am reminded of two adult patients in whom compulsive head-banging was relieved only when they became able to cry.

In this and other papers Searles has described the effects of a mother's intolerance of her child's "basic human aliveness." The parent with a severe ego defect can maintain only a precarious equilibrium and cannot tolerate a relationship with a separate independent person. Any relationship such a parent can have with anyone, including the child, can only be one of rejection or of engulfing narcissistic exploitation in the service of the parent's precarious ego integration. But it is not always vitality and vivaciousness that is intolerable to parents. Indeed, a parent may exploit a child's liveliness to counteract his own depression. The "basic human aliveness" to which Searles refers here implies rather the child's individuation as a separate *autonomous* individual. A suicidal patient can be complying with a parent's need to eliminate this "aliveness," which his parent experienced as an intolerable threat.

I have read this paper five times, and have learned something new from it with each reading. The most significant comment I can make is to urge any readers who have not yet done so to immerse themselves in Dr. Searles's writing.

Author's Response

I find on re-reading this paper, for the first time since submitting it three years ago for publication, that it is still fully consonant with my theoretical views, with one exception: it omits mention of the dimension of the patient's, and the therapist's, suicidal proclivities. If I were writing this paper over again today, I would make at least brief mention of the fact that just as suicide can be a defense against murder, so can murder be a defense against suicide; as Mrs. Glaser, for example, is quoted as saying to me, "I still had bad thoughts toward the baby or myself—either one." In a similar vein, I would suggest today that the therapist's anxiety lest the patient murder him is likely to be based not only upon his reality-based awareness of the patient's murderousness, and upon the therapist's projection (as I have mentioned) of his own unconscious murderous feelings upon the already murderous patient, but also upon some increment of an unconscious longing on the therapist's part to be murdered by the patient. At any rate, I believe the opening paragraph of my paper makes clear that I was not setting out to cover nor even touch upon every major dimension of so broad a subject.

The version of this paper which was read by the discussants did not contain the second of the opening paragraphs I have included here, in which I make clear that I wrote this paper alone; I had thought that this was clearly enough implied, and I regret that I had not made it unmistakably clear to the discussants. It would be most unwarranted for Bisco, Coutu, and Scibetta, whose role in this paper is limited to their having most generously permitted me to include the material from their patients, to be held at all responsible for my own therapeutic techniques and theoretical formulations.

A word employed by Little, "prodigious," nicely describes my task in responding to the thoughtful comments of the nine discussants, all of them persons of wide experience in working with schizophrenic patients and equipped, therefore, to speak with authority about the psychodynamics and psychotherapy of such patients. My task now is similar to that which I have had each time I have faced an audience for an often critical dissection of a just-completed teaching interview. In one respect it is much harder, for I have never had an audience which contained so many comparably prestigious authorities in this field, and in another it is much simpler, for at least I have had time for contemplation.

Toward Rosen, despite some wide differences in theoretical concepts and psychotherapeutic approaches, I have a strong comradely feeling as regards teaching interviews, for he is the only colleague whom I regard as having had more experience than I with the stresses of doing such teaching interviews and then discussing them afterward, in detail, with the onlookers. I surmise that he would concur with my view that, more often than not, one's relationship with the audience proves more challenging than that with the patient himself. It seems to me probable that many experienced colleagues who eschew this priceless teaching technique, ostensibly out of concern for patients' needs for privacy or presumed fragilities of one sort or another, are in actuality unprepared to brave the stresses involved in allowing one's colleagues to witness one's therapeutic, or quasi-therapeutic, work at first hand and subject it to the kind of searching scrutiny in post-interview discussions which these nine discussants, with varying degrees of approval and disapproval, and much clarification and stimulation for me, have provided here.

Incidentally, Bychowski is indulging in a fantasy when he attributes to me a mindlessly sycophantic "entourage"; I have known little, indeed, of the dubious pleasures such a situation might provide. On balance, most of my audiences have been more critical of my interviews than these nine discussants collectively have been. My audiences usually have been comprised largely of psychiatric residents and junior staff members, and persons of this degree of experience tend to be, although not infrequently impressed in various ways, also somewhat shocked, angered, and mystified by some of my responses to the patient. But any long-experienced onlookers are usually relatively understanding of and not alienated by what they see and hear me doing during the interview—are "with" me to just about the extent that most of these discussants have proved to be, and on such occasions I feel fortunate.

For me, the greatest stress involved in a teaching interview with a schizophrenic patient consists in being faced with the potentially terrifying threat of isolation from one's fellow human beings, of being perceived by them as something non-human. One's feeling of strain in this regard is surely in part derived from empathy with the patient, whose illness is designed, as it were, specifically to protect him from the conscious awareness of such a feeling. This component of the interview situation, specifically as regards schizophrenic patients, is so significant to me that I find I cannot work effectively, or with anything like the requisite degree of personal freedom to respond to the patient, unless I feel that at least a small minority of the onlookers will hesitate to write me off as crazy, or as someone who—as I am sure Bychowski or Bak, for example, would say—does "wild analysis," or who is sadistically victimizing a patient viewed by the onlookers as being himself devoid of sadism or other forms of hatefulness.

Now I shall respond to each of the discussants, at varying length, in turn, dwelling largely of course upon their more critical comments, while privately being grateful for their more favorable responses of which, as I hope to have made clear already, I need at least some modicum from my colleagues in order to pursue this kind of teaching activity.

Rosen says that "The patients described, although they were unquestionably psychotic at the time of their acting out, do not seem to me to fit into the classical categories of schizophrenia." I think it could be said that each of the three patients whose interviews are presented at length was functioning, during the interview itself, with a no more than borderline-schizophrenic degree of impairment of ego functioning (although the history in each instance shows what seems unmistakable evidence of frank psychosis on occasion), and one experienced colleague has raised a sobering question as to whether Mrs. Glaser might more accurately have been diagnosed as suffering from a psychotic depression than from schizophrenia. For this reason the paper might perhaps better have been entitled "Violence in Psychotic Conditions." Here I would add only three considerations: (1) I have used the term "schizophrenia" in this paper to include schizophrenia of whatever degree of severity, including borderline schizophrenia; (2) I wanted it to include particularly clear—and frankly, for reader interest, dramatic—instances of violence on the part of patients; and (3) as I am sure Rosen well knows, interviews with frankly schizophrenic patients often consist so largely in non-verbal responses that it is impossible to provide any very meaningful typescript of them. I could not agree more with his long-held position that "psychotherapy should be taught by live demonstration." The verbal data which this paper contains, no matter how faithfully reproducing what I heard in playbacks of the sound-tapes, cannot be more than a relatively pale and dry approximation of the actual interviews.

He mentions that in his own experiences of treating potentially murderous patients, his reaction was not one of violence but in one instance, at least, of great fear. I remind him that I experienced fear in response to each of the three patients described at length in this paper, and I reassert the importance of the therapist's (or interviewer's) projection upon the patient of the former's unconscious—and to me quite understandable, under the circumstances—murderous feeling. This component, no mere idiosyncrasy of mine, is one which I have seen at work in many instances of colleagues' treatment of potentially dangerous patients, as described in supervisory sessions concerning patients I have never seen. With reliable repetitiveness, over the months of supervisory work in such instances, one finds that the therapist has been constricted in his therapeutic endeavor by a need to maintain under repression his own more violent impulses toward his threatening patient, and the treatment regularly goes better when one is able to help the therapist to become aware of his more rageful feelings, as so clearly occurred in the treatment of Mrs. Glaser.

Surely Rosen does not believe that I am advocating the talionic principle as any informed way of dealing with murderers or potential murderers, who of course need psychotherapeutic help in integrating, and thus gaining mastery of, their violent proclivities. To say that it is desirable that the therapist become conscious of his repressed murderousness toward the patient clearly implies, to my way of thinking, that the therapist should *not* act out his own murderous reactions to the patient. But, as I hoped to have made clear, the eminently desirable feeling of personal forgiveness toward a murderous, or potentially murderous, person is hypocritical and spurious rather than genuine if one has not gained access to one's own understandably violent condemnatory feelings toward him on this score.

Brand begins, "The main purpose of the case interviews recorded . . . is to initiate therapy, to draw out some reality factors of the case and some of its emotional tone, and to prepare the patient for rapport with the doctor to whom he or she will be assigned. With that understood, there is no need to be critical of the interviews as therapy sessions." Brand is letting me off a hook here which I am prepared to remain upon, for although these interviews are intended to be useful for teaching, they are intended even more to be of immediate therapeutic value for the patient. I have been asked many times if I would have behaved differently if the patient I had just interviewed were one of my own therapy patients whom I was seeing in my office. My best impression is that the similarities far outweigh the differences, the main difference being that in my office I would often say less, for in the teaching interviews I am frequently trying, through my verbalizing, to make relatively subtle non-verbal events more explicit and perceptible to the audience. In short, these teaching interviews are intended not only to have a catalytic effect upon the patient's therapy—which, I remind Brand, was in each of these three instances (as usual) well under way at the time the interview took place—but also to *be* a form of therapy for the patient.

To Brand's objection, like Rosen's, that the patient in each instance is in complete verbal contact, unlike more severely schizophrenic patients, again I wish to point out that typescripts of interviews like those in this paper are ill-suited to convey the predominantly non-verbal essence of that which proves therapeutic in one's work with the more deeply ill patients. In my previous writings there surely is no lack of detailed descriptions of such work, largely during my 15 years on the staff of Chestnut Lodge, with patients severely ill enough to fulfill Brand's most stringent criteria of massive regression. My first book (1960), concerning the role of the non-human environment in schizophrenia and in normal development, is comprised essentially of clinical examples, from my work and that of colleagues on the Chestnut Lodge staff, of the patient's and the therapist's reacting to one another as essentially non-human. Two of my recent papers (1972a, 1972b), by way of additional examples, detail my therapeutic approach in working with two chronically schizophrenic women, both of them far more ill than any of the three patients described in this paper.

In reference to the relatively moderate degree of illness in these three patients, Brand comments, "It may be for this reason that Dr. Searles does not assume a role of omnipotence, of the powerful parent able to bring his child up all over again, this time under truly loving and beneficent auspices." Here, in advocating what is well known to be a dimension of Rosen's therapeutic orientation, Brand touches upon the area of my main theoretical differences from Rosen, which is dealt with in my paper (1962) "Scorn, Disillusionment, and Adoration in the Psychotherapy of Schizophrenia," in which I report my experience that the patient's genuine feelings of adoration toward the therapist supervene only after the patient's initially predominant feelings of scorn, and subsequent feelings of disillusionment, have been largely worked through.

My paper (1955) "Dependency Processes in the Psychotherapy of Schizophrenia" emphasizes the importance of the therapist's feelings of dependency upon the patient (an emphasis which, so far as I know, Rosen's writings have not included), and my many published discussions (1959, 1965, 1973a) of therapeutic symbiosis, of which I began to speak in 1958, describe the mutuality of feelings of adoration in that crucially therapeutic phase of the treatment. Also, in two recent papers (1973a, 1973b) I discuss the patient's therapeutic strivings toward the analyst, a major dimension of this area with which again, so far as I know, Rosen's and Brand's theoretical concepts do not deal.

For many years, as for example in my paper (1961a) "The Evolution of the Mother Transference in Psychotherapy with the Schizophrenic Patient," I have emphasized the necessity of helping the patient to resolve his transference to oneself as a malevolently omnipotent mother, rather than trying somehow to override this transference by functioning from the outset as a benignly omnipotent mother in the manner which, it seems to me, Rosen (and, I suppose, Brand) would advocate. Lastly in this regard, in two recent papers (1970, 1971) concerning autism, I have described the therapeutic value, for the patient, in the therapist's becoming able to experience the patient as comprising his, the therapist's, meaningful whole world in the context of the therapeutic session. So it can be seen that my theoretical concepts are in major ways very different from those of Rosen and, I gather, of Brand.

Brand's statement that "Psychosis is, in its beginnings and in its depths, an oral problem" I find hard to gainsay; my first published paper (1951), "Data Concerning Certain Manifestations of Incorporation," had to do with oral-incorporative processes, although in trying to understand those most primitive processes which one finds in autism I find it less helpful to think in terms of mouth and breast than in terms of the much less well-differentiated *world* in which the individual is so completely immersed, or with which, alternatively, he is so bleakly out of contact. Little's (1960) writing on undifferentiatedness and Milner's (1952, 1969) writings about her work with deeply regressed patients have proved particularly congenial to my own experience with such patients.

I fully concur with Brand's statement, "Aggression in a parent may be healthy; it may have nothing to do with violence."

Malin says, "I believe that it is extremely difficult for most psychoanalysts to allow their feelings to be expressed in the therapeutic relationship on the level that Dr. Searles suggests is natural for him." I wish to emphasize in this connection that the kind of interaction described in this paper by no means came naturally and easily to me; it was achieved, bit by bit, only in the course of years of great difficulty with constrictingly obsessive-compulsive defenses from which, as I am sure is clear to the reader, I am still far from free. Several of my earlier papers have detailed aspects of my struggle to gain greater freedom, analogously, from the role of conventional psychiatrist and "dedicated physician" in my work with patients, a role which is tailor-made to dovetail with, and thus perpetuate, the schizophrenic patient's sadistic mockery of the therapist who is trying, without descending into such ugly emotions as hatred, to rescue him from his suffering.

When Malin says that "Most analysts . . . would tend to regard [these feelings] as countertransference phenomena which are best handled in self-analysis, or perhaps in a supervisory situation," I quite agree; but this, more than anything else, is what my writings are endeavoring to change. I do not hold a brief so much for the analyst's becoming more verbose, say, or very much more expressive of his immediate feeling-reactions to his patients. But I do strongly believe that "most analysts," to use Malin's phrase, very much underestimate the extent to which their own feelings, in the course of the analytic session, will prove to be priceless data in the analysis of the patient—if, that is, the analyst regards them primarily as valuable clues to what is transpiring at non-verbalized, unconscious levels in the patient-analyst relationship and within the patient himself, and does not assume, guiltily and anxiously, that these feelings are primarily intrusive counter-transference reactions stemming mainly from his own un-explored childhood. It is only as I have come to see—over the years and from an initial base of great caution and undue readiness to write off many of my emotional reactions as aberrant, crazy, and irrelevant to what was going on in the patient—how very frequently such authentic informational value concerning the patient's psychodynamics is inherent in these reactions of mine, that I have moved more and more freely into the kind of interaction this paper details. No, it by no means came naturally to me; but I do hold that the primary value of a training analysis, in its aspect of equipping the analytic candidate to function effectively as an analyst, consists in helping him to become sufficiently in touch with his own emotional life so that when one or another area of this is evoked in his work with a patient he can feel suffi-ciently at ease with it to remain interested in discerning what subtle but real processes at work in the patient, heretofore unanalyzed, have provided the stimulus for this evocation.

It seems to me that Malin and Grotstein have made an excellent point in suggesting, in their 1966 paper to which Malin refers, that it is the way in which a therapist responds to the projection of the patient that allows for modification of these projections to occur. But I wish to reassert here, as I have many times in previous papers, my experience-based conviction that patients' projective (or introjective) reactions (and of course by the same token their transference reac-tions), no matter how psychotically distorted these may seem, can be discovered to be founded in part upon some element of reality. In my very first analytic paper (1949), never accepted for publication, I suggested that "all projective man-ifestations, transference reactions included . . . have some *real* basis in the analyst's behavior, and therefore represent distortions in degree only." A paper (1972a), "The Function of the Patient's Realistic Perceptions of the Analyst in Delu-sional Transference," concerning my work over more than 20 years now with a remarkably delusional woman, discusses, as the title suggests, my discovering to what a remarkable degree her delusional transference reactions, no matter how incredibly exaggerated or otherwise distorted, proved to be responses to one or another heretofore largely unconscious aspect of my own personality-functioning during the sessions.

Malin comments, "I do not agree that Searles's particular approach to the schizophrenic patient is always very helpful. In my experience there are a number of schizophrenic patients who will become very frightened by what would appear to them as a loss of control on the part of the therapist." I am well aware that I myself am not always very helpful to patients, schizophrenic or otherwise, and if on balance the evidence is that I am doing more good than harm, I rest relatively content with my efforts. As for psychiatric residents, for instance, who after seeing me do interviews have endeavored to utilize my approach in their own work with their patients, I am aware that this attempted identification with me—although more often than not it does prove useful, or my teaching interviews would long since have ceased—sometimes does not go well. This tends to happen when a resident endeavors to employ the open bluntness which is one of the characteristics of my approach without having first acquired the requisite personal acquaintance with his own unconscious and the requisite degree of clinical experience. I think that one of the reasons why this at times does not go well is that the therapist in this instance is not equipped to deal with the consequences of his intervention—with, for example, the patient's reacting with increased anxiety and oftentimes with the conviction that the therapist is being the equivalent of the psychotic, sadistic (and so on) parent of early childhood. Some residents find that such reactions in the patient make them increasingly anxious and guilty, and the whole relationship quickly becomes permeated with inadequately dealt-with anxiety. I shall have more to say about this matter in responding to Flarsheim's discussion.

The most difficult thing for me personally in doing teaching interviews with schizophrenic patients is knowing how to cope with the frequently intense threat—how, that is, not only to tolerate it, but to utilize it as communication, as information concerning unconscious processes at work in the patient—lest one come, by reason of one's responses or lack of responses during the interview, to be viewed by patient and audience members alike as something other than human, far more dreadful than a terribly lonely person—something inherently outside the human pale because lacking in the kind of emotional equipment (compassion, kindness, and so on) requisite for membership in the human species. It is precisely this kind of subjective identity experience against which the schizophrenic patient's delusional experiences are serving as unconscious defenses. Just as I find this sort of identity experience difficult in a teaching interview, so may the resident find it impossibly difficult, on venturing a bit out of the relatively safe (for himself) conventional-psychiatrist role in his work with the patient and participating with him in a more tangibly affective manner. But I cannot see how we can help the patient with his largely unconscious, fearful conviction of his own being something other than human if we remain too entrenched in having to demonstrate that we (the therapist) are the kindly, intendedly helpful, rage-free *one* in the relationship.

Malin writes of "The angry, violent attitude that is demonstrated by the violent schizophrenic patient and projected into the therapist . . ." Here is an area in which I sense a fundamental difference, as I have already mentioned, between his concepts and mine. I surmise that he tends to assume that the patient is purely projecting, whereas I always assume the patient's projection to be based upon some increment of reality in the therapist, no matter at how unconscious a level in the latter. I have cited many times in this connection Freud's (1922) drawing attention to the basis in reality of projection: "We begin to see that we describe the behaviour of both jealous and persecuted paranoiacs very inadequately by saying that they project outwards on to others what they do not wish to recognize in themselves. Certainly they do this;

but they do not project it into the sky, so to speak, where there is nothing of the sort already . . ." (p. 226).

Malin makes an excellent point when he suggests that the negative therapeutic reaction on the part of a violent schizophrenic patient can be a way in which the patient is hanging on to the only internal object situation he can handle, that is, the relationship to the primary objects, the breast-mother. Malin perceptively asks, "Are we perhaps dealing with the situation in which any attempt at growth and development means to the patient that this breast-mother must be relinquished, which he perceives as a fragmentation of all inner psychic contents and a disappearance of the self?" This I find a valuable way of describing the importance which the patient comes to have for the therapist also, in what I describe as the phase of therapeutic symbiosis. It is the therapist's need to maintain under *repression* his experiencing the patient as being of such a primitive kind of maternal significance to him that accounts for his own unconscious resistance to letting the consciously desired maturational changes occur in the treatment relationship. From what I have seen both in my own work and in that of supervisees, it is only insofar as the therapist becomes *aware of* this kind of early-mother significance that the patient has for him (as well, of course, as he for the patient, which is much easier to recognize) that he becomes able, more wholeheartedly now, to work toward the patient's further recovery, which, as is now evident, will involve deep feelings of infantile loss not only for the patient but for the therapist also.

Little's comments I find, as in all of her papers which I have read, illuminating and informative, especially her thoughts about the varying degrees of differentiation in each of the patients described here and about the problem, therefore, of differential diagnosis and prognosis.

I know of no other writer besides Little who accepts as fully as I do that what I term a phase of therapeutic symbiosis (or, in Little's phrase, of undifferentiatedness) is essential in successful therapy. It is powerfully strengthening to me to read her statements (in marked contrast to Malin's views, for example, as I see it): "I agree entirely with Searles that the reactions brought about in the therapist are of prime importance. The ability to allow his ego boundaries to dissolve temporarily—to let himself become merged with the patient, and to permit reality and delusional or hallucinatory experience to become indistinguishable—is the only route by which real contact, understanding, and ability to share in an experience can develop." I fully agree, likewise, with her emphasis, in the very next sentence: "But equally important are the ways in which the boundaries can be re-established and the speed and progression of the resynthesis, when it is appropriate." Little's own writings have been most helpful to me in this latter connection, and I wish to recommend Jacobson (1964) as also providing highly valuable formulations concerning the progressive differentiation of the various psychic structures.

Upon reading Bychowski's discussion I had intended to make a spirited response to some of the more savage of his comments, but having heard more recently the sad news of his death I feel that a more moderate tone is in order here.

When he says that "apparently his entourage is also filled with all sorts of violent feelings toward the patients," he was apparently attributing to me, as I mentioned earlier, a sycophantic following which does not in actuality exist. As I have said already, the colleagues who observe my interviews are, on balance, more critical than these discussants are collectively, and I doubt that anyone would regard any of them as sycophantic. Also, I hope to have made it quite clear by now that the kind cooperation extended to me by Bisco, Coutu, and Scibetta does not warrant their being subjected to the sneering term "entourage."

I hope few readers will respond to Bychowski's call for the abandonment of an essentially psychoanalytic approach to such dangerous patients as Mr. Delaney: "One has to ask whether some other therapeutic method, more in the style of conditioning, and of retraining, based, of course, on the dynamic insights, might not be more appropriate."

The gulf between Bychowski's views and my own is so wide

that I cannot attempt to bridge it in this brief space. I am content to leave it for readers of his work and of mine to take from it what they find useful and relevant, and discard the rest. The dimensions of the gulf are suggested not only by the more excoriating of his remarks here, but also by a statement he makes in his book *Psychotherapy of Psychosis* (1952) near the beginning of the first chapter, "The Personality of the Psychiatrist": "not only should he not respond with overt hostility to aggressive manifestations of the patient, *it is also necessary that he should be sufficiently mature so as not to harbor any resentment toward him*" [p. 1, italics added]. This point of view, which would require that a therapist of integrity be either obsessive or schizoid if he were not to disqualify himself from attempting this kind of work, was precisely my emotional orientation toward patients, neurotic as well as psychotic, 27 years ago. As I have already mentioned, I have been spending all these years primarily in a difficult struggle to become less constricted, more open to communications from my own unconscious, and, by the same token, from the patient himself.

I was amused at Bychowski's extending me his "sympathy" for my troubled inner state; well might I need sympathy, after he got through with me. But I am not to be pitied for having become able to let a patient become lastingly a part of me; for me, that is a hard-won accomplishment.

Wexler is a man from whom, I am sure, I can learn much. All that he says concerning efforts at reparation make a great deal of sense to me, and his statement that "no single formulation serves to explain the violence of the schizophrenic patient" is incontestable. I hold that my capacity for integrated ego-functioning is not as fully in chaos as he apparently regards it; but, after Bychowski, Wexler's comments made relatively light reading for me, such that I feel moved only to express the hope that we shall have a chance, sometime, to compare clinical experiences at leisure.

Rosenfeld, in his description of his treatment of the woman doctor who suffered from an at times delusional syphilophobia, mentions that "In the countertransference I never felt that I was the murderous mother, but I was aware of an intense pressure coming from the patient to change me into a punishing, frightening superego which threatened her with death and accused her of not being human." Here I wish to emphasize that, in my own analytic work, neither do *I* feel that I *am* the murderous mother; I definitely am not recommending that the analyst be, or transitorily become, psychotic (i.e., come to misidentify himself as being the patient's mother, for example) in working with these patients.

But I definitely would find it mystifying if the analyst were entirely a stranger to murderous feelings within himself toward such difficult patients as Rosenfeld has treated. Rosenfeld, whose writings have taught me much, as I have many times acknowledged, nonetheless is a prime example of those colleagues who, in my opinion, portray psychoanalytic treatment as though the patient's transference is "pure transference" and the latter's projection "pure projection," without these reactions being based upon any reality in the feelings—murderous feelings, for example—which the analyst indeed comes to experience toward the patient over the course of the often difficult treatment.

Similarly, while Rosenfeld makes a useful point about the importance of assessing the strength of the patient's murderous intent versus the strength of his fear of it and wish to become able to control it, his comment that it may or may not be a "real" desire to kill reflects, in my opinion, his tendency, repeatedly manifest in his writings, to imply that some feelings are not "real." It is important that we regard both sides of the patient's conflictual feelings as *real*, for otherwise we fail to appreciate the intensity of his genuine conflict.

In hypothesizing about the situation where the small infant projects his destructiveness and his fear of it into his mother, Rosenfeld suggests that "It is the mother's capacity to contain both the aggression and the fear of disintegration (Bion) which gradually leads to a lessening of the sense of danger and to a strengthening of the infantile ego in coping with the aggressive impulses." Here again, in line with my foregoing commentary about Rosenfeld's views, I suggest that the mother's capacity to contain the aggression consists in part in her being conscious of, rather than needing to repress and project upon the infant or other persons, the murderous component of her actual feelings toward him.

I concur with Rosenfeld's well-stated emphasis upon the importance of distinguishing between neurotic countertransference on the analyst's part and "countertransference" which is essentially an empathic experiencing of feelings communicated from the patient. This indeed is an ever-present, never completed, and most important task. As I have already said, concerning the evolution of my own analytic position over the years, it is only as I have gained, bit by bit, a degree of increased freedom from an initial too-great readiness to *assume*, guiltily and frightenedly, that this or that emotional response within myself was predominantly of the former (true countertransference) variety, that I have become increasingly able to appreciate the richness and accuracy of the information, at times no less than amazing, which flows from the patient to oneself, largely by non-verbal avenues, and which is made available by largely unconscious empathic processes. In order to come to understand the workings of these processes better than we do at present, it is essential, in my opinion, that we react to such "personal" responses within ourselves not by self-condemnation but by regarding them, until proved otherwise (until proved, that is, more properly a function of the analyst's own unanalyzed childhood history), as inherent and priceless data of the patient's analysis, data for mutual exploration—well-timed, of course —on the part of both patient and analyst, and eminently deserving of inclusion in any subsequently published account of the analysis.

Bak's discussion is brief but telling and requires, therefore, that I respond to it at relative length. It is evident that he is more conservative, analytically, than I—more cautious, more given to emphasizing secondary process. To me he represents that aggregation of relatively classical analysts who are inclined to regard me as a wild analyst and who, from hard-won positions of respect and even dominance over much of the psychoanalytic thinking in this country, have made it difficult for me to get my papers published in our leading analytic journals.

Bak makes the excellent and fundamental point (in emphasizing, as does Wexler, the patient's restitutive effort) that "It is not easy to decide whether the murderous acts represent a breakthrough of aggression with the aim of destroying a person, or whether they appear in the course of restitution, i.e., re-establishing lost contact with the world (objects)." Clinical documentation of this point is contained in a paper of mine (1958) in which I described at considerable length some of the clinical events of my work with a murderously rageful and frequently hallucinating hebephrenic man, and summarized the description by saying, "It was both fascinating to me in a research sense, and deeply gratifying to me as a therapist, to find that, by the end of two and a half years of both his, and my own, becoming more fully and consistently aware of our respective feelings of intense contempt and rage, his hallucinating had now all but disappeared from our session" (p. 204). We had become, that is, much more real interpersonal objects to one another. Similarly, in recent years I have come to realize with increasing frequency that urges toward physical violence, on the part of either a patient or myself, are in the service of our effort to make some human contact with one another in the face of the chilling weirdness attendant upon his most severely schizophrenic ways of relating to me and to others.

Bak's statement that "The lack of differentiation between animate and inanimate objects is not a cause of violence but in a way a consequence of it" might better be expressed, I believe (as I endeavored to describe in this paper), as *both* a cause *and* a consequence. My previously mentioned paper (1972a) concerning delusional transference contains much data from the account of the chronically schizophrenic woman whose analysis is detailed there, clearly showing that her awesome degree of non-differentiation between animate

80 —

and inanimate objects is both a cause and in part a consequence of her violence.

Bak comments that "one cannot help feeling that these subjective reactions of the therapist and supervisor are overdrawn. Instead of using them as *signals* for intellectual awareness, they may be *lived* for longer than necessary." This is a sobering point, with much riding on it—the whole question of whether I do wild analysis and indulge in being crazy along with the patient. I genuinely do not believe that I do, and I believe that Bak, like other persons who have made comparable comments about my interviews with schizophrenic patients, would feel reassured if he were present at typical sessions with neurotic patients—during, for example, the considerable number of training analyses I have done and am doing. I have been a training analyst for 15 years now, and for nine of them have spent most of my working time in that activity. In most such sessions I say little or nothing at all, and find that it is only on landmark occasions—of crucial value, nonetheless, for the analytic work—that I engage at all openly in the kind of interaction which is commonplace in my work (whether as therapist or teaching-consultant) with borderline and more severely ill patients. But I find his comment sufficiently thought-provoking to keep it very much in mind during the coming years in evaluating my own work and endeavoring to be maximally useful to and minimally exploitative of or otherwise harmful to patients.

He goes on, "Also, there is too much emphasis on subjective observation. . . . there is still room for clinical judgment and prognostication, at least partly based on experience." Here I wish to mention once again the inherent inadequacy of transcriptions of interviews. During these interviews I am responding in actuality, to a far higher degree than the reader has any way of knowing from this paper, to tangible non-verbal cues from the patient, cues which I perceive in a context of many previous interviews with other patients who, as regards the particular psychodynamics giving rise to the cue in question, are clinically very comparable with the patient I am presently interviewing. It is this accumulated clinical experience which, hand in hand with an increasingly frequent finding that my own personal responses to the patient are indeed relevant to what is going on in his unconscious, has given me the confidence to conduct these demonstration interviews in a manner which increasingly reveals my "personal" responses in the interview situation.

Another factor in this paper is that each of the three interviews it details was an extraordinarily anxious one for me personally, compared with the vast majority of such interviews I have conducted. I have had other interviews which were equally stressful, but not many. I chose these partly because of what I regarded as their relatively high dramatic potential for capturing the interest of the reader; but one of the prices I have paid by such a selection is that in them I emerge as more threatened with feelings of anxiety and isolation and less comfortably ensconced in clinical experience than is usually the case in my demonstration interviews.

Before leaving Bak's discussion I want to make a point concerning a subject upon which he touches: prognostication. It is easy for psychiatric residents to attribute prognostic omniscience to anyone who has had a great deal of experience in working with schizophrenic patients; his wealth of clinical experience is so great as seemingly to place his clinical objectivity, in handing down a prognostic pronouncement, beyond serious question. But I have found innumerable times that one of the most important lessons to be learned from these interviews, by me as well as by the residents I am teaching, is the subtly distorting impact which the interviewer's unrecognized countertransference has upon the prognostication he tends so loftily to give—and which in most cases, indeed, he is called upon to render.

There is a tremendous tendency, for example, for the interviewer to remain largely unconscious of the hate which the patient engenders in him during the interview, and to act out this hate during the discussion period after the interview by assigning to the patient a gloomy, basically hopeless prognosis, in a hypocritically sad or gloomy manner. In the light of the interviewer's prestige, this is equivalent to his placing a very considerably effective curse upon the patient who, during the just-terminated interview, has succeeded in doing various forms of violence to some of the interviewer's more cherished images of himself.

There is a comparably powerful tendency, on the other hand, for the interviewer not to face, during the interview, his own feelings of disappointment and disillusionment toward a patient who has proven able to maintain a façade of relative health and attractiveness. Thus, after the interview, he is likely to de-emphasize, in his comments about prognosis, the seriousness and tenacity of the pathologic process actually at work in the patient.

The interviewer's relationship with the therapist, and with the resident-group generally, is another important dimension, making real clinical objectivity most difficult to attain in this setting. The interviewer tends to be constricted, partially outside his own awareness, by a concern not to place too frighteningly somber a prognosis upon a patient about whom these other persons have high hopes, founded largely upon a transitory and superficial, transference-based symptomatic improvement in the therapeutic work thus far.

In short, where Bak reacts to what he tends, I gather, to regard as relatively wild analysis on my part, I react with comparable skepticism to his apparent assumption that clinical objectivity, acquired on the basis of no matter how many years of experience, can be maintained with relative comfort and certainty in the face of the intensity of involvement which these interviews need to achieve in order to be of maximal therapeutic and teaching value. Such supposed objectivity could well be regarded as wildly illusory.

Flarsheim comments, "I have had psychiatric residents misuse Searles's writings to justify burdening patients with their own emotional reactions, which are disruptive to the treatment." His reservations are to a degree, in my opinion, justified. In responding to Malin's discussion, I acknowledged that sometimes a psychiatric resident's attempted identification with me does not go well. In the belief that several of the discernible factors involved are not limited to my own experience but are present in the work of supervisors and consultants generally, I shall mention a number of them. I spoke before of (1) the resident's relative lack of familiarity with the workings of his own unconscious and relative lack of clinical experience, particularly with regard to the patient's responses to interpretations. In addition, there are the following factors to be considered in instances where the resident's attempted identification with me proves antitherapeutic to the patient: (2) the resident's partially unconscious, partially transference-derived competitive feelings, contempt, and rage toward me, and consequent unconscious attempt to demonstrate my techniques as being predominantly antitherapeutic; (3) the patient's unworked-through murderous rage at me, in terms of which patient and therapist in effect join together in murdering my intended image as a constructively functioning psychotherapist; (4) frustrated dependency feelings, on the part of both patient and therapist, toward me (who in reality visit their institution, if more than once only, then at best infrequently); (5) the competitiveness of senior staff members toward me, lest I acquire the role of favorite teacher-model for the residents; (6) my own competitiveness toward the resident-therapist, the senior staff members, and also toward the patient—competitiveness heightened by my own relative professional isolation as a full-time private practitioner and occasional consultant, who has found painful the loneliness attendant upon his having left Chestnut Lodge nearly ten years ago, after nearly 15 years of work on its staff, and who has not acquired subsequently a comparable degree of group-relatedness with colleagues. I realized too, some years back, with rueful amusement, that (7) the flounderingly inept resident who is struggling to be Searles is indeed accurately identifying with an entirely real component of my ego-identity —with, that is, the "me" which is struggling to be SEARLES, struggling to fulfill my own ego-ideals as well as the images which the more admiringly hopeful of the audience members apparently have of me.

In this last regard, as the years go by I have become

appreciably less burdened with concern about the audience's reaction. There have been many interviews which have left me aware that the audience was feeling predominantly disappointed and dissatisfied with the interview, but in which I have felt, nonetheless about myself, that given the difficulties posed by the patient's psychopathology, and given my own to-me familiar limitations in ego-functioning imposed by unresolved areas of psychopathology in myself, I have done sufficiently well to feel relatively kindly and accepting toward myself. The audience's expectations, if one is too much at their mercy as a projected, harshly demanding superego, can be cruel indeed.

I fully concur with Flarsheim's emphasis upon the prognostically differentiating role of available capacity for humor in the patient. I would add only my conviction, developed over the years, that *everyone* has a sense of humor, no matter how straight-faced, sadistically mocking, or otherwise unconventional its mode of expression, and no matter at how unconscious a level it is operating. It is relatively seldom, and in my opinion of particularly sobering prognostic significance, that one of my demonstration interviews, even with a tragically ill patient, includes no moments of shared and genuinely amused laughter. So I tend to ask myself, during the interview, not whether this patient has a sense of humor, but rather how is his particular sense of humor being manifested at present, and is he predominantly conscious or unconscious of it.

I am sure that Flarsheim recognizes that, on the other hand, the patient's capacity for humor can be employed unconsciously as a powerful resistance to therapeutic progress. More than once I have seen, in my own analytic patients and others, that a patient particularly talented in the use of humor can postpone, time after time, his becoming aware of wishes to murder me, by proving reliably able to cause me again and again to break up in laughter, the unconscious equivalent of slaying me. Such interaction can serve for both participants as an unconscious means of fending off the recognition of murderous feelings, grief, and other non-humorous emotions

— 85

which need to become integrated in the course of their analytic work. The chronic schizophrenic patient's sense of humor is often manifested, in a manner largely unconscious to both participants, in mockingly sadistic, highly treatment-resistant delusional identifications with the therapist, such as I described in a recent paper (1972a).

Flarsheim's statement that "There are limits to the patient's capacity for actual, in contrast to fantasied, destruction" is surely valid, and to me seems relevant to my impression, mentioned in the first paragraph of the discussion section of this paper, that those patients who most violently damage one's image of oneself have no need to resort to physical violence toward one.

He says that "The therapist's unconscious destructiveness toward the patient can also take the form of an unconscious wish for the patient to commit suicide; this may first be experienced by the therapist as anxiety lest the patient commit suicide." Flarsheim's experience in this regard evidently corresponds to mine. As I mentioned in a paper in 1967,

> . . . the suicidal patient, who finds us so unable to be aware of the murderous feelings he fosters in us through his guilt-and-anxiety-producing threats of suicide, feels increasingly constricted, perhaps indeed to the point of suicide, by the therapist who, in reaction formation against his intensifying, unconscious wishes to kill the patient, hovers increasingly "protectively" about him, for whom he feels an omnipotence-based physicianly concern. Hence it is, paradoxically, the very physician most anxiously concerned to *keep the patient alive* who is tending most vigorously, at an unconscious level, to drive him to what has come to seem the only autonomous act left to him—suicide.

Relevant here, too, are the following passages from my earlier paper (1961b), "Phases of Patient-Therapist Interaction in the Psychotherapy of Chronic Schizophrenia," concerning the phase of resolution of the symbiosis:

> On the other occasions, the therapist experiences a resolution of the symbiosis, or at least a step in this resolution process, not in this quiet and subjectively inscrutable way, but rather with a sudden sense of *outrage* [p. 544].
> . . . One now leaves in his hands the choice as to whether he wants to spend the remainder of his life in a mental hospital, or whether he

wants, instead, to become well. In every instance that I can recall . . . I have found occasion to express this newly won attitude to the patient himself, emphasizing that it is all the same to me. . . . One cares not, now, how callous this may sound, nor even whether the patient will respond to it with suicide or incurable psychotic disintegration; and one feels and says this while casting one's own professional status, too, into the gamble. . . . Thus, in effect, one braves the threat of destruction both to the patient and oneself, in taking it into one's hands to declare one's individuality, come what may [p. 545].

. . . if the therapeutic relationship is to traverse successfully the phase of resolution of the symbiosis, the therapist must be able to brave . . . the threats of suicide or psychotic disintegration on the patient's part, and of the professional and personal destruction to himself which might be a correlate of such outcomes . . . [p. 549].

I am deeply gratified by Flarsheim's appreciation of my work, and in turn find informative and congenial to my own clinical experience all that he says, in his discussion, of the psychodynamics of violence and suicide. Without the kind of professional comradeship I feel toward him, and in varying degrees toward all these discussants who have accorded this paper their thoughtful comments, psychoanalytic work with schizophrenic patients, which at best is formidable despite its many gratifications, would be quite impossible.

REFERENCES

Brand, M. (1968), *Savage Sleep*. New York: Crown.

Bychowski, G. (1952), *Psychotherapy of Psychosis*. New York: Grune & Stratton.

Freud, S. (1922), Some neurotic mechanisms in jealousy, paranoia, and homosexuality. *Standard Edition*, 18:221-232. London: Hogarth Press.

Giovacchini, P. (1969), Aggression: Adaptive and disruptive aspects. *Bull. Phila. Assn. for Psychoanal.*, 19/2:76-86.

Jacobson, E. (1964), *The Self and the Object World*. New York: International Universities Press.

Little, M. (1960), On basic unity. *Internat. J. Psycho-Anal.*, 41:377-384.

Malin, A. & Grotstein, J. (1966), Projective identification in the therapeutic process. *Internat. J. Psycho-Anal.*, 47:26-31.

Milner, M. (1952), Aspects of symbolism in comprehension of the not-self. *Internat. J. Psycho-Anal.*, 33:181-195.

——— (1969), *The Hands of the Living God—An Account of a Psychoanalytic Treatment*. New York: International Universities Press.

Rangell, L. (1952), The analysis of a doll phobia. *Internat. J. Psycho-Anal.*, 33:43-53.

Rosenfeld, H. (1955), Notes on the psycho-analysis of the superego conflict of an acute schizophrenic patient. In: *New Directions in Psycho-Analysis*, eds, M. Klein, P. Heimann, & R. Money-Kyrle. London: Tavistock, pp. 180-219.

Searles, H. F. (1949), (I) Two suggested revisions of the concept of transference and (II) Comments regarding the usefulness of emotions arising in the analyst during the analytic hour. Unpublished.

——— (1951), Data concerning certain manifestations of incorporation. In: *Collected Papers on Schizophrenia and Related Subjects*. New York: International Universities Press, pp. 39-69.

——— (1955), Dependency processes in the psychotherapy of schizophrenia. In: *Collected Papers on Schizophrenia and Related Subjects*. New York: International Universities Press, pp. 114-156.

——— (1958), The schizophrenic's vulnerability to the therapist's unconscious processes. In: *Collected Papers on Schizophrenia and Related Subjects*. New York: International Universities Press, pp. 192-215.

——— (1959), Integration and differentiation in schizophrenia. In: *Collected Papers on Schizophrenia and Related Subjects*. New York: International Universities Press, pp. 304-316.

——— (1960), *The Nonhuman Environment in Normal Development and in Schizophrenia*. New York: International Universities Press.

——— (1961a), The evolution of the mother transference in psychotherapy with the schizophrenic patient. In: *Collected Papers on Schizophrenia and Related Subjects*. New York: International Universities Press, pp. 349-380.

——— (1961b), Phases of patient-therapist interaction in the psychotherapy of chronic schizophrenia. In: *Collected Papers on Schizophrenia and Related Subjects*. New York: International Universities Press, pp. 521-559.

———— (1962), Scorn, disillusionment, and adoration in the psychotherapy of schizophrenia. In: *Collected Papers on Schizophrenia and Related Subjects*. New York: International Universities Press, pp. 605-625.

———— (1965), *Collected Papers on Schizophrenia and Related Subjects*. New York: International Universities Press.

———— (1967), The "dedicated physician" in psychotherapy and psychoanalysis. In: *Crosscurrents in Psychiatry and Psychoanalysis*, ed. R. W. Gibson. Philadelphia/Toronto: Lippincott, pp. 128-143.

———— (1970), Autism and the phase of transition to therapeutic symbiosis. *Contemporary Psychoanal.*, 7:1-20.

———— (1971), Pathologic symbiosis and autism. In: *In the Name of Life— Essays in Honor of Erich Fromm*, ed. B. Landis, & E. S. Tauber. New York: Holt, Rinehart & Winston, pp. 69–83.

———— (1972a), The function of the patient's realistic perceptions of the analyst in delusional transference. *Brit. J. Med. Psychol.*, 45:1-18.

———— (1972b), Intensive psychotherapy of chronic schizophrenia. *Internat. J. Psychoanal. Psychother.*, 1:30-51.

———— (1973a), Concerning therapeutic symbiosis. In: *The Annual of Psychoanalysis*, 1:247-262.

———— (1973b), The patient as therapist to his analyst. To appear in *Tactics and Techniques in Psychoanalytic Therapy*, Vol. 2, ed. L. B. Boyer, P. L. Giovacchini, & A. Flarsheim. New York: Jason Aronson.

Storr, A. (1968), *Human Aggression*. New York: Atheneum.

Szasz, T. (1965), *The Ethics of Psychoanalysis*. New York: Basic Books.

Psychoanalysis of the Rich, the Famous, and the Influential

CHARLES WILLIAM WAHL, M.D.

Dr. Wahl is Clinical Professor of Psychiatry at the UCLA School of
Medicine, and a consultant in psychiatry at the Sepulveda, Oliveview,
and Camarillo Hospitals. He is on the faculty of the Southern California Psychoanalytic Institute. Dr. Wahl is the author of two books,
New Dimensions in Psychosomatic Medicine, and *Sexual Problems
in Medical Practice.* He is a contributor to 23 other books and author of 98 papers, the majority of which are on aspects of psychosomatic medicine and the meaning and theory of the fear of
death.

Discussants

SANDOR S. FELDMAN, M.D.†

The late Dr. Feldman was Clinical Professor Emeritus of Psychiatry at the
Medical Center, University of Rochester, New York. He came to the United
States in 1939. He has published papers in Hungarian, German, and English,
and books in Hungarian and English. His best-known book in English is
Mannerisms of Speech and Gestures in Everyday Life.

ANGEL GARMA, M.D.

Dr. Garma is Founder and Past President of the Argentine Psychoanalytic
Association and Founder and Past Director of the Psychoanalytic Institute of
Buenos Aires. He has written several papers dealing with transference and
countertransference reactions, among them, in *The Psychoanalytic Forum,*
"Group Rivalry between Analysts and Its Influence on Candidates in Training."

ROBERT M. GILLILAND, M.D.

Dr. Gilliland is Associate Professor of Psychiatry at Baylor College of Medicine, and on the Faculty of the New Orleans Psychoanalytic Institute where
he is a Training and Supervising Analyst. He has been in private practice of
psychoanalysis since 1952.

MILTON L. MILLER, M.D.

Dr. Miller is Professor of Psychiatry at the University of North Carolina and
Director of the University of North Carolina/Duke University Psychoanalytic
Training Program. He has been a training analyst for many years and was
formerly President of the Institute for Psychoanalytic Medicine of Southern

California. His recent publications include his article on the poet Shelley in Volume 1 of *The Psychoanalytic Forum*, a new edition of *Nostalgia, A Psychoanalytic Study of Marcel Proust*, a contribution on Balzac, and a review of Weston Barre's *The Ghost Dance*.

LEON J. SAUL, M.D.

Dr. Saul is Emeritus Professor of Psychiatry at the Medical School at the University of Pennsylvania, Emeritus Psychiatric Consultant to Swarthmore College, and in private psychoanalytic practice. He has published more than 150 papers and articles and seven books, the latest of which is *Psychodynamically Based Psychotherapy*.

PAULA HEIMANN, M.D.

A Fellow of the Royal College of Psychiatrists and a Training Analyst in London, Dr. Heimann's publications include investigation of the problems of psychoanalytic training and technique in general; transference and countertransference; the operational use of the countertransference; and early infantile development.

Psychoanalysis of the Rich, the Famous, and the Influential

CHARLES WILLIAM WAHL, M.D.
Los Angeles, California

RECENTLY, ON THREE SEPARATE occasions during conversation with colleagues, I was astonished to hear them make inappropriate disclosures of patient identification or material. It was the more surprising since I knew all of them to be excellent clinicians—experienced, conscientious men who took their Hippocratic responsibilities very seriously. Not one of them seemed to be aware of the inappropriateness of his communication and, most significantly, in each instance the indiscretion related to a person of celebrity or influence.

This set me to thinking about the analysis of the rich, the famous, and the influential, and to consider some of the special characteristics in the analysis of such patients and of the transference and countertransference that can be evoked therein. I began also to look more deeply into what has been my long-standing clinical impression, that many more patients in these three categories had had incomplete, ineffective, or unsatisfactory analytic experiences than any other category of patient.

I remember some years ago having been told by a famous man who had been unsuccessful in two previous therapeutic efforts and who was now my patient, "Both of the doctors were more like friends than doctors. They fawned on me, seemed to want to know me as a friend, and one of them even asked me for an autograph for his daughter." As this third analysis progressed, it became clear that one of the reasons this patient had failed to form a working imago transference in his previous analyses was that an examination of the factors which evoked such interplay in the analyst-patient relationship had been neglected.

In a general consideration of why such patients so often fail to receive a good therapeutic result in their analyses, several factors suggest themselves. Among these it is probably not without significance that our work, uniquely among the specialties of medicine, is intensely solitary in character. Its triumphs and defeats, difficulties and achievements, save only in a most circumscribed and scientific fashion, can never be shared with others. Hence, the analyst's need for recognition and for praise is often painfully aborted. It is thus understandable, if unacceptable, that an occasional departure from grace may take the form of name-dropping, which is perhaps a subtle indication on the analyst's part that he is prized and valued by the great, particularly if the patient he mentions has an impressive, immediately recognizable name and reputation.

This need partakes of the same unconscious dynamism that is seen in the dreams of intimacy and familiarity with a famous person which our patients frequently report. We regularly find upon analysis that these dreams not only are associated with an immediate and pervasive lack of self-esteem, but that they derive from early needs for parental recognition and acceptance which, thwarted and neglected at the time, have been subsequently displaced onto the symbolic figure of a celebrity. The analyst, therefore, may unwittingly play out by name-dropping, or by personal cultivation of a famous patient, his own unresolved sibling rivalries and oedipal strivings by displacing them onto colleagues whom "the great one" has *not* chosen as his analyst. If these countertransference phenomena remain unrecognized and unaltered, major artifacts and impediments in the analysis can result.

An interesting aspect of this dynamism may be activated if the famous person is a movie personality or "sex symbol" of the opposite sex. Here, to be especially chosen by such a patient may sometimes initiate in the analyst a sexual countertransference of special puissance. If this is repressed, and it usually is, it may often be expressed by reaction formation, and may then result in the analyst's persistent avoidance of viewing and analyzing the important fact of the patient's sexual symbology in her life and in her relations with others. Or it may take the form of a small series of chivalrous and quasi-seductive mannerisms which pander to the patient's exterior image, as the analyst, utilizing his special coign of vantage, indulges his own repressed needs to be the great lover.

Another variant may occur, for example, as the analyst, by becoming a kind of *cavaliere servente*, falls for the patient's propaganda and thereby fails to see and respond to the lost little girl who may be hidden under the exterior of the glamorous and seductive woman. Such covert seductiveness by the analyst can produce an overly strong oedipal and incestuous transference in the patient. This can evoke possible acting out, or enormous fright, recoil, and horror as she is excited or repelled by attitudes that recapitulate the incestuous father figure.

Strange and unusual situations can arise in the analyses of patients who are popularly perceived as sex symbols. A colleague once mentioned to me with a smile that he had in analysis a reigning (if dowager) movie queen who had once been the major object of his masturbatory fantasies in boyhood. It is to his credit that despite such an unusual circumstance he brought the analysis of this patient to a successful conclusion.

Analysis of persons of great wealth is fraught with many other covert vicissitudes and pitfalls. On one occasion, a very wealthy patient said to me near the end of his analysis, "In looking back over our work, I think the exploration of money, both as a symbol and as what it has meant in my life, was of great importance in my getting better. Learning that you liked and respected me, not just the fees that I brought, was important also. All my life I have been used to people viewing me as a resource, a symbol, rather than a person. I learned early to pick up the greed and the resentment in their eyes. This always had a great deal to do with my cynical mistrust of everyone."

Apropos of this, it is important to remember that the majority of analysts come from middle-class origins, and as such we are not exempt from the cultural influences and biases that conduce to a suspicion and dislike of the rich. Also, our education has often been obtained at the cost of great privation and sacrifice, and we have sometimes preserved, despite a training analysis which has in other respects been complete and effective, attitudes and views toward money, the rich, and upper-class status that are found so often in upwardly mobile lower-middle-class groups. In particular, we may have preserved even into analytic adulthood, an animated, albeit covert, hatred or envy of the rich. And, hardworking as we all are, it is most easy to pair the noun "rich" with the adjective "idle."

Numerous folk sayings illustrate the persistent bias entertained by the middle class against the upper, for instance, St. Matthew: "It is easier for a camel to pass through the eye of a needle than for a rich man to enter the Kingdom of Heaven." And do we not often hear, "Behind every fortune lies a hidden crime"? A legacy of this bias can be a tendency of some analysts either overly to prize or overly to derogate wealth and social status. A solid personal identity that is founded on who one *is*, rather than on whom one knows or what one possesses, seems often to be more belatedly acquired than are many other aspects of maturity. Perhaps we too share this common defect of character. If so, the rich may, even in their analyses, may be perceived by us less as individuals than as symbols.

Let me illustrate. Do we not regularly discover that our patients' religious and political convictions, which on the surface appear to be logically derived and maintained, are on deeper examination usually asseverated for patently irrational reasons? Such views usually parallel those of a parent or are reaction formations to them. Long after patients learn to identify and to moderate the effect of antecedent paleological influences on other forms of personal value and belief, their political, religious, and sociological convictions have inevitably lagged behind in that scrutiny and in the change that succeeds insight.

Is it too harsh to suggest that as analysts we are not exempt from this phenomenon? We may be equally inclined to accept without logical examination the antiestablishment bias of our own parents (or its converse) and, if so, this must certainly color our countertransference to patients. If a rich patient is seen by the analyst as one "who has had it too good" or as "the exploiter," it is hard to see how such a patient could be perceived other than as an object deserving of covert punishment or depreciation. The analytic transference which gives such great power over the self-esteem and identity of others is susceptible to acting out in countertransference. Its presence is often subtle and unsuspected and, hence, frequently missed.

Actually, it is an important part of the analyst's sociological education to discover that the rich, as members of a small minority, display many of the apparent identification difficulties characteristic of any minority group, such as suspiciousness of outsiders, loneliness, and isolation. They are often deeply locked in their own socioeconomic class, and they possess the narrow outlook that social immobility classically produces, just as we tend to be similarly locked into the professional upper middle class.

Another common finding is the discovery that the rich person has rarely had contact with warm, affectionate, or loving parental figures: seemingly, sustained parental surrogates have often been lost in childhood with a repetitive and frightening immediacy as one governess or tutor followed another.

We sometimes need to be reminded that the rich suffer no less than the poor. They too are human and no less than other patients deserve our sympathetic understanding and best work. It is not always forthcoming.

The wealthy patient's demeanor itself can create an obstacle to warm and sustained analytic interest, for he may be prone to relegate all professionals to a kind of servant status.

Such a posture can be used as a barrier against healthy imago identification with the analyst and impede the development of a positive transference. And it can arouse strong feelings of hostility and resentment in the analyst. If the cultural and psychic roots of this stance are ignored, or if the analyst responds to the derogation personally, perhaps viewing it as a personal assault, then this valuable segment of material is lost to the scrutiny of the analytic process.

Another barrier to analytic progress can be the tempting, or testing, of the analyst by the patient with the advantages that his wealth, influence, or desirable acquaintanceship can afford, such as offers of the use of vacation retreats, private planes, or beach houses, offers to "get it for you wholesale," invitations to exclusive parties or clubs, or the proffering of inappropriate or expensive gifts. It has been said that gratitude is the unanalyzable defense. This wise adage is consistently reaffirmed in the analysis of these patients, who all their lives have been able to buy or bedazzle others with such resources. It can be a unique and valuable experience for them to find that such overtures are ineffective and unnecessary.

A variant of this problem may occur when the analyst, for whatever reasons, promises more of himself as a personal resource to the patient than he can or should deliver. It is tempting to proffer to such patients—especially those who have had deprived and alienated childhoods—oneself, one's house, one's time or family, as surrogate resources. It is easy to forget that what can be a gift in friendship can be a burden or impediment in a therapeutic relationship. Friendship, with its mutual give-and-take, implies gratitude and reciprocation, both of which may be quite beyond the patient's capacity. No classical transference can develop if the analyst is "one of the family." Such pseudo intimacy engenders continuous testing of limits on the part of the patient, or inculcates deep guilt in him at not being able to respond in kind to the proffered warmth.

My few remarks on this subject by no means exhaust the possibilities by which the artifacts of wealth, influence, or position can complicate analysis, and I was surprised to note, on perusal of the literature, that this subject has seemingly never been studied.

Another artifact that has not engaged our theoretical attention—one that puts a heavy burden on the analysis—is that introduced by patients who act out in ways not normally available to our usual patients. For example, a colleague of mine in the East had in treatment a prominent member of the Mafia, who, in a tearful rage following the analyst's painful but necessary interpretation, menacingly threatened, "Doctor, I have had people rubbed out for saying much less than that to me!" (I am pleased to report that my estimable colleague is not only still alive but thriving, and that the analysis was brought to a successful conclusion despite this problem.)

Undoubtedly a further reason why such artifacts as eminence, social class, position, wealth, notoriety, etc., have claimed so little attention in analytic study is that these patients, by their very nature, are rare in professional practice. No professional life is long enough to encompass detailed experience with even a small number of patients in any of these categories, and what one man can learn, therefore, is bound to be partial and incomplete. A larger understanding must await the accumulation of more information from our collective experience. I recommend this area of inquiry to my colleagues as a fruitful endeavor.

Discussion

SANDOR S. FELDMAN, M.D.†

Rochester, New York

This is an outstanding paper, one we have long wished for. It is interesting, stimulating, and beautifully written.

I have had many patients who were famous, rich, or influential, and I agree with Dr. Wahl that attention to his propositions will result in better prognosis for therapy. While reading his paper, several of my own cases immediately came to mind, in which I recognized the transference Dr. Wahl discusses.

Case 1

From the audience, I had often admired a young dramatic actress in Budapest. One day she asked for an appointment to discuss a very disturbing dream. During the session, which was very helpful to her, neither of us made any mention of a fee. Later I realized that I had neglected to state my fee (at that time we did not send bills) because countertransference had influenced me.

Case 2

I was a beginning analyst, and poor. A rich man, suffering from a paralyzing phobia, came with his wife, who had insisted on being present at the interview. I noticed that she stared intently at my rugs. When I recommended analysis for the husband, she decided instead that they would see whether a long trip would help. It did not. When the man then came for analysis, he told me that his wife doubted my abilities because I could not afford first-class oriental rugs. (The cause of his neurosis—briefly—was that he got rich in obnoxious ways.)

Case 3

When I came to the United States, a committee of the American Psychoanalytic Association suggested I go as a "pioneer" to Rochester, New York, where there were no analysts. Though I came as an "immigrant," I was considered a "refugee," and as such had a most kind, considerate, and helpful reception.

One of my first patients was the wife of a rich businessman. Her dominant life interest was money (though she did have several redeeming qualities). She once said smilingly that "we resent that you who have brains should also have money." It irritated her that I charged her a fee, although it was a moderate one.

Case 4

A wealthy head of industry enjoyed his power over his employees and the outstanding status in the community that his position gave him. He needed treatment badly and knew it. He considered me, as his doctor, superior to him, but was troubled about how to address me. By my first name? No. By my last name? Again, no. Finally he compromised: he addressed me as "Dr. S. S.," leaving out not only my last name, but even its initial, "F."

Cases 5 and 6

Two internationally known "classical" scientists needed my help. Both men immediately conveyed to me that they did not consider analysis a science. I do and did. I told them that our differing views would not interfere with the treatment. It did not.

Dr. Wahl's paper will surely remind psychoanalytic readers of other similar cases.

ANGEL GARMA, M.D.

Buenos Aires, Argentina

According to Wahl, when analyzing rich, famous, or influential patients, analysts sometimes make mistakes which cause treatment to be "incomplete, ineffective, or unsatisfactory." From his description, we may deduce that this incorrect behavior on the part of the analyst arises (in general terms) from masochistic submission to his superego and to his castration complex, which leads him to make partial identifications with the unconscious neurotic reactions of the analysand.

The mistakes made by analysts in these cases are of a countertransferential origin. Now, the countertransference reactions of an analyst are provoked by the unconscious neurotic reactions of his patients. To be more precise, the countertransference reactions of an analyst reflect (in a parallel or complementary way) the neurotic reactions of his patients. Therefore, self-analysis of his own countertransferences will show an analyst the nature of the unconscious neurotic behavior of his patients.

Analysts sometimes fail to analyze their countertransference reactions because they are unaware of them. Dr. Wahl's interesting article, which calls attention to them in addition to pointing out some of their special characteristics and latent contents, will help analysts make adequate use of their countertransference in understanding the unconscious of rich, famous, and influential patients.

I shall give three examples of how this may occur in certain cases. According to Dr. Wahl, "the inappropriate disclosures of patient identification or material" show, as revealed by the analysis of "dreams of intimacy," an "immediate and pervasive lack of self-esteem" in the analyst. When the analyst finds himself tending to make "inappropriate disclosures" about his patient and, on conducting a self-analysis of this countertransference reaction, finds a latent content of a lack

of self-esteem, he may deduce that in his patient there is also a
"pervasive lack of self-esteem" which has caused him to
become neurotically disturbed. If the analyst carries this self-
analysis even deeper, he may discover further details about
the origin and neurotically disturbing influence of the patient's lack of self-esteem.

It may be deduced from Dr. Wahl's article that when an
analyst insufficiently or ineffectively analyzes a man of means,
he behaves in this way (at least in some cases) because he is
unconsciously, as it were, submitting to orders of a divine
(superego) nature which oppose his patient's best interests.
For according to popular belief, which Dr. Wahl suggests has
been revived in the unconscious of the analyst, a "rich man"
should not "enter the Kingdom of Heaven"; in other words,
he should be prevented from reaching a state of well-being
such as would result from psychoanalytic cure, since "behind
every fortune lies a hidden crime" which must be punished.

Dr. Wahl further suggests that the analyst may change this
countertransference attitude if he can "be reminded that the
rich suffer no less than the poor" and that, therefore, the rich
"deserve our sympathetic . . . best work." On the basis of
the self-analysis of this countertransference reaction, in which
he will find the above-mentioned contents, the analyst may
deduce that this rich patient, who has provoked in him this
particular countertransference reaction, has become neurotically disturbed because, among other reasons, he feels guilty
about his wealth. He will further deduce that for this same
reason this rich patient will not tolerate his analyst's carrying
out a successful psychoanalytic treatment, since unconsciously
the patient seeks to be redeemed from the guilt he feels at
being rich through his neurotic suffering, in support of which
aim he rejects his cure, or, in other words, causes his analyst to
fail. The working through of this suppressed unconscious
material will facilitate the analytic process in this patient.

Returning to Dr. Wahl's paper, we learn that when an
analyst insufficiently analyzes a woman who is a "sex symbol,"
it is because, in this countertransference reaction, he identifies
with the "lost little girl" that exists in that woman, and con-

sequently submits to a femininity which has destructive contents. If the analyst perceives the countertransference which is driving him to therapeutic failure, and if he can carry out a detailed and thorough self-analysis, he will discover similar psychic contents in his patient. That is, in general terms, he will be able to discover in this woman self-defeating, infantile, masochistic traits, which made her neurotic, and which she continues to act out in her environment.

Dr. Wahl's extremely interesting observations are deserving of more detailed study. In practical, everyday professional experience a thorough self-analysis of countertransference reactions such as those described by Dr. Wahl will undoubtedly allow an analyst to uncover deeper and more detailed psychological contents, opening the way to the discovery of similar unconscious contents in his rich, famous, and influential patients—that is, important contents which motivate and maintain the neurosis of these patients and encourage the failure of the treatment. In this context, it is interesting to recall what Dr. Wahl (1967) said several years ago: ". . . how uniquely neglected has been our scrutiny of countertransference when it has to do with the analyst's feelings of failure and difficulty" (p. 22).

ROBERT M. GILLILAND, M.D.

Houston, Texas

Dr. Wahl reminds us once again of a ubiquitous clinical pitfall, at least to some extent derived from the dehumanizing aspects of our medical educations: the tendency to identify another human being by some single aspect of his current status. Such references as "the tubercular on Ward A," "the bleeding ulcer in the E.R.," or "the post-partum psychosis upstairs" are familiar to all of us. The persistence of such a tendency in a psychoanalyst is indeed sufficient ground for attempting to investigate its meaning and derivations, for if an analyst is captivated by a particular aspect of a patient, be it wealth, fame, influence, or any other of the endless array of characteristics which go to make up an individual, I think it is safe to prognosticate that the analysis is in for some difficulty.

I am somewhat troubled by the designation of rich, famous, and influential patients as "categories," and I am skeptical—though admittedly not in possession of adequate data—"that many more patients in these three categories" have "incomplete, ineffective, or unsatisfactory analytic experiences than any other category of patient." I would not expect any correlation between such phenomena as affluence, celebrity, or degree of influence and the standard nosological entities. If these three attributes have a special potential for leading to complications in analysis for the reasons Dr. Wahl suggests or for any others, my own experience does not bear this out. Since such designations as wealth, fame, and influence have no agreed-upon boundaries, I do not know how many of my own patients, past and present, qualify; but after more than 20 years of psychoanalytic practice, I assume that some of them do. Even if we grant that "such patients" often fail to "receive" a good therapeutic result, one must not ignore other factors which contribute to the failure. The more "special" a patient is to the analyst for any reason, the greater the potential for countertransference difficulties.

Training analyses are not so selective that prejudices about wealth are especially retained, and a "persistent bias" of the middle class against the upper does not mean that this is an invariable residue of all training analyses. The proneness of some analysts overly to prize or derogate wealth is an individual issue, and the characteristics in a patient which may cause the analyst to put him in a "special" category are also individual issues. While the rich certainly are not "exempt from the human condition" and deserve the best analytic attention of which the analyst is capable, so do all patients. The fact that a rich patient sometimes does not receive the analyst's "best work" constitutes no monopoly. There may be some defensive postures which are common among the extremely rich, and these postures may indeed derive from or relate to their wealth, but this is no new phenomenon in the course of an analysis, since every patient elaborates his own defensive constellation in the transference, and it is to be hoped that the analyst will be able to deal with it analytically. Temptation and testing in varying degrees occur in all analyses, and I question whether the analyst succumbs more often to such maneuvers on the part of the rich patient than the nonrich. If the analyst proffers himself, his home, his time, or his family to "such patients," or to any patient, I agree that "no classical transference can develop in such a situation," because the analytic situation no longer exists. I further agree that these remarks "by no means exhaust the possibilities of the ways in which the artifacts of wealth, influence, or position can complicate analysis," just as it is impossible to exhaust the possibilities of the ways in which the artifacts of any arbitrarily selected characteristic of a patient may complicate the analysis.

It is hard to form "long-standing clinical impressions" about patients who are "rare in professional practice," because they *are* rare. I suggest that another reason why "so little attention in analytic study" has been paid them is the fact that the formal characteristics of the analytic problem are no different in their case really—only the content varies, as it does any way from patient to patient.

MILTON L. MILLER, M.D.

Chapel Hill, North Carolina

There is a wistful element in the problem of prestigious patients. Years ago it was accepted that those patients who were wealthy, famous, or politically powerful were indeed people with influence. Psychoanalysts had to be aware of countertransference in regard to these patients, just as they had to take note of their reactions to the weak, the minority group members, those who arouse special guilt, the sexually seductive, and the relatives of close friends—and, perhaps most of all, the acting-out, talented manipulators of other people, regardless of category.

If patients use their prestige to belittle or bribe the thera-

— 105

pist, it may take a few unhappy episodes for the therapist to learn how this has happened to him. The goal of seeing the patient's problem clearly and conveying insight to him is the only professional one. An example is the case reported by Theodore Reik (1948) in *Listening with the Third Ear*. This applicant for analysis was wealthy enough to buy all of Reik's time and to be taken as his only patient, but Reik would have to move from Berlin to Vienna. Reik finally agreed to this, with the rationalization that he would thus be freed for research, and gave up the rest of his practice. Although Reik received payment over a period of six months, the patient never showed up.

Pleasant, luxurious surroundings and prominent connections build up self-esteem. A sense of accomplishment builds up the analyst's self-esteem more effectively. The psychoanalyst's self-esteem may be consciously and unconsciously increased in various ways, enabling him to function better than if he felt depleted. His psychoanalytic skill and his degree of ego integration will help determine the extent of his success in helping the patient overcome neurotic patterns in order to be able to continue developing toward maturity. This is a different order of gratification from that of a narcissistic patient who uses wealth, prestige, or influence in the service of neurotic goals, repeated in the analysis without insight. With the former attitude, the successes of these patients need not stimulate a strong emotional reaction or acting out (e.g., socially) in the analyst, which may obscure his perception of his patient's neurotic tendencies.

Patients have all kinds of successes that the analysts may not have, but the psychoanalyst's profession has its own special rewards and its own incentives for increasing our skills.

The concept of the analyst's upper-middle-class identification may be changing now to correspond more closely to the attitudes of younger patients who wear blue jeans and challenge middle-class traditions. The divisiveness of our youth-oriented society has made phoniness more apparent. There is less incentive now to take sides against a social class or age group, or to seek the approval of a special group.

The main problem with the theatrical star patient is that one is dealing with a manipulator of others. If this patient has built up a remunerative career by surrounding her- or himself with admirers, this method of handling anxieties may next give way to a "flight into health." For the worried therapist and the patient, this may not seem the best way of continuing an established career, and this opens up a whole new set of circumstances that may have nothing to do with therapy. Saving the career, as a practical consideration, may take precedence over saving the total personality.

Analysts also have to face feelings of disgust, indignation, and guilt stimulated by patients who have been severely traumatized by backgrounds of extreme poverty and neglect. Here countertransference is equally important.

The therapist's personal "public relations" cannot substitute for the painful self-analysis involved in every therapeutic situation. Dostoevsky wisely concluded that most men's tragedies were based on their personal pride. It certainly is difficult to satisfy one's professional ambitions by obtaining good therapeutic results; yet one sometimes does achieve this with the famous and rich, as with any other social group. But the urge of the analyst to identify with the fame of his patients is particularly fatuous because of the changing definitions of social success.

Although name-dropping is still one of our national tendencies, it is growing less effective. The kind of idolatry upon which it is based is a quaint relic of outmoded attitudes. In some sections of the country it is more prevalent or differently oriented than in others, but the prestigious names in one group are becoming marks of limitation in another. A more chameleonlike attitude on the part of the name-dropper makes the process less automatic.

The main probem is countertransference in all its aspects, and open discussion of the pitfalls in this area seems an excellent idea. Hunger for prestige and narcissism are among the many contributing factors. The question of exposing confidential material—why, and to whom—is still another problem related to intercolleague transference.

LEON J. SAUL, M.D.
Media, Pennsylvania

Dr. Wahl has performed a service in calling attention in his well-written, straightforward paper to an important and long neglected problem in analytic therapy. However, perhaps the word "countertransference" should appear in the title, for this is the main emphasis of the paper, although it is all part of the general problem of the effects of a patient's position and status in life upon his psychoanalysis.

If a black patient is analyzed by a white therapist, the factor of race must be dealt with from the beginning—not the analyst's feelings, but the patient's. And in addition, the patient's dynamics, transference, and resistances can all be strongly influenced by poverty and prejudice, as well as by wealth, fame, and influence. For example, a wealthy man has a problem with alcohol, and also in his marriage. These stem from a childhood pattern of rejection by his mother and hostility to her, with masochistic acting out by seducing and rejecting women. If this man is an indigent clergyman, the situation will have entirely different effects than if he is very wealthy, able to go to any length in seducing women, and secure enough financially to be completely free of the necessity to support himself by working.

It was, I believe, in one of his first introductory lectures that Freud cited his reaction to a patient of high socal position; he told the man almost rudely to close the door. This was a sort of test: if the patient could not accept a situation in which he was not a great personage, then he would not likely be suitable for analysis. It is to be hoped that Dr. Wahl's call for more research on this increasingly important and most interesting subject will be responded to by sound, perceptive studies.

PAULA HEIMANN, M.D.
London, England

Unfortunately, observations that some colleagues of high professional caliber talk about their patients and reveal their identity, unaware of what they are doing, are not rare. Analysts mention these facts privately, and lament them. It is Dr. Wahl's merit to make them a public concern and to offer and invite analytic investigation of the specific hazards that attend the analysis of privileged patients.

My own experience with "name-dropping" indiscretion started many years ago. The analyst concerned was far senior to me in experience and position, and my first reaction was of surprise. The obvious motive, however, was neither a boast nor a reflected-glory identification with the patient, who was an important and influential man. Instead, the analyst stated plainly the difficulties she had encountered in this analysis. She complained about the patient, but still more about herself. Her communication was, in fact, an appeal for help—again, very surprisingly, considering the difference in our working experience. What was clear to me was that the analyst was struggling with unresolved countertransference problems, and this observation was one of many that led me to explore more carefully the phenomenon of the countertransference and realize its function as a cognitive tool, provided the analyst "recognizes and masters" the difficulties it can cause—as Freud (1937) in his only-too-brief comments on the countertransference demands.

When later I not infrequently met the kind of indiscretion which Dr. Wahl describes, I felt ill at ease and irritated in that special way one does when put in the position of accomplice to an action of which one disapproves. I reacted with a kind of resigned acceptance of just one more example of human weakness, but—in constrast to Dr. Wahl—I failed to mobilize scientific curiosity.

I welcome the opportunity to make up for that failure now.

Dr. Wahl suggests that in an otherwise thorough and success-ful training analysis some areas were not sufficiently worked through, thus leaving the analyst vulnerable. He mentions conflicts belonging to the Oedipus and sibling complexes, broad socio-economic-cultural factors determined by superego influences, ambivalence toward members of the privileged class, insecure self-esteem, etc.

I fully agree with his suggestions and conclusions. I would, though, when considering persisting pockets of immaturity, give more weight to experiences preceding the oedipal phase. Dr. Wahl points to identifications which interact with the transference and countertransference, and stresses two kinds: (1) the superior, powerful patient is identified with the analyst's parent(s); (2) the colleague who is told about such a patient is identified with a sibling. The boasting in the indiscretion can then be rendered as: "Look what wonderful parents I have!" and "Our parents love me more than you (brother, sister)."

A third mode of identification is that of the patient with the analyst himself, and the communication then says: "If this superior patient selected me to be his analyst, it is be-cause I am as good as he is; he is myself." The narcissistic element of reflected glory is particularly strong in this case. These identifications are spurious. In contradistinction to the true identifications occurring during the child's formative years, they do not further the process of growth. They may lead, though, to imitation of mannerisms, and they lend greater rigidity to the existing structures and ego-dystonic, neurotic trends.

There is still another kind of identification worth consider-ing. It is of a different order, since it is based on the analyst's empathic perception (which may remain unconscious) that he has in common with his patient an experience of suffering. I shall say more about this when discussing a clinical example.

If we focus on the fact that the name-dropping is a com-munication which uses spurious identifications, we may ques-tion whether such identification may not be a *façon de parler*, an ad hoc phenomenon intended to convey a special message.

Once we accept this perspective, we are on very familiar ground. It is indeed part of our daily work to be offered an object presentation in lieu of a self presentation. We all know what it means when a patient remembers that the child next to him in class had the shameful accident of messing his pants.

It is not only a matter of past experiences. All our patients frequently talk about another person when in fact they mean themselves. There are many motives for this mode of communication, but a common factor, I think, is unconscious diplomacy. The message is indirect, tentative, a tryout that allows for withdrawal: "It is not I who . . . , it is somebody else." The person chosen to stand in for the self is by no means always superior, as the familiar example of childhood memory shows.

What, however, is the message if the person presented as self is really superior, better than the self, admired and envied, blessed in various ways? Is diplomacy necessary even in these cases? I am inclined to answer in the affirmative. I think the message is the wish to be like that person, coupled with the notion that the object to whom this wish is conveyed has the magical power to make it come true. It is the infantilism in both the wished-for identity and the belief in the omnipotence of the audience that rouses shame and fear and leads to the defensive device of an escape route.

The fragment of an analytic session which I am now going to present consists of four parts. My patient brought two reports on recent experiences and a spontaneous association. To this last I responded with my interpretation.

Dr. Y. was a psychiatrist whose work in a psychiatric hospital consisted largely, and by choice, of psychotherapy on a one-session-per-week basis.[1] He frequently talked about his patients, partly to understand them better and partly because they or something about them represented himself, so that talking about them amounted to talking about himself. I felt

[1] In a study of indiscretions committed by analysts, it is not superfluous to state that the data I shall mention preserve Dr. Y.'s anonymity, as he has confirmed, while hopefully sufficing to illustrate certain problems.

sometimes that I had to pick up one bit of his identity from one patient, another bit from another, and so on, in order to decode the message he ambivalently conveyed.

On a Monday, the first day after a weekend holiday break, Dr. Y. reported that on the preceding Friday he had woken up with a depression so profound as to be totally incapacitating—he was unable to get up, dress, go to work. He thought of me with an overwhelming need for his analytic session, feeling that even if he were to have his regular Saturday session he could not last till then, let alone till Monday. In fact, his melancholic helplessness covered the imperious demand (with rage) that I should be with him at once—and even earlier, before his waking up—and should never have gone away, so that he might never have experienced this terrible need and distress.

However, he overcame his sense of helplessness, did the things he had to do, and luckily found himself with some free time, which he resolved to use for self-help by attempting a piece of self-analysis. As he succeeded in gaining a good deal of understanding, his depression lifted and he felt gratified on various counts: pleased both by the actual evidence of independence and self-reliance and by the evidence of having really acquired and integrated psychoanalytic knowledge, so that he now owned both the psychoanalytic method and its object, his analyst, even in the analyst's physical absence. His depressive rage against me disappeared, and he then looked forward with friendly feelings and expectations to our resuming his analysis on Monday.

This ended his report on the events of Friday. What now came into his mind was a recent incident with Mr. A., a patient whom he had treated for a long time with very good results. (A crucial part of Mr. A.'s history must be mentioned here. In very early infancy he had been abandoned by his parents and brought up by foster parents. When he presented himself for therapy, he was very disturbed. His symptoms included antisocial behavior, delinquency, and perversions. His prognosis seemed poor. However, Dr. Y. had not been discouraged.)

The spontaneous association about Mr. A. was this: For

reasons on both sides, Mr. A.'s therapy was to be interrupted for several weeks. In the session preceding the interruption, Mr. A. very urgently asked Dr. Y. to phone him if he should unexpectedly find a free hour for him.

Dr. Y. spoke with satisfaction of his patient's progress, as shown by his making a request in so open and direct a manner.

At this point, I gave an interpretation, saying to Dr. Y: "Mr. A. has made progress; he no longer feels himself to be the unloved and unwanted child who can only alternate between submission and delinquent protest. Hence his direct request. You wish me to regard your demand for a session on Friday morning as identical with Mr. A.'s, and as indicating that, like him, you too have ceased to feel an unloved and abandoned baby."

It is obvious that Dr. Y.'s claim for identity with Mr. A. was unfounded. Mr. A., when faced with a longish separation, maintained his normal state and hope. He could therefore believe that things might turn out better than they looked now. My patient, however, did not maintain his sanity and hope when he woke up on that Friday morning, and his self-esteem fell disastrously. He collected himself later, re-established object constancy, and recovered, thanks to his own efforts.

Now, Mr. A. was not rich, influential, or famous. But in his reaction to a specific, painful experience he had proved superior to Dr. Y. Mr. A. was no longer a deprived child, and in fact Dr. Y. could take credit for this development. He might even have boasted of his success and savored his triumph over me, a senior analyst, who was seeing him five times a week and had not achieved with him what he had achieved with his own patient. But there was no boasting or triumph, as there had been none earlier when he had described his self-analysis. What he showed was quiet satisfaction and the wish to share this with me. Also, he did not require an interpretation then, but went on to associate Mr. A.'s reaction to separation and waited for me to confirm as unrealistic his claim for identity with his patient.

— 113

My aim in presenting this material is to demonstrate areas of early infantile deprivation. Dr. Y. was not identified with his patient in his reaction to separation from his analyst. He was, however, identified with him in terms of the empathic perception which I mentioned earlier. He had, in fact, experiences of early infantile deprivation in common with his patient.

I wish to mention one more incident before presenting the relevant details of my patient's life and analytic history: At the end of this particular session Dr. Y. did something unusual. Just before leaving the room he turned round and said with great warmth that it was good to see me back.

Now to his history.

Dr. Y. was not an abandoned infant—he was brought up in a good home with loving parents. Mother-orphaned in early latency, he was then exposed to the ministrations of mother-surrogates with a high degree of hostility in their ambivalence. He also suffered from an insufficiently paternal father. Further, during the period of his mother's illness he had received neither appropriate care nor preparation for her impending death.

He began analysis with an idealized mother-transference and with repressed fears lest I should die before the analysis was finished. (He was greatly relieved when I brought this out into the open and continued to be alive.) In the early phases his mother's death dominated our work, and this theme continued to form the background of all subsequent events throughout the analysis. Shortly before the holiday experience, however, I had arrived at some conjectures about defects in maternal care during his very early life. It appeared that, although a much-wanted and loved child, he had suffered maternal deprivation because his mother had been too efficient, too quick. Her nursing activities ended when the infant's obvious pressing needs were fulfilled, while his more subtle wishes remained unattended. She had not encouraged any playfulness or happy idling, nor any mutual enjoyment for its own sake. (She had probably reached her high professional position because of this capacity to attend quickly to pressing needs.)

A memory, valid in itself and also serving as a cover for experiences beyond recall, shows him, perhaps three years old, indignant at her talking on the phone. He took some scissors and started cutting something up—with the desired result that his mother turned quickly from the telephone to her son.

Following the session which I have partly described, Dr. Y.'s melancholic state on that Friday morning came up frequently. The analytic work on his relation to his mother, reflected in the transference, moved between his losing her finally through death and his early losses of her during her lifetime. At some point I wondered what her feeding regime might have been. Without hesitation Dr. Y. said that from all he had been told about her, he felt sure she would have followed the then prevalent rule of strict intervals between feedings. The baby must have suffered somato-psychic frustrations from a loving mother who took her cue from the clock instead of from her infant's signals.

It is noteworthy that Dr. Y. spoke with complete certainty, although he had never broached this matter spontaneously nor associated it in the Monday session with his agitated state on waking up on the preceding Friday. We can now understand it as probably reproducing many an occasion in early infancy when he awoke with hunger distress and missed the maternal presence. It had not occurred to me to offer an interpretation to this effect. I am inclined to think that this was not due to faulty perception but to a sixth sense that protected me from rushing too quickly into a facile interpretation.

The analytic working team cannot be maintained if the analyst is too "clever" and far ahead of his patient's immediate concerns, which as I have tried to show were revealed in his spontaneous association and dealt with his relation to his patient. Thus both the immediately significant issue and the potential growing point were indicated by his spurious claims of identity with the superior patient and by his neglect of his true identity with him, which was based on empathic perception of common suffering. It was this that needed interpretation. His condition per se on Friday was not in focus.

It is my impression that the value of reconstruction as a form of interpretive exploration has not been sufficiently appreciated. It may be that the uncertainty attached to speculations about preverbal experiences acts as a deterrent. However, reconstructions are not arbitrary. They are determined by qualities or events in the transference, and help to make sense of certain of the patient's attitudes, certain character traits, modes of conduct, etc., and, of course, dreams. As the analysis proceeds, we learn whether our conjectures are correct or whether they need modification or withdrawal.

The benefits of reconstructing very early life are worth risking errors that can later be amended. Reconstructions liberate the patient's suppressed and repressed fantasies; beyond that, they encourage his creativity, his capacity for fantasying, for forming images and allowing them to interact with his intellectual functions.

These considerations link up with a point I made earlier. When the analyst refrains from making interpretations too quickly, the patient is given the freedom to arrive at meanings by his own efforts, through the momentum of the analytic process itself.

No analysis can be complete. The best chances, though, for kindling a lasting flame of analytic orientation in our patients and students lie in helping them to experience, in the course of their analysis, how cathexis moves from present to future and past, including the prehistory and the somatic memories which in later life become overlaid with clusters of images, fantasies, speculations.

Pockets of early frustrations may escape analytic scrutiny in patients who impress their analyst, from a global point of view, with the background of a happy home with loving parents. Such patients, moreover, often enough show a capacity for warmth and love in their relationships, including the transference; but unexpectedly, opposite tendencies may appear that do not correspond to their personality and the picture of their parents as presented hitherto. It becomes obvious that these patients' object-constancy is fickle. Without provocation they turn away, and keep away, from their love object. As analysis proceeds, these personality defects can be understood as stemming from defects in maternal and paternal care during the early narcissistic stages.

The more immature the child at the impact of such frustrations, the more nonverbal their re-enactment in a later analysis. The transference assumes a specific, yet confusing, configuration. The patient's conduct is utterly narcissistic, the roles and identities of patient and analyst are easily and quickly changed and reversed, the analyst becomes the patient's "subjective object" (Winnicott, 1971) or "self-object" (Kohut, 1971) and is exposed to bewildering therapeutic demands and analytic tasks. Such demands testify to the analyst's role as his patient's object, while the role of his patient's self tends to lower his self-esteem and deprives him of the sense of a clear baseline for interpretive procedure.

Obviously, re-enactments of our patients' prehistory represent a far greater challenge to our understanding and skill than those pertaining to later phases of development, such as oedipal and sibling conflicts. We need greater psychoanalytic discipline, greater vigilance and critical introspection, closer scrutiny of our countertransference, and deeper self-analysis. It is not surprising if occasionally we slip, lose our analytic footing, and revert to various forms of reassurance.

Whilst I accept Dr. Wahl's reasons for the specific difficulties in analysis of the rich, famous, and influential, I would suggest that the most powerful factor lies in these patients' capacity to seduce their analyst. Dr. Wahl mentions the "propaganda" of the "sex symbol" movie star. As I see it, the really effective seduction emanates from the lost little girl, the deprived infant. Traumatized children tend to provoke their trauma, deprived children their deprivation, and as patients they have an uncanny knack of exploiting their analysts' weaknesses and blind spots. Privileged patients, thanks to their position, their habit of success, their security in many respects, their well-oiled *savoir-faire*, tend to be highly skilled in manipulating people, more so than our less illustrious patients.

If the analyses of patients with great social and economic advantages are less successful than those of middle-class patients, we have to take account of their provocations. The indiscretions under discussion must be seen in a special perspective. The contrast to the usual highly professional work of the analysts concerned indicates that a vulnerable spot has been touched on. Empathic perception of common suffering with a deprived patient can lead to constructive and reparative response to his needs, but if we are vulnerable the deprived patient may seduce us and blur our judgment.

To return to my clinical example: Dr. Y. accepted his patient despite the unpromising prognosis, and worked well with him. When Dr. Y. spoke of his real achievements with his patient and with a piece of self-analysis, he showed no boasting or triumph. But when, for reasons undisclosed, his early deprivations had been activated and his self-esteem severely reduced, he flagrantly denied reality and took refuge in the spurious reflected-glory identification.

Now, at the end of my deliberations, I return to my first experience of a name-dropping analyst. As I said, the unmistakable motive was a plea for help. I suggest that in other instances too such a plea is implied, even though the analyst may manifest self-satisfaction and aggrandizement.

Author's Response

One of the most distinct pleasures that the format of *The Forum* affords is the otherwise unobtainable opportunity to share discussion and dialogue with esteemed colleagues about matters challenging or problematical of psychoanalytic theory and practice. To Drs. Feldman, Garma, Gilliland, Heimann, Miller, and Saul, I extend my warm thanks for their comments, insights, and criticisms. Almost all have focused on a special issue that I believe merits a more detailed theoretical

attention by psychoanalysts. I refer to the concept of transference and countertransference.

Earlier I submitted this paper to one of our learned
journals. The editors indicated their willingness to accept it
for publication if I would change the title to "Transference
and Countertransference Problems in the Treatment of the
Rich, Famous, and Influential Patient." I chose not to do so,
since it seemed to me that such a title would too narrowly
restrict the subject matter; and to exclude from purview issues
that, although sociological and cultural in character, were not
without import in the vicissitudes of analysis with this type of
patient. It would reflect the tendency, as Dr. Gilliland has so
felicitously put it, "to identify another human being by some
single aspect of his current status."

"Transference" in ordinary psychoanalytical usage conveys,
does it not, the concept of *unconscious* projection onto the
person of the analyst of attitudes, postures, and expectations
which had their inception in the patient's past relationships.
"Countertransference," too, is usually restricted to unconscious converse projections of the analyst onto the patient.

It became clear to me in the study of rich and famous
patients that the analyst's attitudes often reflect intrusion of
factors such as these that were not necessarily unconscious,
and were not transference per se as we ordinarily employ the
term (i.e., a transfer of the analyst's genetic dynamics onto
the patient), but were rather a permutation of attitudes,
biases, bigotries, and cultural sets from which the therapist
had not freed himself, and indeed had perhaps not begun to
scrutinize, even though he had been "thoroughly analyzed."

How often is this the case? Pumpian-Mindlin once said in
an analytic seminar that the basic difference between psychoanalysis and psychotherapy may be likened to that of a
lighthouse in that in psychoanalysis the lighthouse illuminates in a 360° arc, while in psychotherapy it is restricted to
illuminating the shoals offshore.

Can analysis be considered complete if bias, bigotry, or
cultural ethnocentricism is left unexplored or intact? An

— 119

analyst who has retained a covert hatred or suspicion of the rich is no less limited in his work than is one who has lingering prejudices against Negroes or Jews. Or, as Milton Miller has said, an analyst with a small ego or an impaired self-esteem, or one with too abject a need for his patient's gratitude and respect, may bring into the analysis an artifact fully as invasive and problematical as any of those of more unconscious provenance. As, however, such artifacts often inhere in the psychoanalysis of these patients, it would seem that the concept of transference and countertransference must be enlarged and expanded to embrace not only those unconscious dynamic factors which the analyst inappropriately projects onto the patient, but also those sociological and cultural factors which operate to limit his effectiveness.

In practice, do we not try to embrace all such factors in our scrutiny of transference and countertransference problems? Saul rightly says ". . . it is all part of the general problem of the effects of a patient's position and status in life upon his psychoanalysis." But countertransference reactions which occur *unnoticed*, as Garma mentions, are the ones that we most often fail to analyze in ourselves.

Perhaps, therefore, as analysts we have a task yet before us; namely, that of addressing ourselves anew to the theoretical concepts of transference and countertransference, and outlining a definition and theory that can embrace the larger concept which we have been discussing here, and which at present psychoanalytic theory does not adequately deal with.

May I extend my warm thanks to my colleagues for these stimulating and useful comments, and their rich and insightful observations. I am especially indebted to Drs. Spellman and Heimann for their additional case examples, which shed still more helpful light upon this fascinating subject.

REFERENCES

Alexander, F. (1950), Analysis of the therapeutic factors in psychoanalytic treatment. In: *Scope of Psychoanalysis: Selected Papers of Franz Alexander, 1921-1961*. New York: Basic Books, 1961, pp. 436-454.

Frenkel-Brunswick, E. (1939), Mechanism of self-deception. *J. Soc. Psychol*, 10:409-420.

Freud, S. (1912), The dynamics of transference. *Standard Edition*, 12:99-108. London: Hogarth Press, 1953.

——— (1914), On narcissism: an introduction. *Standard Edition*, 14:73-102. London: Hogarth Press, 1957.

——— (1937), Constructions in analysis. *Standard Edition*, 23:257-269. London: Hogarth Press, 1953.

Kohut, H. (1971), *The Analysis of the Self*. New York: International Universities Press.

Rado, S. (1956), Adaptation development in psychoanalytic technique. In: *Psychoanalysis of Behavior*. New York: Grune & Stratton, pp. 347-357.

Reik, T. (1948), *Listening with the Third Ear*. New York: Farrar, Straus.

Sullivan, H. S. (1927), Meaning of anxiety in psychiatry and life. *Amer. J. Psychiat.*, 6:646-683.

Wahl, C. (1967), Discussion of paper by R. Little: Transference, countertransference and survival reactions following an analyst's heart attack. *This Annual*, 2:107-125.

Winnicott, D. W. (1971), *Playing and Reality*. London: Tavistock.

The Incredible Sixties:
Psychodynamics of Youth

JOSEPH C. SOLOMON, M.D.

Clinical Professor of Psychiatry, University of California School of Medicine, San Francisco, and a member of the San Francisco Psychoanalytic Society and Institute. He was a practicing pediatrician before entering the fields of child guidance and psychoanalysis. His publications cover subjects ranging from play therapy, psychopathy, psychological aspects of deafness, and fugue states to the psychoanalytic view of existence, ego integration, and the general systems theory in therapy. His book *A Synthesis of Human Behavior* is used as a text in several medical schools.

Discussants

ROBERT COLES, M.D.

A Research Psychiatrist at the Harvard University Health Services, Dr. Coles has worked for nearly fifteen years with black and white children in the South, in Appalachia, and in the urban North. He has also spent many years working with young students involved in the Civil Rights Movement in the South and in Appalachia, and with college students who have chosen to work in the ghettos of the North. His more than 350 articles and books deal with some of the social problems the United States has faced in recent years.

HARRY GIRVETZ, PH.D.

Dr. Girvetz is Professor of Philosophy at the University of California, Santa Barbara, one of the campuses most involved in the turbulence of the late 1960's. Author of *The Evolution of Liberalism*, co-author of *Science, Folklore, and Philosophy*, editor of and contributor to three widely used anthologies, *Contemporary Moral Issues*, *Democracy and Elitism*, and *Literature and the Arts: The Moral Issues*, he is presently completing a work in moral philosophy to be entitled *Escape from Skepticism*. During his many years as a teacher he has been in contact with thousands of students individually and in groups of varying size up to 700.

L. TAKEO DOI, M.D.

Dr. Doi is Secretary of the Japanese Psychoanalytic Society and Professor in the Department of Mental Health, School of Health Sciences, Faculty of Medicine, University of Tokyo. He has written many articles and books, in both English and Japanese, in which the Japanese concept of *amae* appears, which he defines as "the longing for and expectation of dependence or oneness with others or sometimes simply indulgence," and as being derived from a verb which means "to depend and presume upon another's love."

CARLOS NUÑEZ-SAAVEDRA, M.D.

Dr. Nuñez-Saavedra is President and Professor of the Chilean Psychoanalytic Association, Professor of Psychiatry, Chile University School of Medicine, and past Ordinary Professor of Psychiatry, Schools of Medicine and Social Service at the Catholic University of Chile. He has presented numerous psychoanalytic papers on disturbances of consciousness and other topics at various national and international meetings.

WILLIAM L. O'NEILL, PH.D.

Dr. O'Neill is Professor of History at Rutgers University. He has written or edited half a dozen books, the most recent of which is *Coming Apart: An Informal History of America in the 1960s*. It includes a commentary on the culture and politics of the young.

ARNALDO RASCOVSKY, M.D.

Dr. Rascovsky is Honorary President of the Coordinating Committee of Latin-American Psychoanalytic Organizations, Professor of the Argentine Psychoanalytic Institute, National Honorary Member of the Argentine Medical Association, and for 23 years a Member of the Children's Hospital of Buenos Aires. He is the author of *La Matanza de los Hijos* (*The Slaughter of Children*) and other books and papers, many devoted to filicide.

AARON H. ESMAN, M.D.

Dr. Esman is Chief Psychiatrist of the Jewish Board of Guardians in New York, Lecturer in Psychiatry at the Columbia University School of Social Work, and on the faculty of the New York Psychoanalytic Institute. He has for some years been interested in adolescent problems and has written about them in *The Psychoanalytic Forum* and other professional publications.

The Incredible Sixties:
Psychodynamics of Youth

JOSEPH C. SOLOMON, M.D.
San Francisco, California

IF THE FOLLOWING DISCUSSION seems to label American youth of the 1960's as truly pathological, it may be, in part, because as a clinician I see mainly maladjusted people who are seeking help or parents who are distressed at their children's behavior. From these and other sources, I also have the opportunity of gaining a wider overview, and I know that there are many healthy young people to whom none of the following descriptive material particularly applies, except as it has applied to young people from time immemorial. Nevertheless, the youth of the 1960's, and probably of the 1970's as well, present distinctly pathognomonic features which differ from those of any previous decade in this country, including the 1920's. These changes have been manifest at all levels of society, and represent interactions between many changed environmental conditions and alterations in family structure.

Whereas the youth of the 1950's were subdued, passive, and silent, the opposite was true of the youth of the 1960's. They became vocal, rebellious and discontented, openly demanding change. Some of these demands seemed quite reasonable and may ultimately become a part of a changed society, while others were unrealistic and highly charged with emotion.

The young people, for the most part, were convinced that they were progressive thinkers. They believed that the answer to human discontent was to modify or destroy all existing cultural and governmental institutions, and they became highly resentful at the suggestion that much of their behavior was regressive rather than progressive. We cannot yet judge with certainty what part of the present social turbulence is in fact progressive and what is regressive, and scholarly approaches are warranted from many disciplines, including psychoanalysis.

Although the psychoanalyst's expertise is directed mainly toward the intrapsychic phenomena which constitute only a portion of the total picture, it must also be integrated with the culture and environment; and inasmuch as human personality, and especially human behavior, is so intimately linked with cultural phenomena, it is within the psychoanalyst's scope to understand not only the forces operating upon individuals—including social changes and events in the total environment—but also the effect that some individuals have upon society.

The changes taking place in our society are most noticeable among young people, and I will draw from individual case histories of youthful participants in the social movements of the sixties to demonstrate how—and that—today's young people influenced these changes. It may be years, however, depending upon the future turn of events, before we know whether to call the past decade "The Sorrowful Sixties" or "The Significant Sixties."

The manifestations described in the following pages do not necessarily apply to all young people, but they played a telling part in widespread general trends, especially at the college level. Some of these phenomena, aside from racial or ethnic manifestations, were: first, overt aggressiveness bordering on or including violence; second, its opposite, social apathy; and last, sexual license. All of these manifestations are intensified by the use of drugs. College professors noted that their students had become increasingly uninterested, as though the lectures and subject matter were irrelevant to their lives. Did these reactions indicate a philosophical absorption in more idealistic thinking? Or were the students "stoned" on marijuana or LSD? Both questions can probably be answered in the affirmative, and indeed each factor can fortify the other.

Writers who speculate about what might be troubling the

youth of today tend to emphasize external forces. I am concerned here with what goes on in the psychic process of the adolescent or pre-adult. I will not dwell on the family unit, which we have been inclined to blame for all personal problems, but will instead look at the world of the last decade where the adolescent had to make his adjustment.

One such adjustment involved the college experience. Dances, football games, and other such pleasures used to be almost a part of the curriculum, but in recent years "college spirit" has all but vanished in the face of tremendous educational pressures. I shudder to hear the numbers of books a student must read for an ordinary liberal arts course; and increased knowledge in the sciences, sociology, economics, higher mathematics, linguistics—in fact, in all subjects—has made the mere accumulation of information a formidable task. Compound this with the need for superior grades to obtain a meaningful diploma or to compete for postgraduate education, and we can see where ceaseless pressure alone causes many students to wonder whether it is worth all the effort, especially as their emotional tensions reach unbearable proportions.

Also, during the early sixties the Civil Rights Movement began to take shape. In a sense it was a romantic movement; it bore fruit in many quarters and exposed injustices that needed to be righted. Desegregation was the watchword, and many young white people allied themselves with Blacks. Speaking up for the underdog led to the Free Speech Movement, and freedom to speak served as a precursor of freedom to act, especially when speech alone did not quickly bring results.

Far more important in its impact on youth was the Vietnam War. In time of war people tend to unite, forget differences, and join forces against a common enemy. Aggressive impulses, including gripes against the military itself, are channeled into the war effort. But this war was different.

The intelligent student saw no purpose in the Vietnam War, and blamed the Establishment for sending him to kill or be killed when he not only did not feel threatened but had no sympathy for the causes he was called on to support. The protest became intensified as teachers and other adults shared the students' sentiments. Nevertheless, though dissidence increased, the war continued. It had to be someone's fault, and the parent surrogates in Washington were blamed. In many instances, the growing resentment created conflicts with loyalty to country and the need to identify with and defend one's home. In addition, the government's unresponsiveness or, at best, palliative gestures stimulated the frustrated students still further to revolutionary thought and activity. This spirit of revolution which captures many adolescents has its historical source in previous revolutionary movements and in the current resurgence of Black-White conflicts, which lead to new areas of conflict and increased alienation from the Establishment.

In the past, the Marxists found sympathy among the working people. Today, cries of "Workers of the world, unite!" fall on resentful or deaf ears because most working people are likely to be conservative or indifferent. In fact, today they are more likely to join the John Birch Society or the Ku Klux Klan than a socialist rebellion!

In the middle sixties, white students began to feel disappointed and betrayed as the Black militants failed to appreciate their efforts. The Blacks thought that they were being *used* for the revolution and that their own particular aims were not being considered. The desegregation movement began to polarize, with consequent emphasis upon separation, rather than admixture, of races.

It seemed that the very biases and prejudices the Civil Rights Movement attempted to eradicate produced the same prejudices in the opposite camp. This polarization was combatted by a change of leadership among the Black Panthers. Its founder, Stokely Carmichael, envisioned a union of black people throughout the world—hence the term "Black Power." Subsequent Black leadership has veered from this chauvinistic or fascistic attitude toward cooperation with white radical groups to overthrow the capitalistic system, but suspicions remain, especially among Blacks toward Whites. It is difficult to predict what would happen if there were a depression. Would there be open warfare between Blacks and Whites? Or would all impoverished people and their sympathizers unify to overthrow existing governmental and commercial institutions?

All of these movements led to confusion of personal values, of individual identity, and of basic instinctual motivations. Young people, beset by these confusions, sought protective coloring by associating with others equally confused. As a result, their problems became reinforced, and all felt a common interest in searching for solutions. In the following pages I will attempt to coordinate individual psychic determinants, with emphasis on these social determinants, in three arbitrary categories: existence versus nonexistence, identity versus identity confusion, and intimacy versus pseudo intimacy.

Existence versus Nonexistence

In a previous publication, "Alice and the Red King" (1963), I defined the psychoanalytic view of existence, using a patient's dream and a sequence in *Through the Looking Glass* (Dodgson, 1870) to show that existence depends upon being in the mind of another pertinent individual. The fantasies were those of appearing in the dream of another person: if that person were to wake up (meaning the disappearance of the dream), then the person who is dreamed about also would disappear.

I adduced the concept that one's existence, or more specifically, the awareness of one's existence, depends upon internalizing the object who has internalized one. On this ground, I (1970) modified Descartes' concept of *cogito ergo sum*, "I think, therefore I am," to *cogitor ergo sum*, "I am thought about, therefore I am" (p. 79). I emphasized, too, that the concept of the awareness of one's existence is the basis of the need for attention and the desire to be important, and lays the groundwork for the establishment of an identity.

If this phenomenon is not mastered there is an inherent vulnerability for survival, or, expressed differently, a fear of nonexistence. As I have defined it (1965), the ego is the reservoir or bank for the stored memories of mastered experience. Consequently, a failure to attain ego mastery over the basic need for survival renders the individual susceptible to other threats to life. If the sense of another person is necessary to establish one's own existence, it is understandable that to people without this ego mastery the concept of being alone is a most serious threat to survival.

The fear of isolation is coupled with ideas of separation and abandonment. Stronger than the fear of lacking sources of narcissistic supplies (Fenichel, 1953) is the fear of nonexistence. Children who are afraid of the dark may fear threatening intruders, but they also fear nonexistence: "If I cannot see, I cannot be seen; if I cannot be seen, I will disappear." I have been told of a primitive tribe which punishes an offender by ignoring him; unnoticed for an extended period of time, the victim dies.

There are many sectors of our society, especially among young people, in which the concept of nonexistence prevails. Young people, some of whom may have had some feeling of importance during preadolescence, are plunged into the maelstrom of a large university (or, earlier, of a big high school), and become lost. Contacts with parents and parent figures, represented by interested adult teachers, are abruptly terminated. "Nobody cares about my existence, so I do not exist." Add to this the threat of thermonuclear war, or even the actual war in Vietnam, and hopes for the future become dimmed. Many young people say frankly that they do not expect to reach old age; they expect to be caught up in a holocaust that will destroy everyone.

Accompanying this widespread fear of death, or nonexistence, was the young people's perpetual search for a solution. Rebellion and activism was one result of this search; another was the turn to mysticism, manifested by the surge of interest in Zen Buddhism, Yoga, Bahai, Scientology, and meditation.

Many observers believe that the use of drugs activated this mystical orientation; others say with an equal degree of conviction that drugs are merely manifestations of the same forces that create the need for mystical or magical experi-

— 129

ences. However, it cannot be denied that in the countries in which drugs are part of the culture, meditative mystical religions do prevail. The perceptual experience that often comes from the use of drugs does not respond to logical thinking. Rather, it seems to emerge from mysterious sources, and hence gives the impression of being a supernatural or mystical phenomenon. Nevertheless, the use of drugs alone does not explain the contagion of the turn to mysticism in the last decade. Let me cite a case.

Alan is a 20-year-old student who called for help because he was confused, nervous, and preoccupied with bizarre thoughts. He had previously tried various forms of self-help: inspired by Alan Watts, he took up Zen Buddhism and meditation, and also studied semantics, Jungian psychology, and any other form of therapy about which he could read. He turned finally to psychoanalysis because everything else had failed.

His description of his background related a variety of factors to his present symptomatology. He saw his father as interested but passive, especially in relation to the mother, whom Alan saw as both domineering and temper-ridden. The grandmother, who shared in his care, was fixed in the attitudes of an earlier generation; for instance, she threatened to amputate his penis when she found him masturbating. He developed a swallowing tic which conjured up elaborate fantasies which he felt to be the cause of his symptoms, as when a child he thought that he had swallowed his mother's voice, which acted in his stomach like a pair of scissors. This was related to his sexual feelings, as though to have sex meant that he was close to Mother, but at the same time he fantasied that having sex was also dangerous and defiant of her and Grandmother. There were other interesting details of the analysis, but it is Alan's meditation phase which is relevant here.

The magical or mystical quality of his meditation experiences became clear to him during analysis. He conceptualized it as follows:

> All through high school and the beginning of college I felt a sense of aloneness. It was like feeling separate from everyone. This led to my

being preoccupied with fears of death. When I meditated I lost all awareness of my body. I felt instead like I was part of the world. This brought
on a feeling of stillness in myself like I had attained a oneness between
life and death. Really what it was, was a coming to terms with fears of
death. Then you become a part of an external world, like you are im-
mortal. This counteracts the feeling of non-existence.

Although the traditionally accepted religions in our North
American society contain mystical qualities, there was a tendency among many young people in the 1960's to move
toward esoteric religions. There has even been a resurgence of
Hasidic Judaism, which is a mystical religious belief. In the
history of Hasidic practices one sees the same defenses found
among some members of the "hip" culture. The rites consist
of singing, dancing, and incantations against the horrors of
persecution and despair.

The "spiritual awakening" is a necessary component of
most forms of mysticism. This is a true perceptual experience;
it is the essence of "salvation," the nirvana or satori of
oriental religions. It is my conviction that the religious experience is similar to the sensation described by Freud as "the
oceanic feeling" (1928). Since it is out of keeping with
ordinary reality, it is explained as "direct knowledge of God"
or the arrival of "spiritual truth." Psychologically, the feeling
has been described as a rebirth phenomenon, and it probably
represents the memory of the beatific union of mother and
infant. This is compatible also with the concept of the fusion
of life and death, death symbolizing the return to mother (or
mother earth).

As a defensive maneuver, the changed state of awareness
associated with the "mystical" experience is a search for the
magical or metaphysical which denies the problems of the
world of reality. It may be that the decreased incidence of
some forms of schizophrenia, notably catatonia, among our
young people is due to the fact that many cases that would
otherwise appear on the wards of the state hospitals are now
living peculiar lives of esoteric religious experiences, or may be
medicating themselves with drugs, or both.

Although the use of drugs is widespread among young
people, I do not wish to imply that all of them are drug

addicts. In the colleges, heavy drug users are not able to keep up with their studies and they drop out, but many others keep up with their work in spite of their marijuana smoking and occasional LSD trip. The amphetamines and, of course, heroin are too disruptive to the ego for even marginal adjustments to the realities of existence.

Identity versus Identity Confusion

The establishment of a self is equivalent to the knowledge that one exists, which is subsumed under the concept "I am." The term "identity" refers to the design of the ego, which differentiates one individual from another. It is epitomized by the sentence, "This is who I am."

The ego incorporates learning from each orbit or ambit which the individual inhabits. The main orbit or milieu is the home, but others are the school, the church, social groups, etc. During late adolescence there should be a harmonious amalgamation or integration of the various areas of identity formation. The young adult should have successfully fused his family identity and his occupational identity. For example, he might say, "I am a Jones, a Protestant, an American, a White, and an engineering student." If these orbits of identity fail to merge adequately, conflicts ensue which precipitate emotional stress. A case in point is the discrepancy that may occur when one area of identity is at variance with another—for instance, the incompatibility of one's social identity with one's family identity. This type of conflict produces the phenomenon of alienation which has become a matter for wide discussion in our society.

Alienation may refer to breaking away from family ties or identities and casting one's lot with contemporaries who are similarly rebelling against parental influence. It may refer also to alienation from society, the seeds of which may have been implanted originally by the family itself. For example, a mildly liberal family may produce a wildly radical revolutionary son by virtue of his exaggeratedly compliant defiance as an expression of an unconscious need to obey. At the same time he may burlesque the parents in order to release aggression against displaced parental authority.

A Berkeley student who was a patient of mine illustrates the foregoing points. Jason came from a prosperous family on the East Coast. His father had indulged him in preference to his two younger sisters. His mother, an efficient clubwoman type, was active in numerous organizations, often to the neglect of her family. Both parents were mildly liberal, but strictly within the framework of a capitalistic society.

Now 19, Jason felt his principal problem was his need to break away from the influence of his family. In line with this, he considered himself a revolutionary, and wore a beard and shoulder-length hair as physical evidence of the break. He was worried that he might be homosexual and not able to perform sexually with a girl. He used marijuana and mescaline but did not consider himself habituated. Most of his energies were involved in campus politics. A self-proclaimed pacifist, he was noisily hostile to police, to administrators, and to parents.

He said that he arrived at his present state through being made aware of "the inhumaneness of the world," for during his upbringing he had never really understood its cruelty. Now he could defend himself against it only by linking up with something warm and comforting, and he identified himself with the "tribalism of the flower culture." He used drugs to relieve the anxiety that came from feeling pressured. He hoped through drugs to obtain great wisdom about himself and thus to gain sovereignty over himself.

During analysis, Jason had both positive and negative transference reactions. Sometimes I was his rescuer; at other times I represented the hated Establishment. As he worked through some of his feelings, he lived for a while with a somewhat depreciated girl. Later he renewed a high school romance. Although he always kept up with his studies, he began to feel after a time that he was now doing so for himself rather than in compliance with his family's pattern. He chose to terminate therapy after a year and a half. Ashamed to face his friends otherwise, he kept his beard and long hair, but he spoke of cutting his hair upon returning home.

Joseph C. Solomon

In other cases the identity struggle is much more severe and complex than Jason's and involves regressions to extremes of sadomasochism, common among young people. Frequently they are acting against their own best interests even while espousing utopian philosophies. Here is such a case.

Jody, 20 years old, is a brilliant student from San Francisco State College who came to see me because of extreme anxieties, depression, and inability to apply herself to her studies. She had experienced a series of broken romances, the pattern of which consisted of quickly becoming sexually involved with a young man, moving into his apartment, then inviting his abuse and finally getting pushed out.

At the time Jody came to San Francisco State College the campus was relatively quiet, and she found the political activity disappointing. She had come from another big-city college where she had been a real revolutionary, and she was proud of the fact that she had spent several months in jail because of her activism.

She was an only child of rather neglectful parents who frequently fought; the home atmosphere she remembered was one of turmoil and noisy contention. Her father had never been warm to her. When she got into trouble, he wanted to disown her, but her mother persuaded him to maintain interest. The mother was a nurse who "meant well," but was away from home a great deal. She lectured Jody constantly about proper behavior, saying she loved her, but never quite establishing a lasting harmonious relationship with her.

During several months of analysis Jody was in constant turmoil—agitated, restless, and tense. She harangued her parents incessantly, especially her mother. For a time she continued to get involved in messy sexual liaisons. Then she moved into a household where she helped care for the children, and there she formed a good relationship with the mother, who was a bit of a rebellious spirit herself.

Jody attained real calm when the campus turbulence began. She immediately became a leader, participating in all the campus strategy for revolt and going into physical action. It was clear that when the outside environment was tranquil

134—

Jody was inwardly turbulent, and that when there was turmoil outside she was calm within. I pointed out to her that she was addicted to turmoil, the atmosphere of her childhood home.

To this girl, to be calm and to live in a calm atmosphere was very frightening. In effect it symbolized abandonment and death. Turbulence meant life, mother, survival.

There are many instances in which the identity struggle is less subtle and more openly expressed. A Black student from a stable family background may feel little need for personal rebellion. But if he has white friends and does not want to be aligned with militant groups, he is accused of being an "Uncle Tom," of selling out to the "enemy." He has no choice but to join the Black rebellion, and when he does he suffers from abandoning the identity he had established in his home and schools. He may go through many cycles of doubt, first being ashamed to be black, then denying his shame, and finally even developing "Black pride."

Identity problems are particularly prevalent among left-wing Jews. When Israel seemed destined to disappear as a sovereign nation, leftist Jews wore the Star of David on black armbands. They mourned the passing of a symbol of their heritage. But after the Six-Day War was over and it became clear that the Soviet Union was not happy about the outcome, these same people did the flip-flops that characterized reactions to the Hitler-Stalin Pact. They had the choice of repudiating either their left-wing identities or their Jewish identities. Many left-wing Jewish activists denigrated everything Jewish, to the extent of claiming that Jews had outlived history and must disappear "for the greater good of mankind." Others turned from Russian communism to Maoism or Trotskyism, but even these forms were unsatisfactory, for they were compatible with the "Cult of Personality." This in turn is being repudiated now in favor of the "Third World," a movement which forms another identity whose aim is to integrate many areas of thought, including race, religions, and national identities. Thus far, the Third World movement presents no other meaningful program.

It is clear that finding an identity is like finding a self; it is a device by which internalized or introjected images become part of the ego. The epidemic of bohemianism (with some nominal variations, e.g., beatniks, hippies, street people) is one manifestation of the search for an identity. Long hair, originally associated with *soi-disant* artists, gained impetus from the rock-and-roll musicians (Elvis Presley and the Beatles, in particular). But the real impetus came from the anti-war movement. Once assumed, however, the hair and garb led to secondary gains; the costume provided a kinship with others of similar appearance, thereby counteracting feelings of loneliness or isolation. Of course it contained an element of protest, and it would seem that a noteworthy gain was that of exhibitionistic gratification, of being noticed. As such, the exhibitionism is a defensive maneuver to help bring oneself closer to people in the name of alienation.

Although this is a spurious type of identity, it is still an identity of sorts. I call it "spurious" because it is approached through the assumption of negative values and because it appears as a way station toward maturity, without lasting or clearly established goals. The young persons who adopted these altered patterns of living felt that they were doing something original, but in fact in many respects these "new" lifestyles represent a return to historically earlier styles, sometimes simpler communal and agricultural ones. This return to the primitive represents an avoidance of life's complexities and a return to a secure childhood or ancestral existence. Because these patterns of living resemble those of the past, they are best considered "regressive" rather than "new."

Intimacy versus Pseudo Intimacy

The term "intimacy," popularized by Erikson's writings (1950), has been thoroughly misunderstood by many young people and often by their parents as well. I distinguish two types of intimacy: true intimacy and false or pseudo intimacy. The former is an aspect of mature adult behavior; the latter, of neurotic and infantile behavior.

True intimacy, at least in our culture, occurs as the culmination of the union of two partners of opposite sexes who value each other highly and feel intense loyalty to each other to the exclusion of other individuals, including, to some degree, their respective families. It involves complete commitment in all spheres, including the social and sexual, and includes the desire to maintain a lasting and meaningful relationship, establish a home, and produce and rear children.

Pseudo intimacy, on the other hand, is a distortion of the mating impulse. Normal biological drives are diverted, exaggerated, or flaunted in an effort to attain some form of psychic equilibrium. Freud's early teachings gave the impression that dammed-up sexual libido caused mental illness. Some people mistakenly reasoned from this that venting sexual feelings is very "healthy" mentally. This has led some parents to believe that their children should never be "frustrated," fearing that frustrations would produce mental aberrations. To some degree, the same reasoning has been applied even to the expression of violence and aggression. In refutation of this basic mistake, it can be stated quite emphatically that neither "sexual freedom" nor unbridled aggression has decreased in any degree the incidence or prevalence of neurosis. In fact, the opposite seems to be true.

Sexual knowledge should not be equated with emotional stability. It is quite independent of it. Important writing on sex, like Kinsey's (1953) or Masters' (1966), omits that dirty four-letter word, "love." And not only is there much more information available on sex, but we now also have "the pill," which has abolished the fear of pregnancy. These and other influences have given meanings to genital sexuality that did not exist, at least not as openly, in previous decades.

There are other factors besides the pill which have produced a change in cultural attitudes toward sexuality. Modern novels depict sexuality with clinical factuality. Many of them are probably written by people, such as homosexuals or other neurotic individuals, who cannot experience mature intimacy, so that their emphasis is indeed on the pseudo-intimacy I mentioned earlier. The results, however, seem to encourage sexual license. In addition, the movies depict sexuality with an abandon that was seen a few short years ago only at men's smokers.

It may be said that these are all manifestations of our changing culture. However, there is no doubt that this new "freedom" propagates the attitudes which spread like a contagion by imitation and by peer identification.

Because of the availability of sexual contacts and because of the changed cultural attitudes toward sexual relations among young people, the act of coitus has become a widely used defense mechanism. As such, it can be classified with drug use. It is mainly a defense against loneliness, depression, or anxiety.

But it is simplistic merely to state that pseudo intimacy is a defense against loneliness. The manifestations of loneliness are not the same in all people, nor even in the same person at all times. On the one hand, there may be feelings of emptiness, boredom, or ennui, and on the other, feelings of restlessness, turbulence, and turmoil. Sexual gratification—or, if it is unavailable, masturbation or overeating—may offer some satisfaction in an otherwise empty, lonely, or threatening world. In this instance, pseudo intimacy provides a form of excitement comparable to that produced by mood-elevating drugs. But when turmoil prevails, the need for sexuality is for a quieting or pacifying effect; here the parallel to a sedative or tranquilizing drug is obvious. The pseudo intimacy may be similar, but the purposes are different.

The frustrations inherent in problems of growth itself, together with those that loom for youth in the future, impel young people toward substitute gratifications: "Get it now, before it is too late." Sexual freedom, including promiscuity and homosexuality, represents the quest for some sort of internal equilibrium. It is evident that instead of serving to attain such equilibrium, this attitude only exacerbates and perpetuates the problem of the search for gratification.

In many cases, pseudo intimacy serves as a smoke screen against the fear of real intimacy. The superficiality, the absence of commitment, and the casualness of the relationships lend boy-girl union a sense of tentativeness. This tentative quality can create uncertainties and disquiet in one partner, especially if he or she is more firmly committed than the other. The disappointed partner, usually the girl, may feel abandoned or scorned, with consequent reactions of anxiety, depression, or retaliatory acting out in promiscuous pseudo intimacy.

The phenomenon of pseudo intimacy leads in many directions: encounter or sensitivity groups are natural outgrowths of its defensive aspects. Perhaps for some schizoid or isolated individuals these groups serve as entering wedges for the beginnings of human contact. But let me stress the fact that these contacts should be *only* beginnings. They should not be considered as ends in themselves, nor as the *sine qua non* of all human relationships. Some would-be group therapists advocate multiple intimacies as healthier than a close husband-and-wife relationship. They certainly are not healthier for the marriage; I have known several couples whose marriages ended in divorce after they had participated in group sensitivity "training." The pleasurable aspects of pseudo intimacy, instead of being used to help establish real intimacy, become an end in themselves, thereby necessitating the setting up of a new value system.

Can a relationship of pseudo intimacy develop into a true intimacy? The answer is yes. People can grow up emotionally at any time. If lasting values can be found in the marriage after the neurotic ones have been resolved, a real and enduring intimacy can develop. More often than not, however, a true intimacy or a good conjugal relationship does not start with a desperate, defensive type of pseudo intimacy, because if a relationship of pseudo intimacy is established as a gyroscope to help one remain at even keel during the period of troubled youth, then it continues as an unconscious reminder of turmoil and not necessarily as the enrichment of one's life which is characteristic of true intimacy.

Further Remarks

When I lectured to a class of residents, social workers, and psychologists on the subject matter of this paper, I was

— 139

greeted with open resentment and sarcasm. One psychiatric resident made an interesting point. He defended the younger generation and accused me, as a representative of the older generation, of fearing the loss of the children. He said it was the giant who feared nonexistence because he is no longer in the mind of the child, rather than the other way around.

It is true that many parents feel that they have lost their children. At least, they feel they *might* lose them if they do not indulge their offsprings' hedonistic or rebellious demands. In many instances parents actually fear their children, and are at a loss to cope with the behavioral changes that have taken place since their own youth. This sometimes works to the disadvantage of the young people. When the parents or authority figures yield to their rebellious demands, the young people sometimes feel stranded in the absence of a "cause," like the child who at some stages of development needs to disagree just for the sheer delight of disagreeing. Disagreement can sometimes be very vital, and can act as an antidote to the feeling of isolation.

The use of drugs, especially marijuana, hashish, mescaline, and LSD, is sometimes defended on the grounds that the drug experience opens up new areas of awareness and insight into what is happening in the world. My reply is that it is a sad commentary on our educational process if one must become drugged in order to know what is going on in the world. Furthermore, it is difficult to understand how a perceptual experience can really lead to the highly complex conceptual thinking which is necessary to appreciate value systems.

Earlier in this paper, I mentioned that the recent tendency toward classroom uninterest may have been partly due to the fact that some students came to class "stoned." A more noteworthy phenomenon was the readiness to attack or dispute teachers and administrators. Without much actual evidence to draw upon, I would like to offer the suggestion that this aggressiveness may be rebound phenomenon from the tranquilizing effect of the cannabis drugs, comparable to the depression following the use of the amphetamines. It may well be that student violence can be attributed in part at least to pharmacologic effects.

The shocking stories that have emerged about the atrocities committed by American troops in Vietnam may be representative of the changed attitude toward the expression of violence, and the widespread use of cannabis drugs among the troops may partially explain the change. It is hard to say whether atrocities such as these and the hippie murders were due to released aggressions that had lain dormant, or were the result of the toxic effects or aftereffects of drug use.

Besides causing violence, the mind-altering drugs seem to act in other ways. The heavy use of drugs such as LSD, mescaline, or the amphetamines is known to produce psychotic reactions. On the other hand, some schizophrenics or borderline cases seem to get along, in a bizarre way, in a hippie setting. Taking drugs seems either to control their hallucinations, or gives them the appearance of being in some sort of ego control. In fact, it has been said that schizophrenics were welcome in the Haight-Ashbury area because they could hallucinate even without drugs.

Another phenomenon of the sixties which can be discussed from the regressive-progressive point of view is the ubiquitous interest in rock-and-roll music. When a rock group performed in front of the Student Union of the University of California Medical School in San Francisco in the late sixties, one song in particular interested me. It consisted of nothing more than the constant repetition of the words "Baby, baby, baby." The music and the musicians' body movements appeared to be clearly related to a corruption of the "Rock-a-Bye-Baby" lullaby, combined with the tumultuous fervor of rebellion and sexuality. The wild, rhythmic music and the frenetic musicians inspired some listeners to join actively in the dance, generally in a self-centered, autoerotic fashion; others swayed in passive listening, as if being rocked in a cradle. The active participants seemed to say, "I am alive," and the passive listeners, "I am not alone."

Some of the words in the songs of the popular singers are both rebellious and salacious. They clearly demonstrate both

— 141

the sensuous and the defiant nature of bare instinctual expressions. They must have touched off some emotional response in the young people, otherwise they would not have attracted the 200,000 to 400,000 youth who flocked to rock concerts. It was not the music alone that attracted them; it was a total involvement with the mingling of kindred spirits and the massive turn-on with drugs. Regressive? It looks that way. Even the names of some of the bands are hebephrenic irrelevancies.

The clinging to turbulence and rhythmicity is but one aspect of the regressive tendencies. The return to infantile orality, with its drive for immediate gratification, and the magical search for altered psychic states are also clinical manifestations of regression, as well as the hair, the clothes, the disruption of family, and the repudiation of technology—all manifesting varying degrees of the longing for a return to the primitive. Displaced oedipal behavior is clearly evident on all sides, both by acting out in liaisons of pseudo intimacy and by their denial, which is similar to that of children in the latency period, when the main libidinal elements are directed to the group. Here one obtains a protective coloring from the other members, and loyalties are directed toward others like oneself, while the nuclear family loyalties are foresworn.

As children in the latency period set themselves apart from the rest of the world as "we" against "they," so do many of our rebellious young men and women. The "we" do not strive to attain the status of the "they" because the "we" have already enjoyed all the privileges and material things that "they" have. The "we" are fighters for something "better," but are not sure what "better" is. Without going further into the psychic mechanisms involved, suffice it to say that many young people emerge from adolescence with strong feelings of hostility and equally strong needs to deny or repudiate their aggressions. Thus we have the phenomenon of student violence in the name of pacifism, like the Crusaders who killed in the name of the Prince of Peace.

Seen from the eyes of the young people, these attitudes take on a different meaning. They claim to be establishing a new morality. They claim that their parents' values have failed, offering as proof the prevalence of war, poverty, and racial inequality. Air pollution, the destruction of wildlife, and other disturbances of ecology are considered further indications of the thorough corruption and incompetence of the conglomerate of parents, and they look upon the government as a distillation of this conglomerate. The young people berate their parents for inconsistencies, e.g., their permissiveness versus their demands for conformity. They repudiate parental guidance altogether, feeling they are doing something definite in the face of such double messages as "Be independent!" versus "Be like me!", which they consider "dishonest."

The young people, especially those who are hippie-oriented, seek to counteract what they consider parental hypocrisies by being "honest." They say they want to "tell it like it is," and they "tell it" through their music, their conversation, and their poetry. By the use of psychedelic drugs they achieve a "new feeling" which ostensibly opens awareness of thought processes by letting one look into oneself and find "answers" there. This philosophy has many precursors, such as bohemianism, avant-gardism, dadaism, the "beats," and existentialism.

Student intellectuals have for centuries been the vanguard of rebellion, dating back at least to the Goliards in the twelfth century, and later to the French and Russian revolutionaries. We are in a somewhat similar situation today as the attitude of youthful rebellion begins to seep upward into our institutions—the schools, the church, the military, and the arts. Hopefully, salutary changes will take place and benefit mankind.

Summary

I have tried to summarize the psychodynamics of young people of the past decade, in which there are many similarities to youth in general throughout the centuries, but also some unique features that are worth recording. The presentation consists of a correlation of environmental factors with the thinking and behavior of young people. The subject was discussed from the points of view of three arbitrary levels of ego development, namely, existence, identity, and intimacy. The main thread of psychopathology is the state of loneliness and the defenses against it, which have both regressive and adaptive qualities.

Let me add that all is not psychopathology. There is also a spirit of a healthy morality and aspiration for improvement which, tempered by intelligence, experience, and ego mastery, should give renewed hope for the years to come.

Discussion

ROBERT COLES, M.D.
Cambridge, Massachusetts

I have to say right off that I found Dr. Solomon's paper sadly biased and unbalanced, at times extravagant in its claims, at times sour and cranky. And this is a pity, because we badly need the clinician's perspective on this subject. But instead we get sweeping generalizations worthy only of the worst kind of social science—the kind this society of ours has come to live with so very comfortably.

Dr. Solomon begins by letting his readers know that he believes many youths are "wholesome" and "healthy," not at all candidates for his kind of analysis; but soon enough he is talking about "the young people" and he never stops doing so. Which young people? Presumably those who become patients, several of whom he describes. There is no doubt that in doing so he takes risks which any critical reader of his paper is bound to consider. How can such sweeping and unqualified generalizations be made by a doctor who has seen only a limited number of avowedly troubled youths? If Dr. Solomon had left his office and spent time talking with social and political activists of one sort or another, if he had observed them as they did their work, and followed them along over months or years of their lives, he might be in a position to offer us a clinician's estimate of what a number of *somewhat* representative (one can never be really precise and accurate in such research, and no one is asking that of Dr. Solomon) young people are like psychologically, even if they have no occasion to consult someone like him. As it is, he arrives at his conclusions after talking only with those who have chosen to go see him, and he is neither kind nor generous to a whole generation of people, whose "pathognomonic features" he feels so confidently able to describe.

One wonders what other kinds of patients Dr. Solomon sees

in the course of his San Francisco private practice. Elderly businessmen? Middle-aged stockbrokers or lawyers? Over-thirty political conservatives of either sex? And on the basis of his work with those patients has he been willing to offer us, as he does here with respect to "the young people," the benefit of his social and cultural views, so that we can get an idea of the "pathognomonic features" of those Americans who grew up in the fifties and forties and thirties? To single out a small group of patients and then use them to characterize an entire generation is in itself a decisive act—and one worthy of a certain kind of "analysis," political as well as psychological. I wonder, for instance, whether Dr. Solomon, who can become so clinically interested in the music of our young, has seen fit to bring the heavy guns of his clinical language to bear on the kind of behavior one can witness every day, say, in the Wall Street Stock Exchange, as people gaze fixedly at numbers, scurry about frantically, push into each other, try to undercut one another desperately and without evident remorse. I wonder whether he has stopped to "analyze," and then go on to generalize so freely about, what he must probably have heard, or certainly could easily manage to hear, from men who spend their lives inventing hypnotic television commercials aimed at selling God-knows-what to God-knows-whom in this "free-enterprise" society. I wonder whether he has thought of taking a careful clinical look at some of the military personnel stationed in Air Force bases near San Francisco. What kind of mind allows a person to work day in and day out to keep our bombers flying over Vietnam? What kind of mind keeps one continually fighting this competitor and that competitor—not only in business, but also in the professions?

Many young students have begun to question all of this, but Dr. Solomon seems to see in their sharp and unsparing analysis only evidence of neurosis. Incredibly, he can talk about "extremes of sadomasochism, common among young people," at a moment in this country's history when bombs are pouring out of B-52's on defenseless Asian peasants, and a nation like ours allies itself with governments like those of Greece and Spain. He talks about "student violence," suggesting that it may be a "rebound phenomenon from the tranquilization effect of the cannabis drugs," but there are people in this and other countries who for years and years have had no difficulty in expressing their violence without the stimulus of cannabis. (I wish Dr. Soloman had also offered a little bit of evidence for that speculation of his about cannabis, but there is no space here for an example-by-example analysis of all his unsubstantiated arguments.) I refer not only to bomb-dropping and saber-rattling, but to the violence we all have to live with intimately every day—the violence done to our air or water by corporations headed by individuals whose "minds" Dr. Solomon might want to think and write about one day; or the violence done to those who get killed driving badly made automobiles, each such car the product of corporate policies and "attitudes" established and executed by such individuals, none of them "students," of course, nor subject to a description like "the young people." Perhaps they might be classified as the middle-aged, middle-class "normal" people who don't see psychiatrists—*and* don't have to worry about being labelled and written about in psychiatric papers by the likes of Dr. Solomon or me.

I have little more to add here, because what I might want to say would require pages, other than to express my surprise and dismay at phrases like "hebephrenic irrelevancies" as applied to rock-and-roll bands (but not to some of the things said by some of our nation's leaders or those who ape them?) or remarks like: "College professors noted that their students had become increasingly uninterested." Which college professors? After saying what? And to whom?

Alas, one shrugs one's shoulders at the "methodological" problems Dr. Solomon presents to us—and maybe one also has a right to demonstrate that "judicious indignation" which Erik H. Erikson (writing in *Childhood and Society*, Dr. Solomon's first reference) mentions as being at times utterly necessary and valuable.

HARRY GIRVETZ, PH.D.
Santa Barbara, California

We must be careful not to treat healthy youthful protest against sham and hypocrisy as if it were pathological, remembering that involvement in the more unhealthy manifestations of the counterculture is for many young people only temporary. We must not forget our own youthful—often antisocial and nearly self-destructive—indiscretions. With these caveats, I must say that in general I applaud Dr. Solomon's refusal to be fashionable and to go along with those who regard the young as the sole repositories of virtue and wisdom (much as orthodox Marxists regarded the proletariat), encouraging them to drown in an ocean of self-pity, and filling the air with *mea culpa*.

However, I must confess that I cringe before the task of explaining what happened in the late sixties, and I tremble for those who try. Clearly, it is dangerous to generalize not only about all of youth but about all college students, or even all students who have joined the counterculture. Dr. Solomon reckons with this, although perhaps not enough. Also, it is easy to be misled. I do not agree, for example, with those professors referred to by Dr. Solomon who found "that their students had become increasingly uninterested, as though the lectures and subject matter were irrelevant. . . ." And to the extent that this is so, the explanation could be quite simple: the fact that many have been attending college or remain there only in order to avoid the draft, or the fact that it is harder to concentrate in the midst of a campus crisis. Neither do I agree that students these days are under unusual academic pressures; some of us are apprehensive about a tendency in some quarters to relax standards.

Although I welcome the appearance among college students of an active social conscience and endorse their rejection of some of the specious values they find in our society, I worry with Dr. Solomon over mindless militancy, a tendency to confuse difference (and even freakishness) with identity, counter-culture escapism, and the kind of instant hedonism that manifests itself in sexual permissiveness and the drug scene. But the etiology of such phenomena poses serious problems and is bound to provoke argument.

I must confess that I am not sure I see how such expressions as "the fear of nonexistence" or "the failure to obtain ego mastery over the basic need for survival" increase our understanding of the need for affection and recognition, the dread of loneliness and isolation, or the old-fashioned feeling of homesickness which Dr. Solomon also subsumes under the concept of "nonexistence." That last malaise, whether designated by my homespun term or as Dr. Solomon's "fear of death," surely afflicted some of his and my generation of college students as well as students of the 1960's. Neither am I sure that the statement, "the concept of the awareness of one's existence is the basis of the need for attention and the desire to be important," although it seems to affirm a causal relationship, really says anything. (In any case, I do agree with Dr. Solomon—as I always have with Professor George Mead, who told us so long ago—that self-consciousness is a social derivative, and that we find and become aware of ourselves through the regard of others.)

In our quest for an explanation we must be careful not to cite causes that were operative long before the recent wave of disaffection and continue to be so now that the more militant and extreme manifestations of disaffection have subsided. Too often, attempts to describe the psychodynamics of unrest fail because they deal in such constants. For example, loneliness, the need for recognition, what Dr. Solomon calls the failure to achieve "ego mastery"—surely these antedate the phenomena for which we are here attempting to provide an explanation, and I doubt that there is evidence to indicate that they were more acute during the late 1960's. On the other hand, we can all agree that involvement in the most unpopular war in our history has been a decisive factor in bringing disaffection among young Americans to a climax, especially since its impact has been greatest on them. We can also agree that the de-escalation of the war has contributed to the prevailing calm. Still, many of us share a strong suspicion that, while a complete end to the war might restore peace permanently to the campuses, it would not close the disproportionate gap that separates this generation from the preceding one. I think we must look primarily to the social psychologist for explanations, and Dr. Solomon's silence on a number of questions confirms this.

Have liberal and "reasonable" parents structured the family so democratically and rationally (in the sense that decisions are never arbitrary and are always justified with reasons) that their offspring, upon leaving home, suffer a kind of culture shock and rebel against a world which tells them what to do without inviting them to participate in the decision or taking the time to give them reasons? They often encounter that kind of world at the university.

Can it be that the unprecedented width of today's generation gap is brought about by a unique situation, namely, loss of those guidelines on which parents in the past were able to rely for resolving problems so difficult as to challenge the powers of even the most intelligent and sympathetic adults?

Parents today have burdens of decision and choice which condemn them in advance to inadequacy. It is not simply that the rules change at an unprecedented pace, but that in many areas among so-called emancipated groups there no longer are any rules. Parents are on their own, and the result is bafflement and bewilderment in complex situations which leave fathers and mothers discredited and even rejected.

The result is not necessarily rebellion. As Kenneth Keniston (1965) has written in *The Uncommitted,* parents are to be "understood," even pitied. Otherwise, the consequence, as he points out, can be disastrous:

> . . . from his parent a child has traditionally learned the meaning of adulthood, of maleness and femaleness, of work, play, and social membership. By identifying with his parents, by internalizing their ways of doing things, by imitating their behavior, he has known how to become an adult. . . . With no exemplars, no objects of identification, and an obdurate refusal to accept them, the result is often that perplexity, self-fragmentation and confusion we see in many young men [p. 233].

Not only parents but today's young people have burdens of choice and decision rarely faced by their parents when they were young. The parents—and surely the grandparents—of those who have joined the counterculture generally knew what occupation they would follow, whom they would marry or date (at least with respect to class and ethnic background), how they would worship, what political party they would join, what the content of their education would be (unconfused by the relevance kick), etc., etc. We have found no substitute for the rules and regulations that have been jettisoned and for such collective "wisdom of the past" as they may have embodied—granted that that wisdom was sometimes dubious. An older generation took its standards for granted and adhered to them too routinely; a younger generation has thrown them over too uncritically, has not yet found new ones, and worst of all, is unsure of the role of standards as such in the guidance of conduct. In sum, this and future generations are in need of a new ethic—an ethic which tells them why the alternative to moral dogmatism is not skepticism, subjectivism, or some other debilitating form of relativism. The current breed of moral philosophers hasn't been of much help. Perhaps wise healers like Dr. Solomon can come to the rescue.

L. TAKEO DOI, M.D.

Tokyo, Japan

Perusing Dr. Solomon's paper, I feel that I am on familar ground because his description of American youth would apply equally well to Japanese youth. As a matter of fact, I too once wrote a paper on this world-wide phenomenon of youth unrest (trying, however, to explain it from a different angle from his).

I would like to state my basic agreement with Dr. Solomon's viewpoint, which perhaps proves that I belong, like him, to the older generation. At any rate, I am glad to know that he has had the courage to call a spade a spade and that he didn't yield an inch to the audience who greeted him with open resentment and sarcasm when he lectured on the subject of this paper. It is indicative of our present age that the psychoanalyst is forced to take a moral stand almost against his will—a trend quite opposite to that which Freud faced in the Victorian age.

Much as I admire the strength of this paper as reflecting the author's moral fiber, it has a weakness, too. The weakness lies, in my opinion, in the fact that Dr. Solomon makes much too sharp a dichotomy between mental health and pathology. He says that he describes pathology because he sees mainly patients, that all is not psychopathology, and that there is also a spirit of a healthy morality and aspiration for improvement. But then he doesn't provide a viable concept that can embrace both the pathology and the health of contemporary youth. I think that is why this paper gives the impression of being only "descriptive," in spite of the author's concern with the psychodynamics of young people.

I shall explain my point by taking up Dr. Solomon's three categories: existence versus nonexistence, identity versus identity confusion, and intimacy versus pseudo intimacy. It is obvious that in all three categories the first term signifies a positive value and the second a negative, and that contemporary youth often distinguish themselves by negative values. I don't dispute this, but would like to emphasize—as I think the author doesn't sufficiently—that many young people nowadays plunge into negative values precisely because they are searching for a decisive solution.

Now what kind of decisive solution do they want for themselves? I can't describe it better than by saying that they are seeking a complete renewal of everything on this earth. Is this not equivalent to a wish for rebirth? One could maintain that it is a disguised manifestation of such a wish. Interestingly, Dr. Solomon also mentions "a rebirth fantasy," in connection with mysticism, and notes that the latter has become a fad among contemporary youth. I believe, however, that the wish for rebirth is not confined to mystically inclined people or psychotics, but may have a broader application—it may also be the basis of the struggle for identity or intimacy. A confused identity or a pseudo intimacy ensues from this struggle only when the wish for rebirth becomes an aim in itself.

I think the wish for rebirth is present in everybody, whether manifest or not. It often serves as a hidden incentive for those who enter psychoanalysis. Also, unless we recognize the existence of such a wish it is impossible to account for the almost universal belief in reincarnation, one form of which, for example, was Nietzsche's doctrine of eternal recurrence. In this regard I might also mention an expression commonly used by the Japanese when they have been rescued from a dire predicament, when they feel they have been given a second chance: "I shall live from now on as if I were reborn." It is characteristic of the Japanese to be able rather easily to act out a make-believe of rebirth, whether individually or nationally.

Is the wish for rebirth pathological in itself? Taken literally, it certainly sounds absurd. When Jesus preached rebirth in the Kingdom of God, Nicodemus expressed the classical objection: "How can a grown man be born again? He certainly cannot enter his mother's womb and be born a second time." Still, the concept can be understood on a higher spiritual level, as Jesus implied. Or, as Buddha taught, it can be relegated to the ordeal of reincarnation to which man is subjected repeatedly unless and until he reaches Nirvana. At any rate, the wish for rebirth does not seem pathological so long as man either uses it as an incentive for change or makes room for it outside of everyday life. But it may lead to pathology if man tries to realize it in this life, as in the case of psychotics who actually hallucinate their rebirth, or of agitated youth who, renouncing the possibility of personal rebirth, yet dream of a complete renewal of everything on this earth.

It should then be the psychoanalyst's task to identify the wish for rebirth as such even in its disguised forms, and thus to save it from pathology. I do not say that we should save it for the sake of religion; this, after all, is the province of religious people themselves. As for the psychoanalyst, he should rest content if he can make a Nicodemus out of a man too heavily inebriated with the heady wine of rebirth.

CARLOS NUÑEZ-SAAVEDRA, M.D.
Santiago, Chile

Dr. Solomon's paper is stimulating, exciting, and also somewhat puzzling: stimulating as a psychoanalyst's contribution to understanding a multiphasic sociologic phenomenon; exciting as it evokes the phenomenology of youth by *considering young people as a biological and historical entity*; and puzzling as it presents a psychodynamism that comprises such a vast sector of humanity; it is somewhat like walking through a labyrinth.

In the first pages, Dr. Solomon guides us firmly through this labyrinth. He does not hide his doubts and vacillations, demonstrating throughout his work that he is conscious of the difficulties. This becomes most obvious when the demonstrative force of the thesis begins to weaken as many of the ideas being developed do not adjust adequately to his pursued objectives. But this is not surprising. The fulfillment of such an ambitious project demands a clear conceptualization which in a case like this is difficult to attain.

As Dr. Solomon remarks, the behavior of youth in the United States lends itself to broad comparisons with that in other countries. I will concentrate on the Chilean scene after some general observations.

In his introductory remarks we can see that Dr. Solomon follows the trend of thought of those who have tried in the past to establish a psychoanalytic characterology or a psychoanalytic anthropology: Freud initially with "Civilization and Its Discontents" (1930), "Analysis Terminable and Interminable" (1937), "Beyond the Pleasure Principle" (1920), "Group Psychology and the Analysis of the Ego" (1921), "Totem and Taboo, Part 3: Animism, Magic, and Omnipotence of Thought" (1912-1913), etc.; then Marcuse, in his philosophical and political discussion of psychoanalysis,

Teilhard de Chardin, Adorno, and many others. We must also mention Fenichel and his methodology for the establishment of a psychoanalytic characterology, as well as the work edited by Kruse (1957), *Integrating the Approaches to Mental Disease.*

Dr. Solomon makes some pertinent distinctions lest his discussion might seem to label 1960's American youth as exclusively pathological. He states, nonetheless, that they show pathognomonic signs observable "at all levels of society and [which] represent interaction between many changed environmental conditions and alterations in family structure."

The signs that he calls pathognomonic characterize 1960's youth as "vocal, rebellious and discontented, openly demanding change." He says that most of the young people "were convinced that they were progressive thinkers" and "believed that the answer to human discontent was to modify or destroy all existing cultural and governmental institutions," and that "they became highly resentful at the suggestion" that this conduct might be "regressive rather than progressive." He admits it is difficult to be precise about which part of the current disturbance is to be considered progressive and which regressive; yet he specifies that some of the demands are reasonable while others are "unrealistic and highly charged with emotion," and that these latter, which he says can be observed in all social levels, although not necessarily found in all young people, play a "telling part in widespread general trends, especially at the college level." He adds to these features: "first, overt aggressiveness bordering on or including violence; second, its opposite, social apathy; and last, sexual license." He then states that "all these manifestations are intensified by the use of drugs."

After having presented the principal characteristics of the problem and stating that they express the interaction between "changed environmental conditions and alterations in family structure," Dr. Solomon defines his position as an investigator concerned with what goes on in the psychic process of the adolescent or pre-adult who has to adjust to the social changes of the last decade.

In spite of the introductory statements, the methodology employed is dubious. Indeed, the problem calls for a multidisciplinary approach based upon the sociocultural-historical-political level involved. Since these methodological difficulties in psychoanalytic research on characterological problems have been the most difficult to surmount, we must necessarily accept that they become even more complex when the research is directed toward the characterological traits of a vast sector of humanity. I do not wish to continue analyzing the methodological problems implied, but will review two other points.

1. What is regressive or progressive in the conduct of the sixties' youth, or in actual social disorder? I think this could be answered merely by applying the standards of the psychiatric clinic. Yet psychiatrists and psychoanalysts must remember that neurotic conduct that implies regression is sometimes a ciphered message of protest, as Frieda Fromm-Reichmann once said, admonishing psychiatrists that it was their task to decipher this message. Perhaps she was thinking of John Stuart Mill's words: "There is nothing more true than the fact that any advancement of the human situation is solely due to discontented characters."

I do not wish to praise badness; I simply note that the distinction between what is regressive and what progressive might not be as interesting for a psychoanalyst as his commitment to discern the content of protest and its causes, and that this same criterion applies to the problem of current social disorder. Thus, we must consider the political activity of youth in another light.

The ideology or political activity of a patient can be studied by the analyst just as can any other manifestation of his psychic life. But when the analyst wants to explain the political conduct of youth as a whole, he must bear in mind the gestalt principle that the whole is more than the sum of its parts if his contribution is to be of value as part of the necessary multidisciplinary approach.

2. Although Dr. Solomon says he will not insist on the family unit, I think it is necessary to note briefly that the

importance of paternal authority has visibly diminished proportionately as the authority of the social collectivity has increased. This means a serious alteration in the functioning of the psychic apparatus as Freud conceived it; it could perhaps explain the different symptomatology of actual neurosis; it could demonstrate yet again how the analysis of neurotic symptoms reflects the current morals of the epoch.

The characteristics pointed out by Dr. Solomon as peculiar to youth of the sixties are observable on a larger or smaller scale not only in North America but in the rest of the world as well. Even though each country has its own sociopolitical structure, these characteristics still depend on something more fundamental—a sociocultural change of worldwide dimensions.

If this be so, it would be useful to attempt a comparison, bearing always in mind the limitations I have noted. On this basis, I will offer some comparative reflections on Chilean youth, dividing the characteristics according to Dr. Solomon's description: (1) rebellion and aggression against the establishment; (2) social apathy and disinterest; and (3) sexual license.

Rebellion and Aggression Against the Establishment

In several countries rebellion and aggression against the establishment started before the decade of the sixties with the appearance of angry youth, a group of whom concentrated on social changes and demanded educational reforms.

In Chile, the tendency to political participation has always been an outstanding feature among students, especially at the university level, to such an extent that it has sometimes been scornfully referred to by foreign observers. But for the Chileans it is natural.

In the last few years there has emerged in Chile a clandestine ultra-left movement which remained underground until the change of government in 1971 but now is demanding drastic measures to hasten the revolutionary process. There also arose in Chile in the sixties a small ultra-right movement which attracted attention inasmuch as it sustained a much more conservative ideology even than that of its young adherents' parents, most of whom belonged to the highest social levels.

I have been able to make but minimal psychoanalytic observations of members of these ultra groups. I can say only that they confirmed once again the psychoanalytic teaching that certain forms of political and religious activity have a symptomatic value which must be measured in the context of the total neurotic symptomatology of each particular case.

According to Dr. Solomon, knowing how a group of three psychical categories—*existence, identity,* and *intimacy*—operate in the adjustment of youth to social change would enable us to understand their participation in social movements. Dr. Solomon's formulation is correct. But we must remember that these categories express an even more fundamental motive in man's psychic life from birth to death: the need to live his life with a sense of omnipotence. This universal need for omnipotence is the real architect of man's history, with all its horrors and all its greatness.

In his work "Group Psychology and the Analysis of the Ego" (1921), Freud reveals many of the secrets of the interaction of individuals within a group, but there are still many troublesome questions. Bringing them to light is our fundamental and everlasting duty, which Dr. Solomon has gone far toward fulfilling.

Social Apathy and the Youth of the Sixties

The aggressive and violent expressions of youth engaged in the social struggle can be attributed to purely psychopathological motivation only when it touches the extremes of the indiscriminate and arbitrary, of the brutal and unjust. On the other hand, social apathy and lack of interest in creative activity, expressed in arbitrary criticism that leads to aberrant and escapist conduct, does undoubtedly involve psychopathology.

When such conduct acquires group dimensions, it requires both quantitative and qualitative measurements: Quantitative, because when peculiar to determinate groups it is especially conspicuous; in its extension it seems exhibitionistic, and presumptuous, much more widespread than it is, and we run the risk of generalizing it as applicable to youth at large, which is obviously unjust. Qualitative, because it is also necessary to evaluate group conduct according to the level of the socio-economic-cultural-technical strata in which it appears, distinguishing between it and those culturally critical positions which imply, on the contrary, a truly philosophical reflection, despite a superficial appearance of apathy.

The critical negation of the culture, as expressed in the context of regressive conduct intensified by the use of drugs, is not new. In Chile it has been observable as a group phenomenon affecting mainly that sector of the youth of the sixties living in large cities. Its origin cannot be explained in terms of a specific sociological movement of national character. Psychiatric examination of members of these groups does reveal a deep and varying pathology, but in my opinion this group character responds to more complex motivations than can be thoroughly understood by the mere psychoanalytical approach to individual cases. I say this while particularly bearing in mind all the socio-cultural and economic problems of a country like Chile, to whose severe problems we must unfortunately add endemic alcoholism.

Sexual License

In Chile, as in other countries, we see a change of attitude toward sexual matters which, in the sense of Freud's critical view of the cultural morality, can be considered as progress. Clinically, in Chile sexual license of a neurotically conditioned group character, which could be considered peculiar to youth of the sixties elsewhere, has not been observed.

I cannot end my discussion without expressing thanks to Dr. Solomon, for his presentation has been a stimulus for me to continue my studies concerning the correlation of environmental factors and the behavior of young people. I say this as both psychoanalyst and citizen of a country which today is going through a critical moment of its history; that is, I speak as a psychoanalyst working in the midst of a political and social convulsion whose effects upon the concepts of existence, identity, and intimacy are an enigma.

WILLIAM L. O'NEILL, PH.D.

New Brunswick, New Jersey

Dr. Solomon's paper shows, I think, how hard it is to generalize successfully about large populations on the basis of limited clinical evidence. Analyzing small numbers of disturbed individuals may provide insights into deviant behavior, but it is no substitute for the larger empirical studies that produce sociological and psychological profiles of significant groups. There is already a huge literature, much of it by social scientists, on youth in the 1960's. A bibliographic survey (Altbach) published as long ago as 1968 includes 44 printed pages of citations on student politics alone. Although I have not read most of these, and find it difficult even to summarize those I have, there is some agreement among social scientists that there were at least two generations of student activists in the 1960's, neither of which resembled Dr. Solomon's two case studies. The first generation, those active before 1968, consisted of upper-middle-class children with professional fathers, who were superior students majoring in the social sciences and humanities. Most of their families were liberal or radical, and supported their children's militancy. There was no generation gap. The second generation, a larger group active in the late sixties, had backgrounds more representative of the middle class as a whole, but they also tended to be superior students majoring in the humanities and social sciences. Their parents were less likely to approve of their political activities. Few experts seem to agree with Dr. Solomon that pathognomonic features were an important part of college life in the 1960's.

A further problem in this paper is that Dr. Solomon never really makes clear who his subjects are. He lumps together student activists, hippies, street people, and others, but the evidence suggests that different elements in the youth culture had different origins and attributes. Hippies do seem to have been social misfits, passive, disturbed, unable to function effectively in normal environments. Student militants, as I have indicated, were opposite types, the graduate student radicals I knew personally being notably intelligent, academically successful, and with no more than the ordinary number of personal problems so far as I could tell.

I don't feel that Dr. Solomon's attempts to relate youth movements to the national environment—still less to centuries of history—succeed. He suggests that increased academic pressures created anxieties leading to rebellion. Yet academic pressure declined from the mid-sixties on, and by the decade's end many universities were concerned with grade inflation. Professors seem to have lowered their standards, enabling student grade averages to rise. Or perhaps graduate teaching assistants, who grade most papers in large universities, were responsible for the higher averages. At Harvard University, for example, two-thirds of the 1971 senior class graduated *cum laude*. Dr. Solomon also repeats the common excuse that students became lost in the larger, impersonal multiversity, and so rebelled. No doubt some student activists fit this pattern, but as we saw, most student radicals were good at coping with the university environment. Moreover, surveys taken at the University of California after the Free Speech Movement found that most students at Berkeley were quite satisfied with their situation. Indeed, since California has colleges and universities of all sizes, most Berkeley students came there precisely because it was large and exciting.

Dr. Solomon misses the point in saying that student intellectuals have been the vanguard of rebellion. Whatever the case elsewhere, American college and university students have historically been passive and conservative. Their most notable political trait until recently was a slavish adherence to the conventional wisdom. Even in the 1930's, when for the first time activists appeared on campus in some strength, militant students were invariably affiliated with, and took their direction from, adult political organizations. The surprising thing about student activism in the 1960's was its largely autonomous character.

The youth revolt of the 1960's is now a part of history. At its peak it never included anything like a majority of college and university students, and had almost no influence among the non-students who were a majority of the college age population. As the feeble efforts in April of 1972 to demonstrate against the escalated air war in Indochina showed, a constituency for campus radicalism no longer exists. It is doubtful, therefore, that clinical evidence gathered even a few years ago will tell us much about student activism, today, for the old pattern no longer holds.

I must compliment Dr. Solomon on the calm and rational tenor of his essay. His subject is still an emotionally charged one, and many discussions of it are flawed by partisanship and bad temper. There is only one point here that I must take strong issue with. Dr. Solomon implies that young Jewish radicals criticized Israel after 1967 because Moscow did. On the contrary, all authorities agree that Russia had virtually no effect on the New Left. In fact, most young radicals scorned Russia and regarded it as counter-revolutionary. Their position on Israel hardened because their growing identification with Third World peoples, including Arabs, led them to see Israel as the aggressor in the Six-Day War, and because the Palestinian Liberation Movement seemed to resemble other admired revolutionary movements, such as those led by Che Guevara and Ho Chi Minh. They may have been misled, but certainly not through Communist influence.

ARNALDO RASCOVSKY, M.D.

Buenos Aires, Argentina

Taking into account the genetic factors that gave birth to the youth of the 1960's, there are good reasons to believe that a great many of their expressions which Dr. Solomon considers maladjusted are merely manifestations of a corresponding adaptive reaction response. To catalog these youth as pathological is to adopt a gerontocratically a priori position. Such youth emerged as the natural consequence of recent sociocultural developments, such as the devastation of modern warfare, the extreme shattering destructiveness of atomic weapons, the brutality of contemporary initiation rites that subject adolescents to the ordeal of military service and war, the meaningless university careers which compel young people to spend one of the most fruitful periods of life storing up an overwhelming quantity of information and cramming for exams under high academic pressure and humiliating and obsolete requirements, only to find themselves in the end ill-equipped to cope with reality; and last but not least, the calamitous contemporary rupture of the parental function by which motherhood has become more an illusory attitude than a reality. Which attitude, then, is in fact more pathological—that of the youth of the 1950's: "subdued, passive, and silent," or that of the youth of the 1960's: "vocal, rebellious and discontented, openly demanding change"?

We may question the validity of considering progressive or regressive behavior as indices of evolution. There are reasons to support the belief that the evolution of a superior species is accomplished at the cost of fetal regression of the preceding species. Volk and his followers have shown through comparative anatomy that the human being looks very much like the anthropoidal fetus. It seems that we have to accept the fact that evolutionary modification calls for a previous regression to earlier stages where the creative powers are to be found, and from which the modified evolution would spring. Therefore, the belief of young people that "they are progressive thinkers" could be the first step in their struggle against the obsolete establishment. It should be noted that under present conditions maladjustment, implying as it does a search for a less filicidal and frustrating reality, is a necessary prerequisite for change. Both categorizations, "The Sorrowful Sixties" and "The Significant Sixties," seem appropriate as definitions of the past decade. The former holds true for the decadent gerontocracy that loses ground as the younger generations become aware of the sacrifice of their lives, instincts, rights, and creativity that has been imposed on them. Similarly, the latter points to youth struggling against such slavery and bondage.

The characteristics shared by the youth of the 1960's, according to Dr. Solomon's excellent synthesis, are overt aggressiveness, social apathy, and sexual license—all intensified by the use of drugs. With respect to aggression, the influence of the above-mentioned environmental factors on young people is only too obvious; they are simply responding to the aggression that has been inflicted upon them ever since they were infants. Aren't those about twenty years of age thrown into the most dreadful hell of violence when they are sent to war? Hasn't the establishment provided all sorts of examples of extreme violence through television, radio, comics, and movies? Isn't it true that the average American child between five and 14 years old has watched 13,000 crimes of violence on television? Are we aware of the violence universally inflicted upon children when they are deprived of their most basic rights?

Teaching that fails to interest young people is teaching that is alien to their lives and remote from their present and future aims. Do the initiation rites, represented by prolonged and but slightly useful secondary school and university studies, justify the total employment of one of the most productive periods of a person's life—from ages 15 to 25—when the result is an insecure individual, poorly furnished with pseudo knowledge, ill-equipped to face reality?

In Argentina—and as far as I know in most Latin-American countries—teaching is deficient, obsolete, and humiliating, demanding an expenditure of time disproportionate to the results. To illustrate: The School of Medicine offers no connection between the subjects taught and the morbidity of the environment in which the would-be physician is expected to practice. For instance, although mental disease has the highest rate of morbidity, including as it does psychoses, neuroses, addictions, perversions, suicide, psychopathy, delinquency, and so forth, it is given very little importance in the programs of study. The same is true of the majority of pseudo-formative university specialties which are imposed as initiation rites upon the young who aspire to enter into adult society. Dr. Solomon has reason to shudder before the quantity of books that a student must read! The accumulation of information has become insupportable and impossible unless the students have already surrendered their minds to authority.

At present, not only the university is being judged in this respect, but all other areas of society as well. It has become increasingly evident that the fundamental unconscious motivation underlying all war is the sacrifice of the young, the Vietnam War in particular having proven irrefutably that young people are being used as propitiatory victims in this generational sacrifice demanded by the sociocultural process. Thus, the young soldier feels closer to his young enemies than to his own superior officers; he is aware that he is at war to serve interests other than his own. For the young American, the historical exploitation of the colored people amounts to an unconscious variant of the child's exploitation by his parents. The confusion of personal values, of individual identity, and of basic instinctual motivations can be better understood in the light of the ambivalent and ambiguous imposition of a sociocultural organization based on the slaughter, abuse, and exploitation of the weak, symbolized by the child.

Existence versus Nonexistence

Quite correctly, the author remarks that awareness of one's existence depends on the primary object relationship, that is, the relationship with the mother, the origin of the possibility of existence. When this relationship is inadequate, the feeling of isolation which ensues is coupled with a sense of separation and abandonment. The failure to resolve these feelings leads to regressive rebellion, and mysticism and drugs activate this regression, contributing to denial of the unbearable external reality by withdrawing into one's self. The cases Dr. Solomon reports show a threatening and mutilating parental reality, in Alan's case embodied in his earlier images that induce him to return to a previous fetal union with his mother, which is less persecutory than the threat of being annihilated by the actual external mother. Through regression, Alan regains the feeling of oneness with the universe, the oceanic feeling of being in the amniotic fluid, thus counteracting through hallucination the annihilating feeling of nonexistence. Drugs, which are partly the result of identification with parents who smoke or are alcoholic, block the increase of anxiety and place the addict in an artificial intrauterine nirvana, with sorrowful consequences.

Identity versus Identity Confusion

The achievement of a satisfactory identity depends upon introjection of the parents and identification with them. As the child grows he accumulates other identifications from the environment, but the basic pattern of identification is originally laid down in the initial relationship with the mother. It is very important to stress this fact when dealing with the identity problems of our time, because the impoverishment of the mother-child relationship plays a decisive role in the activation of further identity conflicts. Abandonment is the main pathogenic agent in a deficient parental introjection and identification. We witness then a regression to primitive bisexuality, caused by the lack of a specific sexual differentiation based on identification with the parent of the same sex.

Intimacy

Mature genitality depends on the pregenital bases of sexual development, and these are closely related to the individual parents' behavior and attitudes; but child abuse, mutilation, disparagement, neglect and abandonment, and the underrating of the maternal function characterize our society as a whole. Circumcision is performed upon 80 per cent of the male population of North America, and this early trauma is serious enough to be taken into account when referring to sexual patterns. That is why we believe that when trying to understand the reasons for the superficial and immature sexuality of the youth of the 1960's, a more penetrating light should be focused on the problem. Contraceptives have contributed to lessen the asocial consequences of premarital sexual life, and their use has been facilitated defensively. It is true that pseudo intimacy is a defense against loneliness, but why is there so much loneliness? A child who has had satisfactory parental companionship in his early years feels accompanied throughout his lifetime. Failing this, sexuality then tends to find ways of appeasing anxieties, mainly of a paranoid nature, that have arisen from an early lack of maternal support and presence.

Why did this phenomenon become so conspicuous in the sixties? Aren't these the children who were born during and after World War II? Wasn't abandonment more frequent because fathers had to leave home to go to war? Weren't these children brought up deeply immersed in the ethics of war? Aren't they the children who heard about or suffered from the repercussions of the atomic bomb, of Hiroshima, Nagasaki, and the bombing of London? Didn't they witness the merciless killing of young people in Europe, Korea, Vietnam? Aren't they the children of pseudo liberated women who permanently underrated the maternal function? The cultural monster demanded that women work in the office, the factory, the school, the shops—the price of which was the abandonment of the child and the neglect of the most essential human function: gestation and generational transmission. Motherhood was perverted, and with it the essential roots of the generational process. Civil ethics were replaced by military ethics to such an extent that in some countries female armies were created as an expression of the masculinization of women and the loss of their most precious function, maternity.

The youth of the 1960's is one of the most striking outcomes of these ethics, and we wonder whether this is not the beginning of a singular human variety, amaternal or without parents—that is, without love.

JOSEPH C. SOLOMON

AARON H. ESMAN, M.D.
New York, New York

The youth scene of the 1960's has exerted on behavioral scientists of all disciplines and persuasions a fascination in direct proportion to its flamboyance and complexity. Psychoanalysts in particular have felt themselves challenged to deal with the events of this period, and their efforts range from relatively dispassionate studies such as those of Erikson and Greenacre to highly personal statements pro and con, such as those of Liebert on the one hand and Bettelheim on the other. Rarely have analysts been obliged to deal so extensively with matters outside the province of their consulting rooms—and often outside their professional competence—as they have been in their attempts to make sense of the turbulent behavior of the young people they have seen and read about during the kaleidoscopic years following the election of John F. Kennedy.

Dr. Solomon's study represents another valiant effort to encompass the social and psychological phenomena of this era, and in many respects he has grasped the essentials. Certainly his delineation of some of the social influences on the process of adolescing and identity formation during the sixties—the Civil Rights Movement, the fear of the Bomb, and, above all, the Vietnam War—is astute, as are his frequently perceptive observations about the age-old developmental problems of the adolescent who seeks to cope with the enigma of existence, the crisis of identity formation, and the demands of intimacy.

I fear, however, that Dr. Solomon's courage and perspicuity are somewhat vitiated by an ill-concealed distaste for virtually every aspect of the picture he is attempting to interpret. His disclaimers to the contrary notwithstanding, he appears to regard the whole business—rock music, drug use, campus protest, mysticism, sexual "license" (*sic*)—as pathological and a bit distasteful to boot.

168—

Now Dr. Solomon is, as a citizen, an adult, and a liberal humanist, entitled to his feelings about the whole messy sixties scene. But as an analyst, a scientist, and a scholar, he offends, it seems to me, by his lack of objectivity and by what can be fairly called countertransference reactions, resulting in such personalized comments as his (supposedly) jocular references to "that dirty four-letter word 'love,' " his allusions to "*soi-disant* artists," and his suggestion that sexually frank modern novels are mostly written by "people . . . who cannot experience mature intimacy." His statement that "many" students "keep up with their work in spite of their marijuana smoking and occasional LSD trip" ignores recent studies showing that most such students consistently do at least as well academically as their nondrug-using peers and, in essence, show no adverse effects that can be measured from their scholastic performance. Indeed, he does not indicate that it is, by and large, the brighter, more reflective students at the schools with the highest academic standards who appear to be involved in the current normative pattern of moderate use of cannabis and sporadic experimental use of hallucinogens. And his suggestion that overt aggressive behavior and sexual "license" are intensified by such drug use is simply unsupported by everything we know about the pharmacology of marijuana and the psychedelics.

The result of Dr. Solomon's—doubtless inadvertent—bias is, I think, a failure on his part to empathize with some of the special problems of young people living through the recent past and the present. He does mention the terrible burden of keeping up with the information explosion and the growing complexity of technology. He does not, however, seem to appreciate the effects of certain related social currents of the time on the process of becoming an adult. I refer, first, to the endless extension of the educational process—the process of *becoming* itself—and the associated impressment into higher education of innumerable young people who have no real interest or aptitude for it. Second, I refer to the decline in influence and credibility of the traditional cultural sources of values. Both of these have served, I believe, to leave many young people in a state of limbo, deprived of the opportunity to form an ego identity and of the possibility of integrating a firm, consistent, and supportive ego ideal. Thus, in my view, the appeal of the mystico-religious systems, including the drug ethos, derives less from existential anxieties than from the desperate value-hunger of many young people who, having decathected the values associated with their parents in the course of the normal adolescent individuation process, are left bereft of socially given, believable models. (Who can believe in our current crop of political or religious leaders?) Many such young people have turned, thus, to new and exotic leaders, often only slightly older contemporaries, who are able to play on their phase-appropriate wish to experiment and their undeniable tendency to regression. Blos has, however, emphasized precisely the necessity of such freedom of regression for the healthy resolution of adolescent conflicts.

Dr. Solomon is much concerned with what he calls "pseudo intimacy," which he appears to define as any relationship other than a permanent heterosexual marriage. Apart from the judgmental quality in this definition, which a priori excludes the possibility of true intimacy in a homosexual relationship, Dr. Solomon fails, I believe, to see how the establishment of truly intimate, stable relationships is complicated and interfered with by the drawing out of the educational process and the prolonged delay in the attainment of adult socioeconomic status. Coupled with the uncertainties imposed by the draft, the Bomb, and the economic situation, many young people are unwilling or unable to make binding commitments of the kind Dr. Solomon, looking backward, sees as normal. Are they then to defer sexual relations and amatory experimentation until their life situations permit them to make such commitments? Indeed, as Toffler points out in *Future Shock* (1970), living as we do in a world that increasingly promotes transience in residential, work, and interpersonal commitments, the kind of impermanent, casual relations Dr. Solomon is concerned about may represent youths' groping search for a realistic adaptive pattern.

Dr. Solomon is, of course, correct in his repeated admonitions about the need to await further returns before we pass judgment on the long-range consequences of the sixties' youth scene. One might add that the same could be said of other aspects of that troubled and tempestuous decade—aspects referable to the behavior and psychology of the adult world. In a decade that saw the unutterable madness and immorality of the Vietnam War represented as rational, respectable, political conduct, who indeed can pass judgment on the behavior of the young?

Author's Response

I very much appreciate the discussants' contributions. In one form or another they hinted that there is a marked difference between "healthy" reactions and psychopathology. At times the borderline is not clear-cut, especially when the young persons are asked to adjust to cultural pathology. The emphasis of my paper is upon intrapsychic processes, but it was necessary to include some remarks about mass psychology and the existing environmental and social forces, even though my expertise is greatest in the first-mentioned.

As to the question of regression versus progression, I am more than willing to concede that it may be necessary first to regress before we can make the big leap forward. This should not in any way refute the observation that much of the behavior of the young people (which I only partially described in the paper) was in fact regressive. This is neither an insult nor a manifestation of "countertransference," as Dr. Esman suggests, but is as near as I could possibly get to a dispassionate observation. Furthermore, it cannot be said that the students who displayed the reactions I described were merely a few isolated neurotic individuals. Hundreds of thousands of students and nonstudents were involved, not all to the same extent, to be sure, but enough to discern distinct behavioral patterns.

Although they came from backgrounds of varying stability and values, the youth showed sufficient concordance of feelings and attitudes as to constitute "a movement." A lynching could be considered a social action when there is some agreement among the participants as a group, although it would be abhorrent as an individual performance. The individual superego can be superseded by the less responsible superego of the mob. We also speak of nations as having personality characteristics, such as German paranoia or Hungarian sado-masochism. Obviously not every German is paranoid, nor every Hungarian a sado-masochist. Social psychology takes into consideration historic events, economic conditions, food supply, religious traditions, and many other factors in describing group behavior. Admittedly my remarks do not represent a thorough sociological study. In this, I defer to my discussants, especially Dr. O'Neill.

My impressions were not gathered exclusively from the analyses of a few disturbed young people. I did learn a great deal from them, not only about themselves but from their observations of their contemporaries. I made a few personal observations of the total scene and was constantly bombarded, as was everyone else, with reports by the various news media. Particularly enlightening, from more than the merely descriptive point of view, were the observations of my sons, who were close to the "normal" students, for the older, a physician, is a full-time faculty member at Stanford University (Department of Psychiatry) and the younger, an architect, is a full-time faculty member at the University of California at Berkeley (School of Architecture). I also analyzed the parents of young persons, a few of whom were university and junior college faculty members. Admittedly these observations cannot compare to the extensive study of large numbers of students and nonstudents and their families. I hope that my observations can be considered to be more intensive than extensive. Both approaches have their weaknesses.

I am particularly intrigued by the concept of rebirth offered by Dr. Doi. His statement that many young people plunge into negative values precisely because they are searching for a decisive solution is extremely astute. He sees the rebirth phenomenon as an attempt to obtain a complete renewal of everything on this earth. To a lesser degree, I suppose, every phase of ego development is a minor rebirth, although not always as violent as the student rebellions. Each critical learning period has the capacity for either progression or regression of weaning and growth, or a return to primitive behavior.

The release of archaic impulses shown by many adolescents or pre-adults can be described symbolically in oedipal and preoedipal terms. We could say that the destruction of buildings may have represented the wish to destroy or mutilate Father. Free speech may have meant "speaking up" to parents, dirty words violating the incest taboo. Perhaps the student action was an attack on Mother for betraying them (government contracts) or on the intruder (Bank of America). In any case Mother (alma mater) was not sacrosanct. By the same token we can speculate that the police needed to rescue Mother from her unruly children.

Although my paper stressed the similarities in the reactions of the youth of the sixties, I should say more about the differences. There is no doubt that the stable young men and women knew what was going on, perhaps participated in a few peace marches and honored picket lines, but were not grossly affected. They managed to stay out of trouble, rode out the storm and sought to return to their academic pursuits; the more unstable students used the turbulence to bring some of their conflicts to the surface or to seek escape mechanisms. Aside from these personal matters there were other social determinants.

The boys and girls who came from rural or small-town communities, where people are accustomed to meeting each other's needs, fared better than many others, as did big-city students who had mastered the techniques of group living. The most dissident youngsters seemed to have come from the suburbs. It was they who most depreciated adult values, especially money. They came from the most affluent and homogeneous communities, and when confronted with racial and economic differences, in addition to the other social problems, became the most rebellious. They said they did not want to return to exurbia and repeat the patterns of their parents. They were able to say this because they felt that job security was assured.

Let us now reassess the sixties by looking at what is happening in the early seventies. The college campuses are relatively quiet, following a brief cultural lag during which the large universities settled down while the turmoil moved on to the smaller colleges. How do we account for this change? Was it merely cyclical, or were there some other forces at work? I should like to offer a few ideas on this subject.

Some of the young people gave up their rebellious attitudes because they felt that the situation was hopeless, that it was useless to expend further effort to affect changes that were not forthcoming. Others felt they had won, that the Vietnam War was coming to a close through their efforts. Student morale improved with curriculum changes that provided for more student participation. Less pressure was exerted for high grades and more emphasis placed on real learning. The whole academic atmosphere changed to a great extent from the attitude of the authoritarian medieval church to that of ancient Greek intellectual discourse.

Another factor in the change was economic. Whereas in the sixties many jobs were available, this was no longer true in the seventies. The educational system was no longer held in such contempt; students who had dropped out now returned to school wiser and more sober. It was no longer so easy to get jobs, so they came back to finish their education. These returning students, as well as the older Vietnam War veterans, influenced the oncoming classes by their application to serious academic pursuits, sobered by the sad fact that many of them will have a hard time getting jobs after graduation. Student teachers, for example, begin to think seriously of what lies ahead when they are told that only one out of five will be able to obtain positions in their profession.

In the matter of intimacy and pseudo intimacy, there are indications of a swing back to older forms of morality. Whereas the common practice had been for students to "shack up" together in unsupervised apartments off-campus or in coeducational dormitories, there is now a tendency to return to gender-segregated dormitories. The novelty of "the pill" has worn off, and, some girls are becoming reluctant to use it because they have heard of some of its dangers.

Fraternities and sororities still do not control campus activities and are held somewhat in disrepute by the large mass of students, as in the sixties, but they too have changed. The strict lines of white Protestant, Catholic, or Jewish fraternities no longer exist; there is an admixture now not only of religions but of races. Orientals, Blacks, and Chicanos are finding their way in limited numbers into the once sacrosanct fraternities. Fraternity boys and girls have engaged in some of the campus protests and have become nearly indistinguishable from the other students in dress, long hair, and beards. And in off-campus social life the debut is no longer what it used to be. Debutante parties are either ignored by the girls or are deemphasized to a great degree.

Changes in our social institutions have had a great deal to do with the changed attitude of youth, a principal one, to the credit of the Nixon administration, being the 18-year-old vote. In my opinion this was an important factor in allaying the youth rebellion. The feared swing to the left of the young voters did not materialize; they were disarmed from fighting the establishment by suddenly becoming members of the establishment. Large numbers of 18- to 21-year-olds voted to reelect President Nixon. Once they were given a sense of responsibility and acceptance into the ranks of adulthood, they became as fearful of change as their parents.

Another factor in reducing political agitation was the rapprochement between the United States and Red China. Some of the campus radicals had carried the Mao Book and openly held the philosophy of the People's Republic to be the only hope of the future. Their ardor seemed to diminish to a great extent when they saw materialism and compromise as tangible forces in international relations.

Problems of racial identity still disturb our troubled youth. The Chicano takeover of student politics at Santa Clara and the rioting at the University of Southern California are cases in point; there may be others. From the point of view of reaction formation or the "backlash," many white students resent the softened attitude to Black students. They resent the lowered academic requirements for admission and the lessening need for maintaining scholastic excellence. Furthermore, the policy of quotas is abhorrent to many people. They feel that higher education should be offered only to students who are capable and willing to make use of it.

Although the early seventies can be regarded as a relatively quiescent period, perhaps because of changes in the social atmosphere, we can look back upon the sixties as a period of history, at least in our country, where young people took it upon themselves to say something. The real meaning of what they were saying, or how they said it, is not as important as the fact that they tried to express themselves. But this is still a far cry from the student activists of Japan and South America, where the voices of young people are central to any political action. I do not disagree with those who maintain that many of the affirmations of youth were based upon reality, and that the spirit of rebellion is a universal phenomenon of youth. What I tried to describe in my paper is the hypertrophy or distortion of the psychodynamics of the youth of the 1960's. Some of the manifestations were indeed "incredible." The spirit of rebellion has not been extinguished; who knows when it will erupt again? External circumstance could touch it off at any time.

I have emphasized college students in my discussion of the psychodynamics of youth, but a word should be said about high school youngsters and the young people who were not in school. Both of these groups are influenced by the college youth. Going to college, at least junior college, seems to be an integral part of our society. The people who go into factories or construction work with a minimum of formal education are mostly those who didn't "make it." High school students tend to imitate their big brothers and in some instances outdo them in their oppositional attitudes, especially as these manifest the beginnings of the breakaway from family dependence. The unemployed noncollege young people are a disgruntled lot. Many of them drift into delinquency or crime. The working young people often rationalize their situation by adopting a hostile attitude to the college group as an expression of their resentment at having to take a lower place in our social stratification. This feeling persists into later years; witness the antagonism of the "hard-hats" toward the students, and their constant battle for higher wages in order to attain positions of ascendancy over their "educated" brethren.

It is true that in discussing the psychodynamics of youth I concentrated on the student population. I did so because as the more intelligent members of the youth society they are likely to be more sensitive to the nuances of environmental forces. Even on the campuses some of the most disruptive were also the most intelligent. I agree with the discussants who spoke of "normal adolescent rebellion." This was not the subject of my paper; I was discussing the particular form that this took in the 1960's. I quite agree that breaking windows, smoking "hash," and "shacking up" are analogous to the football rally, the hip flask, and necking. The twenties, as the aftermath of World War I, may have resembled the sixties; youth is youth and similarities prevail. But as a psychoanalyst who treats varying degrees of people's problems or problem people, I can only state that in the sixties there was an exacerbation of both.

REFERENCES

Altbach, P. (1968), *Student Politics and Higher Education in the United States: A Select Biography.* St. Louis: Center for International Affairs, Harvard University & United Ministries of Higher Education.

Dodgson, C. (1870), *Through the Looking Glass.* New York: McGraw-Hill, 1946.

Erikson, E. H. (1950), *Childhood and Society.* New York: Norton.

Fenichel, O. (1953), *Collected Papers.* New York: Norton.

Freud, S. (1912-1913), Totem and taboo. *Standard Edition,* 13:1-161. London: Hogarth Press, 1953.

——— (1920), Beyond the pleasure principle. *Standard Edition,* 18:1-64. London: Hogarth Press, 1955.

——— (1921), Group psychology and the analysis of the ego. *Standard Edition,* 21:69-143. London: Hogarth Press, 1961.

——— (1928), Future of an illusion. *Standard Edition,* 21:5-58. London: Hogarth Press, 1961.

——— (1930), Civilization and its discontents. *Standard Edition,* 21:64-148. London: Hogarth Press, 1961.

——— (1937), Analysis terminable and interminable. *Standard Edition,* 23:216-254. London: Hogarth Press, 1964.

Keniston, K. (1965), *The Uncommitted.* New York: Harcourt, Brace & World.

Kinsey, A. C. (1953), *Sexual Behavior in the Human Female.* Philadelphia: Saunders.

Kruse, H., Ed. (1957), *Integrating the Approaches to Mental Disease.* New York: Hoeber-Harper.

Masters, W. H. et al. (1966), *Human Sexual Response.* Boston: Little, Brown.

Solomon, J. C. (1963), Alice and the red king: The psycho-analytic view of existence. *Internat. J. Psycho-Anal.,* 44:63-73.

——— (1965), *A Synthesis of Human Behavior: An Integration of Thought Processes and Ego Growth.* New York: Grune & Stratton.

——— (1970), Cogitor, ergo sum. In: *Hope: Psychiatry's Commitment,* ed. A. W. R. Sipe. New York: Brunner/Mazel.

Toffler, A. (1970), *Future Shock.* New York: Random House.

Some Superego Considerations in Crime and Punishment

STUART S. ASCH, M.D.

Dr. Asch is Clinical Professor of Psychiatry at the Mount Sinai School of Medicine of the City University of New York and a member of the New York Psychoanalytic Society. He is on the faculty of both the New York Psychoanalytic Institute and the Columbia University Psychoanalytic Clinic. He is on the Editorial Staff of the *Journal of Psychiatry and Law*. In 1969 and 1970 he chaired an interdisciplinary colloquium on "Psychoanalysis and Jurisprudence" at the winter meetings of the American Psychoanalytic Association. He has written several papers dealing with the vicissitudes of the superego as exhibited in certain forms of behavior and in depression.

Discussants

PAUL CHODOFF, M.D.

Dr. Chodoff is a Fellow of the American Academy of Psychoanalysis, Member of the American Psychoanalytic Association, and Clinical Professor of Psychiatry at George Washington University. In addition to his private practice, he serves as Consultant to the National Institute of Mental Health, Walter Reed General Hospital, and St. Elizabeth's Hospital in Washington, D.C.

H. MICHAEL ROSOW, M.D.

Dr. Rosow is Senior Faculty Member and Analyzing Instructor at the Los Angeles Psychoanalytic Society and Institute, and Associate Clinical Professor of Psychiatry at the University of California, Los Angeles. He has been Psychiatric Consultant to the California Department of Corrections at the Medical Facility at Terminal Island, and to the Parole Outpatient Clinic since 1954. He is the author of "Integrated Individual and Group Therapy" and "Some Observations on Group Therapy with Prison Inmates."

NORMAN TABACHNICK, M.D.

Dr. Tabachnick is Associate Chief Psychiatrist at the Los Angeles Suicide Prevention Center, Training Analyst at the Southern California Psychoanalytic Institute, and Clinical Professor of Psychiatry at the University of Southern California. His major research interests have been in various clinical and theoretical aspects of self-destruction and related issues. He has published a number of papers on these and other topics.

JOSEPH E. LIFSHUTZ, M.D.

Dr. Lifshutz is Lecturer in the School of Social Welfare at the University of California at Berkeley. During 1965-1969 he was Chairman of the Extension Division of the San Francisco Psychoanalytic Institute. He is in private psychoanalytic practice, and from 1968 to 1970 was involved in a psychotherapeutic confidentiality case in California, resulting in a State Supreme Court decision significantly improving the atmosphere of confidentiality for the practice of psychotherapy and psychoanalysis.

FREDERICK J. HACKER, M.D.

Dr. Hacker is Clinical Professor of Psychiatry at the University of Southern California Medical School, and Clinical Professor of Law in Psychiatry at the USC Law Center. He is Chief of Staff of the Hacker Psychiatric Clinics in Beverly Hills and Lynwood, California. Dr. Hacker has given over 2,000 psychiatric opinions about criminal offenders on Superior Court appointment, and is currently on the panel of psychiatrists for the Federal Court. For many years, he was advisor to the Austrian government on law and penal reform. He is President of the Sigmund Freud Gesellschaft in Vienna, and his 1964 book on criminology and 1971 book on aggression are expected to appear in the United States in the very near future.

JEAN ROSENBAUM, M.D.

Dr. Rosenbaum is a Faculty Member and Supervising Analyst in the New Mexico Psychoanalytic Association, and for many years has done research on the vicissitudes of individual and group aggression. Several of his hundreds of articles and seven books explore various aspects of violence.

PHILIP G. ZIMBARDO, PH.D.

Dr. Zimbardo is Professor of Psychology at Stanford University and Fellow at the Center for Advanced Study in the Behavioral Sciences. His research relevant to Dr. Asch's paper is in the area of psychologically coercive techniques used by the police to elicit confessions, and in the psychology of imprisonment. In a recent simulation of a prison, he discovered the remarkably pervasive pathological influences generated in such an institutional setting.

Some Superego Considerations in Crime and Punishment

Stuart S. Asch, m.d.
New York, New York

We would expect the analyst's occupational familiarity with feelings of guilt and the need for punishment to qualify him to offer some educated opinions on crime and punishment. Yet, to judge from the psychoanalytic literature, criminal acts—especially acts of violence—are among the most rarely studied of all the varieties of human behavior and social problems that have been investigated by psychoanalysts.

Most of the more recent psychoanalytic work in this area deals with "delinquency," an artificial category comprising the various antisocial acts that have been committed by pre-adults. But delinquency is only one very particular aspect of the problem of crime, and involves many factors that are significantly different from those we face with the adult criminal.

Freud's contribution to criminology consisted of four articles. Of two of these, which were short pieces of jurisprudence (1931; Jones, 1957), Strachey (1959) comments, "In both of these instances he wrote to deprecate any half-baked application of psychoanalytic theories in legal proceedings" (p. 102). In a similar vein Freud (1906) wrote "Psychoanalysis and the Establishment of the Facts in Legal Proceedings," in which he disparaged the value of word-association tests for the establishment of guilt or innocence. In his 1916 paper, "Criminal Out of a Sense of Guilt," he did make a valuable contribution to criminology, which I shall discuss in more detail later.

There is also a marked dearth of analytic comment on

systems of punishment,[1] despite the fact that society's punishments of crime have become not only increasingly expensive and cumbersome but, even more disturbing, increasingly ineffective.

On the surface, there may be some justification for the almost negligible involvement of analysts in these areas: we are usually not consulted in such situations; we tend to have personal biases against engaging in such work; and, of course, we must remain alert to the dangers inherent in applying findings in individual intrapsychic phenomena to problems of group psychology. That is, we cannot readily compare the relationship of the superego to the ego with society's restrictions on individual behavior, since the two restricting agencies (superego and society) are not at all the same and do not function in the same way. This latter reasoning contributes in part to the continuing dichotomy between law and psychiatry—namely, that the law deals with the external relations between the individual and society, while psychiatry concerns itself with the individual's internal relations with himself.

But however valid these considerations may be, evaluative study of crime and punishment is now more essential than ever, and my intention here is to review those criminal acts and varieties of criminals about which analytic theory has already achieved some understanding. In addition, I will discuss the various aims and the present effectiveness of legal punishment. Finally, I will suggest some modifications of existing systems of punishment, based on the theoretical conclusions I have reached through extrapolations of analytic theory in combination with published experiences of law enforcement agencies.

I am aware of the serious abrogation of civil liberties that the policies resulting from my conclusions might entail, and I am not recommending them. Rather, I present them with the aim of provoking further thought and study in this important area, in which psychoanalysis so far has had very little to say.

[1] One notable exception is Karl Menninger's (1968) study, *The Crime of Punishment*. Menninger is critical of the present system of criminal sanctions, which is based in effect on the questionable belief that "the punishment must fit the crime, not the criminal."

Crime

Our first tendency is to believe that the reason a normal adult does not commit a crime is that he has a personal internalized law-enforcement agency, a fully developed and completely stable superego. But, the more we observe human behavior, the more we come to recognize that the mere existence of a well-developed superego does not preclude the commission of antisocial acts. And as we become more sophisticated in our knowledge of ego psychology, and recognize that crime or antisocial behavior can occur with *any* kind of character structure, we begin to modify further our definition of a "law-abiding" psychic structure.

Since crime is limited neither to the psychotic, who may be unable to appreciate the meaning of his act, nor to individuals with serious defects in superego development, whom we might call the "real" criminals, it may be helpful to set forth the various determinants of criminal acts to be found in the relatively "normal" character, in neurotic characters, and in individuals with severe superego defects. (The psychotic criminal presents a completely different problem, outside the scope of this paper.)

Even in the "normal" individual, the person with a well-developed superego, the equilibrium of intrapsychic structures is not static; rather, it is dynamic and constantly shifting. As a result, even emotionally mature individuals may at times engage in the acting out of what they themselves, in other circumstances, would deem to be unacceptable impulses.

To give some examples: Pressures of frustration can intensify drives to the point where usually forbidden impulses are acted out. Ego control can be weakened by fatigue or by alcohol or other drugs. Superego restrictions themselves can be evaded in several ways, such as by participation in group action, thus making possible the commission of crimes that would have been unthinkable for the individual, as the example of the Nazis has already taught us.

Projecting the superego onto others makes it easier to negate its authority. Minor income tax evasion is a classic example in our culture of the shifting of responsibility away from the self—i.e., away from an intrapsychic constellation—by displacing it onto the government. The internal regulatory agency having displaced responsibility onto the "outside" agency, no misconduct is felt to have taken place, if the evasion is not challenged, and the need to suffer painful guilt feelings is thereby avoided.

The superego also tends to be more tolerant of forbidden acts when they are committed at a distance. This calls to mind Freud's (1915) citation of Rousseau's "Chinese Mandarin": If, by an act of will and without being discovered, one were given an opportunity to kill an old mandarin who lives in China, with great profit to oneself, but without having to leave Paris. . . . Freud wouldn't have given much for the mandarin's chances in that case! " 'Tuer son mandarin' has become a proverbial phrase for this secret readiness to sin, present even in modern man" (p. 298). I doubt that many of us would feel comfortable if put to such a test!

Antisocial acts resulting from intrapsychic conflict are familiar to analysts, especially to those who work with younger patients. Identification with the aggressor, aggressive misconduct as a denial of feminine identification through acting out, the acting out of unconscious antisocial wishes of the parent—these are among the more common dynamic mechanisms that can lead to the commission of antisocial acts.

The strict, inflexible superego—the so-called "strong" conscience, which is actually a primitive structure mainly dominated by the law of talion and its simple tenet of an eye for an eye—is an unreliable bulwark against the antisocial impulse. Such a harsh conscience may even of itself provide the stimulus for antisocial behavior.

Some individuals commit crimes in order to be punished for the guilt they already suffer from a primitive conscience that has archaic elements demanding punishment for fantasies and wishes as though they were realized acts. It is this neurotic group that Freud (1916) characterized as "criminals from a sense of guilt"—individuals in whom there is a pre-existing feeling of guilt, of unknown origin, and for whom the commission of a forbidden act results in mental relief, for then "his sense of guilt was at least attached to something" (p. 332). We are all familiar with this phenomenon in children, who are "often 'naughty' on purpose to provoke punishment and are quiet and contented after they have been punished" (p. 333).

I am reminded, in this context, of the well-known tendency of obsessional patients to indulge in sadistic acts. Their rigid and strict control of impulses is under the domination of a primitive, archaic superego based on early anal-retentive experiences. Their conscience operates under Ferenczi's (1925) concept of a "sphincter morality" (p. 267) which will tolerate the most sadistic and cruel behavior so long as that behavior is completely controlled. These obsessional characters, therefore, judge their own sadistic acts by their form rather than by their content: the acts must be performed neatly and cleanly, and without any great show of feelings, since such affects would make them "dirty" (and thus, forbidden on that basis alone).

Neurotic determinants of crime should also include the dominant conceptions of those highly narcissistic individuals who, although not necessarily psychotic, view themselves as "exceptions," and as such, "above the law." For very particular reasons—perhaps because of some congenital deformity (as in Freud's example of Richard III [1916]), or because of some special ability they feel they have—they believe themselves to be *entitled* to gratification forbidden by the law. Leopold and Loeb, for example, were convinced that their high I.Q.'s made them "exceptions" to the laws against murder.

We tend to think of the "real" criminal, the sociopath, as essentially different from those I have described. His criminal act is not the result of intrapsychic conflict; it is committed for material gain, and because he feels he can "get away with it." The sociopath, with his defective superego development, deals with his impulses by keeping one eye on "the policeman on the corner." Since his controls remain external, he can evade them more easily than he could an internalized law enforcement agency. Such failure on the part of these character structures to develop a stable and reliable superego should be considered in any evaluation of the efficacy of various systems of punishment or prevention.

It is unusual, however, to find a criminal who acts as if there were absolutely no superego restrictions on his activities. We usually find ourselves dealing with *areas* of defect rather than with a total agenesis. Most criminals have their own particular kind of antisocial activity; often they look down on other forms. It is the "lacunae" of the conscience, in Adelaide Johnson's term (1949), that tolerate such misconduct, not the absence of conscience altogether.

I should like to emphasize some ancillary characteristics of such "real" criminals. Internalization and identification require good object relations, along with some ability on the part of the ego to neutralize aggression. Thus, the superego's failure to develop into a reliable and stable structure implies previously existing difficulties with incorporation and identification that have resulted in problems in ego development. Where there is a failure of superego development, we should expect to find defective ego development as well.

My impression is that such sociopathic characters often tend to exhibit, in addition to their superego defects, two main defects in ego functioning: one, a primitive narcissism, which is expressed in a conviction of their own heightened worth and invulnerability; and two, a localized defect in reality testing which interferes specifically with their ability to evaluate realistically the risks to themselves. (Aichorn [1935] has similarly stressed that the criminal often achieves a generally high level of adaptation to reality, yet is unable to use it appropriately, especially in the service of social adaptation).

If such criminals *are* caught, their very ego pathology limits the value of punishment as a deterrent to future criminal acts. Their fantasy is that it was just by "bad luck" or someone else's error, etc., that they were caught this time, but that it won't happen the next time. And sometimes the narcissistic need to *prove* their ability not to be caught drives them to repeat the crime as soon as they can.

Heightened narcissism and specific defects in reality testing may be a consistent pathological combination in these sociopathic character structures. It may be just this combination, together with the defects of conscience (for they experience little if any guilt in connection with their actions), that gives them the freedom to commit a specific crime. They will be deterred only if they recognize an immediate or unavoidable danger of being caught.

Accordingly, the failure of such "real" criminals to internalize prohibitions suggests that *deterrence* is the watchword and that their particular form of antisocial behavior can be kept in check only through fear of an *external* law enforcement agency.

Still another group of antisocial acts that do not fit readily into any single category are the impulsive and so-called senseless acts of pure violence. These are rarely available to analytic observation; yet they are alarmingly on the increase, and I am convinced that they constitute an extremely valuable and necessary area of study.

We are all probably quite familiar with the violent acts committed by the person with impulsive character disorder, and we understand that it is his poor ego control that leads to his seeking direct and immediate gratification of his aggressive drives. A more detailed examination, however, discloses at least two other dynamic explanations for violence:

1. With some individuals, the impulsive violent act is a means of heightening self-esteem. Through impulsive, senseless destructiveness, such a person is demonstrating his refusal to submit to *any* restrictions, even those of his own superego.

2. Another important function is the need to ward off terrifying episodes of depersonalization through some violent act that serves to recathect the self-representation. The sudden and tremendous discharge of energy through an act of violence seems to serve this purpose for some personalities.[2]

---

[2] I suspect that many "senseless" acts of violence have a similar basis to that of "wrist scratching." This is a special form of behavior whose specific aim seems to be to ward off frightening feelings of depersonalization by means of an act of violence (Asch, 1971).

It is important to remember that a poorly structured superego does not necessarily imply a criminal character. For example, although we no longer accept the classical picture of the female superego as grossly deficient, it seems clinically true that women present a more diffuse, less reliable superego structure than do men. This has been considered an inevitable result of the special circumstances of female castration anxiety and oedipal resolution (Freud, 1925; Greenacre, 1952); yet, on this theoretical basis, we would have the right to anticipate a higher delinquency and criminal rate among women.

Actually, of course, the figures show just the opposite. The ratio of delinquency among girls with that among boys ranges from estimates of one to four down to one to ten. Even allowing for the fact that "delinquency in girls" excludes those boys whose delinquency is a defense against their feminine identifications, such statistics still reveal a tremendously significant differential.

Among adults, the sex disparity in crime is even greater, particularly in crimes of violence, which are quite rare in women (infanticide is a very special exception) (Asch, 1968). Byrne (1966) states that "about ten per cent (of women in prison) fit the standard description of a criminal: they have robbed or murdered or forged checks or kidnapped or committed arson. The other ninety per cent have infringed on the public order [i.e., through prostitution, alcoholism, drug addiction, etc.]. Their acts are crimes against themselves, or to borrow a phrase from the moral theologians, sins of weakness, not of malice" (p. 25).

This sex disparity in criminal behavior is an extremely curious phenomenon which, so far as I know, has never been adequately explained in psychoanalytic terms. The recent findings with regard to XYY chromosome karotype—a chromosome abnormality associated with tall, thin, acned males, that seems to be associated with aggressive behavior—offers a possible genetic basis for sex-linked criminal behavior (Telfer et al., 1968), but there are no figures available that place criminals into categories according to their neurotic conflicts or the type of psychic structure that has produced their pathology.

Freud suspected that his category of "criminals out of a sense of guilt" might constitute the major group. I tend, rather, to agree with Franz Alexander's (Pollack, 1964) feeling that such people are in the minority. Although it seems likely that most crimes are committed by "real" criminals, with severe superego imbalance, "homogeneously anti-social and non-conflict-ridden or non-guilt-ridden" (p. 461), there is a tendency once again to believe that the criminal really *does* have a superego that is effective enough to arouse a sense of guilt. This idea has been revived because the solution of many crimes has been found to result from something so obvious about the way they are committed that the attention of the authorities is inevitably directed to the appropriate criminal. This reasoning may be valid, but we must keep in mind that it is based only on those crimes so solved, while the great majority of crimes seem to be successful and remain unsolved. The fact that only about one law violation in a dozen is detected (Menninger, 1968) immediately restricts the crime statistics to a select group of criminals—namely, those who are caught. Even among these, many are found out only because of informers.

A guilty conscience or a need to be punished are not necessarily the only reasons a criminal will leave clues leading to his apprehension. The persistence of this self-defeating method of operation can also be explained by way of the repetition compulsion, in which the same pattern is repeated each time, along with a narcissistic overvaluation of the self and a magical belief that one will not be caught. This is similar to the explanation of the familiar phenomenon of young children who run to the same "hiding place" every time they do something wrong: they do so not necessarily because they want to be caught, but more often because their narcissism and reality testing have not developed sufficiently to enable them to appreciate the futility of such a repetitive action. They are surprised each time to be found so quickly by the parent.

Punishment

"Power tends to corrupt and absolute power corrupts absolutely." Lord Acton's remarkably insightful dictum may be viewed in metapsychological terms, employing Rapaport's (1960) useful "nutriment" concept which he developed in connection with his conceptualization of ego functions. It seems to me, however, that one of the most important differences between the superego and the other two intrapsychic constructs is that while the energy of the drives is appetitive (as is also perhaps the energy of the ego, although to a lesser extent), the energy of the superego does not seem to be self-sustaining.

Clinical findings suggest that unless some outside agency creates standards or sets up restrictions with punishments—i.e., unless there is a fairly stable ego ideal or law enforcement agency—the tendency does exist gradually to override one's conscience, usually by means of rationalizations that themselves tend to become less and less necessary (possibly even in proportion to the severity of the legal standard; it would be interesting to investigate this). In structural and economic terms, this means that under constant pressure from drive derivatives the superego—or at least that part of it which serves as the conscience—requires *external* nutriment for maintenance. Otherwise, it atrophies or regresses. This weakened superego may then tolerate the emergence of drive derivatives that have been only partly warded off by defenses. Absolute power to regulate one's own conscience by oneself *does* corrupt, if one is left without at least the intermittent outside support of that "policeman on the corner."

Clear and specific rules of behavior, with known punishments for misconduct, are helpful aids even to the well-developed conscience. Constantly carrying the responsibility for good behavior is a heavy and painful burden; it is a relief to shift the pressures arising out of conflicts of conscience to the outside, to "share" these with society. There is an economic advantage, too, in terms of the energy that is released when the superego is freed from the task of constant surveillance in certain proscribed areas.

Accordingly, from a psychoanalytic point of view, it is reasonable and even necessary to place legal restrictions on certain *overt* conduct. At the same time, because of the varying effects of punishments on different character structures, I question strongly whether we should place full reliance on punishment and imprisonment as *deterrents* to crime, or even whether we should be satisfied with the existing precept, "Let the punishment fit the crime."

It is evident that rules of behavior, in combination with some system of sanctions, are helpful for even the relatively stable superego. For instance, it is socially valuable to make the act of stealing illegal for the "normal" individual, for his superego requires only moderate outside control. For him, mild to moderate legal censures, when combined with censures from his own conscience, may be quite sufficient for good law enforcement, whereas severe punishment could easily provoke ego regression leading to the weakening of ego controls and perhaps even to the committing of further antisocial acts. The neurotic criminal, on the other hand, may well *have* to repeat his crime, no matter what punishments society has set up. In such a case, punishment is useless as a deterrent.

Thus, if the punishment of a misdeed is to be really effective, certain aspects of the offender's character must be considered, as well as the offense itself.

In short, I would conclude that it is socially valuable to make the act of stealing illegal, but the way in which society deals with the wrongdoer once he is apprehended should depend on factors other than the crime itself.

With the sociopath, whose psychopathology is directed against society, the problem is quite different. These individuals commit crimes for material gain rather than as the result of intrapsychic conflict. Since they lack a consistent conscience within, they actually do require a "policeman on the corner." An increasing incidence of crime in New York City subways was dealt with recently in just this way: when police-men were placed on each train, crime was almost completely eliminated. However, such extreme maneuvers are, for obvi-ous reasons, impractical for large areas.

It seems reasonable to expect that severe external punish-ment would also serve to deter antisocial impulses in those individuals whose defective superego is incapable of limiting behavior through arousing fears of painful guilt reactions. But, while it is apparent that the very real policeman on the corner can effectively deter the sociopath who has no "internal policeman," it is not at all clear that punishment can do so. This is in contrast to the healthier group, for whom minimal to moderate punishment does seem to be effective as a deter-rent. "Suffering, the currency by which we buy off guilt, is more effective for the non-criminal, and less effective in changing the criminal's psychological system of credits and balances" (Pollack, 1964, p. 462).

The aim of punishment, as imposed by society, is to "ex-press a formal social condemnation of forbidden conduct, buttressed by sanctions calculated to prevent it" (Wechsler, 1955). When punishment is imposed by the family unit (a microcosm of society), it has similar aims along with a per-haps more specific pedagogic function: to internalize the con-demnation of the forbidden conduct, so that the recalcitrant individual can eventually come to control his own behavior and so avoid repeating his previous defeat in such a conflict.

Within the individual psychic apparatus, however, the aim of punishment is quite simply to avoid or remove the feelings of guilt produced by the aggression of the superego, which is directed against the self-representation. Although this intra-psychic conflict can be anthropomorphized as a conflict be-tween a punitive parent and a wrongdoing child, and although it is in fact partly derived from such a conflict, the intra-psychic aim of punishment shows significant differences from society's aims in devising punishments.

A need for punishment exists within the individual when guilt is aroused in response to the mental representation of "forbidden conduct," whether such conduct is acted out or not. This differs from society which demands punishment for the forbidden act alone, without its being accompanied by a sense of guilt. When the individual punishes himself, it is in order to appease his superego and to allay his guilt. This is a strictly personal situation, which may have little relationship to society's demands.

Society has evolved a system of punishments with a variety of aims in mind: (1) reformation of the criminal psyche; (2) deterrence from future crime; (3) retribution by society; (4) protection of the community by incarceration of the criminal.

Reformation. The courts today tend to favor "the use of corrective and educational measures either in addition to, or in substitution for punishment proper" (Friedman, 1965) in their dealings with certain categories of crime, such as those involving the sexual psychopath, juvenile offenders, and the insane. "These statutes are premised on the ability of the relatively new science of psychiatry to identify, isolate, and treat such individuals" (Lindman and McIntyre, 1961, p. 298).

Such enlightened views and statutes seem more appropriate and humane than are purely punitive measures such as imprisonment. Encouraging as these attitudes are, there is inherent in them one basic flaw—lack of provision from the bench for the implementation of these directives, for the courts have tended to be completely unrealistic in their evaluations of psychiatric facilities. For example, "the philosophy [behind laws with regard to sexual deviation] is that these offenders should be treated rather than punished. Lack of treatment destroys any otherwise valid reason for differential consideration of the sexual psychopath. It would appear that the law is looking to medical knowledge for solutions to problems in this area, only to find that such knowledge is as yet non-existent or imprecise" (Lindman and McIntyre, 1961, p. 307). (I would add that facilities for such treatment, when they exist, are too often inadequate.) Further, "Even under the indeterminate sentence, the key to release is whether the offender has been a well-behaved prisoner. But the good behavior of a mentally ill offender in the highly structured prison society provides no assurance that he will so behave in the unstructured free society" (Brennan, 1963 p. 240).

Deterrence. Just as the healthy individual ordinarily avoids transgressing his own moral code so as to avoid superego censure and guilt, so society hopes to deter wrongdoing by posting specific punishments, with the expectation that the punishment will have a double effect: convincing the lawbreaker not to repeat his transgression, and at the same time serving as a "cautionary tale," a warning deterrent to other members of society.

The punishment itself must be consistent and real if it is to serve as a deterrent. For instance, once the public has a more than reasonable doubt that the city will indeed seek out those who have failed to pay their traffic fines (as is true in New York City), then a large number of violations will recur, no matter how heavy are the fines levied on those who do pay up.

Unfortunately, threats of punishment do not restrain a majority of lawbreakers, including those whose crimes are expressions of an "irresistible impulse," the product of an ego that has poor control over acting out. If an impulse is intense enough, it will be acted out by a person with such a character structure no matter what the law. Many sexual crimes and those committed by drug addicts are in this category of "irresistible impulses."

On the basis of what we do know of the psychopathology of the sociopath, there is little reason to expect that consistent and real punishment will deter him from crime. His infantile narcissism, plus the defects in reality testing that I have postulated to be usually associated with his superego "lacunae," lead him to overestimate his ability to evade the policeman, and temptation thereupon leads him to the commission of further crime. With such a psychopathology the sociopath is not particularly deterred by any threat of punishment, nor is he even deterred, after actual punishment, from repeating such acts.

Nor will severity of punishment induce morality, for morality is *not* fear of punishment "from the outside." Morality requires an internal policeman and an internalized judge.

Official statistics tend to bear out these beliefs. Seventy per cent of those sentenced to state and federal institutions have had previous sentences, and over 50 per cent of them have further difficulty with the law *within a few weeks or months after their release* (Radzinowicz, 1961). "The similarity of success and failure rates, as measured by the after-conduct of offenders, irrespective of whether they were put on probation, fined, sentenced to short term imprisonment, or to longer corrective detention is indeed striking" (p. 136).

The efficacy of punishment as a warning deterrent to other members of society also remains open to question. In effect, punishment seems to be an effective deterrent only if there is an effective superego, good reality testing and judgment, relatively stable control over impulses, and a mature narcissism. Paradoxically, punishment may be of the greatest value when we are dealing with a relatively healthy individual who commits a crime under stress, while it may have little deterrent value for the habitual lawbreaker.

Retribution and revenge. In primitive law, the purpose of retribution was to satisfy the desire for revenge, in contrast with modern law, whose purported aim is to recompense for injury. However, American law still takes revenge very much into account, as in our system of "exemplary damages"—the monies that must be paid to the victim in addition to the full compensation he is awarded for the actual loss suffered.

Revenge requires that the criminal suffer, not to enable him to expiate his guilt nor as a form of penance, but rather to serve the need for vengeance on the part of the victim and his surrogates, society. This aim of punishment is perhaps the one that is least acknowledged in present-day jurisprudence, probably because it constitutes, after all, only a modern version of the age-old law of talion: "An eye for an eye, a tooth for a tooth."

When the brutal murder of eight nurses in Chicago came up in conversation among a social gathering of analysts, their almost unanimous reaction was that the murderer should be executed. There was no question of recognizing the apparent psychosis of the criminal, nor did there appear to be any question of using the McNaughten rule to protect such an obviously mentally ill person. It seems clear that unless a criminal of this kind is punished, and punished harshly, society feels cheated and the fabric of civilization, which is based on the renunciation of direct instinctual expression, is felt to be threatened.

Uncompromisingly cruel as this attitude appears, psychoanalytic theory does offer some justification for revenge as a basis for punishment. Taking revenge may support the individual in his constant struggle to ward off his own antisocial impulses; it may contribute to the counter-cathexis against his antisocial drives through displacement and projection of such impulses onto the criminal. Furthermore, legalized punishment provides a socially and morally acceptable outlet for destructive aggression. Unlike war, which excessively stimulates aggressive impulses (thereby of course defeating the purpose of any form of legal punishment), this is a well-regulated and carefully structured outlet.

If individuals generally were to tolerate wrongdoers, they might have greater difficulty controlling their own antisocial impulses. The weaker one's own control over an active impulse, the more strongly must one attack a lack of control in someone else. The nursery school toddler who has an "accident" becomes the object of much sharper critical comment from his peers (who have only recently, and insecurely, achieved sphincter control themselves) than he receives from his teachers. This aggression and repugnance, felt in any social group toward a member who "breaks the code," is indicative of the need to ward off temptation to make allowances for the same gratification in oneself.

Incarceration to protect society. The criminal who indulges in crime for material gain may do so because of character defects that cannot be altered by punishment. This means that the protection of society may turn out to be the only practical aim of punishment for such character structures and that we should perhaps be prepared to consider the possibility of indefinite confinement for such criminals.[3]

These ideas are not at all applicable to the more normally developed individual whose misconduct is not a manifestation of severe superego and ego defects. But such individuals *do* go to prison, and I feel it important to discuss briefly how prison life can damage the individual, thus adding yet another complicated category to the problems of crime and punishment.

As I stated earlier, such persons might be damaged by penal life, even to the point of leaving prison as hardened criminals. Schoenfeld (1966), among others, has elaborated on the destructive effect of present-day prison life, with its debasement and demoralization of the individual. The prisoner is at the mercy of his jailers, many of whom have strong sadistic tendencies; further, ego regression is both forced and fostered by monotony, lack of stimulation of ego interests, regimentation, and the loss of freedom.

Perhaps most debilitating is the enforced homosexuality that characterizes prison life. In a personal communication from Dr. M. Franzblau (1967), a psychiatrist attached to a federal prison, I learned that within the first 24 hours of a new prisoner's arrival, he is approached by a veteran inmate and informed, "I have bought you; you belong to me." This "possession" includes the right to demand and receive complete sexual and moral submission.

An investigation of the Philadelphia prison system, completed in July, 1968, includes this report on the scope of sexual assaults: "Virtually every slightly built young man committed by the courts is sexually approached within hours

---

[3] This is not at all a new idea in criminology. It was a chief tenet of the "positivist doctrine" of Enrico Ferri, a leader of jurisprudence at the beginning of this century. He insisted that the only valid determinant of the type of treatment the criminal should receive was the offender's "state of danger"—how likely he was to *repeat* his offense against the community (Radzinowicz, p. 17). Alexander (Pollack, 1964) has arrived at an identical and equally drastic conclusion: "As long as an offender remains a danger or menace to society in *any* way, he should not be allowed free and full access to that society" (p. 463).

after his admission to prison. Many young men are overwhelmed and repeatedly 'raped' by gangs of inmate aggressors. . . . After a young man has been sexually assaulted, he is marked as a sexual victim for the duration of his confinement, and this mark follows him from institution to institution until he returns to the community embittered, degraded, and filled with hatred" (p. 3).

The same investigation revealed that many homosexual rapes occur while young men are being transported to and from court in sheriff's vans. Tremendous emotional resources would be necessary to be able to withstand such assaults on one's identity and self-esteem, assaults that are likely to continue throughout the years of confinement in prison.

It is apparent that imprisonment, as the punishment of choice, should be carefully and individually evaluated. It may well be that our own society overrates its value. Brennan (1963) states that "the U.S. places greater reliance on imprisonment than does any country in the world" (p. 240). To our 178 prisoners per 100,000 civilians, England, by contrast, has only 65 per 100,000!

It is apparent, too, that psychoanalysts have much further work to do in the areas of crime and punishment.

Summary

In contrast to the drives, and even the ego functions, which seem to have their own intrinsic sources of energy, the superego seems to require at least intermittent *external* reinforcement. Without such forms of nutriment, the functions of conscience atrophy and regress. Constant and complete responsibility for one's own good behavior is a heavy and unrealistic burden.

In examining what we as analysts do understand about the problems of crime and punishment, I have presented several general hypotheses:

1. *Legal sanctions* may be most valuable and effective for the normal and the neurotic individual. Such sanctions may well be of *less* value in dealing with those antisocial character structures that display severe ego and superego defects.

2. *Punishment*, beyond a moderate degree, seems to be of little value for the relatively healthy or the neurotic wrong-doer. Suspended sentences, fines, etc., might be more effective deterrents to them than more severe punishments such as imprisonment.

3. Perhaps we should place less reliance altogether on punishment and imprisonment as *deterrents* to crime. The normal superego requires only moderate outside control, while the neurotic criminal may well *have* to repeat the crime, no matter what we do.

4. In relatively healthy people, imprisonment may be so traumatic to their narcissism that the resulting ego regression could create *more* pathology than had previously existed. These individuals might well be *made into* "hardened" criminals by prison.

5. The psychic structure of the "real" criminal, to whom we must attribute marked superego defects, is also characterized by circumscribed yet serious ego defects in reality testing and judgment, as well as by a pathological primitive narcissism.

6. The deterrent and reformative value of punishment and imprisonment seems to be quite limited with these "real" criminals. Their pathological narcissism and defects in reality testing and judgment, as well as the presence of magical thinking, impede their learning from experience.

7. Retribution as an aim of punishment may have an analytically justifiable basis. Some form and degree of retribution may be necessary in order to help society keep its own aggressive impulses in check—in part through gratification of its aggression in the act of punishment, in part through the strengthening of counter-cathexis by way of the recognition that such impulses are unequivocally forbidden.

8. In addition to such theoretical justification for visiting severe punishment on the habitual criminal, prolonged imprisonment seems also to be a logical conclusion. Here the aim of imprisonment is to devise some way of isolating the criminal for the protection of the rest of society. For this

purpose prison itself is not necessary, and other forms of communities separated from society might be considered.

We as analysts do not as yet really understand the psychic structure of the sociopath, and we know all too little about either crime or punishment.

Discussion

PAUL CHODOFF, M.D.
Washington, D.C.

Leaving out the psychotic criminal, Dr. Asch classifies committers of crime into "normals" who may, under the pressure of certain circumstances, act out unacceptable impulses; neurotic characters whose criminal acts stem from such neurotic determinants as a need to seek punishment to assuage irrational feelings of guilt; and "real" criminals, the sociopaths with defective superego development. Left out of this classification are the numerous crimes committed by individuals who are in tune with the customs and values of the subculture which they inhabit, and who are behaving normally and acceptably in the terms of that subculture.

One cannot say that these individuals are normals who have fallen prey to unacceptable impulses, since they find what they do acceptable, and so does their culture. They are not neurotic, and one cannot describe them as having superego defects unless one considers superego structure to be independent of the cultural values which it precipitates and transmits—a position which I do not think Dr. Asch would take.

I think it is extremely difficult to differentiate the behavior of this group from that of the so-called real criminals or sociopaths, a designation which does not have a great deal of empirical support and which runs the risk of being used as a label to justify the values of the dominant culture. I fear that when Dr. Asch suggests the use of indefinite separation from society for those whom he classifies as incorrigible sociopaths, he is providing society with a psychiatric rationalization for its failure to deal fairly and effectively with the economically depressed and minority groups to which these individuals belong.

STUART S. ASCH

H. MICHAEL ROSOW, M.D.
Beverly Hills, California

I appreciate the opportunity to discuss Dr. Asch's succinctly stated ideas regarding the criminal's dynamics and society's system of punishments. Before launching into a discussion of the criminal and his acts, it is essential to recognize the distinction between the captured criminals, the inmates, and the vast majority of criminals who are never apprehended. I believe any discussion of the dynamics of criminals is almost meaningless without keeping this distinction in mind. The former, who constitute a small minority of offenders—only one is punished for every thousand crimes committed (Menninger, 1938)—are the unsuccessful criminals who are caught not only once but over and over, repeatedly. These recidivists (the recidivist rate is as high as 80 per cent) permit themselves to be apprehended because of their emotional disturbances and general ineffectualness. Their incarceration is often as much a result of their helpless ignorance of legal procedures and their poverty (inability to acquire competent legal counsel) as of the offense committed.

Distinguishing between the apprehended inmate and the "successful" offender may be one factor in explaining the high ratio of men to women in prison. Vice squads are less interested in arresting lesbians than male homosexuals: a man undressing in full view of passersby is arrested as an exhibitionist; when a woman is similarly engaged, it is usually the gaping male passerby who is picked up as a peeping tom. Such double standards (and there are of course others, favoring men) result in distorted statistics if we confuse the number apprehended with the frequency of any particular offense.

As for the successful offenders, we can only speculate on their dynamics, since their ego-syntonic success keeps them away from psychiatric scrutiny. Only those whose offenses are ego-dystonic (some shop-lifters, sexual deviants, etc.) have been investigated and their dynamics described.

Another distinction to be kept in mind before we can discuss the "dynamics of criminals" is to differentiate two groups with vastly different dynamics: those who commit crimes against property and other persons, and those who commit "crimes without victims" (e.g., homosexuals, marijuana users, etc.).

Assuming that Dr. Asch is discussing the captured offender against persons or property, I believe that any psychoanalytically oriented therapist working with inmates would readily recognize the dynamic constellations described. Nor is the list by any means a complete one. In a paper (1955) about my experience as a consultant at the California Department of Corrections at Terminal Island, I described many of the mechanisms that Dr. Asch noted; other dynamic configurations were also detailed, though they need not be repeated here. A common denominator was a background of an intensely traumatic and emotionally deprived childhood, with frustration of early security needs leading to a profound sense of personal inadequacy and a "basic mistrust." Surprisingly, less than 10 per cent could be considered sociopaths; most were borderline acting-out characters, except that their acting out was of an antisocial variety. A useful operational definition of their personality disorganization is that it is one which compels dramatic criminal acting-out behavior. For them no other adaptive coping behavior is available. Discharge of the strain of intolerable tensions often resulted in violence. They know they must either break out violently, or be broken. Evidence that many violent, often senseless, crimes constituted a desperate defense against depression or a schizophrenic break was noted at the Facility at Terminal Island; when incarceration prevented such a criminal acting-out defense, a psychotic break often did ensue.

We found "crimes out of guilt" more frequent than is usually believed; during intensive group therapy many men became acutely aware of their previously unconscious guilt feelings.

But we must always keep in mind the "criminogenic" role of society acting on those emotionally disturbed people, analogous to the role of the schizophrenogenic mother in the pathology of the schizophrenic. Here too we see the same old double bind of contradictory messages in operation: the overt "Thou shalt not commit crimes of violence" and the covert approval and encouragement of violence. Films of the most sadistic violence are rarely X-rated, to say nothing of the bombing and napalming which we see night after night and year after year on our TV screens in living (or should I say, dying?) color. Military books are never censored; in fact, most of us have been taught that history is chiefly a succession of wars, and the most successful killers become our heroes.

To explain criminal behavior on the basis of inner dynamics alone, without taking into account social, economic, and racial factors, is simplistic. Pressure from both determinants is required to trigger the explosion. As Menninger (1968) states, society's crimes against prisoners are enormous; the entire legal process demands a radical change in its gestalt. For example, observe the charade of the defense attorney and the prosecuting attorney. Both are interested in their batting averages: the goal of the D.A. is to get convictions; the defense wants to score by getting the prisoner off free. Psychiatry is exploited by the defending attorney to improve his score by obtaining a verdict of "not guilty by reason of insanity"; the prosecution in turn is intent on defeating this ploy. The interests not only of the prisoner but of society become irrelevant in this contest. Thousands of our tax dollars are spent in getting a man into prison; very little is spent in trying to help him learn how to stay out of prison.

Which brings me to the second part of Dr. Asch's paper— "Punishment." I do not believe that the cold war between psychiatry and the law is due to the fact that "the law deals with the external relations between the individual and society, while psychiatry concerns itself with the individual's internal relations with himself." I believe the basic difference is that the law wishes to establish blame and punish the culprit, while psychiatry is concerned with understanding and helping through therapy. There is no place for vengeful punishment in recommending disposition. This does not mean, however, that one necessarily condones behavior because one understands its underlying dynamics. Limit-setting and penalties to the point of indefinite incarceration to protect a man from injuring himself or others may be warranted. At the California facility and elsewhere, it has been demonstrated that such an approach prevents recidivism; punishment does not. For example, at the Boys Industrial School in Kansas, a treatment-oriented milieu program succeeded in lowering a 65 per cent recidivist rate to four to nine per cent. A similar program is in operation at the Draper Correctional Center in Elmore, Alabama, and in other states (Wolfe, 1966).

We must realize that only those with a relatively normal ego can be deterred by threats of punishment; when there are enormous dynamic forces primed to explode into crime, threats of punishment are ineffectual. (Incidentally, I disagree with the statement that "psychiatry concerns itself with the individual's internal relations with himself." It is also concerned with his relationship with others.)

I do agree that even if we could achieve a more enlightened attitude toward offenders, and even if we understand their dynamics, it is an exercise in futility if we lack provisions and facilities to implement these good intentions.

At present a man is sentenced and sent to prison, where he is subjected to anti-therapy: he is dehumanized, his "basic mistrust" is strongly reinforced, and he becomes bitter and vengeful. No "reformation" is possible until our prisons are replaced by institutions in which the entire staff has a therapeutic attitude toward the inmates. Without this, no "therapy" can be effective. Nor is this a utopian dream; the California Department of Corrections has established such a medical facility, and Menninger (1968) describes similar ones. As I described in my 1955 paper, they are effective in preventing recidivism when used in combination with a psychiatric outpatient parole clinic. If we can convert our psychiatric-hospital snake pits into community mental health centers, we can convert destructively ineffectual prisons into institutions which help men to tolerate their anxieties and develop alternative coping techniques.

Just as the threat of punishment fails to deter, punishment itself fails to prevent recidivism, because punishment is vengeance. There is no doubt that it serves to find a scapegoat and helps "normal" citizens control their violence by serving as a counter-cathexis. But I thoroughly disagree with Dr. Asch that some justification for revenge as a basis for punishment can be found in psychoanalytic theory. All it offers is understanding and explanation of the need most of us have for punitive revenge; it does not at all justify or condone it. Legalized punishment does *not* provide society with a *"morally* [my italics] acceptable outlet for destructive aggression."* It is as immoral a criminal acting out as the offender's criminal acting out. Society, like the inmate, will have to find better and more adaptive ways of coping with its aggression, not only because it is immoral to vent its rage on a helpless prisoner, but because in so doing it practically guarantees that the prisoner will commit another crime against the society which behaved so stupidly.

To cite the approval of the death penalty by a group of psychoanalysts in one particular case creates a false implication which must be challenged. It invokes the authority of psychoanalysts, and therefore indirectly of psychoanalytic theory, to support the idea that punitive retribution is defensible. I interpret the reaction of the analysts quite differently. In a social setting, where critical judgment is less apt to manifest itself, the analysts' reaction is evidence of the readiness in all of us to vent our lust for vengeance and counterviolence when some particularly heinous crime lulls our superegos into accepting and justifying our own sadistic joy in exacting retribution in kind.

Recently, when I read of the brutal, senseless killing of a four-year-old only child, my gut reaction was to kill the monster who committed this cruelty. But then the voice of reason—quiet but persistent—made me realize that vengeance would neither bring the child back to life nor prevent further similar crimes.

Vengeance merely escalates violence. The incident exposed my readiness to justify experiencing the pleasure of sadistic, vengeful retribution. We must all guard against our readiness to utilize a seemingly justifiable excuse to warrant the release of the Eichmann present in all of us. Psychoanalysis teaches us to recognize and acknowledge the existence of these irrational impulses waiting to be rationalized and discharged in reactive response to some heinous crime or in justification of some ideology. We must learn to regard such passions as dangerous and obscene, instead of viewing them ego-syntonically as justifiable. Of course, there is no guarantee that we shall be able to control or sublimate such drives, but unless (to paraphrase Freud) we let ego be where id is, we forego any hope of change. How much more humane, civilized, and pragmatically more effective was the reaction of the anti-Nazi French farmer in the documentary film *The Sorrow and the Pity*, who refused to seek vengeance on the informer because he believed that if he stooped to the level of the Nazis he would feel like a Nazi himself. The classic film *M* expresses similar rational sentiments.

In California and elsewhere a faint breeze is blowing in the right direction: pre-release work-furlough programs and many other progressive steps have been instituted. These must be better supervised and overlapping responsibility must be avoided to prevent any misuse of these privileges, because even occasional failures serve to cast doubt on all progressive programs and enable reactionary attitudes toward prisoners to prevail.

While we applaud these humane reforms, I believe that unless radical measures are taken ("radical" meaning to get at the root) to replace prisons with therapeutic and innovative facilities, we are building up to more Atticas, more polarization within the prison, and making sure that on release someone else will be mugged, raped, or robbed.

In such a facility the psychoanalyst would be in a position to help: through his understanding of underlying dynamics he is in a position to recommend the most effective disposition.

Such an environment would be conducive to the development of newer techniques.

To quote Karl Menninger (1968): "Prisons are evil places, evil in conception, evil in operation. They are operated for the wrong purpose and in the wrong spirit, and often (not always) by the wrong people" (p. 81).

Our prisons, however, are models of enlightenment compared to the often described (and quickly ignored) horrors of our jails. Jails, supposedly for people who have committed misdemeanors or who are awaiting final disposition of their case, have no program at all for their inmates and are invariably overcrowded and filthy.

Unless we develop institutions with a therapeutic atmosphere, manned by properly trained, qualified, and adequately paid personnel to replace prisons; unless we can forego the sweetness of revenge (abandon the pleasure principle in favor of the reality principle), we have no right to complain of the inevitable penalties to society and to ourselves as members of the society. Unless we can learn to reinterpret "an eye for an eye" in terms of restitution rather than retribution, we will guarantee the continuing failure of our punitive and vindictive attitude toward inmates. We must change, not only to help inmates but to save ourselves.

NORMAN TABACHNICK, M.D.
Beverly Hills, California

I congratulate Dr. Asch on a very fine paper and extend my warm thanks to him, because I agree that psychoanalysts have paid too little attention to issues of crime and punishment. It is important for us to consider these areas for two reasons, of mutually reverberating significance. One, as members of society we have an obligation to contribute what we can from the vantage point of our discipline to the understanding and remedying of society's problems. Two, our general psychoanalytic theory and practice will be enriched as we study the superego in relationship to the other intrapsychic agencies, and the meaning of crime and punishment from a psycho-analytic viewpoint.

In his paper, Dr. Asch has made two significant contributions: he has reviewed much psychoanalytic literature and thinking on the subjects of crime and punishment, and, using material from a broad variety of sources and contributing his own considerations, he has come to certain tentative conclusions regarding deterrents and punishment. In moving toward conclusions in such a relatively uncharted field for psychoanalysts, Dr. Asch risks (and probably invites) dissenting viewpoints. I hope he will respond to my further observations with the knowledge that, although they are at variance with some of his ideas, they were stimulated by his good work.

I feel that an issue Dr. Asch has not sufficiently considered is this: "Crime" may be a positive adaptational response to the vicissitues which a particular society offers to a particular individual. Much of the psychoanalytic theory which Dr. Asch quotes and then uses in his further formulations have a distinctly middle- and upper-class bias. What do I mean by this? The subjects who came to be analyzed and the analysts who did the analyzing and then wrote psychoanalytic theory were all middle-class people; and more important even than their social class was the fact that they were "winners" in the world of their day (even as most analysts and analysands are "winners" in our world today). By following the approved procedures, rules, and laws of their time, they had managed to achieve life styles which were both gratifying and gave them relatively high status in their society. (True, one may argue that all or most analysts and all patients have significant difficulties in life. However, generally speaking, I believe my assertion that analysts and analysands are among the "winners" in society is correct.)

Now it is precisely this class of "winners" who have the most power in the society. Therefore, it is they who formulate the procedures and laws which maintain the social order, to their own advantage.

For example, let us consider laws against stealing. Businessmen and manufacturers make certain agreements among themselves concerning delivery of goods, prices, etc. By keeping to these agreements, they mutually prosper. If one party to such an agreement steals (that is, breaks the law), the others do not prosper. Therefore, generally speaking, it is to the advantage of these "winners" in society to observe the law against stealing.

But the situation is very different for certain subgroups within our culture who might be called "losers." By my definition, "losers" means the people who do *not* benefit from observing the laws and procedures which have been developed and given status by the "winners" in the society. For example, a person of a lower socio-economic class may find that if he follows the accepted rules and procedures in regard to paying taxes, honoring his promises to pay and avoiding stealing, he will be in a much worse position than if he violates laws and approved procedures. For him, "living by his wits" may secure more of the necessities and amenities of life than would "playing the game according to the rules." Dr. Asch points out that so few of the total number of crimes are solved that it really might be held that crime *does* pay. But particularly to lower-class people who may justifiably feel themselves shut out of the power structure, with relatively little opportunity to get into it, the choice may be between stealing and cheating (which at least gives them a chance to gain certain material benefits) and "playing the game" (with no chance at the good things in life).

Along these lines, let us remember that "crime" is not an absolute, but like most concepts is a *defined* entity. I can think of no "crimes" which do not fit that formulation. Homosexuality, a crime in some societies, has not been and is not considered a crime in all. Murder is very often considered a crime, but not invariably so. Suicide is considered a crime in some jurisdictions but not in others. I make this point to emphasize that "crime" cannot be profitably looked upon merely as an impulse of the individual to act against authority or as a synonym for impulsive activities which are not subject to control. It is only those activities which certain segments of society have found it advantageous to control that become "crimes" when some member of the society doesn't go along with the "rules."

I believe this formulation is compatible with much of the material Dr. Asch has brought to our attention. For example, why is it that there is a certain group of people to whom that "external nutriment" for superego maintenance results in keeping "within the law," while there is another group of "sociopaths" who do not respond to external nutriment in the same way? I suggest that the law-abiding folk are "winners" who are reminded by laws and threats "which side their bread is buttered on." The "losers" pay no heed because the "winners'" rules have no positive value for them.

Dr. Asch makes another statement which is compatible with my ideas: "Internalization and identification require good object relations. . . ." I believe that there are potentialities for and precursors of many identifications in each human being. For the "winner," identification with "law-abiding" introjects attains dominance because they afford a means of realizing some of the individual's goals. For the "loser," attempts to move forward through "law-abiding" identifications gradually prove to be unsuccessful, and so the "criminal" or "sociopath" identifications prove more valuable for him. "Obeying the law" is thus not a constant which makes all people feel equally good when they comply with it and equally bad when they repudiate it. I believe this point of view may be more useful in understanding "psychopathic" behavior than formulations which stress increased narcissism or superego lacunae.

Let me give an example which I believe supports my point of view.

Recently, the Los Angeles Suicide Prevention Center undertook a program of rehabilitation with "criminals," i.e., parolees who have been convicted of various crimes and have served some prison time. What they all have in common is that, according to our laws, they have been drug abusers or "criminals." Previous experiences with criminals of many types, including those with drug histories, indicate an extremely high rate of recidivism. However, that rate in our program seems to be at least 50 per cent lower.

We have focused on a "total" program to integrate our clients with the rewarding aspects of society. We not only see them for a good deal of counseling, but, perhaps even more important, we make quite active efforts to get jobs for them and help them establish good social relationships, including even the formation of family-like groups. We have been active in helping them avoid subsequent brushes with the law. These are activities at which most "winners" are quite adept, but, as we have discovered, our clients unfortunately are not.

My interpretation is that we are giving our clients positive experiences and positive feedback in regard to their living in a law-abiding way; in more technical psychoanalytic language, we are providing good introjects for them. We are also showing them that a "law-abiding" kind of life can pay off.

Psychoanalysts have often thought of themselves as possessing the ability clearly and objectively to see things as they "actually" are. They often write and act as if their values and biases do not affect their observations and conclusions. However, much recent research shows us that we are not at all value-free, but instead hold strong biases which are often representative of the groups of which we are members.

This whole trend of thinking suggests that psychoanalysis is more closely connected with social forces than the instinct-dominated earlier psychoanalytic theory led us to believe. To me, however, pointing out the possible influence and impact of societal, environmental, and cultural forces does not imply that drives of an "instinctual" nature do not exist. However, such thinking certainly indicates that whatever the intensity of those drives, they can be very importantly affected by external or environmental forces.

JOSEPH E. LIFSCHUTZ, M.D.
Orinda, California

Dr. Asch is to be commended for this worthwhile effort to delineate the different qualities of criminal acts as committed by different character types. He reminds us of the arduous course toward "mature" superego development and of the ever-present regressive process threatening psychic equilibrium. His idea that normal superego processes require external "nutriment" reminds me of Erikson's concept of ego virtue: that each phase of ego development requires external validation for optimal consolidation of the particular ego "virtue" or strength. Dr. Asch calls our attention to the vulnerability of ego and superego processes to narcissistic regressive disorganization, and to how important are our relations with the external world for the maintenance of psychic balance and integration.

His comments about the effect of imprisonment—the debasement, demoralization, and dehumanization of the individual—are all too true. During my legal efforts with respect to confidentiality some years ago, I was held in contempt of court and had to spend three days in a fairly modern county jail in California. Although I was in no way personally abused during my imprisonment, I must say that the ordinary person cannot grasp the profound humiliation, the forces toward total obliteration of one's personal identity, that begin to work immediately as one passes through the locked steel doors.

Freedom is totally lost, and one is completely at the mercy of anonymous, indifferent guards. Whatever system of enlightened punishment or imprisonment may be devised in the future, the human worth of every prisoner must be nurtured no matter how serious his crime.

Which leads to the dilemma of punishment. Here I think Freud's cautionary remarks should be recalled. As Strachey puts it: ". . . he wrote to deprecate any half-baked application of psychoanalytic theories in legal proceedings." I agree that long imprisonment for convicted persons with normal or neurotic superegos will do more harm to them *and* to society than good, while those with genuinely sociopathic superegos remain continuing dangers to society. But great caution is needed, I think, to keep psychiatrists and psychoanalysts from battling from opposite sides of the adversary process in court. The result is often the public demeaning of our professional image. Possibly an independent, impartial panel of psychological authorities might be available to advise judges as to the neurotic or sociopathic character structure of the prisoner. Such a function would be similar to the one now served by probation departments. Possibly the answer is more severe punishments, longer sentences, for recidivism. My guess is that the greater the recidivism, the more likely the individual is to have sociopathic superego defects.

Further intensive psychoanalytic research in the area of crime and punishment should yield fruitful results, deepening our understanding of this dark area of human experience.

FREDERICK J. HACKER, M.D.
Lynwood, California

Surprisingly, acts of violence are varieties of human behavior rarely studied in psychoanalytic literature. This is how Dr. Asch begins his interesting observations, which range widely over topics of psychoanalytic structural theory, psychology of punishment, penology, and social policy. To be sure, all these fields are related to each other, although their systematic interconnection is not always completely clarified in this paper, which also does not attempt to explain the remarkable reluctance of psychoanalysis to face the problem of aggression with the same sober detachment and realism with which it views other problems of intrapsychic and social life.

It was Sigmund Freud who established the tradition of partial scotomization of aggression in psychoanalysis, but it was also he who broke with it when he "discovered" the potentially destructive and self-destructive evil in man by conceptualizing the death instinct and aggressive drives. Movingly, Freud described the internal obstacles blocking the recognition of innate self-destructive tendencies and the difficulties of dealing with the various, often hidden forms of man's aggression against himself and others. To this day many psychotherapists refuse to follow Freud in what they consider his speculative, metaphysical aberration regarding the death instinct, which they cannot see clinically and hence consider a superfluous conceptual tool. These "love-only" analysts have no choice but either to deny altogether all biological basis for human behavior (which ultimately also leaves the "hard" scientific facts of learning perception and social influence unexplained) or to consider only progressive growth and development to be normal, genuinely human facts. The biologically equally "given" phenomena of aggression, decay, and death must then be relegated to pathology, or to mishap. Aggression is thus at best considered a symptom, a sign of illness indicating loss of control, while aggression in its strategic, attention-arousing, consolidating, structuring, or if you insist, in its constructive aspects is totally overlooked. Then the way is clear to consider one's own or society's aggression as either non-existent or, by the device of label change, as defensive and inevitable, while projecting all "real" aggression onto the outsider, the criminal, the enemy who (deplorably, even most analysts agree) ought not to be studied but punished, or at least by all available means rendered incapable of doing any further damage.

Asch recognizes that deterrent external structures, like legal threats and sanctions against undesirable behavior, are a necessary superego nutriment. Every society expects optimal internalization of its prohibitions (which cannot be enforced anyway without such internalizations), but no society so far has believed that it can afford to depend on internalization alone or has dared abolish all external threats. Certainly, even the normal superego needs societal support and nutriment, all the more so since the relationship between superego and restricting societal agencies is interdependent and intertwined, a two-way street. By internalization of formerly environmental restrictions, the superego becomes (partly) the internal policeman, but society's morality and laws are also (partly) the externalized and organized projection of former superego manifestations. Morality, law, and social institutions confront any individual child born into a culture with the overwhelming force of near-inflexible, immutable fate, yet indubitably the sum total of the social system and all of its parts is not given but made, designed and developed by human wishes and human fears, documents or monuments of man's rationality and irrationality (particularly of man's proclivity to rationalize the irrational), and hence subject to blind or conscious human influence in principle and practice.

The main issue of criminology is not whether attempts at deterrence are justified and legitimate (clearly they are, and they would exist even if they were not) but whether they work effectively. Like everybody else concerned with the subject, Dr. Asch has observed that deterrence and punishment in their present form fail miserably and dangerously, particularly with those offenders for whom they were specifically designed, such as neurotics, sociopaths, etc. (Sex offenders and white collar and organized criminals could easily be included in this list.) The phenomenon of deterrence which does not deter represents the current failure of social controls by our system of punishment, ultimately epitomized in the scandal of our prisons, often exposed and never remedied, as dramatically described in Karl Menninger's recent book *The Crime of Punishment* (1968). Asch provides not entirely novel but illuminating observations on the dehumanization and cruelty of prisons, on their failure to rehabilitate offenders or to protect society. Incidentally, this writer has never been able to resign himself to or completely explain the patent oversimplification by which "society" (whatever that may mean) is cast in the role of the "good guy" and the criminal in the role of the "bad guy." In equally primitive manner this casting is sometimes reversed. What about those violent acts committed in perfectly good conscience, supported by society, collective ideology, and individual rationalization, which, in loss of life and happiness, in cruelty and danger, exceed anything brought about by violence disapproved of by society or by superego? In other words, what about those crimes in which superego and society function not as restricting but a facilitating agencies?

After having pointed out the inhumanity and ineffectiveness of punishment based on the collective need for revenge in prison and otherwise, Dr. Asch feels obligated to stress that "psychoanalytic theory does offer some justification for revenge as a basis for punishment" and that "retribution as an aim of punishment may have an analytically justifiable basis." If Dr. Asch means to claim that the collective need for retribution, in spite or because of its destructive irrationality, has a meaning and can be interpreted, he is obviously correct. If he intends to indicate that the use (or abuse) of the so-called criminal as scapegoat supports the (presumably noncriminal) individual in his constant struggle to ward off his own antisocial impulses, he is again completely right. Putting the same by now somewhat trivial insight into psychoanalytic jargon, "It [the taking of revenge] may contribute to the counter-cathexis against his antisocial drives [are there any social drives?] through displacement and projection of such impulses onto the criminal," is somewhat gratuitous. But should a human being or a group of individuals be victimized as scapegoats in order to support the defensive structures of other individuals or groups? If so, then prejudice, race-, class-, and minority-hatred, and all the other forms of satisfaction of the need for an enemy upon whom to project one's own conflictual aggressions are "justified," "even analytically justified."

Well, unfortunately they are. Just ask the self-righteous law-and-order individual, the prejudiced person, and the racist. That is precisely why we still have prejudice and race hatred and retribution and the scandal of our prisons. Does it come as a surprise that prejudice, violence, projection, even paranoid projection, will fulfill important, at times even stabilizing, intrapsychic and social functions for those who have been manipulated into becoming violent, prejudiced, and paranoid? Does that insight, well known to all behavioral

— 217

scientists and often exploited by politicians and demagogues, represent psychoanalytic justification? In the language of the aggressor, victimization is called by different names (even, and particularly, if the aggressor mistakes himself for the defender of virtue and other higher values); in fact, this is precisely the label change and label swindle through which violence attempts to mask its brutal appearance.

The attempts to "advance" psychoanalysis, from a "subversive" science (in principle analytical and critical, hence frequently on the side of the oppressed) to the presumably mature respectability of social acceptance, should themselves be critically analyzed in order not to pervert the original psychoanalytic message of hope into its opposite; there is every reason to be genuinely alarmed when the grossest inhumanities of man toward man are first described and analyzed with scientific detachment in order then to justify the existing unconscionable brutality in terms of the needs of the irrational and cruel oppressor.

Dr. Asch concludes with the statement that we know all too little as yet about either crime or punishment. We also know much too little about our own attitudes, which have made crime the overwhelming problem that it is today and punishment the hypocritical safety valve for unresolved conflicts of the punisher. We should beware that our expert knowledge designed for understanding (possibly forgiving) and changing does not become a tool to justify and encourage man's individual and collective destructiveness and self-destructiveness.

JEAN ROSENBAUM, M.D.

Durango, Colorado

A minor criticism which could be made of this essay is that it suggests that there is little analytic material available on the subject, revealing an incomplete survey of the literature. This general comment applies to all polemical authors. It is as if they have to establish the fact that little or nothing has been written on a subject in order to justify its study. In this case a review of Abraham's work on anal sadism, Bettelheim's book on how to handle a Nazi, or my own past comments in *The Psychoanalytic Forum* on concentration camps might have been useful. On the whole, however, Dr. Asch accomplishes his aim of "provoking thought" very well, and I found the essay quite stimulating.

Proceeding with this Socratic approach, let us first examine the premise that superego and society are "not at all the same." Putting aside the possibility of a visitation from God, where does Dr. Asch suppose conforming parents get their standards from? There is a profound relationship between group (societal) and personal (parental) superego which many writers (among them, Lindner and Waelder) have pursued, including this discussant in papers on "groupicide" and "psycholdanalysis" (*sic*).

The most provocative analytic hot potato Dr. Asch drops in one's lap is his observation concerning the relationship between the diffuse nature of the female superego and the low incidence of female crime. Freud commented on the former, but I am unaware of anyone ever before contrasting this with the latter. If Dr. Asch is right, the committing of crimes, especially the more serious crimes of violence, has much less to do with the cultural whims of the superego and much more to do with sexual disposition than we have heretofore believed. I first became intrigued with this subject many years ago when, as chief psychiatrist at a women's state prison, I became very much aware that man's potential for destructive behavior was markedly different quantitatively and qualitatively from woman's. This subject was pursued at some length, though certainly not exhaustively, in my study on "groupicide" in which I concluded, well before the women's lib movement, that men aren't fit to rule.

I do think that the reading list of such a study should not be limited to the biographical index of the Berlin and New York psychoanalytic associations, not because the list is not a sound one—it is—but because it is so political. There is much fruitful psychoanalytic work going on outside that sterile area of influence.

I agree with Dr. Asch that present systems of punishment do not work, but not for the reasons of structural theory that he struggles with. I think the human equation is much simpler than the arithmetical one. That is, punishment doesn't work when a person has nothing to lose.

Furthermore, Dr. Asch is deploring prison from the viewpoint of a gentleman. Jail's not so bad for a desperate person with no sense of psychosignificance, living in a filthy, chaotic society. Ninety-five per cent of criminals come from such an environment. To them enforced camaraderie, three meals a day, shelter, and safety are scarcely punishment. The brutalities on the inside are far less random, intensive, and existential than out on the streets. "It's bad out there, man," one eight-time loser told me.

We also have to face the reality of man's need for revenge rather than trying to rationalize it away with theoretical maneuvers. As I write these comments I can hear a television news program in the next room reporting a major attack by North Vietnam on South Vietnam, a joy-kill that has been going on for 40 years despite French and American attempts to referee. In one form or another it will probably go on for another 40. Let the boys have their fun, men. Political, nationalistic, or romantic analytic daydreaming will not alter the basic elements of murderous tit for tat.

Substituting something else (prisoner-of-war camps?) for prison is an old idea and not a very realistic one, unless accompanied by massive geographical relocation, as in the success story of Siberia or England's transportation of her criminals to Australia and America (if one can consider America a success).

A really effective public relations program came to mind as I was reading Dr. Asch's comments on homosexual rape in prisons. I have already indicated that the usual American criminal (there aren't nearly as many repeaters in Turkish prisons) doesn't find hard time that hard. But one thing every red-blooded American male is terrified of is passive anal penetration. If one could somehow advertise in some persuasive but of course tactful way (perhaps on cigarette packs?) that the automatic consequence of serious crime is the unspeakable horrors of rectal rape, one might see a vast decrease in the crime rate. Perhaps free records of the nightmarish noises could be distributed with gasoline or with educational movies shown to high school boys. *That's* why there are so few repeaters in Turkish prisons!

PHILIP G. ZIMBARDO, PH.D.
Stanford, California

Before outlining a few of the many intriguing issues which emerge from Dr. Asch's perceptive analysis of the nature of crimes and the functions and consequences of punishment, I find it important to mention several other of his provocative ideas which should be researched more fully: Antisocial acts focus and externalize guilt by giving an undefinable inner tension a label, a structure, and a rational source outside the guilty individual; external punishment provided by prisons and social institutions may have an effect opposite to that intended by absolving the individual of any need for self-generated punishment; and laws are intended to protect both the "ego" and "superego," as well as "society."

For me, two central concerns relevant to the ideas expressed here are (1) the dispositional *versus* situational attribution for crime and antisocial acts, and (2) the general preference for punishment over reward across a variety of "training" situations, despite the demonstrated superiority of reinforcement for modifying behavior.

John Stuart Mill (1848) cautions us that "of all the vulgar modes of escaping from the consideration of social and moral influence on the human mind, the most vulgar is that of attributing the diversities of conduct and character to inherent natural differences." Personality-trait theorists and some psychoanalytic thinking has given support to the popular notion that the place to look for "evil" is within evil people; the locus for antisocial behavior is to be found in the character structure (or lack of it) of the deviant, in weak or too-severe superegos, in high F people, etc. To the average person, as well as to our legislators and correctional personnel, the dispositional hypothesis is appealing because it places the responsibility for evil not upon them (society), but solely upon the individuals in question. The solution to the problem of antisocial behavior then need not involve extensive reordering of social, political, or economic priorities, but only of the defective individuals—it is they who are to be re-educated, rehabilitated, cured, treated, rescued, and so forth. Such thinking has been perpetuated because it lets society off the hook both for the cause and the prevention of crime— and, of course, it is cheaper.

A situational or transactional attribution, on the other hand, looks to social forces in the situation which impinge upon the individual, and moves the locus of the elicitation of stimulus for antisocial acts out of the privacy of the psychic structure into the public domain of the social matrix.

There is a growing body of empirical evidence in psychology supporting the proposition that antisocial, deviant, evil behavior is primarily under the control of social, situational stimuli. That is, the most accurate predictions of whether a person will inflict pain upon a fellow human being (without provocation), will cheat, lie, steal, etc., come from an analysis of his/her transaction with prevailing norms in the immediate situation. We observed pathological, extremely antisocial behavior in college students who were "normal" on every dimension we could measure, in response to the pathological influences of absolute power relations which characterized the prison we created (simulated at Stanford University in 1971). The greater predictive utility of situational rather than dispositional analyses of antisocial behavior finds strong support in the demonstration by a third-grade Iowa school-teacher, Mrs. Elliott (1970), that merely labeling children "superior" or "inferior" on an arbitrary basis of eye color makes them hate and discriminate against their former

friends. Stanley Milgram's (1974) research on blind obedience to authority clearly places the "blame" not on personality variables but social-situational ones.

A re-emphasis in psychoanalytic thinking on the present
(acute) environmental influences on behavior appears to be
called for to balance the over-reliance on hypotheses relating
historical influences to chronic, internal, hypothetical disposi-
tions.

My second point centers around the hypothesis that people
prefer and choose punishment and coercive tactics of behavior
control over reward and supportive tactics, even though they
know intellectually that reinforcement has been proven to be
more effective. Some evidence for this speculation comes
from a questionnaire study of preference for various tactics of
behavioral change across situations, as well as from a labora-
tory study and observations of diverse training situations by
Curtis Banks, Susan Phillips, and me. From what we have
seen we have begun to develop a theoretical model which
predicts both the conditions under which punishment rather
than reward will be used and the variables which account for
the relative preference of the one over the other. To illustrate,
let me suggest a few of the variables and processes we have
isolated.

To reward a "trainee" effectively demands knowledge of his
history as well as his current state of deprivation, interests,
etc.—the reward must be tailored to some qualitative features
of the target subject. Punishment, on the other hand, requires
only a limited knowledge and a simple conception of human
nature—the quantitative determination of how much pain
can the person take. Thus, to reward, you must individuate
the other, which is not desirable in some situations, is impossible in most hierarchical, authoritarian institutions, and
demands considerable effort, patience, and skill on the part of
the trainer. Related to this is the question of who gets credit
for any observed change in behavior. If you use punishment,
the punisher clearly is responsible for the outcome, if it is the
desired one; if reward is used subtly (if the desired response is
evoked gradually), then it appears to those who do the ac-

— 223

counting as if the trainee is responsible for changing his or her own behavior. If one's job depends on such an accounting, then it is probable that punishment will predominate. Furthermore, we believe that rewards are administered only when the agent of change anticipates that the target of change has the capacity to reciprocate, if only by a smile or a compliment; that there is something the other can do which is meaningful to the trainer. Once the trainer believes the other cannot reciprocate or has nothing to offer that he wants, then the trainee is perceived in a dehumanized way and punishment becomes the preferred mode of relating to that person.

Finally (for this limited discussion), punishment must be dominant in any situation where behavior is under the social control of *rules*, be they explicit regulations or implicit expectations. What follows from adhering to a rule, doing what is expected of you, what you are supposed to do? Nothing! You have done what any reasonable person should and your behavior goes unnoticed and typically unreinforced because it is not special. But if you fail to keep a rule, punishment follows. Rule-binding situations (whether they be in formal, total institutions such as prisons, mental hospitals, or colleges, or informal ones, such as the family) become zero-negative game situations. You're ignored if you do and damned if you don't. Indeed, some extremely deviant behavior in such situations comes from individuals with strong needs for social recognition behaving differently from the standard and being "singled out" for punishment. Punishment for some people living in these situations may be the only way to receive the ultimate social reinforcer—recognition of one's uniqueness by someone of high status. Do we gain anything by labeling such people "masochists," or are we in a better position to recommend social therapeutic techniques by analyzing the rational conditions which elicit this apparently irrational, antisocial behavior?

I lend my support entirely to Dr. Asch's call for increased concern among analysts to the problems of criminal behavior and social attempts to control it. The state of our prisons and the administration of "justice" are among the most important and neglected areas of concern for us all. How can we change *our* behavior to do something about them, *now?*

Author's Response

Most of the discussion revolves around two points: (1) the humanistic conflict over the relative importance of societal as against intrapsychic forces in producing criminal behavior, and (2) the presentation's failure to denounce whatever element of retribution is to be found in systems of punishment.

Although the influence of society was never disregarded or even belittled by Freud, his emphasis on internal conflict was necessary to direct attention to an area that had been almost totally disregarded before. The expertise of the analyst today remains essentially in this area, and while it certainly includes the individual's conflicts with the environment, it is the sociologist who has the territorial claim to societal problems on a group scale. When Gladstone felt that a religious revival was necessary and insisted that government politicians should be in the vanguard of this movement, Macaulay objected to the government taking a role in religious education on the grounds that while bread is certainly more essential to society than music, if pianists therefore became bakers society would end up with both poor bread and poor music.

For similar reasons, I have, for the most part, avoided analysis of and opinions about social groupings. My discussions have been fairly limited to problems derived from, or immediately affected by, functioning of the individual psychic apparatus.

Of course, I too believe the socio-economic "have-nots" are entitled to an improvement in their status. I also agree that it seems likely that this would decrease the incidence of criminal activity. However, I do not believe that crime would disappear if economic inequities disappeared. We have long since abandoned Marx's naive conviction that thievery results from socio-economic disparities alone. Dr. Tabachnick's "winners" in our society exhibit a fair amount of criminal or antisocial behavior themselves. In line with one thesis of my paper, it may well be that the more power and prestige they have, encouraging them to consider themselves "above the law," the more easily their potential criminal activity breaks through, if the internal restrictions of their superegos are not supported by the same external restrictions and laws ("nutriment") as those of "lesser" people.

Understanding the antisocial behavior found among the white-collar class, and certainly in the executive class, still requires understanding of the individual psychic structure and its particular conflicts.

Dr. Zimbardo is among those who imply that changes in society will be sufficient to change the individual psyche. He apparently believes the "label 'masochist'" is meaningless, since such behavior can be modified by corrective "social therapeutic techniques." Those of us who have worked with such personality problems, however, have recognized for a long time now that masochism, once developed into a character trait, is unchanged by any environmental manipulation.

It is of course understood that there is a close relationship between the societal and the personal superegos, but while they may have similar aims at times, they are certainly not identical. Even in a closely knit group, the gamut of behavior observed is quite wide.

Dr. Hacker's statement encompasses several of the discussants' claims that psychoanalytic theory is being used to justify vengeance. My aim was to explain *why* retribution is important to the individual struggling with his own antisocial impulses, and further, why *some* form of retribution can perform a useful socializing function for the *non*-offenders. In addition, retribution in my context means only that the criminal must receive *some* form of punishment. I certainly do not mean to justify punishment by humiliation, torture or death. The example I gave of the group of analysts in a social setting who impulsively favored capital punishment for a particularly heinous crime was not intended to justify cruelty, but rather to emphasize that we must not deny the existence of what may be a universal impulse, the need for retribution. Our problem then is to find forms of punishment that are reasonable and uncontaminated by sadism.

Dr. Chodoff is concerned specifically that the suggestion of indefinite separation of incorrigible psychopaths could provide society with a psychiatric rationalization for prejudicial treatment of minority groups. I can only agree with his concern. The history of Devil's Island presents a case in point. This was originally planned with the humanitarian aim of protecting society from incorrigible criminals by isolating them on a fertile island where they could live freely, do farming, etc. It was of course a dreadful failure. The guards sent to keep them on the island, and especially the senior administrator, had such complete power that the overseers became corrupt themselves and finally overly restrictive and cruel. This is a sequence of events which was anticipated by Lord Acton's "power tends to corrupt," and which my presentation elaborates upon. Dr. Chodoff's concern is justified, and the administration of any penal system should be carefully restricted by some system of checks and balances. Society's "good guys" also need policemen, just as the police in turn need a civilian review board.

In contrast to this pessimistic view, Dr. Rosenbaum believes our present systems of punishment are unsuccessful because "punishment doesn't work when a person has nothing to lose." Solzhenitsyn presents the same argument in *The First Circle*. However, it was probably more valid in his context, where the Russian political prisoner was deprived of family and freedom for an indefinite period of time. It is hard to accept Dr. Rosenbaum's claim that a majority (he suggests 95 per cent) of criminals find prison life preferable to the harsh deprivations of reality outside. Other than O'Henry's derelict, who preferred the jail's Christmas dinner, I have not been aware of many people battering down the Bastille gates to be admitted. His statement leaves me at a loss to understand the intense efforts of those indicted to avoid prison.

Most of the discussants have agreed with my emphasis on the inadequacy, even harmfulness of our present correctional facilities. They have urged that more time and money be spent on changing our penal system. In these times, however, when the public is reluctant to increase even its share of local school taxes, it seems unrealistic to assume that enough funds will be made available for prison reform. But the future may not be so bleak. More realistic approaches may be possible, even if for the wrong reasons. For example, in New York the crime rate has reached such proportions that the prisons cannot possibly contain the increasing number of potential inmates. One can hope that the community will now be forced to adopt more *selective* methods of handling offenders, and find alternatives to the wasteful expense of more prisons.

Dr. Tabachnick's examples of decreased recidivism in response to his special rehabilitation program is quite consistent with analytic formulations on superego pathology. Some superego variants are mainly a result of identifications with family or group norms that accept certain kinds of antisocial behavior. Such superegos are to be distinguished from those with a more pervasive pathology. This is similar to the distinction Aichorn makes in *Wayward Youth*. Analytic theory would anticipate that such morality can be modified if new identifications are made with objects whose values include being law-abiding. Such identifications require clients with an ability for libidinal investment in new object relations (which Dr. Tabachnick's group is apparently able to attract).

It would be of great value to see if this distinction can be confirmed clinically: *Does* the group of recidivists who are resistant to such changes consist of those with specific defects in ego and superego development? It should be possible to evaluate defects in the ego's function of relating to objects, for example.

Dr. Rosow suggests that one factor in limiting the number of women in prison in contrast to men may be that vice squads are less tolerant of male sexual deviants. Actually, sexual perversion, other than homosexuality, is almost unknown among women, for sound dynamic (*not* cultural) reasons. The important male preponderance appears in crimes against other persons and property, rather than "crimes without victims" (I agree with Dr. Rosow's distinction).

Finally, Dr. Rosow's work on violent, senseless crime occurring as a defense against depression or psychosis is intriguing. This is an area I too have been interested in, especially violence as a defense against depersonalization (viz. my paper on "Wrist Scratching and Anhedonia").

Most of these phenomena are concerned with the vicissitudes of the aggressive drives. It is here specifically that the sociologists, and some psychiatrists, tend to over-emphasize the effects of societal pressures. They look on aggression as a reaction phenomenon only, as a response to external aggressions or frustration. Dr. Hacker disputes this view elegantly. Many psychological structures and much of human behavior cannot be understood without appreciating aggression as a basic human drive. Society or the family can only stimulate, modify, or rechannel these drives.

By neglecting to consider aggressive drives in man as independent and possessing their own appetitive thrusts, we are susceptible to one-sided societal orientations (such as the "labeling" theory) and the confusions emphasized by Dr. Hacker.

REFERENCES

Aichorn, A. (1935), *Wayward Youth*. New York: Viking Press.

Asch, S. S. (1968), Crib deaths: Their possible relationship to post-partum depression and infanticide. *J. Mount Sinai Hosp.*, 35:214-220, 1968.

—— (1971), Wrist scratching as a symptom of anhedonia: a predepressive state. *Psychoanal. Quart.*, 40:603-617.

Brennan, W. J. (1963), Law and psychiatry must join in defending mentally ill criminals. *Amer. Bar Assn. J.*, 49:239-243.

Byrne, B. (1966), The revolving cage. *Jubilee*, May, 1966, pp. 24-30.

Davis, A. J. (1968), Report on sexual assaults in the Philadelphia prison system and sheriff's vans. *Phila. District Attorney's Office & Police Dept.*

Elliott, J. (1970), *Eye of the Storm*. ABC-TV Merchandizing, Inc. Film.

Ferenczi, S. (1925), Psychoanalysis of sexual habits. In: *Further Contributions to the Theory and Technique of Psychoanalysis*. London: Hogarth Press, 1950, pp. 259-297.

Freud, S. (1906), Psychoanalysis and the establishment of the facts in legal proceedings. *Standard Edition*, 9:103-114. London: Hogarth Press, 1959.

—— (1915), Thoughts on war and death. *Standard Edition*, 14:273-302. London: Hogarth Press, 1957.

—— (1916), Some character types met with in psychoanalytic work. *Standard Edition*, 14:311-333. London: Hogarth Press, 1957.

—— (1925), Some psychical consequences of the anatomic distinction between the sexes. *Standard Edition*, 19:248-258. London: Hogarth Press, 1961.

—— (1928), Dostoevsky and parricide. *Standard Edition*, 21:175-196. London: Hogarth Press, 1961.

—— (1930), Civilization and its discontents. *Standard Edition*, 21:59-243. London: Hogarth Press, 1961.

—— (1931), Expert opinion in the Halsmann case. *Standard Edition*, 21: 251-253. London: Hogarth Press, 1961.

Friedman, W. (1965), *Law in a Changing Society*. Baltimore: Penguin Books.

Franzblau, M. (1967), Personal communication.

Greenacre, P. (1952), Anatomical structure and superego development. In: *Trauma, Growth and Personality*. New York: International Universities Press, pp. 149-164.

Johnson, A. (1949), Superego lacunae. In: *Searchlights on Delinquency*, ed. K. R. Eissler. New York: International Universities Press, pp. 225-245.

Jones, E. (1957), *Life and Work of Sigmund Freud*, 3. New York: Basic Books.

Levin, M. (1956), *Compulsion*. New York: Simon & Schuster.

Lindman, F. T. & McIntyre, D. M., Jr. (1961), *Mentally Disabled and the Law*. Chicago: University of Chicago Press.

Menninger, K. (1938), *Man Against Himself*. New York: Harcourt Brace.

—— (1968), *The Crime of Punishment*. New York: Viking Press.

Milgram, S. (1974), *Obedience to Authority*. New York: Harper & Row, 1974.

Mill, J. S. (1848), *Principles of Political Economy*, ed. D. Winch. Baltimore: Penguin Books, 1970.

Pollack, S. (1964), Franz Alexander's observations on psychiatry and law. *Amer. J. Psychiat.*, 121:458-464.

Radzinowicz, L. (1961), *In Search of Criminology*. Washington, D.C.: Harvard University Press.

Rapaport, D. (1960), On the psychoanalytic theory of motivation. *The Collected Papers of David Rapaport*. New York: Basic Books, 1967, pp. 853-915.

Rosow, H. M. (1955), Some observations on group therapy with prison inmates. *Arch. Crim. Psychodynam.*, 1 & 4.

Schoenfeld, C. G. (1966), In defense of retribution in the law. *Psychoanal. Quart.*, 35:108-121.

Strachey, A. (1959), editorial comment. *Standard Edition*, 9:102. London: Hogarth Press.

Telfer, M. A. et al. (1968) Incidence of gross chromosomal errors among tall criminal American males. *Science*, 159:1249-1250, 1968.

Wechsler, H. (1955), Criteria of criminal responsibility, 22. *University of Chicago Law Review*, p. 374.

Wolfe, B. H. (1966), Reshaping convict behavior. *Think*, 32:25-29.

Healthy Parental Influences on the Earliest Development of Masculinity in Baby Boys

ROBERT J. STOLLER, M.D.

Dr. Stoller is Professor of Psychiatry in the Medical School at the University of California, Los Angeles, and a Member of the Los Angeles Psychoanalytic Society and Institute. His research is concerned with the development of masculinity and femininity.

Discussants

CHARLES W. SOCARIDES, M.D.

Dr. Socarides is Associate Clinical Professor of Psychiatry at the Albert Einstein College of Medicine in New York. In addition to supervising residents he teaches the third-year seminar course on "Sexual Development and Sexual Disorders." He is the author of over 30 papers, most of them dealing with the etiology and treatment of serious sexual disturbances. His book *The Overt Homosexual*, first published in 1968, has subsequently appeared in German and French editions as well as in paperback.

MARGARET S. MAHLER, M.D., SC.D. (MED.)

Dr. Mahler is Clinical Professor of Psychiatry, Albert Einstein College of Medicine; Chief Consultant to the Child and Adolescent Services of Roosevelt Hospital, New York; former Director of Research of the Masters Children's Center; and Past President of the New York Psychoanalytic Society. *Separation-Individuation*, published in her honor, is a collection of her approximately 80 papers published before 1970. Volume I of her book *On Human Symbiosis and the Vicissitudes of Individuation* has been translated into four foreign languages to date. Dr. Mahler has written extensively about the genesis and problem of self-identity.

JANICE DE SAUSSURE

Madame de Saussure is a Training Analyst and a past Vice-President of the Swiss Psychoanalytic Society. She is in private practice of psychoanalysis in Geneva.

IRENE M. JOSSELYN, M.D.

Formerly Training and Supervising Analyst with the Chicago Psychoanalytic Institute, Dr. Josselyn is now a Geographic Training and Supervising Analyst with the Southern California Psychoanalytic Institute. She is a child analyst,

232 —

and the author of several articles and four books on various aspects of child and adolescent psychological development.

JOHN BOWLBY, M.D.

Dr. Bowlby is an External Member of the Medical Research Council at the Tavistock Clinic, London, and has held various offices in the British Psychoanalytical Society. He has conducted research on the effects on personality development of separation from and loss of a parent. His publications include *Maternal Care and Mental Health* and a number of papers on the child's tie to his mother, separation anxiety, and mourning. He is at present engaged on a three-volume work entitled *Attachment and Loss*.

Healthy Parental Influences on the Earliest Development of Masculinity in Baby Boys

Robert J. Stoller, m.d.

Los Angeles, California

This is an interim report on work and thinking in progress. The data that are the source of these ideas require more confirmation, but I feel that the tentative findings may be strong enough that it is not a waste of time to present them.

Although research on gender identity in our Clinic[1] has been conducted exclusively on people with marked aberrations of masculinity and femininity, the purpose of this research has been to understand the development of masculinity and femininity in more normal people. Though possessing a body of information to which the contrasting scales of common sense and psychoanalytic theory can be applied, for some years I could not get the perspective into more normal development that severe psychopathology can so dramatically give. Recently, however, it has been possible to observe certain processes at work in families that produce children with severe problems of gender identity, processes that are skewed versions of forces which in happier circumstances produce masculine boys and feminine girls. Although most of these observations confirm what others have long since reported, there are some new findings.

The reader should know the ground rules for this report. First, the question of biological forces contributing to masculinity will not be considered, although this is the focus of much exciting and controversial research. There is still argument as to whether and to what extent biological factors con-

[1] Gender Identity Research and Treatment Clinic, Department of Psychiatry, School of Medicine, University of California at Los Angeles.

234—

tribute to masculinity; I will not review the subject but wish only to indicate that my not discussing it here does not mean that I consider it irrelevant.

Second, the data are from a relatively culturally homogeneous group of patients; thus, whatever conclusions are reached cannot be shown to apply to more than white, middle-class Americans of the last 30 years.

Third, there are too few cases for the findings to be considered more than suggestive. To me, however, they are very suggestive, for the same findings keep coming up in one case after another. Still, it is necessary that many more people must be studied in great detail before one's sense of conviction becomes overpowering.

Fourth, this summary concentrates on aspects of identity development which have been peripheral to the main areas of psychoanalytic interest. It is not necessary now to review or even consider the crucial aspects of the development of masculinity which are familiar to the reader—such immense areas as the contributions of conflict and defense to the development of masculinity, the crises in the development of identity and the process of identification that center around such experiences as weaning, toilet training, castration anxiety, and the production and resolution of the oedipal complex in males.

Fifth, the data are derived from secondary observations, not from the more powerful immediacy of watching mothers and fathers actually at work with their infant, impressing upon his malleable psyche those forces that will shape fundamentals of his gender identity. At best, we have directly observed the parents exerting these effects upon four- and five-year-olds and have noted that what we see with our own eyes is the same as what the parents described as going on from the early times before we arrived on the scene.

Generalities Derived from Cases[2]

Gender identity is that part of identity concerned with masculinity and femininity: it is the algebraic sum of, or the balance between, one's masculinity and femininity (not

[2] For reports of particular cases illustrating these points, see Stoller, 1968.

maleness and femaleness). At its core, and the earliest part to develop, is a taken-for-granted conviction that one is a male; that is, that one's assignment to the male sex was anatomically and ultimately psychologically correct. Given this core gender identity, one then builds on it as a result of one's happy experiences, of conflicts which end in mastery, of conflicts which end in compromise formations, and of conflicts which end in failures to develop a particular piece of masculinity.

Except in the most unusual case (certain congenital hypogonadal states) (Stoller, 1968), once the biological substrates have been laid down prior to birth gender identity is essentially learned (Money, 1955; Money, Hampson and Hampson, 1957; Stoller, 1968). As with other learning in the first few months of life, there is a growing consensus that the earliest stages of learning and of identity formation are produced by conditioning (Mahler, 1968) (and, I believe, by the related but different process, imprinting). However, when the beginnings of islands of primitive bits of memories and fantasies develop, memories influenced by fantasies begin to conglomerate and eventually form ego and identity nuclei. With these come the construction of more sophisticated psychic structures, the permanent foundations of identity; and more and more, as frustration, separation, and individuation progress, these foundations are the result of conflict between the infant's primitive wishes and the opposing demands of his mother (society). Habitual styles of dealing with conflicts solidify, serving eventually as solutions (defenses)—which brings us to those areas familiar to the psychoanalyst and beyond the subject of this study.

From the study of aberrations of gender identity, let me remind you of findings that point to non-conflictual, non-defensive origins for the sense of maleness.

The conclusion reached from studies of the development of core gender identity is that one's conviction regarding the feeling that he is a member of his assigned sex is directly the result of his parents' unquestioning belief that he is a member of that sex (Money, 1955; Money, Hampson and Hampson,

1957; Stoller, 1968). This not only holds for normal males and females but is also true of hermaphrodites, who test the hypothesis so well. Thus, we use a first group of patients—the anatomically intersexed—as a variable to study normalcy: If an infant is born intersexed but its parents have no question that it is a male, the child will have no question that he is a male (even when he is in fact almost completely a biologically normal female, as in hyperadrenalism [Money, 1955]). However, if the appearance of hermaphroditism causes the parents to be fundamentally uncertain as to the child's sex, then the child develops an uncertain (hermaphroditic) gender identity (Money et al., 1957; Stoller, 1968).

We can therefore say that one factor contributing to the development of gender identity is the parents' conviction that the assigned sex was the proper one.

A second group of people in whom pathology illuminates the normal are transsexual boys, boys who wish to be changed into females. This condition is brought about by a situation such as the following: a chronically depressed woman, in whose own childhood there was a period of several years during which she yearned to be a male, keeps her infant son so close to her physically and psychologically (as a cure for her depression) that the growing child has no impetus toward separating and differentiating from his mother's (female) body. His father is passive and distant, both physically and psychologically, and so the little boy not only does not have a male to whom he can turn as a source of masculinity, but there is no one to counteract the *excessively* blissful mother-infant symbiosis.

As such a little boy develops, his mother, instead of encouraging masculinity and discouraging non-masculine behavior, is thrilled when she sees her little son dress in women's clothes, show keen sensitivity regarding cosmetics, hair styles, feminine carriage, and express artistic sensibilities, such as gracefulness in dancing, musical and painting abilities, and any other manifestations that are not aggressive, "dirty," sexual, "nasty," vigorous, or intrusive.

Thus, from earliest infancy into school days (and beyond, if

— 237

the process is not interrupted by someone in the outside world), such a mother, moment by moment, all day long and every day, guides with her approval and disapproval[3] the selection process by which children pick up from the outside world those attitudes, feelings, and behaviors which are defined in a society as masculine or feminine. When a mother respects masculinity and encourages it in her boy, he will enjoy developing such qualities; unfortunately, the transsexuals' mothers discourage masculinity and encourage femininity. All this occurs unimpeded, without trauma or conflict in its earlier stages.

In the "experiment" that produces a transsexual boy, the pathological parental attitudes made me aware of familiar, taken-for-granted, more normal attitudes. Watching mothers who encourage symbiosis for too long and too intensely alerts one to notice how mothers of masculine boys do the opposite. The latter women, while encouraging the symbiosis in the first months of life, are able to sense when it is time to let their boys begin to separate from them and how to do this efficiently and lovingly without damaging the child. Boys destined to be masculine are not only encouraged to separate from their mothers' bodies but also are rewarded for masculine behavior at the same time as they are discouraged from feminine behavior and fantasies. It is also easily observed that fathers who wish their boys to develop in a masculine way make it worth their while, checking feminine behavior by disapproval or even physical punishment (Bieber et al., 1962).

From these studies I believe one can recognize *some important healthy early parental factors which contribute to the development of masculinity in males:*

1. The parents' unequivocal conviction that the infant is a biologically normal male, which is confirmed in the infant by the sensations it receives from its genitals as well as seeing them. However, the infant is not immediately aware that his

[3] Here, with her disapproval begins conflict—but not much. The inducements these mothers offer to their sons to avoid what mother feels is masculine behavior are far greater than the vague possible advantages the sons might sense in disobeying her and becoming masculine.

particular genitals are male genitals. That takes him a year or so to learn from his parents, by their unquestioned acceptance of him and his anatomy as male. Only then do the concepts "I have these genitals" and "I am a boy" become fused into the concept "These are male genitals, which proves I am a boy."

(Parenthetically, it always happens that way, but it is not inevitable. Imagine this grotesque situation: A mother brings up her son in total isolation from all other humans and all outside information, telling him unequivocally that his penis and testes mark him as a female, and then raises him to behave in a feminine manner appropriate to girls. If he were turned loose with girls at age five, he would wonder why *they* were abnormal. My thesis is that assigning sex to an infant is a social, not biological, act, and that the infant's gradual coming to know that that assignment is beyond question is not biologically induced but *learned*.)

2. Encouragement of phase-adequate separation from mother's body, with mother not only feeling but also expressing her pleasure at her infant's capacity to separate from her body (Greenacre, 1960; Mahler, 1968; Winnicott, 1960).

3. Encouragement of phase-adequate individuation (development of the knowledge that one is a unique individual with precise, definable, valuable, and permanent attributes—i.e., development of identity), with mother and father feeling and expressing pleasure at their infant's capacity to become a distinct individual (Greenacre, 1960; Mahler, 1968; Winnicott, 1960).

4. Encouragement by mother at the appropriate time to do masculine things ("masculine" defined for the child by expression of attitudes that mother has learned from society and by her own style of interpreting these attitudes), her capacity to accept masculinity in males, and her relatively unambivalent pleasure in the boy's maleness and masculinity. Such encouragement by his father is also, and increasingly, helpful as the child separates from his mother.

5. A masculine father who is present physically and psychologically, as a model for identification. He should also act as a

shield to protect his son if the boy's mother has any "reflex" anti-masculinity that she unthinkingly directs at her son for being male. If she enjoys her husband's masculinity, the boy will find it especially easy to identify with his father.

6. Mild seduction by his mother, which makes it clear that he is an external object clearly differentiated from her body and psyche, an object which she wants to possess again, but this time not as a content of her womb but as a male with his own identity. This will not only reinforce his sense of identity but will also make heterosexuality more attractive to him. (This is an aspect of point 3, above.)

7. Minimal seduction by his father. I am using the word "minimal" with two meanings, the first that more than "minimal" may lead to pathology, the second that there must be *some*, not *none*. If it is minimal but still pleasurable, then it may encourage identification (as can be seen in the hero worship of older children). If the seduction is more than minimal, or if it is too directly linked to physical contact, it may encourage the boy to identify with his mother in order to be a more suitable object to be loved by his father.

It is obvious that if these parental influences play an essential part in the development of masculinity, then we have displaced—as have so many other workers using different data—the oedipal situation and its castration anxiety as *the* crucial force introducing masculinity. I do believe that conflicts, especially threats to one's masculinity and sense of maleness (which go far beyond the mere fear of losing one's genitals), are also essential contributions to the development of masculinity, but as I said earlier, these factors need not be reviewed now, for our immediate focus is on the more egosyntonic forces presented here.

Discussion

CHARLES W. SOCARIDES, M.D.
New York, New York

Stoller's psychotherapy with young patients in the Gender Identity Clinic at the University of California in Los Angeles is praiseworthy. However, his theoretical assumptions on the origin of gender identity disturbances can be misleading and contradictory in my opinion.

I feel it is imperative to scrutinize his concepts carefully because of the unfortunate proliferation of clinics now offering gender identity transformation, otherwise known as sex "reassignment" surgery. In this connection, it is significant to note that UCLA itself, despite its Gender Identity Clinic, has thus far carried out only one transsexual operation, due to an interdepartmental memorandum prohibiting such procedures on anyone except intersexes.

First of all, I am puzzled by what Dr. Stoller means when he states that he possesses a body of information to which the "contrasting scales of common sense and psychoanalytic theory can be applied."

According to Stoller, "The conclusion reached from studies of the development of core gender identity is that one's conviction regarding the feeling that he is a member of his assigned sex is directly the result of his parents' unquestioning belief that he is a member of that sex." He applies this formulation both to hermaphrodites, i.e., anatomical intersexes (embryological defectives) as well as to transsexual boys (anatomical normals). It is his belief that both of these groups develop faulty or pathological gender identity from "non-conflictual, non-defensive origins." Simultaneously, he mentions the importance of the earliest stages of learning, identity formation, "primitive bits" of memories and fantasies, ego and identity nuclei, "sophisticated psychic structures," the importance of frustration, and refers to the separation-individuation phase. Furthermore, he rightly concludes these "foundations are the result of conflict between the infant's primitive wishes and the opposing demands of his mother (society)."

It is obvious that one cannot have it both ways. In view of the above quotes it is difficult to understand why he eschews psychoanalytic in-depth studies. He fails to mention important work by others on the origins of homosexuality, transsexualism, fetishism, and other perversions. Some of these investigators are beginning to regard such conditions as a demonstration that failure to traverse the separation-individuation phase results in gender identity aberrations. They may well be the core difficulty out of which the sexual perversions emerge.

Other psychoanalysts, disregarding the very discipline which equips them to help the sexually disordered, deny that homosexuality, transsexualism, and even obligatory masturbation (Socarides, 1971, citing Marmor) are anything but "natural and normal" sexual patterns. Stoller does not take this position.

When Dr. Stoller says that an anatomic intersex has no conflicts, I ask if he has studied such an individual in depth analysis. Only thereby could he discover whether or not there are unconscious motivations which led this individual to a faulty gender identity. Without such investigation, he cannot conclusively state that conflicts, defenses, severe anxieties, etc., do not exist. When a child is assigned a wrong gender identity, one contrary to anatomy, we know that he *may or may not* eventually assume the correct one. Kubie and Mackie (1968) made this point succinctly in their article, "Critical Issues Raised by Operations for Gender Transmutation."

Although I have no experience with intersexes, I have seen many transsexuals, both in private practice and at the Albert Einstein College of Medicine where I supervised their psychotherapy. In 1969 I published a psychiatric evaluation and in 1970 the only psychoanalytic study of transsexualism.

Stoller states that mothers who encourage symbiosis produce a feminine boy—a boy who, contrary to anatomy, is convinced he is a girl—and that no conflict led to this outcome. In my opinion, this position may well be erroneous. The mechanism by which this conviction arises and which Stoller misinterprets is the persistence of the primary feminine identification with the mother, a preoedipal identification. The child who later becomes transsexual shows the greatest degree of conflict of all the sexual deviants. He is overwhelmed with anxiety, paranoidal fears, incorporation fears, body ego deficiencies, overwhelming fears of engulfment, and paranoidal fears of attack. Typically, this man's history shows strong homosexual wishes in early adolescence; characteristically, he disavows his penis and urgently desires anal penetration by men. Later he may go through a transvestite phase but this does not alleviate his anxieties, until finally, through the "help" of modern medicine gone astray, he is aided and abetted in implementing his insistent, overriding wish, often a delusional or semi-delusional belief, to become a person of the opposite sex.

The transsexual is, in fact, unable to neutralize his anxiety through homosexuality, transvestitism, or any other sexual deviation. Ultimately, he resorts to self-murder and attempted rebirth through transsexual procedures. His pathology is extreme, not minor. The apparent "absence of conflict" that Stoller describes is in reality a monument to severe and overwhelming psychic defeat.

I am hopeful that Stoller will take additional steps to revise *some* of the theoretical aspects of his important clinical work, bringing them into line with the positive contributions he has made to the welfare and healthy maturation of youngsters suffering from gender identity disturbances. It is more than time to reverse the dehumanizing and antipsychoanalytic trend toward irreversible mutilative surgery in these cases of severe psychosexual pathology.

MARGARET S. MAHLER, M.D., SC.D. (MED.)

New York, New York

Dr. Stoller's very condensed paper is a most timely and valuable challenge to us to reflect on the area of gender identity. He draws conclusions as to the importance of "healthy parental influences on the earliest development of masculinity in baby boys," basing those conclusions mainly on extreme deviations of gender identity among boys resulting from severely distorting interactions with the parents.

Since his article is meant to initiate thinking about this question among others and to encourage discussion of his germinal propositions, I should like to begin by making a comparison with a few impressions that have been conveyed to us through our research of ten years' duration on the separation-individuation process as we have seen it in normal or average mother-infant pairs and their interaction from the baby's fifth to 36th month.

On the basis of our experience, we are inclined to say that the important contribution that the parents (especially the mother) make during the preverbal period, in terms of coenesthetic empathy, to the general question of the identity formation of their sons (and also of their daughters) may help us to understand the minor deviations—or rather, uncertainties—of the toddler's gender identity at the age level at which he develops what I have termed the second level of intergration of the sense of identity, namely, *sexual*; or in Dr. Stoller's term, *gender identity*.

We found that, as far as the children themselves (boys and girls alike) were concerned, their awareness of the anatomical sex difference begins much earlier than was hitherto believed. The inborn and early environmental variables that lead, as early perhaps as at the end of the second and the beginning of the third year, to the second level of identity formation— namely, *gender identity*—are, however, quite numerous; they are also much more complex than one can deduce from what appear to be Dr. Stoller's deliberately oversimplified statements.

In our experience, the mother's unconscious attitude toward her own "self"—especially her belief in her femininity or in her own "good" or "bad" motherhood, her feminine "self-esteem," as well as her castration complex, her penis envy, her penis awe (Greenacre 1953), and the defenses concerned with all these—significantly affect her attitude toward her young male child, as Dr. Stoller's work has borne out.

Even normal or average mothers (in our limited sample) seemed every so often to regard their infants' whole body as a most precious part of their own body—more or less clearly as their penis or penis substitute (this fantasy seemed to occur not only with baby boys but with baby girls as well).

There were also mothers who seemed to regard their little son's penis from the very beginning as the symbol of his own masculinity, attaching to it either positive or negative emotional valence (both of which probably depend upon their general attitude toward the male).

Abandonment of the first of these fantasies at the time of beginning differentiation (subphase one, from the baby's fifth to tenth month), and certainly by the time of the toddler's practicing period (10-15 months of age), seems a very important environmental factor in the development of the sense of identity of the baby boy as well as of the baby girl.

This renunciation by the mother is, as Dr. Stoller has indicated in his own way, one of the crucial factors in the baby's development of sound gender identity, and a prerequisite for it.

Our experience with nearly two score of mother-infant pairs, however, indicated quite strongly that the normally endowed baby boy's own contribution to the determination of his gender identity must not be underestimated.

From my own rather limited experience, it is difficult for me to believe that transsexuality ever takes place in the baby's earliest stages without severe trauma or conflict, and particularly without some contribution in that direction being made by the baby's constitutional predisposition.

It is essentially characteristic of every average or normal boy or girl that what Dr. Stoller calls "excessively blissful mother-infant symbiosis" does not exist beyond the fifth month. This is because, purely maturationally, it is automatically dissipated during the developmental process by the ego's inner resources. That is to say, symbiosis does not continue to be blissful for the infant beyond the fourth or fifth month—whether or not the mother or the father wants it to remain so!

We became convinced that, given average parents and good inherent (gonadal?) endowment in the baby boy, the mechanisms by which to achieve what Greenson (1968) has so felicitously called "disidentification from the mother" are operative, sometimes even against formidable environmental odds.

I also believe, as Dr. Stoller does, that, especially among boys, the active presence of the father, especially by the end of the second and in the third year, importantly reinforces the little boy's gender identity. Here the father's readiness to be identified with—not by way of what Dr. Stoller has described as "punishment for feminine behavior," but rather through his gentle rough-housing and playing with the toddler—gives the latter the opportunity to identify with the male parent in a way that has a far greater influence than psychoanalytic metapsychology in its earlier ages had anticipated (cf., Greenacre, 1966; Mahler, 1967; Abelin, 1971).

Our mothers (our sample is by no means large and varied enough, ethnically or otherwise, to lend itself to generalizations) could be somewhat artificially divided into three main categories:

1. Mothers who cherished their baby boy's body as if the son were part of themselves (which seemed to be not very different from the way in which they regarded the body of their baby daughter). This put certain obstacles in the way of the baby's individuation, at both levels of identity formation.

2. Mothers who rather early behaved in an unmistakably contemptuous way toward the phallicity of their baby sons. This happened as early as the differentiation subphase (five to

ten months and beyond), and was marked by hostility toward the *phallic* self-assertions and self-esteem of the baby boy and the male toddler—especially during the phallic phase, but also much earlier.

3. Mothers who rather unambivalently enjoyed having a baby boy "in his own right." These mothers promoted and enjoyed the toddler son's delight in the practicing subphase (10 to 15 months), encouraging the growth of his masculine prowess and also, importantly, permitting the father to assume his decisive role as the main image for identification.

Let me repeat, however, that while it is true that the mother's, and also the father's, "healthy" unconscious and specific fantasy about, and attitude and behavior toward, their baby son may play a major role in the development of the son's gender identity, one must not underestimate the average infant's and toddler's innate capacities to arrive at his or her gender identity.

The widespread indefiniteness about gender identity—and concomitantly the luxuriant growth of overt bisexuality and homosexuality in present-day society—has been greatly augmented by the parents' own uncertainty about their gender identity. The minor deviations of course need careful consideration, which Dr. Stoller's important contributions ought to promote significantly.

JANICE DE SAUSSURE
Geneva, Switzerland

Stoller's paper, which highlights the main findings of his research, presented more completely in his book *Sex and Gender* (1968), is one of a growing number of current works which are extending the boundaries of psychoanalytic thinking by stressing the multiplicity of factors involved in individual development. Of particular interest in this connection is Stoller's emphasis on the importance of parental influence during the pre-oedipal period, when objects are experienced more frequently as part of a two-way linear relationship rather than in the more familiar triangular oedipal structure which forms the core of our psychoanalytic theory.

In discussing this paper I intend just to mention some of the thoughts which it stimulated. The first is an elaboration of item one of the concluding statements concerning healthy parental factors which contribute to the development of masculinity in male children. As part of his statement that it is essential for the parents to have an unequivocal conviction that the infant is a biologically normal male, Stoller adds that this conviction is then confirmed by the infant's experience of his own body through sight, touch, and inner sensations. Such confirmation does not automatically progress favorably, however. The extent to which the child is permitted to have the necessary experiences depends on the parent's attitudes toward the child's body. This in turn involves the parents' unconscious and conscious feelings about their own bodies. It is axiomatic to say that parents need to be secure about their own gender identity and relatively satisfied with it if they are to help the child to establish his. When this is not the case a mother, for example, may prevent her child from developing a clear and accurate body image by setting up prohibitions against the processes by which he comes to know his body, i.e., through seeing and touching his genitals and experiencing and recognizing the sensations thus provoked. She may also interfere with his possibilities of seeing and touching the bodies of his peers, thus depriving him of the means for becoming aware of his similarities to or differences from them.

As a result of uneasiness about bodies, particularly with reference to sexual differences, some mothers tend to create mysteries about bodies. This was perhaps more prevalent some years ago than it is now, and may be a more common reaction with girls than with boys. However, when it occurs it tends to confuse and hinder the development of a child's precise image of his own body and to encourage a resort to fantasies as a basis of establishing his body image. This in turn creates a sense of uncertainty and insecurity about both internal and external body images. Although in point two Stoller mentions that it is not essential that an infant be aware that his genitals are male genitals, still a psychologically correct gender identity will certainly be reinforced by the ability of both his parents to apply the term "male" or "female" to those bodies which are also so labeled by society. Otherwise an eventual conflict with society will undermine the earlier acquired confidence in gender identity.

In his concluding paragraphs three, four, and five, Stoller particularly emphasizes the importance of a mother's ability to encourage her male child to separate from her and to value him as a male object. The problem of appropriate timing for such encouragement is specifically mentioned in paragraph five. In this connection I should like to raise a question concerning the effect of mothers who are overly eager to push the infant into separation and independence. These may be mothers who experience the infant's dependency and desire for a symbiotic relation as threatening, either in the sense of draining them of energy or of depriving them of time for themselves for other activities and relationships. This type of maternal reaction is becoming more and more common. Some of these mothers may also resent being forced into an identification with their infant which they experience as painful because it involves them in a regression to a dependent state. These mothers, because they identify too strongly with the infant, feel such a strong pressure to gratify the child's needs that they experience intense and persistent anxiety. They may then be impelled to push the child into independence in order to reduce or avoid this anxiety. Among other mothers, particularly those who experience their male child as a penis substitute, there are some for whom an infant represents an inadequate or inferior penis. Often they cannot wait for the child's natural growth processes and they try to force a premature development of masculinity.

Whatever the causes of a given mother's behavior, it seems to me that the effect of insisting on too early a separation from the mother and development of masculinity may well retard and confuse the child in his acquisition of gender identity. The child who is obliged to renounce dependency needs before they have been adequately satisfied may build up a general resistance to development, and this can include a reluctance to accept his own gender. In such cases there is not so much a confusion between masculinity and femininity as there is between masculinity and sexually undifferentiated babyishness. If the child identifies masculinity with mother's expectations and demands which he feels unable to meet, then the fact of being a male becomes equated with discouragement, failure, and frustration. Consequently, gender identity becomes difficult for the child to acquire and to integrate into his awareness of himself as a masculine being.

IRENE M. JOSSELYN, M.D.

Phoenix, Arizona

Dr. Stoller's interesting paper offers many potential fields for further exploration and discussion. Omitting from consideration, as does Dr. Stoller, the significance of biological factors in fostering final gender identity in both sexes, I would like to respond tentatively to his final question regarding the oedipal situation. His use of the term "situation" is significant, suggesting the possibility that the *situation* normally creates the oedipal conflict rather than the reverse.

I would agree that gender identity, as manifested in our culture, regardless of the biological factors involved, is essentially the result of a learning experience. As Dr. Stoller points out, parents and others normally respond to the male or female child according to its gender and subtly or overtly encourage gender-appropriate behavior, the latter defined by the culture. This, among other influences, promotes identification with the parent of the same sex. Unless his identification with the father is optimally encouraged, the male child has a more difficult task than the female child. The first intense relationship for both sexes is with the mother. As the male child becomes aware of his gender, and what is positively responded to in that role, he can no longer identify primarily with his mother, as he is often inclined to do, but must shift to identi-

250 —

fication with his father. It is not surprising that if the mother does not encourage this shift, does not indicate her appreciation of his struggle for an appropriate gender identity, and/or if he does not have an adequate and available father figure with whom to identify, he will continue to follow in the path of his original identification. This struggle can often be observed in the relatively normal toddler.

The oral and anal stages of normal development can be explained in part on the basis of neuromuscular and neurosensory developments. So far there has not been conclusive evidence that the oedipal period has a similar, parallel biological basis. Pleasurable masturbation and erectness of the penis, for example, suggest that a sensory responsiveness in the genitalia is present perhaps from birth. Is not the oedipal "situation" in part the result of identification with the parent of the same sex and the oedipal conflict then a partial response to that identification, leading to rivalry with that parent as the male child sees a male way to assure a continual relationship with his mother?

Such a theory would in no way be incompatible with the metapsychological formulation of the conflict during the oedipal phase or the effect of the resolution of that conflict; it merely suggests the forerunner of the conflict and its solution. It also by no means offers a definitive explanation of all roots of the oedipal situation. Some cultures do not foster early gender differentiation, but the boys still become men and the girls women in those cultures. Our own forefathers tended to dress and treat boys and girls alike until a more advanced age than is now customary, but the many Little Lord Fauntleroys did eventually become boys. However, one does find an interesting suggestion in the literature in regard to the age at which the oedipal conflict develops. At one time it was thought to occur at approximately the age of four or five, but one increasingly sees manifestations of it in children in our culture prior to that age. This would suggest that a culture may facilitate early gender identity and thus the evolvement of the oedipal "situation." The biological factor must offer, as Dr. Stoller suggests, a foundation upon which that development occurs.

I would, however, agree with Dr. Stoller that many developmental steps that have by some been attributed to the existence and resolution of the oedipal conflict actually have begun to take shape prior to that phase of psychological growth. I would conceptualize these as taking embryonic form at the time the child becomes aware of himself as a separate entity. It is my impression, for example, that at that time not only does gender awareness begin to take shape, but the superego, the ego-ideal, and many other characteristics of the human personality begin to become manifest.

JOHN BOWLBY, M.D.

London, England

Dr. Stoller's study of the development of gender identity has benefited us in several ways. First, we are now much better informed about the problem itself and some of the conditions that bring it about. Second, his work testifies to the value of a research strategy that selects a particular problem, gathers empirical data about it, generalizes cautiously, interprets the findings in as parasimonious a manner as possible and, when necessary, reformulates theory to fit the new findings. Third, his findings are an important contribution to the movement within psychoanalysis that recognizes that personality development, whether healthy or pathological, cannot be understood except in terms of the interactions that occur between an individual and his family of rearing, and consequently that the study of these interactions is as necessary a part of psychoanalytic science as is study of intrapersonal processes.

In my own thinking about personality development and functioning (1969), I have found it useful to postulate that during childhood each of us builds up two working models, one of self and another of environment (especially of the significant people in it), on the basis of which we plan and act.[1] Information used in the construction of an individual's working models is derived from three sources: personal experience, parents, and others. Information from each source may be more or less valid and more or less compatible with information from other sources. A matter of much interest is to discover how influential the information from each source may be in comparison with that from other sources.

Stoller's findings show unmistakably that, in some cases at least, the information reaching a child from his parents can have great influence on the development of his self-model, even when the information is demonstrably false and incompatible with information from other sources. In addition, Stoller's findings support the hypothesis that a self-model, once developed, tends to persist and to become relatively insulated from new information. Some psychoanalysts interested in the field of personality development and family interaction suspect that a number of other personality deviations, e.g., phobia and schizoid personality, can be understood as due in part to a child developing a non-valid and internally inconsistent self-model as a result of his receiving false information about himself from one or both parents.

If one takes that position, as I do, it becomes necessary both to explain why a parent should systematically communicate false information to a child and also to define the nature of the sanctions that a parent uses to insist that the child accepts it. These issues raise far-reaching questions about the psychopathology of parenthood and can be answered only in terms of the parent's own difficult and unhappy childhood. Adverse experiences, whose effects I have been especially interested in (1973), such as receiving little affection as a child, or losing a parent in early life, make it easy for such a person, when she[2] becomes a parent, unconsciously to look to the child as someone who will mother her, and so to invert

---

[1] A model may be more or less valid, more or less self-consistent, more or less conscious, and more or less open to change. The working model of the self is conceived as an elaborated representation of the physical and psychological characteristics that an individual believes himself to have.

[2] Although fathers sometimes behave in the ways described, the pattern occurs more frequently in mothers.

the normal parent-child relationship. In order to ensure that she receives mothering from her child, a mother may behave as though she were devoting herself to him, and as though he were demanding it, whereas closer scrutiny shows that in fact she is making incessant demands on his time and attention which he may deeply resent. To the novice clinician, the resulting relationship may look as though the child were incapable of developing his own autonomy (in Mahler's terms, to go through the process of separation-individuation), whereas in fact his mother is unconsciously prohibiting it.

As a rule a principal feature of this inverted relationship is that the mother insists that her child accept a (false) view of himself as a person who cannot prosper without her care and a (false) view of herself as someone who is constantly sacrificing herself for his benefit. Some of Stoller's cases, e.g., that of Lance in Chapter Nine of *Sex and Gender* (1968), suggest that a mother's encouragement of her son's feminine proclivities and self-model may be an additional and special aspect of the fairly common phenomenon of a mother seeking to invert the relationship she has with her child.

Stoller's paper postulates that in the development of a valid self-model, no less than in the development of an invalid one, parents exert great influence. This suggestion is in keeping with the findings of a number of empirical studies of personality development during adolescence (e.g., Peck and Havighurst, 1960; Offer, 1969) and seems more than likely to be true.

Author's Response

On receiving, and before reading, the discussions of this paper, I was uneasy. Four and a half years have passed since it was written, and not much less since I last looked at it and submitted it to *The Forum*. Additionally, it was purposely written, as Dr. Mahler recognized, with deliberately oversimplified statements. Issues taken up in other papers and other aspects of the subject already well established by psychoanalytic data and theory are barely noted, much less discussed. And I continued to use a style of writing that has

254 —

made some analytic colleagues uneasy. To them I seem simplistic, having forsworn (with some hedging) technical psychoanalytic language if nothing would be gained by using it, or if there is no consensus in psychoanalysis on the meaning of a word, or if the word allegedly refers to a reality I cannot grasp, or if there is a common English word with the same meaning. (Leites, in *The New Ego*, has dealt devastatingly with the issue of analytic syntax.)

This paper, then, may seem a blunder to those who cannot believe that a psychoanalyst could talk about the earliest stages of personality development without using theory built from such concepts as cathexis, narcissism, or object representations. Yet I do not believe that enlarging concepts into metaconcepts will help us to extricate ourselves from the problem of not knowing what goes on silently inside an infant's psyche, the main methodological problem in my research. Concepts do not close gaps in argument; they only ease the pain.

Now, having used this forum for ax-grinding—unprovoked by any of the discussants—let me deal with issues they raise.

I am surprised and pleased that most agreed with the point that seems to me the most important and controversial in the paper, which is the implication that, for understanding personality development, we make even heavier use of the data and concepts relating to non-conflictual learning than analytic theory has done. One of Freud's astonishing contributions was to demonstrate how complicated "learning" can be, how much more intense, conflictual, and trauma-ridden it is, how unconscious forces dominate, modify, and distort the incorporation of reality. That being now established—the great battles behind us—analysts can afford to turn their attention to the study of other influences on the learning process. Were it not for the bad blood between psychoanalysts and academic learning theorists, we might more easily absorb their work— such as that on conditioning and imprinting—and weave it into our construction of personality development. Dr. Bowlby has been one of the greatest contributors to this advent; perhaps he will agree that psychoanalysis has been more sullen than graceful about considering the work of learning theorists.

Yet there is reason for approaching most learning theory cautiously; one wonders, on reading of non-conflictual forces in development, if the author does not recognize or has abandoned the position that trauma and frustration, conflict, resolution of conflict, and the unconscious forces and defense mechanisms enlisted in this process participate heavily in character structure. Perhaps this concerns Dr. Socarides when he reminds us that these factors are at the root of perversions. He knows I agree with him on this, and that I also agree with his thesis, which he expressed years before I did, that "the primary feminine identification with the mother" predisposes men to perversion.

Our main disagreement is on one precise point only: he believes that transsexualism is not merely sexual aberration but perversion, while I, although I agree with him about the nature of perversion, do not believe that transsexualism is etiologically or structurally a perversion. In order to clarify this stance, I have often written on the differential diagnosis of gender disorders, commenting especially that while I think most of those who request "sex change" procedures are perverse, i.e., motivated by severe unconscious conflict, I have come upon a small group—the most feminine of all—who do not seem of this sort. If, however, one considers as the overriding criterion for diagnosis that the patient requests "sex change," then, on calling all patients in this group "transsexuals," one will of course find, as Dr. Socarides has (and as have the rest of us), that most of these people are anxiety-ridden, suffer a multitude of perversions, sometimes are paranoid, and are otherwise disturbed. But those are not the transsexuals to which I refer in this or other papers.

To take up all of the points Dr. Socarides makes would only be to rewrite papers in which I have already dealt with many of them. Instead, let me extract what seems to me the crucial issue in his discussion and bring it forward into my thoughts on Dr. Mahler's comments, where it again appears, in a more subdued form: "From my own rather limited experience, it is difficult for me to believe that transsexuality ever takes place in the baby's earliest stages without severe trauma or conflict. . . ." I am so eager for data, and "rather limited experience" is ambiguous. I have never seen, in a family producing the extreme femininity I call transsexualism, the alleged blissful mother-infant relationship I describe nor heard reported the traumatic mother-infant relationship others assume. So I would settle not just for "rather limited experience" but simply for *one* observed case. Unless someone has actually made these observations, I do not see how my hypothesis is disproved any more than I can claim—in the absence of such data—that it is proved.

Dr. Mahler's research method and dedication to careful observation is the model that may rescue us, though it measures the crucial weakness of my research: my ideas on transsexuals are gathered from data generated several years after the fact. At the earliest, I have talked with families of severely gender-distorted children only when the children were already four or five years old. While there are ways of improving the reliability of one's information on how these infants were handled from birth on, conviction never quite sets in. When I claim there was an excessively close symbiosis, it is because I see how the mothers and their sons act at age four or five or later, at which time it seems to all of us in our research team that the symbiosis still exists and is too intense, too close, and lacking the barriers to intimacy necessary for separation and individuation of masculinity. We find the same in the stories the boys tell, draw, or play out with the toys in the playroom. We hear it from the fathers and from the grandparents. And I learned of it, and what I think are its origins, in the analysis of a mother who had such a son. Then, to cross-check the findings, I have compared those people I call transsexuals with others who also request "sex change" or cross-dress or try to pass as women or prefer intercourse with a person of the same sex, but who do not fulfill the criteria I have described elsewhere for that restricted group I call transsexuals. And in comparing these other groups—including analyzing their mothers—I have not found these later residues of this excessively close symbiosis. So I feel comfortable enough with the hypothesis—but not too comfortable.

In emphasizing these parental influences I have, for two reasons, said little about the infant's contribution, which Dr. Mahler underlines. First, this really cannot be measured by family histories or even the analyses of mothers, my main tools. Second, we cannot experience the inner mental life of preverbal infants so that we know what the infant makes of himself vis-à-vis his mother. I do think, however, that if one were lucky enough to stumble upon a family into which a transsexual-to-be infant boy has just been born, Dr. Mahler's research methodology would be a marvelous help. She has watched the communication between mothers and infants and seen how the behavior of each changes as a result.

Just a word about her idea that there is a constitutional predisposition in male transsexualism. So far, no method has revealed biological abnormality in those people whom I call transsexuals. Besides, we do not know how to measure constitutional predisposition; we can only guess at it. There is, however, a constitutional factor I have invariably found to be present: these infant boys are, from birth on, beautiful and graceful and warmly responsive to their mothers' mothering, so that the excessive intimacy is easily established. I presume that if the infant had a constitutional "push" away from mother, she would be defeated in her efforts to link herself indissolubly with what otherwise she molds into her perfect, feminized phallus.

So, we must all line up on one side or the other. There are those—the majority of analysts—who do not believe a major deviation in character structure can occur without trauma, anxiety, conflict, and neurotic resolution of conflict (Dr. Mahler is not one of these), and those who believe that areas of personality development can originate in non-conflictual situations. For a time we analysts will have to let it rest at that, but I do believe that those who bet on the conflict theory as the root of all deviation (not meaning here only sexual deviation) are going to have to invent more epicycles to make their universe run than will the rest of us. They may have to say, as for instance they do now about extreme femininity in males, that unobservable anxiety is only a mask for overwhelming anxiety and that unobservable trauma is really psychosis-producing trauma. In such a philosophic system, there is no place for an absence: absence can always be explained as powerful, silent presence; this is one of the great epistemological flaws of psychoanalytic theorizing.

Mme. de Saussure, with whose remarks I am in agreement, notes an aspect of the development of masculinity that could bear study, using the method of Dr. Mahler and her colleagues to collect data: the issue of premature or excessive expressions of "masculinity." My hunches regarding this come from such disparate and vulnerable sources as Shakespeare's *Coriolanus*, cigarette ads, and the study of female transsexuals, those most masculine of females. In the families of the latter, I found massive, premature disruption of the mother-infant symbiosis. These mothers, usually because of severe depression, were unable to provide intimacy, in their femaleness and femininity, that normal mothering provides; this little daughter was forced to mature too soon and too much, the maturity measured by the child's capacity not only to bear the premature separation but to appear to thrive under this trauma. Masculinity resulted when such an influence was coupled with father's encouraging the process and offering his own masculine interests as a source of positive identification.

And so I wonder if societies do not define masculinity— with a harshness that may have made great warriors but not great humans—by the capacity one displays for being free from mother's attraction, that is, not showing a yearning to merge with her in the blissful closeness experienced in infancy.

I am pleased that Dr. Josselyn has carried further the implications of separating out the oedipal "situation" from the oedipal "conflict." Perhaps even at this late date, when it is so old-fashioned, we can still benefit from the study of this crucial event. For instance, we might search out data that manifest the egosyntonic and non-traumatic in the child-parent relationship and distinguish these, in observation and theory-making, from those that are conflictual. Let us hope that painless and creative aspects of child development are not beneath the dignity of psychoanalytic theory and observation. The role of non-conflictual identification has still not been quite thought through in our theory of child development. Because our work keeps us immersed in pathology, I think that we tend to find only identification that is the result of trauma, frustration, and loss. With that emphasis, we not only lose a bridge to the findings of non-psychoanalytic workers; we run the risk of leaving our theory incomplete. It would be exciting to see a complete study, already begun by Freud, built upon Dr. Josselyn's question, "Is not the oedipal 'situation' in part the result of identification with the parent of the same sex, the oedipal conflict then partially a response to that identification?"

Dr. Bowlby's comment on the influence of powerfully delivered information, even if "demonstrably false and incompatible with information from other sources," stirs in me the old, fascinating question—exploited by philosophers and science-fiction writers, not to say playwrights and psychotics—whether what we know in the core of our being to be reality (whether the reality of ourself or of the outer world) may not at any point (or at all points) be false. Before we get too carried away with the apparent madness of the transsexual, who, in the face of the blatant reality of his body, says he feels the opposite within, let us wonder whether some of the givens of our own identities may in time be found "false" by new realities. We need only think of Lorenz's geese and ponder on the implications of Bowlby's own work to appreciate the transsexual's predicament. We need not do so if transsexualism is, as Dr. Socarides and others suggest, a delusion and not merely a false belief. That idea reflects a larger question, inherent in Bowlby's work and, in a different way, in mine: Are psychoanalysts doomed forever to trust that anything alien to their personal system of belief is not simply deviant but delusional? And, on the way to answering that question: Will we ever develop methods of research to permit us to answer such a question? Psychoanalysis, as we practice it, is not up to *that* task.

I regret not having discussed the many other rich ideas with which my colleagues have been so generous. But this is enough.

REFERENCES

Abelin, E. L. (1971), The role of the father in the separation-individuation process. In: *Separation-Individuation. Essays in Honor of Margaret S. Mahler*, ed. J. B. McDevitt & C. Settlage. New York: International Universities Press, pp. 229-252.

Bieber, I. et al. (1962), *Homosexuality*. New York: Basic Books.

Bowlby, J. (1969), *Attachment and Loss, 1: Attachment*. New York: Basic Books.

———— (1973), *Attachment and Loss, 2: Separation*. New York: Basic Books.

Greenacre, P. (1953), Penis awe and its relation to penis envy. In: *Drives, Affects, Behavior, 1*, ed. R. M. Loewenstein. New York: International Universities Press, pp. 176-190.

———— (1960), Considerations regarding the parent-infant relationship. *Internat. J. Psycho-Anal.*, 41:571-584.

———— (1966), Problems of overidealization of the analyst and of analysis: their manifestations in the transference and countertransference. *The Psychoanalytic Study of the Child*, 21:193-212. New York: International Universities Press.

Greenson, R. (1968), Dis-identifying from mother: its special importance for the boy. *Internat. J. Psycho-Anal.*, 49:370-374.

Kubie, L. C. & Mackie, J. B. (1968), Critical issues raised by operations for gender transmutation. *J. Nerv. Ment. Dis.*, 147:431-443.

Leites, N. (1971), *The New Ego*. New York: Science House.

Mahler, M. S. (1967), Abstract of discussion of Greenacre (1966). *Psychoanal. Quart.*, 36:637.

———— (1968), *On Human Symbiosis and the Vicissitudes of Individuation*. New York: International Universities Press.

Money, J. (1955), Hermaphroditism, gender and precocity in hyperadrenocorticism: psychologic findings. *Bull. Johns Hopkins Hosp.*, 96:253–264.

Money, J., Hampson, J. G. and Hampson, J. L. (1957), Imprinting and the establishment of gender role. *Arch. Neurol. Psychiat.*, 77:333-336.

Offer, D. (1969), *The Psychological World of the Teenager*. New York: Basic Books.

Peck, R. F. & Havighurst, R. J. (1960), *The Psychology of Character Development*. New York: Wiley.

Socarides, C. W. (1969), The desire for sexual transformation: a psychiatric evaluation of transsexualism. *Amer. J. Psychiat.*, 125:1419-1425.

———— (1970), A psychoanalytic study of the desire for sexual transformation ("transsexualism"): the plaster-of-paris man. *Internat. J. Psychoanal.*, 51:341-349.

———— (1971), J. Marmor's position is examined in the review of *Dynamics of Deviant Sexuality*, ed., J. H. Masserman. *Psychoanal. Quart.*, 40:689-692.

Stoller, R. J. (1968), *Sex and Gender*. New York: Science House.

Winnicott, D. W. (1960), The theory of the parent-infant relationship. *Internat. J. Psycho-Anal.*, 41:585-595.

Extra-analytic Transference: A Two-way Tide

JOSEPH M. NATTERSON, M.D.

Dr. Natterson is Associate Clinical Professor of Psychiatry at the University of Southern California. He is a Training Analyst in and Past President of the Southern California Psychoanalytic Institute. He has published papers on the psychology of fatal illness, emotional characteristics and problems of medical students, technical problems in psychotherapy, and other aspects of psychiatry and psychoanalysis.

Discussants

LAJOS SZÉKELY, PH.D.

Dr. Székely is in private practice and on the Faculties of the Swedish Psychoanalytical Institute and the University of Stockholm. For many years he was Consultant at the Municipal Child Guidance Clinic of Stockholm, and subsequently at Danderyd (near Stockholm) and at the Psychiatric Clinic of Söder Sjukhuset. He has written on scientific creativity and other subjects.

EDITH BUXBAUM, PH.D.

Dr. Buxbaum has an impressive background in psychoanalytic education and service. She is a child analyst and a training analyst, and has written a number of papers related to the topic of transference.

A. LIMENTANI, F.R.C.P.

Training Analyst and Chairman of the Education Committee, British Psychoanalytical Society, Dr. Limentani is a Fellow of the Royal College of Psychiatry and for the past 12 years has been Consultant Psychotherapist at the Portman Clinic, London. He has published papers on acting out, drug dependence, selection for psychoanalysis, and problems of analyzability.

ALBERT MASON, M.D.

A British-trained psychoanalyst of the Klein Group, Dr. Mason came to the United States five years ago. He is Associate Clinical Professor of Psychiatry at the University of Southern California and on the Faculties of the Southern California Psychoanalytic Institute and of the Los Angeles Psychoanalytic Society and Institute, where he teaches a course on "The British School of Psychoanalysis."

LUCIA E. TOWER, M.D.

Dr. Tower is Emeritus Clinical Professor of Psychiatry of the School of Medicine of the University of Illinois and a Training Analyst and Staff Physician of the Chicago Institute for Psychoanalysis. Her special interests, besides teaching, have centered around psychosomatic medicine and problems of countertransference.

LEO STONE, M.D.

On the Faculty of the New York Psychoanalytic Institute and Past Director of its Treatment Center, Dr. Stone has had a long-standing interest in problems of transference and the analytic situation. Of his published materials dealing with these subjects, particularly relevant to Dr. Natterson's paper are his book *The Psychoanalytic Situation: An Examination of Its Development and Essential Nature*, and an article, "The Psychoanalytic Situation and Transference: Postscript to an Earlier Communication."

Extra-analytic Transference: A Two-way Tide

Joseph M. Natterson, M.D.
Beverly Hills, California

> It is a good divine that follows his own instructions. I can easier teach twenty what were good to be done, than be one of the twenty to follow mine own teaching.
>
> —Portia, in *The Merchant of Venice*

In this paper i will use actual clinical occurrences to establish my observations that some transferences follow a course other than what, to my knowledge, has been expressed to date in the literature on this subject, and that their management requires somewhat different measures. As my ideas and recommendations are developed, I hope the analyst-reader will try to view them without preconception and will ask himself whether they conform to his own observations and interventions.

Intense, significant, autonomous transference reactions toward persons and situations outside the analytic relationship are regular occurrences throughout the course of extended psychoanalyses. In day-to-day practice they are handled effectively and discriminatingly by experienced psychoanalysts. But in specific discussions of technique, these phenomena tend to be overlooked or incompletely elucidated, or regarded as unfortunate nonanalytic complications which require deviation from established technique.

The psychoanalytic situation is complex, and efforts to simplify it are both understandable and desirable; however, there are times when such reductionist efforts not only result in glossing over certain complicating and important facts but prevent us from recognizing and exploring them.

I do not challenge the firmly established fact that hidden

transferences to the analyst may find displaced expression toward extra-analytic objects. The method of free association permits the analyst to observe these displacements, to draw valid inferences as to the submerged transference attitudes directed at him, and, through interpretation, to make the analysand conscious of them. But some transferences follow a different course, and, accordingly, they must be managed differently. We can understand their dynamics and see how they influence the analytic relationship by dealing with three essential issues: (1) the occurrence of more or less autonomous transferences outside the analytic relationship; (2) how these transferences may flow into the analytic relationship; (3) the correct method of dealing with these events; and some related unanswered questions.

The term "transference" designates reactions ultimately based on events in early life being re-experienced in the present, without conscious understanding. Psychoanalytic technique is designed to identify, interpret, and extinguish or reduce these transferences; but if the analyst attempts to define and interpret all transference reactions *only* in terms of the analytic relationship, he may impede the process of psychoanalytic cure, because a priori assumptions about dealing with transference, inflexibly followed, may have an inadvertent paradoxical effect of increasing, rather than reducing, resistance, through the corrosive effect these assumptions may have upon the therapeutic alliance.

For instance, instead of a growing, exuberant zest for open communication (aside from transient and shifting affective states), a sullen sense of not feeling understood may insidiously develop in the patient, masked by a falsely compliant attitude in which he vainly hopes to achieve his goal by telling the analyst "what he wants to hear" rather than "telling it like it is." Also, if the analyst follows such an unvarying practice, it may often be insufficient for the achievement of sensitive, tactful, and elegant interpretations, just as exclusion of the immediate external life situation of the patient from the analyst's formulation may also detract from the effectiveness of his interpretation. This latter factor can be especially pertinent early in the analysis, when the therapeutic alliance needs to be nurtured.

Just as the analyst should move fluently from present to past and from past to present in his response to the patient's productions, so should he also be sensitive to similar reciprocal resonance between the intra-analytic and the extra-analytic aspects of the analysand's ongoing psychological experiences. *With each transference interpretation, the analyst must make an important and delicate decision regarding the locale of the transference.* To a large extent the decision will be determined by the patient's associations, but the analyst's own frame of reference will also be a conditioning factor in the decision. The following example, reported to me by a colleague (Comess, 1969), will illustrate the point.

Mr. G. had seemed to be in a state of high resistance for several months. He dealt almost exclusively with his marital difficulties, in a repetitive and apparently unproductive way. The analyst's efforts to bring the unhappy and discontented emotions into the analytic relationship were consistently unsuccessful and he was aware of increasing frustration, on the conscious basis that the analytic work was not progressing.

In this morning's session he suddenly became aware that his attitude and interventions had become increasingly critical toward the patient, in the manner of a disappointed parent berating a recalcitrant child. He discussed this transference-countertransference development with Mr. G., indicating that he had not accorded Mr. G.'s marital situation sufficient autonomous importance and had been attempting prematurely to relate it to the transference neurosis.

Immediately, and visibly, the patient's silent tension ebbed, to be replaced by an abundance of associations reaching deep into early childhood, all demonstrating his feelings as a chronically disappointed child whose complaints evoked parental impatience and angry criticism. He could now better understand his relationship with his wife, and for the first time could appreciate these same previously disguised dynamics in his relationship with the analyst.

In retrospect, the analyst could see that if he had been

more open and less ready to regard the patient's productions merely as displacement and resistance, the crucial insight might have been achieved much sooner.

In this instance the analyst failed to perceive immediately that the transference reaction to the wife deserved a position of temporary relative autonomy and primacy and that the patient's repeated emphasis on the relationship with the wife contained important clues to, *as well as* serving, the resistance. As the analyst became aware that by insisting first on connecting the patient's associations with the analytic relationship he was in fact playing up to the patient's unconscious sadomasochistic needs, he was then able to break up the log jam.

In a cross-sectional sense the question of whether the patient was displacing attitudes from the analyst became almost irrelevant, for the patient's experiencing and observing egos were involved mainly with his wife. If the analyst had accepted this earlier, the similar transference fantasies regarding him might have emerged sooner, and without the painful transference-countertransference impasse. Thus, the long-range goal of thorough elucidation of the dynamics of the analytic relationship is fostered rather than impeded by the analyst's readiness to accept transference *wherever it is immediately located.* No either/or choice is required of him.

Greenson (1967) writes: "Another question should be raised concerning the extent to which the transference neurosis totally replaces the patient's neurosis. I have had the experience that some aspects of the patient's neurosis become displaced onto a figure in the patient's outside life, who then appears to function as a supplementary transference figure. For example, many of my male patients fall in love romantically with a woman during the course of their analysis. This is a transference manifestation but occurs outside the analysis" (p. 187).

Later in the same paragraph, Greenson promises to discuss the technique of managing such manifestations in a forthcoming second volume, clearly indicating his recognition that transference reactions of considerable magnitude frequently do occur outside the analysis. Also, he tentatively implies that they may not be expressions of the transference neurosis, and that specific techniques may be required for the analysis of such manifestations.

Loewenstein (1958) reports some related but somewhat different experiences: "Another very important empirical rule calls for the interpretation of transference manifestations in preference to other parts of the material. There exist differences of opinion on this point. Some analysts consider this rule valid for all transference phenomena. Others believe that merely transference resistance should be analyzed first, whereas the remaining transference phenomena should be analyzed only toward the end of the analysis. In a few rare cases, however, neither view seems applicable. Manifestations of very violent, ambivalent transference resistance, particularly such as repeated habitual modes of behavior toward other persons, may prove completely unanalyzable when approached directly. A detour over less intensely cathected reactions outside the transference area may be required to overcome this type of resistance" (p. 207).

Loewenstein's cases, unlike Greenson's, suffer from a specific ego defect which prevents explicit focus on the transference neurosis. He affirms that in such cases the success of the psychoanalytic work may hinge on interpreting *outside* rather than *within* the analytic relationship. In my opinion, this carries the misleading implication that in the absence of such ego defects interpretation can and should be carried out exclusively in terms of the transference neurosis. Yet both authors clearly acknowledge the significant occurrence of transference reactions outside the psychoanalytic relationship in the course of psychoanalytic treatment.

In his paper "Transference Outside the Psychoanalytic Situation," Haas (1966) states that ". . . it is not only justifiable but indispensable to analyse and interpret the behavior of the patient towards other persons, that is, his interpersonal relations in the frame of the transference" (p. 422). By "other persons," Haas, of course, means persons other than the analyst. He goes on: "This point of view seems obvious and yet we find that it is not sufficiently appreciated, although this may be far more true in theory than in actual clinical practice" (p. 422).

Delicately but unmistakably Haas here contends that psychoanalysts do not always preach what they practice. However, in his illustrative case material and specific recommendations he emphasizes that "transference outside the analytic situation acquires special significance in the therapeutic procedure of such cases where the transference to the analyst remains superficial, 'uneventful'" (p. 426).

Unfortunately, Haas does not deal specifically with the necessity of recognizing and interpreting such extra-analytic transference in typical psychoanalyses, wherein the transference to the analyst *is* intense and *not* superficial, for there are many ways in which significant and observable extra-analytic transference reactions may strongly affect the relationship to the analyst. I will discuss and illustrate four of them.

1. *The transient, minor variations in the affective coloring of the patient's attitude to the analyst, induced by external events.* From day to day, the analysand may begin his session with widely varying affects: tension, sadness, boredom, exhilaration, irritation, and so on. Very often, perhaps more often than not, the analyst is included in these feelings. These initial attitudes may recede as the hour progresses, or they may persist through the entire session. A certain number of these reactions are evoked by external events—their shifting, transient, and unpredictable nature increases the likelihood that they are—rather than being expressions of the transference neurosis. If the analyst so assesses their nature, he should not attempt to squeeze such superficial reactions into some awkward formulation involving the analytic relationship, for such forced interpretations can generate tension and resistance.

On the other hand, if the analyst hears the patient out and perhaps makes some simple acknowledgment that the mood is a spill-over from the outside event, then different and deeper thoughts and feelings may emerge, more pertinent than the event itself to the analytic relationship and to the patient's neurotic problems. Thus, minor transferences flow into the analysis from other sources.

To perceive the relative superficiality and evanescence of such reactions permits the analyst to respond to them easily and fluently; he will not be misled into premature and incorrect interpretations of the transference neurosis. The patient will feel accepted and understood, even in his chameleon-like variability and inconstancy.

2. *Deeply moving reality experiences which cause a basic shift in the transference attitude in the analysis.* The following clinical incident illustrates this kind of event.

Dr. J. is 39 years old, married, a specialist in internal medicine. Depression, tendencies toward obsessional rumination over his masculine and professional adequacies, and subnormal assertiveness brought him to analysis when he was 36. He is an only child whose father, now retired, had been a successful, shrewd, and bombastic businessman.

During these three years of analysis, in which Dr. J. had experienced moderate symptomatic improvement, his childhood memories consistently dealt with the controlling, ill-tempered, and capricious father, who made life miserable for the long-suffering and kind mother as well as for the boy. When irritable or frustrated, Dr. J. regularly thought of me as a polite version of his father. He consistently idealized his mother and had never expressed negative or erotic feelings for her. There was a rather sustained corresponding idealization of me as the analyst.

Then, in his own practice, his favorite patient unexpectedly developed a severe recurrence of her chronic colitis. Dr. J. came to his analytic session feeling terribly guilty, as though he were "a failure," "a boy trying to do a man's job." And with intense shame and embarrassment he recalled, for the first time in the analysis, incidents of physical intimacy with his mother during puberty: squeezing blackheads on her nose, and once being in bed with her and fingering her pubic hair, with his typically angry father nearby. With these recollections, he immediately felt a wave of affection and sympathy for his excluded father, a sad wish that his father could have been strong enough to prevent the seduction, and a novel sense of resentment toward his seductive and guilt-inducing mother. He became aware that he had overreacted to his patient's decompensation, and his anxiety and guilt in that area diminished.

At his next session, Dr. J. reported that after the previous analytic hour he had learned that his barber had gone bankrupt. That night he *dreamed*: The barber shop is closed; the barber is bankrupt. He awoke with a recurrence of depression, guilt, and apprehension.

The barber seemed to symbolize aggressive, guilty, and erotic feelings toward both parents. Associations dealt mainly with Dr. J.'s need for the analyst to be strong and capable of helping him through this crisis in his practice, with anxious expectations that I would fail him as his father had in the fateful childhood incident.

These psychoanalytic events were gradually followed by a striking shift in the available transference. His previous black-and-white view of the analyst was abolished, and his frequent but elusive doubts about me now became explainable. Similarly, he abandoned his previous equating of the analyst's quietness with weakness. Quietness was now equivalent to strength and guidance, bluster and noisiness equivalent to the hapless father. From this time onward, his fearful fury toward me began to reach the surface, until the previously repressed negative mother-transference had become an open and negotiable part of the analysis.

It appears that a sudden, painful, and surprising change in an eroticized relationship, which had previously been satisfying and idealized in the analysand's professional life, induced a significant shift in the transference to the analyst, with much therapeutic gain for the patient.

3. *Life situations which may accelerate emergence of the transference.* An event in the patient's outside life which brings a budding transference attitude into full bloom is exemplified in the following clinical vignette.

Mr. M. is 28 years old, single, a musician and writer who

initially sought analysis because of sexual and occupational impotence. His father had been a successful businessman and his mother a celebrated theatrical personality. His sister, and only sibling, was two years older than he. The father had been a World War II pilot and absent during most of the patient's preoedipal life. The mother was compulsive, ineffectual, irritable, and domineering in the home. Mr. M. felt strongly attached to his mother, but was uncomfortable with her and tended to avoid her. He saw his father as a pleasant but relatively unimportant figure in his life. His sister seduced him during his puberty, and they had sexual intercourse regularly over a period of several months. This situation was completely controlled by the sister, which was also reflected in their copulatory position.

Initially in the analysis, the patient's resistance was mainly manifested by his bored, indifferent, blasé, and imperturbable manner and attitude toward the analysis, the analyst, and almost everyone else in his life. He reported unusual and sometimes illegal sexual practices and drug use, but with languid indifference, as though he were describing a dull meal. As the resistance was reduced, an attitude developed of friendly devotion and idealized respect for the analyst. Homosexual memories from childhood and adolescence became abundant, and noteworthy relief of his symptoms occurred. Concomitantly there was an abundance of angry and anxious associations to his sister and mother. For the first time in his life he began to enjoy sustained potency in a relationship with one woman, although it was stormy and ambivalent.

As Mr. M. normalized his sexual life, he began to take more seriously the question of aggressive competition with men. Hints of a rising undercurrent of aggressive challenge toward me were now in evidence, but these had not yet achieved threshold level.

At this point, in his third year of analysis, Mr. M. made an important decision: He would leave his secure, remunerative job and go into an independent business venture in the same field his father had been in. (It should be noted that during the previous year he had been taking flying lessons and, like his father, had become a proficient pilot.) With pride and enthusiasm, he visited his parents to share his exciting plans with them. His father reacted by becoming very concerned over his son's long hair, accusing him of not looking like a man, and, insisting that long hair would cause him to fail in business, approached him with scissors in hand.

Although Mr. M. said he was still greatly disappointed and depressed by the incident, he reported it in a remote and languid manner, typical of his behavior at the onset of treatment. I told him that his latent expectation of a damaging attack from me had been activated by his father's behavior, that there was much anger toward me coexisting with all this, and that he was handling his fear and rage by his old defense of passive retreat. Instantly, he experienced a mounting rage toward me and began ranting about quitting (a frequent theme of the recent past). As his rage increased, his words became blocked, and he wanted to tear his shirt. Suddenly, he recognized that he felt exactly as he had before treatment, when he would sit at his typewriter unable to think of anything to write, and also that he felt crushed, simply not equal to the task of indicting me. As the hour approached its close and he realized more fully the negative father-transference feelings toward me, he became amused at the fact that in recent fantasies he had even been constructing an image of me as a very conservative Republican, like his father.

This incident, in which a poignant external event catalyzed a germinating transference attitude in the analysis, was a turning point for the patient. He became increasingly free in expressing feelings of a competitive nature toward me, with associated insights that have strengthened his masculine identity and reduced the prior strong feminine identification.

4. *Transference directed to objects outside the analysis.* This final category concerns externally directed transference which helps to conceal significant transference to the analyst by the dramatic appeal of the external event and by the induction of a superficial but deceptive transference attitude to the analyst.

The analysand is a 41-year-old successful politician who had

274 —

begun analysis a year and a half previously following a brief, acute episode of coronary insufficiency. He had been smoking three packs of cigarettes per day, and a chronically bad marital situation had become an incessant nightmare prior to the heart problem. He was the second son of an Idaho sheep rancher, deceased. The mother had since remarried. The older brother had died in combat in Korea. The patient had felt that members of his large extended family blamed him as being indirectly responsible for the deaths of his father and brother.

In his childhood and adolescence he regarded his parents as ideally and lovingly mated, although in retrospect he sees them as having been addicted to saccharine phoniness, suppressing their real feelings. After a boisterous childhood and puberty, he became a compliant, excessively sweet, sexually and aggressively inhibited person. In college he started pre-ministerial training, but when he realized that such a career would be too frustrating, he withdrew and prepared for a career in politics. His intelligence, his capacity for constructive community work, and his appealing, genial personality helped toward his success.

Even before marriage, he realized that his wife-to-be would thwart his masculine needs, but he felt inexplicably drawn to her and experienced much guilt and anxiety whenever he contemplated pulling away from her. The marriage more than fulfilled his negative expectations. After years of futile fidelity he began a series of extramarital adventures, but these afforded him no significant relief. Then, recognizing the connection between the coronary insufficiency and his emotionally turbulent life, he decided that he needed inner clarification and strengthening, and entered analysis.

In the first year and a half he talked at great length about his wife's immaturity, implacability, and unavailability, and about his tension at public gatherings and committee meetings, in which he was always fearful of being disliked or depreciated. He behaved like an ideal boy scout in the analysis: pleasant, reasonable, and uncomplaining at all times about the analysis and me. His dreams of this period tended to portray me as either very supportive or very dangerous. Nonetheless, there was slow progress: a good therapeutic alliance was established; he became aware that he felt more like a boy than a man; he became somewhat more assertive professionally; and he was able to extricate himself sufficiently from the sadomasochistic marital embrace so that the marriage became more tolerable, although still barren. Only minor transient coronary symptoms occurred.

Then one morning he entered my office and asked in an unusually timid and deferential way, "Is it all right if I leave five minutes early today, because I have to get to an urgent legislative meeting?" Immediately I commented on his finding it necessary to behave appeasingly in order to tell me that he had to leave early. He explained that it was because of what had happened with his wife the previous night. Lately he had been feeling much better, she had seemed warmer toward him, and he was beginning to contemplate resuming a sexual life with her. Then, last evening, he had taken it upon himself to suggest to a neighbor, whose wife was recuperating from a recent injury, that their small children play together regularly. His wife became utterly furious and "shot me down." His affectionate and erotic feelings vanished and he became depressed and pessimistic. As he approached my office for this appointment he wanted to *tell* me that he was leaving early, but he became tense and guilty and had to revise it to *implore* me—he just felt he didn't have the right to assert himself with me, for if he did, I would shoot him down as his wife had done the night before when he had asserted himself.

Initially I evaluated this behavior with me as an acute passive-masochistic response to his fantasy of my castrating him, triggered by his wife's behavior. However, as exploration proceeded in subsequent sessions, a more important and subtle meaning emerged. For some time he had been experiencing wishes for tender, physical closeness to me but was unable to mention them, from guilt and shame. He recognized that his wishes for affectionate closeness to his wife had become a vehicle for the suppressed urges toward me. His appeasing behavior was thus not only an attempt to avoid castration, but also an indirect plea to me to behave lovingly, unlike his wife, and thereby gratify the unexpressed wishes. Thus the incident with the wife was both an unconscious communication of and a screen, through displacement, for unacknowledged longings for the analyst. That same emotionally evocative encounter with the wife appears also to have been a crucial link in the chain of events leading to the direct emergence of important transference longing for the analyst which had heretofore been stringently warded off.

As these largely father-based longings were worked through, the patient, for the first time in the analysis, began to express long-suppressed anger and criticism toward me. The assertive increment thus gained has not since been lost.

I feel that this last example demonstrates how complex and instructive the interplay of transference attitudes, both internal and external to the analytic relationship, can be. As indicated in this case, more than one level of meaning can be discerned if careful attention is paid to the flow of transference in such situations.

The psychoanalytic literature, from Freud to the present, is replete with case reports wherein reactions to events in the current extra-analytic life situations are prominent. The reader is often left with the impression that for analytic purposes such reality events are merely static associative units which provide clues for the analyst, analogous to the fingerprints which have meaning to the detective only insofar as they help him identify the real culprit. The best-known recent texts on psychoanalytic technique, by Glover (1955), Menninger (1958), and Greenson (1967), fully emphasize the essential value for the psychoanalysis of abundant material from the ongoing life of the analysand, but of the three authors, only Greenson offers clear clinical suggestions about the technical approach to the reality data, and he does so with some apparent reluctance.

I have tried in this paper to show that knowledge of intra-analytic wishes and fantasies is increased rather than diminished by an attitude of respect toward extra-analytic neurotic responses, especially when this attitude includes the basic implicit question, "What is the real and complete meaning of this reaction?" To exclude the possibility of significant external transference reactions once the analytic relationship is well established on the basis, for example, of the decathexis of external objects would seem to be employing a metapsychological assumption to fly in the face of empirical evidence. Relatively, the patient's neurotic investment in the analyst does increase, while his neurotic investment in the rest of his life decreases. But the territory between relative and absolute can sometimes bear a rich harvest of useful insight. The purpose of this paper is not to substitute one focus of attention for another, but rather to *extend* the analyst's attention to an additional area of transference relevance without de-emphasizing the central importance of the analytic relationship.

Certainly, if the analyst places too much emphasis on the autonomous role of transference reactions outside the analysis he may become excessively interested in such externals and relatively neglectful of the intra-analytic process. And even if his wish is to elucidate the transference neurosis, his interest in the autonomous meanings of the external events may cause him to overlook very crucial displacement tendencies of the analysand who thereby succeeds, as we saw in the case illustrations, in concealing his transference to the analyst.

It may be argued that each type of situation offered above is simply one form or another of displacement from the transference relationship to the analyst, and that the attempt to accord autonomous transference meaning to these extra-analytic events is a misleading emphasis on epiphenomena. In this context, I do not think that displacement can be discussed as separate from transference, for the concept of transference itself is based in part on displacement from early life to adult life, in order to maintain the infantile amnesia.

An identical function is served by displacement from the analyst to external objects, namely, to maintain in repression these same infantile conflicts which attach themselves to the analyst during the course of the analysis. It therefore becomes difficult and inconsistent to assume that displacement from the analysis has occurred in situations in which transference flows from the outside into the analysis. The repressive purpose of displacement is not accomplished if the transference appears in the analytic relationship.

If the above reasoning is unacceptable, then some other explanation should be offered to support the position that a transference attitude is first displaced from the analyst to an outside object and then returned to the analyst as a manifest attitude. It is more logical to be parsimonious and regard the primary transference event as having occurred outside the analysis. *The evidence does not support the assumption that when a transference neurosis is established extra-analytic transference reactions no longer occur.* Had all of the cases illustrated been reported in full rather than as selected clinical facts pertinent to the earlier discussion, the situation probably would be seen to be mixed, with transference moving in both directions, as is the case in any field of action.

Several conditions are necessary for the valid determination of an extra-analytically engendered transference reaction which influences the transference to the analyst. First and foremost, the analyst must accept the possibility of such a sequence of events. Second, a listening attitude of evenly hovering attention and open-mindedness will enable him to be alert to such developments. Next, it is an important clue when dreams and associations indicate that the transference to the analyst has undergone an acute change which was not predictable or not adequately explainable on the basis of the existing analytic relationship. Reality events of great meaning for the analysand are obviously particularly apt for the evocation of such reactions. Finally, since the event may be part of a mixed picture, it may be necessary to recognize the presence of such a trend even while concentrating the interpretive action on the analytic relationship. For example, the analyst may parenthetically note in his interpretation that the external event has contributed to the quality and intensity of a reaction. Or, if he does not elect to do this, he may still be influenced in his timing, choice of words, and tone by his simply understanding that more is going on than just a neurotic reaction to the analyst himself.

Summary

There are a number of significant but often neglected ways in which extra-analytic transference reactions may affect the relationship to the analyst.

First are the transient, minor variations in the affective coloring of the patient's attitude to the analyst, induced by external events.

Second, massive transference responses, elicited by some life situation of an acute and significant character, may cause a drastic and deep shift in the intra-analytic transference attitude.

Third, life situations may conveniently coincide with developing transference to the analyst and may accelerate its emergence.

Fourth, transferences directed to objects outside the analysis may serve as a complex screening device to obscure crucial transference reactions to the analyst.

Transference reactions to situations and persons outside the analysis are illustrated by case histories and described as often having meaning other than, or in addition to, the usually inferred displacement resistance.

For optimal recognition of and response to such situations, the analyst must accept the possibility that transference flows into, as well as out of, the analytic relationship throughout the analysis; he must approach the patient's productions without preconception so that he may be open to recognizing this development; he must be alert to dreams and associations which indicate an unpredicted, acute change in the transference; and he must remain aware of the presence of such a trend even while focusing his interpretive action on the analytic relationship.

The inclusion of such a perspective in the analyst's approach reduces resistance, improves the therapeutic alliance, and adds to the depth and breadth of the psychoanalytic experience.

Discussion

LAJOS SZÉKELY, PH.D.

Nacka, Sweden

I agree with Dr. Natterson that one of the most difficult tasks in the art of analysis is to distinguish between the intrusion of an autonomous extra-analytic transference into the analytic situation and the displaced expression of hidden transference to the analyst toward persons outside of the psychoanalytic situation. I confess that it is much harder to see the issues clearly in my own analyses than it is to detect and clear them up in the analyses conducted by my supervisees.

That transference is a universal mental phenomenon which lies at the base of perhaps all human relationships was already hinted at in one of Freud's (1905) early communications on this topic, in the famous postscript to the case of "Dora": "Psychoanalytic treatment does not *create* transferences, it merely brings them to light . . ." (p. 117). Two decades later, in "Autobiographical Study" (1925), he declares again that transference ". . . is a universal phenomenon of the human mind . . . and in fact dominates the whole of each person's relation to his human environment" (p. 42).

As with transference within the analytic situation, transference manifestations in relation to other persons must therefore be regarded as unavoidable. Nevertheless, some analysts seem to have overlooked Freud's dictum and interpret all transference manifestations exclusively in terms of the analytic situation.

Dr. Natterson has given a great deal of thought to this subject. He warns that if the analyst misinterprets some serious extra-analytic involvement of his patient, the patient will feel that he is not being understood. This can disturb the working alliance of the patient-analyst relationship, or, even worse, a seemingly complaint attitude develops toward the analyst, preventing progress in the working-through. I can corroborate Dr. Natterson's findings.

He describes four typical instances in which extra-analytic transferences to persons in the patient's daily life have a bearing on the development of the transference within the analysis. It would have been interesting if Dr. Natterson had discussed in this context the phenomenon of acting out. I believe we can learn much about the two-way stream of the transference phenomenon from the analyses of adolescents and children.

I consider the greatest merit of Dr. Natterson's paper to be his raising of these fundamental points. Firstly, some analysts have difficulty in seeing clearly and interpreting adequately the intra- or extra-analytic locus of the transference reaction *hic et nunc*; furthermore, they seem to have difficulty in determining in which direction the transference is moving. As the author rightly observes, the question is seldom raised in the literature on therapeutic technique. And I wonder, without being able to answer, what importance the analyst's countertransference has?

Secondly, we usually distinguish between mere transference reaction and transference neurosis proper. Bird (1972) in a recent paper very succinctly discusses the difference between them. The term "transference reaction" refers to all sorts of feelings, expectations, attitudes, etc., which represent reprints or new editions of the past. These are cathexes displaced from one object to another, repeating the past in the present. Via the flow of extra-analytic transference into the analytic situation, the boundary between two separate object-representations—that of the analyst and of some other person—becomes diffused. Of course, the transference can also flow in the opposite direction; that is, intra-analytic transference may also flow out of the analytic situation. However, the self-representation of the subject and the representation of the analyst have remained clearly separated. This is not the case in the transference neurosis proper; here the patient includes the analyst "somehow in the structure or part structure of his neurosis" (Bird, 1972). The boundary between the patient's self-representation and the representation of the analyst is lost, "and for the moment and for the particular area affected by the transference neurosis, the [analyst] comes to represent *the patient himself* . . . or more specifically, some element of [the patient's] ego, superego, drives, defenses, etc."

It seems to me, from the short clinical vignette from the analysis of Mr. G., that his case fits Bird's metapsychological description of the transference neurosis proper. Mr. G.'s relationship to his wife has been disturbed not only as a result of displaced transference reactions but also by his seeming to have included his wife in some part of his neurotic structure. The boundary between Mr. G.'s self-representation and his wife-representation has become diffuse as a result of regression.

If transference, in Freud's words, "is a universal phenomenon of the human mind, and in fact dominates the whole of each person's relations to his human environment," then we must admit the possibility not merely of transference reactions, but even of transference neurosis proper, outside of the psychoanalytic situation.

The term "transference neurosis" has been used hitherto in two different senses: as the name of a diagnostic group (hysterias and compulsive-obsessional conditions) as distinguished from the narcissistic disorders, and as the neurosis which displaces the patient's neurosis during the therapeutic process (as distinguished from mere transference reactions). If Bird's above-mentioned metapsychological description of the transference neurosis proper is correct, transference neurosis is not limited to the psychoanalytic situation, and the term is redundant.

From our experiences over the last decades, we have come to realize that since hysterics and obsessive neurotics are not the only ones who develop transference neurosis during psychoanalytic therapy, the term as referring to a diagnostic category has lost its meaning. Furthermore, cases with character disturbances, chronically depressive people, and borderline personalities are very prone to include people from their everyday lives in their infantile self-representations. We must therefore re-examine our use of the term "transference neurosis."

Dr. Natterson has most usefully called our attention to the care that must be taken in determining the direction in which and the area from which transferences—both reactions and developing transference neurosis—are moving from moment to moment during the course of treatment.

EDITH BUXBAUM, PH.D.

Seattle, Washington

Natterson's paper concerns itself with extra-analytic transferences which are incorrectly handled by the analyst. He warns that such "reductionist efforts" to "squeeze" every expression of feeling toward another person into a transference interpretation increases the resistance and may jeopardize the transference, and ultimately the analysis. Natterson's advice is well taken; it is not new and has been dealt with frequently in the literature, obviously because the mistakes he points out tend to be repeated by the beginning analyst, and often enough by experienced analysts who treat patients with preconceived ideas rather than by observation based upon the analyst's free-floating attention.

Natterson's approach to the problem is rather reductionist in itself. Transference is a universal phenomenon and the most difficult aspect of analysis (Bird, 1972). Freud (1925) says, "It must not be supposed, however, that transference is created by analysis and does not occur apart from it. Transference is merely uncovered and isolated by analysis. It is a universal phenomenon of the human mind, it decides the success of all medical influence and, in fact, dominates the whole of each person's relations to his human environment" (p. 42). Accordingly, Silverberg (1948) does not limit transference to the psychoanalytic therapy situation, but rather treats it as a specific dynamism that may enter into any interpersonal relationship (Orr, 1954, p. 632); Horney (1939) advocates horizontal interpretations of the patient's disturbances in current interpersonal relationships, including the analytic relationship, as opposed to vertical interpretation that relates everything back to infancy and childhood, and warns that any rigidity in the analysis may render it utterly unproductive, which agrees with Sylvia Payne's (1946) opinion that "any stereotyped transference interpretation will be liable to interfere with the progress of the case" (p. 15). Fenichel (1939) says somewhat impatiently, "Interpreting of transference . . . [is] no special problem . . .: the surface first of all, the defense before the instinct" (p. 73). Obviously, if one analyzes from the surface, extra-analytic relationships will be included in the material if the patient has any meaningful human relations at all. The concept of transference is taken here in its broadest sense, which considers all human relations as derived and displaced from the first love-objects. The transference neurosis has to be considered as a special form which concentrates neurotic reactions upon the analyst. Some people are reluctant to use the term "transference neurosis" and prefer to speak of an accumulation of transference reactions which pass kaleidoscopically through the analysis.

During the analysis we observe transitions from father-transferences to mother-transferences, from positive to negative; but other people who were of importance in the patient's life, past and present, also enter the transference picture. Sometimes it is possible to see one figure as a later edition of a previous one; at other times we find that the patient has introduced a different scene of his life. Edoardo Weiss (1946) says, "At times it is advantageous to have a 'divided transference'" (Orr, 1954, p. 644). We speak frequently of a "split transference." Some patients see their love-objects split into good and bad, e.g., a good mother and a bad mother; they will most likely also split the transference, one part of which can be transferred to a person outside the analytic situation. However, such patients will frequently feel that they themselves also have two sides, at least. (Laing, in "The Divided Self" [1969], deals extensively with this aspect.) In the course of therapy they may recognize such split object representations

— 285

as projections of the two sides of themselves, the instinctual and the superego. Edoardo Weiss (1946) considers the advantage of a "divided transference" to be the possibility of "keeping the therapy close to the patient's real problems by realistic counterbalancing of analytic and extra-analytic transference reactions and interpretations [which] tends to give the patient awareness of his emotions, to make insight more realistic and convincing" (p. 49).

Annie Reich (1958), in a panel discussion on "Variations of Classical Technique," like Edoardo Weiss, seems to welcome the split transference temporarily, saying, "The analyst remains outside for a time—and is not completely the butt of unsatisfiable libidinal demands and aggressive impulses until slowly, with the progress of the analysis, a shift of cathexis and the establishment of a genuine transference can be achieved" (p. 230). She attributes this split to a particular form of superego pathology.

In the same panel, Bouvet (1958) speaks about distance and rapprochement. He discusses "distance" as something that the patient needs in order to facilitate the establishment of the transference. At times in particular cases he analyzes the patient's transference to extra-analytic objects, considering the therapist as "the projection of a beneficial image of an idealized kind, which will help the patient throughout his analysis" (p. 213). As long as this kind of distance is needed, the analyst is confined to reflecting the patient's feelings and ideas. As the need for distance diminishes and the patient begins to allow a rapprochement, interpretations and interventions become possible. "The source of distance in relationship is projection. Since projection is unconscious and is almost always present, the significant object is transformed into a likeness of the subject or of internal objects" (p. 212). This concept has been more recently elaborated on by Kohut (1968).

In his paper "The Transference Neurosis: Comments on the Concept and the Phenomenon," Hans Loewald (1971), like Bouvet, discusses the emotional distance which some patients have to maintain, so that "much analytic work may have to take place at a considerable remove from the transference arena itself. . . . It probably indicates that such patients have to maintain a kind of narcissistic screen behind which significant inner reorganization may take place . . . as though the poignant interactions and passions of the transference have to be filtered through this protective screen in order to be bearable and useful" (p. 66).

Such great sensitivity on the part of the analyst is far removed from the transference interpretations at any cost, which feed the analyst's narcissism and at best don't help the patient, and very often hurt him. It is in the nature of the analyst's empathy with the patient to demand more from the analyst than a knowledge of psychoanalytic technique; the empathy is an aspect of the analyst's countertransference. Whether we consider transference to be a universal phenomenon of the human mind, as Freud calls it, or an ego function, as Bryan Bird calls it, the analyst too has the tendency and the ability to develop transference reactions. His advantage over the patient is his awareness of this tendency. When he develops transference reactions to his patients, we call them countertransferences. When the transference of the patient becomes a resistance, we have to be aware of it, make it conscious by analyzing it. It may be resolved to a degree, but apparently does not entirely dissolve. It existed before the analysis and persists after the analysis. It "never goes away," Bird says. The countertransference also has to be made conscious and resolved as far as possible in order not to disturb the analytic function of the analyst; it differs from transference in that it is necessary for the analyst as well as for the patient. It is part of the instrumentarium which makes it possible for the analyst to identify temporarily with the patient, to fantasy within the patient's life experiences in order to extract their meaning, and finally to read the patient's nonverbalized needs with empathic understanding in order to be able to help the patient to gain control over them.

Different analysts have different ideas regarding the problems of extra-analytic transferences and countertransference. They point to the complexity of the problem. They offer the theoretical framework for the intuitive understanding which Natterson demonstrates. And however valuable intuition may be, it cannot be taught or even discussed without such theoretical understanding.

A. LIMENTANI, F.R.C.P.

London, England

The value of a clinical paper is often judged by the wealth of immediate recollections it evokes of cases and situations similar to those described, which give rise to feelings of familiarity and *deja vu* in the reader. Dr. Natterson's paper elicited such a response in me, but with it came a growing feeling of uneasiness which was not dispelled by a careful perusal of the clinical material and theoretical conclusions. In the end, I was left with a conviction that Dr. Natterson had overstated his case (and he actually has a good one when he criticizes the relentless interpretation of the transference to the exclusion of any other aspects of the patient's life), and that his belief that teachers do not always practice what they preach is a dangerous generalization if used to promulgate technical innovations or variations on accepted techniques which are based on unclear and unsupported theoretical formulations.

Paradoxically, I gained the impression that perhaps the author's approach, in many respects, is not in fact unlike that of most analysts. Unfortunately, his insistence on the use of the term "extra-analytic transference" does not contribute to clarity, as in my opinion the term "transference" should be restricted to certain phenomena observable in the course of, and arising from, psychoanalytic treatment. While no one would question the author's contention that "intense, significant . . . reactions toward persons and situations outside the analytic relationship are regular occurrences throughout the course of extended psychoanalyses," to speak of "autonomous transference reactions" is to confuse the issue, as the reader immediately thinks of some acting out of the transference. But this is not what Dr. Natterson intends to discuss. It is not simply a matter of semantics; it seems to me that the choice of terminology in this instance is used in support of the thesis that the transference is to be interpreted wherever it is to be found. No one would disagree with this, but I believe the majority of analysts, quite wisely in my opinion, would interpret the transference in the "here and now" situation, knowing that the only truly emotionally significant interpretations are those which include a direct reference to the analyst.

A consequence of Dr. Natterson's thesis is that the analyst has the added preoccupation of searching for the "locale" of the transference, which may not turn out to be quite so simple as he seems to think. Patients are apt to respond very quickly to the analyst's offer of an interpretation of the extra-analytic transference (for the purpose of this discussion I am prepared to use the author's terminology) by bringing more and more associations or prepared material concerning their involvement with large numbers of people and real life situations, couched in such a way as to provoke more and more similar responses from the analyst. Each interpretation is received as if it were a revelation, and it is usually coupled with expressions of gratitude for the insight gained, which in my opinion is false insight, as it is seldom followed by anything faintly resembling synthesis.

Dr. Natterson's complaint that some analysts ignore the patient's reactions and behavior patterns in relation to his external environment, on the other hand, is justified. When this happens, the analyst's technique as well as his rapport and understanding of the patient must be at fault, but it is not always easy to know how to utilize this material. Should things go smoothly, there will be no difficulty in detecting the transference significance in the patient's associations, and I would then think that it was quite in order, and probably common practice, to begin an intervention with some reference to the "extra-analytic transference." But in times of stress, when patients demand that we take notice of real aspects of their lives, or in the face of heightened resistance when the transference is altogether obscure, the greatest possible pressure is brought to bear on the analyst in matters of theory and technique. At these times the sessions take place in a stagnant atmosphere punctuated by the patient's complaints about our lack of interest and understanding, followed by demands for enlightenment which cannot be met, coupled at times with enticements to alter our approach.

As my experience increases, so does my conviction that to interpret outside the transference or the analytical situation is at best rather a waste of time, and at worst actually hinders the analytic process. It seems obvious to me, for instance, that a direct interpretation of an incident between a father and son, taken in isolation, might easily be misunderstood to seem as if we were taking sides with either party. I also believe that any attempt by the analyst to cover up the fact that he does not know what is going on will not be missed by the patient. Does this mean then that I would never offer an interpretation to a patient about his behavior toward his boss or his wife or son? I have already hinted at the answer—I would certainly do so, but only when I am satisfied that the subject matter is somewhere in the transference; and I would do so even on the strength of a vague intuitive feeling, but in these circumstances I pay particular attention to the way I express myself. I regard this type of intervention as a prelude to a transference interpretation which is meant to foster attention and interest in the "here and now" as well as indicating to the patient that there is also an opportunity for gaining more insight into his real-life situation. When the intervention is felt to be well-timed and appropriate, the patient responds by working around it, and finally old and new transference features will become recognizable.

Turning to Dr. Natterson's two-way tide proposition, I am indebted to him for raising an issue which will often prove to be the testing ground for the inexperienced. All analysts must be aware of the tremendous difficulty in stemming the flow of transference material outside the analysis, and equally they cannot be unaware of the amount of skill and patience involved in bringing well-established old or recent patterns of behavior into the analytic situation, where they can be examined in a "white-hot state," as Winnicott would have said. But the real test of analytic expertise comes when we need to distinguish between acting out, which is clearly the result of neurotic conflict reactivated by the transference (here I am using the term "acting out" in the classical sense, i.e., pertaining to analysis), and reactions arising from the patients' daily lives and interactions with their environment. In this context I am slightly puzzled by the author's statement that "the evidence does not support the assumption that when a transference neurosis is established, extra-analytic transference no longer occurs." I wonder on what evidence this statement is based.

But to revert to the points at issue, it is an important part, if not the essence, of analysis to investigate any sudden or new departure from our patients' established ways of living and behaving. We are trained to expect little help from them, for they have an interest in concealing their acting out just as they have an interest in keeping real emotions outside the analytic room. Dr. Natterson, well aware of this, has a word of warning for those analysts who appear to be excessively preoccupied with the patient's real life. But his main criticism is clearly directed toward those analysts who misapply the technique by creating a feeling in the analysand that only the transference matters. Such criticism applies especially to the more ardent followers of the Kleinian school who do not hesitate to give deep transference interpretations in the earliest stages of the analysis, when it is doubtful that the patient is really able to feel or understand them.

This particular approach stands out very clearly in the course of seminars attended by students of different psychoanalytical persuasion. The relentless interpreters soon clash with those students who are inclined to follow Dr. Natterson's line of argument, particularly in the early phases of the analysis. My own personal view is reflected in my supervisory work, in which I encourage students to intervene only when they are reasonably sure about the transference, and to reject at all costs any attempts by the patient to draw them into a discussion or interpretation of their "extra-analytic transference," so tempting to the over-enthusiastic and inexperienced student who is often at a loss how to keep things going, particularly in the early phases of a psychoanalytic treatment. It is not always easy to know how to make appropriate noises while waiting for our opportunity, and it is even more difficult when the countertransference is eluding our attention. Dr. Natterson gives us an excellent example of this in his clinical description of Mr. G., when the analyst finally had to acknowledge that his attempts to relate to the transference neurosis had been premature.

Responses to a clinical presentation vary a great deal; for instance, I would like to know more about what it was in the "here and now" situation that forced the analyst to intervene prematurely. Some of us would also be inclined to think that a limited transference interpretation as opposed to an interpretation of the transference neurosis might have been more appropriate. (Unlike the author, I prefer to make a clear distinction between the two types of interpretation.) Should this assumption be correct, it is just possible that analyst and patient might have found an earlier solution from the impasse they were in.

I was also very much interested in the fact that the analyst's admission that he had neglected something in the analytic situation should have provoked such massive dynamic changes in the transference and in the patient's relationship with his wife. Dr. Natterson says that "by insisting first on connecting the patient's associations with the analytic relationship, he was in fact playing into the patient's unconscious sadomasochistic needs." I would suggest that in these circumstances the analyst's admission could well have been experienced by the patient as an act of masochistic submission. This I believe is in keeping with the plasticity of the sadomasochistic relationship, in which the partners' roles are very rapidly exchanged, a phenomenon which can be observed at the very moment the symptom makes its appearance in the analysis. The preconscious awareness of his countertransference had guided the analyst into making an intervention which eventually led to further verbalization of an important slice of the patient's psychic life.

Mr. G.'s case reminds me of a similar occurrence in the course of the analysis of a man who throughout his life had engaged in a series of sadomasochistic relationships with women, which in some respects repeated certain features of the father-son relationship. He had spent several weeks describing in minute detail the violent verbal exchanges between himself and his new wife, *interspersing* his customary terse remarks on the effect a dominating and intrusive father had on his character formation. In the early stages of these repetitious expostulations a transference interpretation had been flatly rejected, and rightly so. In this awareness I found it possible to refrain from further comment during the period when all life and momentum seemed to have gone out of this normally lively analysis. Slowly things began to change and move, and I experienced a greater urge to intervene. Eventually this feeling turned into a conviction that it was time to do so, although I had as yet no clear vision of what the transference situation was really about. Much to my dismay and surprise the patient greeted this interpretation with laughter, pointing out that I had spoken in the same foreign language that he was currently using with his wife. This had never happened before and was an obvious clue to the countertransference: the patient's need was that I should take up a sadistic role, and this I could only manage to do in the guise of his wife.

Both of these clinical cases are relevant to this discussion, because where sadomasochism is prominent the two-way tide is difficult to achieve. Although a transference neurosis may be fully developed, the symptomatology tends to continue its autonomous existence outside the analytic situation, as Dr. Natterson rightly points out. In these and other cases where the transference is tenuous or seemingly non-existent, analysts are tempted to believe that a different or special technique should be used. Here we see perhaps an unwillingness on our part to admit that not all patients are suited for psychoanalysis. Furthermore, it is not often realized that a variation of the technique could also mean an abandonment of psychoanalysis as such, but I must emphasize here that Dr. Natterson is in no

— 293

way advocating this. Nevertheless, in my opinion, his proposition must be resisted because it threatens three most important tenets of psychoanalytic therapy: (1) that we should do our utmost to maintain a reasonable degree of neutrality; (2) that we should bide our time so that we can make use of the transference profitably; (3) that we should not be afraid of not knowing.

We must thank the author for a valuable and thought-provoking paper on important matters of technique. We are stimulated to ponder again the mysterious essence of the transference, the meaning of interpretation, and, above all, what we do in our consulting rooms. This is something that we should keep under constant review, and I am particularly grateful to Dr. Natterson for having forced me to do precisely that.

ALBERT MASON, M.D.
Beverly Hills, California

In drawing our attention to the fact that many problems in the handling of transference still remain to be elucidated, Dr. Natterson has given us much to think about. It is also true, however, that the discussion of transference is the discussion of the whole of psychoanalysis, and I will have to content myself, therefore, with making only one or two points stimulated by this paper.

I certainly do not intend to play the game of re-interpreting someone else's interpretations, which is both easy to do and pointless. One has to accept that the analyst on the spot is in the best position to make a correct interpretation. In criticizing his interpretation, it is easy to forget that the information he conveys to us about his choice of interpretation of necessity omits numerous other observations that he made at the time. He has neither the space to report all these observations nor even the means, as many of his conclusions are based on information which is subtle, barely perceived, and frequently even unconscious. So rather than criticize Dr. Natterson's conclusions, I would like to point out some alternatve possibilities concerning the problem he describes.

I have only one specific criticism concerning the clinical work described. The analyst had been experiencing certain difficulties with the patient, Mr. G., and was also aware of a countertransference reaction which he now felt illuminated the problem. Now, as I understand it, instead of using the countertransference as an aid to understanding the problem and interpreting what the patient was doing to the analyst, the analyst conveyed his *actual* countertransference feelings to the patient. "He discussed this transference-countertransference development with Mr. G. . . ." Note "he discussed," not "he interpreted." In other words, the analyst conveyed to the patient what was going on in his own mind. I do not think this is ever justified; in fact, it is a breach of analytic technique, and I believe that any "improvement" which may follow is the result of the patient's now feeling that his fantasies of omnipotently controlling the analyst have in fact succeeded in their aim.

Whenever patients succeed through exerting pressure on the analytic setting in producing a breach of technique, a shift in material will always follow. The pressure can be of many varieties, ranging from crude threats, seduction, helplessness, and outright demands, to many varieties of analytic "sticking" or bogging down. The aim is to force the analyst to abandon analysis in favor of other things: appeals, exhortations, attacks, advice, sex, personal communications, etc., or, as I believe happened in this case, "frank communication about the analytic difficulty."

These attempts to drive the analyst to action rather than to interpretation are usually accomplished by the mechanism of projective identification. In the case under discussion, I believe this was possibly an attempt to put into the analyst the anger and helplessness felt by the patient, much as he did with his parents, either because he could not deal with these feelings or because he used them as an expression of hostility toward the parents, or both. If the parents cannot deal with these projections, as evidently they could not, the patient then reintrojects them, and is forced to deal with these un-modified projections by reprojecting them into subsequent objects, the analyst being the latest of these. This process will no doubt continue until someone can accept the projections and deal with them in a different way, or, as Bion would put it, by "detoxifying them." Understanding (which implies containment) and subsequent interpretation, which is the detoxified return, would fulfill this need. The patient would then introject a different object to identify with, and thus have the beginnings of a real change of psychic structure, as distinct from a mere change of behavior.

One can always alter a "stuck" analytic situation by a move, however slight, away from analysis, but real development, which depends on a change in the psychic structure and un-conscious fantasy of the patient, can follow only from specific understanding of the fantasy and correct interpretation of it.

To return now to the main theme of the paper, the prob-lem presented to the analyst when extra-analytic transference cannot be successfully linked to intra-analytic transference:

Melanie Klein described two stages in the development of the child, which she called the paranoid-schizoid and the depressive positions. She deliberately chose the term "posi-tion" to emphasize the fact that the phenomena she was de-scribing were not simply passing stages like the oral or anal stages, but were specific configurations of object relationships, anxieties, and defenses. These configurations persist through-out life, and any problem, such as the Oedipus complex, for example, can be viewed as falling into either of these con-figurations. In Klein's view, therefore, it would follow that the transference relationship will be of a paranoid-schizoid or a depressive pattern, and will fluctuate between these positions according to the stages of the analysis.

Now, when the child is in the paranoid-schizoid position, it characteristically splits its object into a good and a bad. Into the good object it projects its libidinal feelings, and into the bad its hostile feelings. It also wishes to acquire the good object by any means possible, i.e., fusion, ingestion, or inva-sion, and to get away from the bad object.

During this period, therefore, the analyst may be seen at times to be ideal and at others persecuting, and fluctuations between these attitudes will occur until, after careful analytic work, it can be shown that the good object and the bad object are the frustrating and gratifying aspects of the same object. Integration now occurs, ushering in the depressive position with its characteristic anxieties. However, this is a difficult accomplishment for many reasons, which include the fear of annihilation, the inborn polarity of instincts, fears of confusion, etc. Therefore, the bringing together of these primary splits will occur only after the patient's anxieties have been worked through. Now, a common version of the split described above is one in which one object can be good—for instance, mother—and another, bad—for instance, father—or vice-versa.

In the transference, this kind of split will be represented by the analyst acting as one part of the object—the good part, let's say—and the mate as the other part.

Now, when this kind of transference is present, there is no point in interpreting that the extra-analytic and intra-analytic transferences are the same, or trying to link them directly as representing the same object relationship. To the patient, they are, in fact, the opposite of each other. When this dynamic is present—and I believe Dr. Natterson may be describing situations in which this is so—a link can be made between the extra- and intra-analytic transferences only through the extensive work of shifting the patient from the paranoid-schizoid to the depressive position, i.e., working at integrating the different views of the object.

This kind of integration has to be done slowly and carefully and may take years to accomplish, but gradually the analyst can show that the extra-analytic transference is a split-off part of the transference proper (the intra-analytic transference). In other words, the analyst can only bring the good and bad aspects of the object together by working through the anxieties that split the object in the first instance, and that continue to keep it split.

A split object relationship can also be present as a result of a retreat from depressive anxieties when they are too much for the patient to tolerate and deal with healthily. This retreat from the depressive position is accomplished by the use of a constellation of defenses which Klein called the manic defenses. Now, if the split is due to manic defenses, the different aspects of the object will come together only by the correct working through of all aspects of these manic defenses. The manic defenses defend the patient from experiencing the pain of dependency, which leads to ambivalence and guilt, and also from oedipal anxieties, which are immediately present when the depressive position is entered, for whenever the object is felt to be whole and separate, it is also felt to be capable of relating to another object as well as to the patient. So a split transference may be a manifestation of a retreat from the depressive position, as well as a fixation in the paranoid-schizoid position. In this case, the manic defenses will need to be worked through before integration can be achieved, and with it, the coinciding of intra- and extra-analytic transference. I am of course talking only of the situation when these do *not* coincide—both mate and analyst can sometimes be bad objects and the good object elsewhere (the real mother, girlfriend, etc.).

From another standpoint, one might say that Dr. Natterson sees the transference problem as a vicissitude of the transference neurosis; and while this may be present, the possibility of a transference psychosis should also be considered, calling for a different approach.

Melanie Klein has demonstrated that psychotic mechanisms are in evidence not only in psychosis but in normal development, and so will play a role in "normal" analysis and normal transferences.

When a patient is fixated at these psychotic points or has regressed to them, the transference becomes puzzling if viewed from the standpoint of neurosis, and conversely will become comprehensible when seen in the light of more primitive anxieties and the defenses against them.

LUCIA E. TOWER, M.D.
Chicago, Illinois

That transference phenomena are more or less ubiquitous is a logical deduction to be drawn from our definition and theory of transference. This ubiquity is a part of the everyday experience and observation of analysts, and also enters into many of the perceptions of ordinary persons as, for example, the young wife who tells her friend, "My mother is coming and every time she comes, I get very nervous. My husband says I behave badly to him, and he's right. She doesn't do anything out of the way, but somehow or other she just makes me very nervous." I like the fact that Dr. Natterson has chosen to look at this ubiquity in connection with certain types of rather common clinical experiences, and that he talks in terms of a "flow of transferences" and deals with them as two-way phenomena in the therapeutic situation and, by inference, in ordinary life situations. Much of this is in keeping with some of my own ideas about the nature and importance of "two-way" transferences.

Some therapeautic situations present not merely a "flow" but a real "flood" of transferences. In such clinical situations, the technical problem often becomes not how to bring out transference material, but how to evaluate and handle the many extra-analytic transferences which may obscure material pertinent to the developing transference neurosis. It is indeed interesting that our literature contains virtually no discussions of the meaning and management of the extra-analytic transferences. I have taken at face value Dr. Natterson's statement that this is an almost wholly neglected field in our literature. It is a subject to which I've often given casual thought, and have always assumed that any transferences—no matter where or how manifested—brought into the associational material were somehow or other grist to the analytic mill, so to speak. I welcome Dr. Natterson's addressing himself to this topic.

JOSEPH M. NATTERSON

As I look back over my experiences in supervising psycho-analytic candidates and residents in psychiatry, I have generally been disposed to attempt with the student a differential diagnosis between a reported transference which apparently exists in its own right and one which manifestly or subtly represents a displacement from the transference in the treatment situation. I will concede that if the "unconscious is timeless," in terms of the deepest unconscious interactions in an analysis, a transference brought in from an extra-analytic source must ultimately be related to what will eventually appear as a neurotic transference development in the relationship of the patient to the analyst. In this sense we would be forced to regard any and all extra-analytic transferences as displacements from or forerunners of transferences in the therapeutic situation. I do not, however, think that it is practical or helpful to interpret a bit of transference material which is not now in any detectable relationship to the current transference situation in the analysis as a displacement from that transference. A simple example would be the common clinical experience of a bad marital situation in which it is obvious that the patient is already under the sway of a severe transference neurosis to the partner in the marriage. To deal with material from such a source prematurely as a displacement from the transference in the treatment would be a grave technical error. An insoluble therapeutic impasse might result if authoritative and persistent interpretations of displacement from the analysis are substituted for empathic dealing with a difficult situation "out there" by insisting that it actually is "in here." True enough, the same mechanisms will eventually appear in the transference in the treatment situation, mechanisms which have long since been understood in the marital situation as being wrong "out there." They can *now* be interpreted in the treatment situation in terms of what the problems are here and now in this situation. Much so-called wild analysis consists of ill-advised compensatory ambitiousness along such lines. I once dealt too drastically with a most intelligent but very ambitious young resident who had made an interpretation of passive homosexual transference to a man who was on the verge of a paranoid break. It took him some time to get over his anger at me, but he survived and, some ten years later, has become a competent, sensitive, fully trained analyst.

Looking back over my own past work, I think that my most conscious use of extra-analytic transference phenomena has been in facilitating the course of the analysis proper through one of two major procedures. The first is that of reducing the intensity of an oncoming frightening transference affect through distancing (when appropriate) by interpreting a transference "out there" which one senses will soon be experienced in, and interpretable in, the relationship "in here." The second is the inevitable necessity, especially in the early phases of an analysis, to make use to some extent of educational measures (i.e., re the analytic process) or to foster intellectual mastery (which is, of course, in itself another form of distancing), thereby helping the patient to feel that transference reactions are frequent occurrences and not to be feared. This strengthens his observing ego and eventually leads to a state of mind in which he can turn insights into his reactions "out there" onto what is going on "in here." I have repeatedly had the experience—as I am certain has every other analyst—that a careful interpretation and discussion of a transference problem "out there" has resulted in relaxation of tension, followed very shortly by a quite spontaneous "You know, I am beginning to be aware that what you have been telling me has a lot to do with some feelings I have been having about you which I have been confused about." It now becomes academic whether the specific extra-analytic transference was a "displacement" from the treatment situation, or whether it existed in its own right and would have recurred regardless of any treatment.

One truly novel idea is presented in Dr. Natterson's paper, namely, that a transference reaction occurring outside the treatment situation may in some subtle way intrinsically influence the development of the transference relationship in the analysis proper, but it is unclear just how Dr. Natterson thinks this happens; there are unelaborated indications that it involves some countertransference changes as well. It would be easy, of course, to attribute this, as I have just pointed out, to the reduction of resistance against transference in the treatment by increased mastery of transference outside of the treatment. But I think this is not what Dr. Natterson considers to be the central mechanism of the alteration of the transference within the treatment by extra-analytic transference, and his four categories of influences from extra-analytic transference further confuse the issue. For example, in (1) "transient minor variations . . . induced by external events," does he mean *any* external event, or only the external event of an extra-analytic transference? In (2) "deeply moving reality experiences . . .", does he mean non-transference reality experiences, or only those which manifest more or less intense extra-analytic transference? Also in (2), he does not make clear what he considers to be the relationship between the change in the transference and whatever interpretations were made of extra-analytic transference.

In numbers (3) "life situations," and (4) "objects outside the analysis," there is a similar, for me at least, lack of clarity as to the difference between "reality events" and "external transference events" in terms of what he experienced as having led to changes in the transference in the treatment situation itself. In other words, is resistance against the analytic transference reduced, and functioning of the observing ego facilitated, by empathic consideration of problems of living or by the understanding through interpretation of extra-analytic transference? I myself would conjecture, by both, but I am not clear as to the focal point here in *his* opinion of these matters.

Dr. Natterson has, however, brought to our attention a new area of technical challenge, some very interesting clinical material to support his main thesis, and some stimulating theoretical questions. We should thank him for directing our attention to a long-neglected area in our theory of treatment.

LEO STONE, M.D.

New York, New York

Dr. Natterson's interesting specification of the transference originating (independently) outside the analytic situation and "flowing into" the therapeutic transference (with lesser variants) is a special and discrete emphasis of his own which merits attention. One may view this question (1) from a broad theoretical-conceptual-semantic point of view (with apologies for the condensation); and (2) from an inevitably related (but not always congruent) clinical-phenomenological point of view.

It may be assumed that in everyday life, even among relatively healthy individuals, all important relationships include variable quanta of transference affect (in some instances, perceptual modification or emphasis) along with the relatively "autonomous" sensory-cognitive reactions and appropriate ego-syntonic drive impulses, largely responsive to the mature perceptions. In neurotic character disorders, the transference elements may indeed be preponderant in certain decisive references.

Ordinarily the give-and-take and relatively free mobility of everyday life (as to environmental responsiveness, satisfactions, alternatives, punishments, aggressive outlets, and other modalities) preserves the intrapsychic distribution of transference and reality, with the former in a minimal role. Where undue frustration, seduction, and infantile associative reverberation (or similar conditions) occur, not to speak of the dynamic-economic predisposition to transference regression (equivalent to the latent predisposition to neurosis), morbid intensification of transferences in relation to important objects may also occur, often occasioning the outbreak of clinical illness.

Where such illness leads to psychoanalytic treatment, the relationship to the analyst, apart from technical considerations (active sense), includes the emotional atmosphere of neutrality and the pervasive rule of abstinence. I cannot, of course, discuss these in detail. However, it is my clinical and theoretical conviction that in contrast with the responsiveness of everyday life, this state of "deprivation-in-intimacy," even when judiciously applied and maintained, fosters regressive reactivation and deepening of transference wishes, with increasing concentration of such wishes on the person of the analyst. One hopes that, in an optimum situation, the depth and tenacity of such regressive wishes will correspond to the nature and depth of the original illness. That iatrogenic moments may also be important is a consideration that has interested me for a long time.

Even when a full-blown transference neurosis has been established, recapitulating (with current adaptations) the essentials of the infantile dramatis personae and interplay of psychic forces, the patient remains (or should remain) an adult in his cognitive and other automonous ego capacities, and also in those large aspects of his instinctual economy not diverted into the analytic process and relationship, in their ultimately limited channel of expression (essentially speech). Certainly we rely always on the "observing" portions of the patient's ego for the very furtherance of the analytic process. That this may be submerged, as in psychosis or in severe transference regressions, acute or chronic, is nevertheless an equally important fact, indicating the potential continuum between the (process) spheres of the ego.

With these general dynamic-economic considerations in mind, I can not fault, in principle, the idea that actual transference reactions can originate in the patient's daily life outside the analytic situation. That they may "flow into" the analytic situation, if such process includes active technical adroitness on the part of the analyst, may be accepted in a practical process sense. Transference(s) have a prior latent existence in the patient in relation to old object images, and in themselves represent a distribution from the original primal object. It is therefore unlikely, a priori, that *any* transference reaction is fundamentally *unrelated* to others. A further question is: How often is such origin *actually* independent of

304 —

the fully established analytic relationship? Apart from the question of the "mutative" value (Strachey) of interpretations directed toward specific transference reactions, how often is one *certain* of the very existence (or "quantity") of the transference element outside analysis when one has no direct access to the situations and objects under consideration?

That the ebb and flow of daily life (certainly its large-scale catastrophes or triumphs) influences mood and responsiveness in analysis, and that it also plays a role in instinctual economy, "for good or ill"—this may be accepted without reservation. However, these vicissitudes may be massively in the sphere of *reality*, and act as reality influences on the patient's system of aggressive or libidinal gratification, or frustration or self-esteem. The impact on the ongoing analytic transference process would thus most often be economic, although events of unusual power can occasion reorganizations which may indeed mobilize new layers or segments of transference (just as they may affect other aspects of personality structure). These events do not, however, necessarily invest persons *outside* the analysis with transference. When Dr. Natterson insists on the analyst's interest in and receptive attention to the patient's external reality, he reiterates what I believe is a widely accepted and (in my view) indispensable principle of analytic technique. No patient can take a serious interest in his warded-off infantile life if his current reality is neglected. But this does not often have much to do with "outside" and independent transference reactions as such.

The phenomenon of "acting out" (of multiple possible origins) is, of course, a major problem of resistance. Except in loose (although related) nosologic extrapolation, this difficult phenomenon refers to, and derives from, the analytic transference and takes impetus from its dynamics. Ambivalence or other instrinsic "incompatability" within the therapeutic relationship may (sometimes temporarily) "require" a parallel object in the outer world. And indeed the individual's family and other elements of his environment may be conscripted by his unconscious to play transference roles complementary to the shifting role of the analyst (as a simple example: wife as mother, children as siblings, with analyst as father). For the adult individual's reality sense cannot be stretched too far; and the analyst cannot be simultaneously a whole family of ancient objects.

Why do I believe that the pathologic or benign process phenomena mentioned immediately above are, in a practical sense, far more frequent and important than the principal phenomenon described by Dr. Natterson, once the patient is genuinely involved in the transference neurosis? The therapeutic transference (in its usual sense) is, in my view, a phase-appropriate derivative of the primordial transference, which is in itself a reaction to primordial separation. The analytic situation, of all human relationships, most nearly parallels the original situation of relative separation, with speech as the essential bridge of mastery. It has thus a unique power to excite transference reactions and, in due course, the transference neurosis. In this process, the ego-dystonic regressive infantile elements in object relationships tend to be concentrated actually or potentially in the therapeutic relationship (and its ancillary objects). This, it is true, is my theoretical position. However, this position was arrived at through empirical observations. Neither subsequent personal observations nor the material in Dr. Natterson's paper would lead me at present to alter this view.

Thus, while I would concede the theoretical possibility of independently originating external transference reactions (based on progressive pathologic process, accidents of life, or interpretative lag) and the desirability of open-minded alertness for them (not to speak of the indubitable and perennial importance of the patient's reality experience and the analyst's respect for it), it would seem to me that the greater and usually more imperative technical challenge still lies in the recognition (sometimes anticipation) of the relationship of most such transference experiences (i.e., those characterized by inappropriate infantile elements) to the ongoing transference neurosis, whatever the appropriate technical approach to these may be. (Coercive, tactless, unrealistic interpretations are, of course, never acceptable.) In other words, with full regard for a theoretically possible alternative, the pre-eminent questions should remain, "What does this mean in relation to the ongoing transference?" or "What have I missed in the developing transference undercurrents of this analysis?"

I must close without direct discussion of the author's case material, but the fact that the cases are not reported "in full" does vitiate their demonstrative significance. I do not find in them adequate clinical support for Dr. Natterson's central and essential thesis. On the other hand, I would not, even if space permitted, wish to exploit inadequate data ("my view" of each case) to oppose or qualify the author's interpretation of the material.

Author's Response

The six distinguished discussants have read my paper thoroughly, thought deeply about it, criticized it carefully—sometimes ruthlessly—and consequently have provided me with much food for thought.

I was particularly pleased to see that almost every discussant believed that interpretation outside the analytic relationship can be appropriate. This acknowledgment is particularly important since all the discussants agree, as do I, that the exploration and understanding of the regressive events within the analytic relationship constitute the *sine qua non* of a psychoanalysis.

Dr. Székely's views regarding extra-analytic transference are virtually identical with mine. His comments about the "possibility not merely of transference reactions, but even of transference neurosis proper, outside of the psychoanalytic situation," is quite intriguing, and I hope that he will elaborate upon this idea in the future. Dr. Székely inquires why I do not raise the issue of acting out, and other discussants are interested in the same point. When I alluded to the well-known tendency to displace intra-analytic transference, I was, of course, also thinking of the acting out aspects.

Dr. Székely wonders about countertransference as a factor in the non-recognition of extra-analytic transference; I agree that it is one of the factors. Narcissism and the consequent rigidity of conceptualization and intervention may play an important role in many such situations. In addition, however, inattention to extra-analytic transference may be the result of an analyst's theoretical orientation or of special characteristics of his psychoanalytic education.

Dr. Buxbaum apparently regards my paper as intuitive and somewhat naive. I cheerfully accept both designations. (Whether my naiveté is exceptional is a matter about which she and I might disagree.) I am particularly grateful to Dr. Buxbaum for referring to the views of Eduardo Weiss on the value of a "divided transference" and to those of Bouvet and Loewald which deal with the need for distance. These do indeed add a conceptual and theoretical dimension to the technical problem of dealing with significant extra-analytic transference.

Dr. Bird's instructive paper appeared after I wrote my own, and it is important that Drs. Buxbaum and Székely mention it. In his paper Dr. Bird makes some tantalizingly brief references to cases that he treated for years in which the patients were totally preoccupied with exterior life problems. They apparently were helped, but without the development of "any significant transference relationship." The paucity of clinical material makes a critique of his explanation impossible, but I would like to ask two questions. First, did he interpret transference reactions to persons in the patients' current lives, and second, did the patients experience significant reduction of their neurotic conflicts without the development of any transference relationship to the analyst?

Returning to Dr. Buxbaum's remarks, in which she constantly reiterates how immensely complex transference phenomena are, she does not categorically reject the notion of autonomous extra-analytic transferences. My impression is that she would regard them as non-existent or, if they do exist, as epiphenomenal.

My paper was primarily written in an effort to solve what I regarded as a problem in technique; the theoretical elements were secondary in my mind and were intended to support my technical recommendations. There may have been an understandable confusion about this point which led Dr. Limentani to think that I might be attempting some drastic modification of psychoanalysis. He says, "Paradoxically I gained the impression that perhaps the author's approach, in many respects, is not in fact unlike that of most analysts." Dr. Limentani's reaction is not paradoxical; it is precisely the impression I wished the reader to have. I have no reservations about the centrality of the analyst in the transferential events of an analysis. Dr. Limentani does seem ambivalent about my technical recommendations. He says he has become increasingly convinced that interpretations outside the transference or the analytic situation either waste time or hinder the analysis. Yet elsewhere he says he certainly would make an interpretation involving the patient and his boss, wife, or son if he senses that this kind of intervention is a "prelude to a transference interpretation." The latter statement agrees with my point of view.

It was Bertrand Russell, I believe, who stated that a tolerance for ambiguity is the most necessary characteristic for the survival of modern man. Dr. Limentani obviously shares this view when he emphasizes that the analyst should be unafraid of not knowing. My notion of autonomous extra-analytic transference was not intended to achieve premature closure. In fact, the content of these discussions indicates that it has stimulated many more questions than answers.

The gist of Dr. Mason's discussion is contained in his statement, ". . . gradually the analyst can show that the extra-analytic transference is a split-off part of the transference proper (the intra-analytic transference)." This is seen from a Kleinian point of view, as a retreat from the depressive position. I wish Dr. Mason had indicated how, during the extended period of splitting, he deals with the extra-analytic transferences. For example, are there situations in which the splitting occurs between two extra-analytic figures and the interpretations are made with reference to those persons, excluding the analyst (even though the analyst assumes that they ultimately reflect conflicts concerning him)? Or does he, instead, interpret to the patient that these exterior transferences are part of the warded-off transference to himself? My impression is that he may do either, his choice depending upon the exigencies of the moment. But without Dr. Mason's explicit statement, one cannot be certain.

It is fascinating to witness the wide range of views entertained by the discussants regarding the transference neurosis, ranging from Dr. Székely's suggestion that a transference neurosis involving someone other than the analyst may occur during the analysis, to Dr. Mason's opinion that all extra-analytic transferences are split-off derivatives of the transference neurosis to the analyst.

Dr. Tower's lament over the confused quality of my categorization of extra-analytic transferences is laudable rather than lamentable. The primary process qualities of transferences render clear and consistent delineation very difficult. I intended the categories to be useful but not necessarily definitive; perhaps they were neither. Dr. Tower's criticism, then, leads back to an essential point, namely, that extra-analytic transferences exist in myriad and subtle forms requiring counterpart responses from the analyst. Dr. Tower's experience has taught her that interpretations of transference outside the analytic relationship to relieve anxiety through distancing or through intellectual mastery (another form of distancing) are particularly valuable in the early phases of an analysis. This view is confirmed by other discussants. Dr. Tower also finds that interpretation of extra-analytic transference can be useful in preparing the analysand for effective work on the transference relationship to the analyst. My own experience has been very similar. In contrast, Dr. Limentani suggests quite the opposite effect. At the moment I cannot explain this discrepancy.

Dr. Stone's characteristically profound discussion admits the theoretical possibility of autonomous extra-analytic transferences, while questioning their likelihood on an empirical basis. His arguments are closely reasoned and persuasive enough *almost* to lead me to relinquish my proposition. However, I again return to the question I raised in my paper:

What accounts for a transference reaction which first appears in an exterior context, then swiftly becomes directed to the analyst without intervening interpretation? Dr. Stone either has not observed such an event or would question that it is in fact a transference reaction (". . . how often is one *certain* . . . when one has no direct access to the situations and objects under consideration?"), or perhaps would regard it as a manifestation of the transference neurosis which inexplicably (due to the unavailability of explanatory data) appears first in an extra-analytic context, since "it is therefore unlikely, a priori, that *any* transference reaction is fundamentally *unrelated* to others." If interpretation were first required in order to bring the transference feelings into the analytic relationship, then of course I would make the usual assumption that feelings have been displaced for resistive purposes. Since I am not certain that Dr. Stone's views cover *all* possible alternatives, I must continue to consider my idea of at least relative autonomy to be tenable.

Three and a half years have passed since I submitted this paper for publication. At that time I was struggling for a more sophisticated understanding in dealing with the infinite richness and complexity of transference phenomena which occur during analysis. It was implicit in my thinking that the analytic process itself is primarily responsible for the emergence of these powerful regressive experiences. It seemed useful, on the basis of my experience, to postulate the existence of autonomous extra-analytic transferences. I thought it might contribute to our understanding of transference and thereby increase our skill in dealing with it. Now, several years later, I am less preoccupied with the concept, but it has proven very useful in my clinical approach.

To all the discussants I offer my most sincere thanks for their scholarship and clinical wisdom. I have been enriched by their ideas, and I am sure that corresponding benefits will accrue to my patients and students.

Joseph M. Natterson

REFERENCES

Bird, B. (1972), Notes on transference. *J. Amer. Psychoanal. Assn.*, 2:267-301.

Bouvet, M. (1958), Technical variation and the concept of distance. *Internat. J. Psycho-Anal.*, 32:212-222.

Comess, L. (1969), Personal Communication.

Fenichel, O. (1939), *Problems of psychoanalytic technique*. New York: Psychoanalytic Quarterly.

Freud, S. (1905), Fragment of an analysis of a case of hysteria. *Standard Edition*, 7:3-122. London: Hogarth Press, 1953.

—— (1925), An autobiographical study. *Standard Edition*, 20:3-74. London: Hogarth Press, 1959.

Glover, E. (1955), *Technique of Psychoanalysis*. New York: International Universities Press.

Greenson, R. (1967), *The Technique and Practice of Psychoanalysis*, 1. New York: International Universities Press.

Haas, L. (1966), Transference outside the psychoanalytic situation. *Internat. J. Psycho-Anal.*, 47:422-426.

Horney, K. (1939), *New Ways in Psychoanalysis*. New York: Norton.

Kohut, H. (1968), The psychoanalytic treatment of narcissistic personality disorders. *The Psychoanalytic Study of the Child*, 23:86-113. New York: International Universities Press.

Laing, R. (1969), *The Divided Self*. New York: Pantheon Books.

Loewald, H. (1971), The transference neurosis: Comments on the concept and the phenomenon. *J. Amer. Psychoanal. Assn.*, 19:54-66.

Loewenstein, R. (1958), Remarks on some variation in psychoanalytic technique. *Internat. J. Psycho-Anal.*, 39:202-210.

Menninger, K. (1958), *Theory of Psychoanalytic Technique*. New York: Basic Books.

Orr, D. W. (1954), Transference and countertransference: A historical survey. *J. Amer. Psychoanal. Assn.*, 2:621-670.

Payne, S. (1946), Notes on developments in the theory and practice of psychoanalytic technique. *Internat. J. Psycho-Anal.*, 27:12-18.

Reich, A. (1958), A special variation of technique. *Internat. J. Psycho-Anal.*, 39:230-237.

Silverberg, W. (1948), The concept of transference. *Psychoanal. Quart.*, 17:309-10.

Weiss, Edoardo (1946). Manipulation of the transference relationship. In: *Psychoanalytic Therapy*, ed. F. Alexander & T. M. French. New York: Ronald Press.

Projective Identification, Analyzability, and Hate

FREDERICK KURTH, M.D.

Dr. Kurth is Associate Faculty Member of the Los Angeles Psychoanalytic Society and Institute, and Assistant Clinical Professor in the Department of Psychiatry at the University of Southern California.

Discussants

R. E. MONEY-KYRLE, PH.D.

Dr. Money-Kyrle is a London psychoanalyst in private practice, and the author of *Man's Picture of His World* and other works.

PETER H. KNAPP, M.D.

Dr. Knapp is Professor and Associate Chairman and Director of Research at Boston University School of Medicine, and a Member of the Faculty, Education Committee, and Research Committee of the Boston Psychoanalytic Society and Institute. He has two longstanding interrelated interests: one in psychosomatic medicine, and the other in psychoanalysis as a research method, and has written 45 papers devoted mainly to these two areas.

MARK KANZER, M.D.

Dr. Kanzer is Clinical Professor of Psychiatry and Past Director of the Division of Psychoanalytic Education at the Medical School of the State University of New York (Downstate). He has published numerous papers on analytic technique, including one appraising the Kleinian limitations in dealing with the superego as an instrument of therapy, entitled "Superego Aspects of Free Association and the Fundamental Rule."

MARJORIE BRIERLEY, M.B.B.S.

Dr. Brierley is a Member of the British Psycho-Analytical Society and a former training analyst, now retired. She continues to assist the Editor of the International Journal of Psycho-Analysis and the Publications Committee as and when required, and is on the Editorial Board of *The Psychoanalytic Forum*. A collection of her papers, *Trends in Psycho-Analysis*, is in the *International Psycho-Analytic Library Series*.

DONALD MELTZER, M.D.

Training Analyst of the British Society and Institute of Psychoanalysis, Dr. Meltzer practices adult and child analysis in Oxford, teaches at the Tavistock Clinic, and is the author of *The Psycho-Analytical Process* and *Sexual States of Mind*.

Projective Identification, Analyzability, and Hate

FREDERICK KURTH, M.D.
Beverly Hills, California

IN LINE WITH JOHN SEELEY'S (1967) VIEW that "the future of psychiatry is bound up so much more with clarification of theory than with inventions of practice" (p. 65), I shall first submit in this paper that recent clarification of theory by Meltzer (1967) and his co-workers changes the practice of psychoanalysis in ways a mere invention could not. I believe that making projective identification a major configuration in the psychoanalytic process changes the concept of analyzability, and I shall illustrate what I feel is at issue regarding analyzability with material from the analysis of a young man.

Second, I shall discuss the relationship between *violent* projective identification and hate.

Specifically, Meltzer's clarification of theory, his spelling out the centrality of projective identification in the *analytic process*, has direct bearing on the concept of analyzability. Furthermore, this centrality assigns a fresh priority to "hate." Within the conceptual framework of projective identification, hate achieves structural status. It is not viewed simply as a regressive phenomenon, or the sum of anti-libidinal forces, or a manifestation of instinctual diffusion. Hate becomes understood in the profound sense that, I believe, Freud was already describing in 1915 when he wrote "that love and hate, which present themselves to us as complete opposites in their content, do not after all stand in any simple relation to each other. . . . *Hate, as a relation to objects, is older than love* [italics mine]. It derives from the narcissistic ego's primordial repudiation of the external world. . . ." (p. 139).

As the first aim of *love*, Freud says, "we recognize the phase

314 —

of incorporating or devouring—a type of love which is consistent with abolishing the object's separate existence" (p. 138). Hate, however, according to Freud, is prior to this mode of doing away with an object. There is yet an older form of annihilating premised on hate, and it is activity in this mode which is reflected in the mechanism of violent projective identification.

This is not to say that projective identification, an exceedingly complex mechanism, is actuated only by hate. The infant may use projective identification for protective purposes, or for communication. Projective identification may be the first step of an introjective transaction leading to growth. In this paper, I shall call the projective identification which is linked to hate "violent projective identification," to differentiate it from projective identification which is derived from other motivational forces. I shall make a suggestion regarding these other forces later in the paper.

Violent projective identification, examined prismatically, reveals such elements as envy, persecutory anxiety, possessive jealousy, deficiency of trust, intolerance of separation, etc. (Meltzer, 1967). It is particularly linked with the spoiling qualities of envy and the paranoid grievances external reality nurtures simply because it is there (Freud's [1915] "primordial repudiation of the external world" [p. 139]).

Melanie Klein first described projective identification in 1946. She spoke of "phantasied onslaughts" on the mother, in which the infant expels in hatred "split-off parts of the ego into the mother" (p. 300). This, she says, "leads to a particular form of object-relation. I suggest for these processes the term 'projective identification.'" Klein writes, "In so far as the mother comes to contain the bad parts of the self, she is not felt to be a separate individual but is felt to be *the* bad self. Much of the hatred against parts of the self is now directed towards the mother" (p. 300).[1]

[1] In his 1950 paper on confusional states, Rosenfeld describes, in somewhat different language, similar processes in the schizophrenic. He writes: "I suggest that under certain external and internal conditions when aggressive impulses temporarily predominate, states may arise in which love and hate impulses and good and bad objects cannot be kept apart and are thus felt to

As a projection of the hated parts of the self, according to Klein, the mother as a differentiated object ceases to exist. This projection is not an attempt to get something of value from the mother, or to communicate with her, or to be protected by her. It is, Klein says, an "onslaught." She explains that in containing the bad parts of the self the mother is no longer experienced as a separate individual; she is related to as though she herself were the bad self and not the containing mother who holds in safekeeping those parts of the child which it finds unbearable. Even if the violent projection is initiated in order to get something from the breast, it is nonetheless an "onslaught" in that it aims not simply to *get from* the breast but to get "it" *away* from and out of the breast. It is a violent taking away designated to leave the breast exhausted and incapable of replenishment.

Other authors since Klein have contributed to further understanding of projective identification, particularly Rosenfeld, Bion, and Segal, as well as Paula Heimann, Betty Joseph, Grotstein, and Malin. Segal (1967), for example, in an article on analytic technique states: "It is to be emphasized, however, that the analysis of the paranoid-schizoid object relationships and defenses is not confined only to the analysis of the psychotic and the prepsychotic. The schizoid defenses [she is speaking specifically of projective identification at this point], though originating in the earliest stages of development, are repeatedly regressed to and revived . . ." (p. 205).

The decisive fact is not that the mechanism of projective identification is used in the more severe psychopathologic conditions—although in these conditions it is more extensive—but rather that it occupies a pivotal position in the analytic process generally, and in each individual analysis to a lesser or greater degree.

In his book *The Psycho-Analytical Process*, Meltzer (1967) describes projective identification as a fundamental modality

---

be mixed up or confused. . . . When libidinal and destructive impulses become confused, the destructive impulses seem to threaten to destroy the libidinal impulses. Consequently the whole self is in danger of being destroyed. The only escape from this danger lies in the ability to differentiate again between love and hate" (p. 53).

in the psychoanalytic process generally, its inevitability as a major mechanism guaranteed by the structure of the mental apparatus itself and the history of this structure's development. In earliest life, as Freud emphasized throughout his work, psychic pain presents a basic problem for the mental apparatus. According to Meltzer (and in this he is following Klein and Bion), "the most primitive form of relief of psychic pain is accomplished by the evacuation into the external object of parts of the self in distress" (p. 21). This evacuation of the self into the object results in "geographical confusion"; that is, the self is confused with its object. Furthermore, following intrusion by the self, the object is felt to intrude in turn, and this leads to further confusion within the self.

Meltzer describes projective identification as "a massive attack on the individuality of objects" (p. 16). This "blurs the boundaries of self and object . . . and produces attendant geographical confusion" (p. 20).

The analysis of a homosexual man (Mason, 1968) provides a particularly clear example of such a "massive attack": "He felt that all boundaries and fences should be abolished, and once chose to go for his holiday to North Canada where there were no boundaries between sea and land, as it was all frozen. No trees projected into the air, and there was even no differentiation between air and land, as they were both snow-filled. There was no night and day, and, heavily swaddled in furs, there was no difference externally between him and a woman, or between his back and front" (p. 6).

Mason's patient, in my view, evidences violent projective identification; but whatever its motivational source, the inevitable and ubiquitous manifestation of projective identification changes the concept of analyzability. The patient I have chosen to illuminate what I feel is at issue on the matter of analyzability also demonstrates violent projective identification.

That this patient is psychotic, however, is irrelevant. Even though, as Freud (1918) implies, it is the psychotic states which enable us to see what would otherwise remain invisible, a main thrust of Meltzer's work (as well as that of others already referred to) is that the primitiveness of projective identification does not limit its pervasiveness in the transference.

I submit that the clarification of projective identification is a conceptual advance, a "clarification of theory" of the sort that Seeley feels is necessary to advance psychiatry. This clarification makes possible more accurate work in the analytic process; it entails no "invention of practice."

In "normal" patients, the clues indicating a state of projective identification are often subtle, even downright banal—a silence, or a frequent "you know" interlarding the patient's talk, or his stating he has "nothing to say" or "nothing on my mind," or leaving out key details so that the analyst feels mildly confused. In saying "you know," the patient implies that he knows about the analyst and his ways of thinking. The patient is thereby able to conduct himself as though he were the only person present: separateness has been destroyed.

Somewhat surprisingly, perhaps, violent projective identification can also occur quietly, particularly in the "nonpsychotic" patient. It steals in and occupies the transference silently. It may betray itself only by a wisp of condescension ("I'm sorry, I didn't hear that, Doctor"), or of earnestness ("I was thinking about what you said in yesterday's hour"), or of cooperation ("I really wanted to come today"), etc. The fact that seemingly intact neurotic patients employ such a violent psychotic mechanism serves only to make it more elusive. In its presence, however concealed, any interpretative work not directed to the state of projective identification is pointless. Without differentiation any relationship, much less an analytic one, is impossible. Silence on the part of the analyst is also pointless, and tends to make a bad situation hopeless.

Clinical Material

The patient is 21 years old, in his first year of analysis. He has ideas of reference (people are talking about his being feminine), occasional auditory hallucinations (voices talking about his being queer), and had initially a profound disturbance of volition (unable to work). Currently he is self-supporting, and pays for his analysis himself. Three years ago he had two cosmetic rhinoplasties which he feels completely ruined him. He blames his intense anxieties when he is with people on his ugly face.

On a Friday he brought in a dream:

"I'm in your office. The session's finished and I'm sitting on the couch. A man comes in and you begin talking to him. You're very friendly. You're laughing and joking. Then I notice you have the same self-consciousness that I have and that you're just like me!"

He said he awoke from the dream "completely confused. I didn't even know the month." He then went to the bank, where the teller remarked good-naturedly that the patient "really seemed out of it." He said to me, "I didn't know anything. I was in a daze. And no matter how I tried I couldn't seem to do a thing about it."

In dream and fantasy, the patient is patently inside of me. I have the same "self-consciousness" that he does. My self is the same as his. When he looks at me, he sees the same self as when he looks inside himself. To get this inside view, he obviously must be inside of me. In his fantasy I now no longer exist as a separate object, with an inside space specifically my own. We both observe me the same way: from the inside.

Furthermore, he is unable to distinguish between his inner world of dreams and fantasies and the outer world. He wakes up, but remains in the timeless world of dreams ("didn't even know the month"). Even the bank teller notes the confusion. He observes that the patient is "out of it," spatially dislocated. He is unable to find his way out of his dreams into the real world.

The patient then makes the observation that he can't do a thing about extracting himself from his dazed and confused condition, "no matter how I tried." His state of projective identification is as deeply rooted in his unconscious as is the dream. He can no more alter this state than he can consciously write the script of his dreams. In fact, his projective identification *is* the dream, continued into his waking life. And there is nothing he can consciously, by force of will, do

— 319

about it. Actually he is more helpless than in a nightmare, for he can't escape by forcing himself awake.

What about analyzability under these circumstances? That he came to the hour, that he brought in a dream and associations to it, does not change the fact that this patient *is not awake*. How does one interpret a dream without awakening the dreamer? Or, to put the question of analyzability another way, what can an ego psychology contribute to the therapeutic process in the absence of a waking state?

Zetzel, in a 1955 paper, drew a line between those analysts who stressed the role of the ego and the analysis of the defenses and those who stressed primitive fantasies and early object relations. As examples she cited Sterba (1934) and Bibring (1937) who are "intimately involved with development of the ego-psychological approach, postulating a therapeutic split and identification with the analyst as an essential feature of transference" (p. 370), in contrast to Melanie Klein who "emphasizes the role of early introjective and projective processes in relation to primitive anxiety ascribed to the death instinct and related aggressive fantasies" (p. 371).

The "ego-psychological approach" led to the concept of the therapeutic or working alliance, with analyzability depending in large part on the patient having sufficient ego resources to enter into such an alliance. In a 1968 paper Greenson writes, "The patient must have the capacity to form a relatively reasonable object relationship to the analyst and also maintain contact with the requirements of the analytic situation" (p. 17).

For the Kleinians, however, analyzability does not depend first and foremost on a "sound therapeutic alliance based on the maturity of the patient's essential ego characteristics," but rather on the analyst's capacity for dealing with primitive fantasies and the primitive anxieties fueling them.

As my patient demonstrates, projective identification is a primitive mechanism that is linked to the deepest levels of the unconscious. With its presence, an "essential ego" (Zetzel's term) is not in a waking state, regardless of whatever "as if" ego functions are custodially in use.

Under conditions of projective identification, it seems to me that analyzability depends on the ego state of the analyst, not of the patient. The patient is, as it were, helplessly dreaming. Projective identification adds further to the analyst's burden in that it is useless for him, under these circumstances, to deal with any other aspect of the transference; if he does, he merely sets in motion a futile "as if" analytic relationship.

On Monday, coming for his hour, the patient saw me in the street. Tuesday he brought in a dream:

"I'm coming down the hall toward your office. When I get to your door, I notice it doesn't have a doorknob but a padlock. Someone has broken in, for the door is splintered. I come in and sit down. Then I notice the walls are flimsy, and I get the feeling they might collapse. I'm frightened I'll be trapped inside."

He spoke of our having met on the street the day before. "It was a tremendous *shock*! I was really stunned. You looked so different. Up here you're more like a regular guy—more my age."

I interpreted to him that the dream was a reversal: someone had not broken in, but had broken out. I had escaped; with a shock, he found me living freely a life of my own in the street. In the dream he reverses this. He forces his way back into me, breaks into my pad, and rips off my lock.

The sense of shock the patient felt at seeing me accompanies the transition into reality (however brought about) from a state of violent projective identification. This transition is as startling to a patient as being suddenly awakened, and when it occurs there is no mistaking it. When a patient describes looking at the world around him following such a transition, he indicates it is with a feeling of pristine astonishment. One patient compared it to stepping from a dream world into the middle of a busy intersection. Another patient said: "I just can't describe it. I don't know what happened to me. It was like waking up. All I know is that as I got into my car it was all different. I mean, the car was the same and all, but it was as though I had been asleep and woke up."

My patient then associated to what had happened in my

waiting room a week before, the previous Tuesday. He had arrived a few minutes early and was waiting for me to come out to receive him for his session. Suddenly a man (a drug detail man) came into the waiting room. Terrified, the patient leaped to his feet, mumbled apologetically for getting the time mixed up, and fled down the hall. "I just flipped out," he said. (Note that what actually happened here to the patient on that Tuesday happens to me in his dream the following Friday: his dream of a man coming into my consultation room— a further manifestation of projective identification. In his dream, however, I laugh and joke with the intruder—a point I shall come back to in a moment.)

This material, I believe, throws light on the patient's ideas of reference. His alleged femininity refers to his particular state of violent projective identification: he is inside the mother's body, having forced his way into her. This internal reality is now represented by the analytic mother and the geography of the analytic setting. To see this mother "on the outside," in the street, is "shocking"; to be caught inside her, however, is "terrifying" (the patient leaping to his feet when the drug detail man came into the waiting room).

The "onslaught" which underlies his violent projective identification is now directed toward himself with a vengeance. (As I said earlier, ". . . following intrusion by the self, the object is felt to intrude in turn." To this I might now add "and what the object contains, such as the father's penis.") He is attacked by the father's penis (man entering waiting room-mother) or, equally terrifying, he can be trapped inside the mother (waiting room walls may collapse).

He deals with the father's attack in two ways. The first, of course, is flight. The second, more sophisticated, he uses in the Friday dream: in it he has me, representing himself, laughing and joking with the intruder; that is, homosexually seducing him. This of course makes him "queer," the very accusation he hears the voices lodge against him.

The "intrusive identification" this patient demonstrates, which results in intense persecutory and claustrophobic anxieties, is a constant configuration in violent projective identification. Again, the fact that this mechanism is wholly un-conscious places the responsibility for dealing with these anxieties on the analyst. There is no point, in my view, in casting about for alliances with one part or another of the patient's ego, except for the patient finding his way to the consultation room. Only the analyst, with a cartographer's persistence and preciseness, can make clear to the patient the psychic spatial confusions.

Unless the projective identification is immediately and con-tinuously interpreted, the analytic process deteriorates rapidly. Either the analyst becomes a persecutor whom the patient runs from or else tries to seduce, thereby stirring up intoler-able homosexual anxieties; or claustrophobic terrors propel the patient from the couch into a "flight into health"; or acting out supervenes; or the patient settles in (particularly schizoid patients) until this fundamentally interminable situation becomes intolerable; or, as not infrequently hap-pens, the analyst falls back on an "invention of practice," such as group therapy.

This reference to group therapy is not made fatuously. Three patients (not psychotic, according to current diagnostic criteria) worked with me for several years in group therapy before beginning analysis. It is apparent from their analytic work that these patients are dominated by violent projective identification. As mentioned earlier, projective identification reaches to the deepest levels of the mind; yet, perhaps con-trary to expectations, it frequently conceals its presence. This is why I do not think the technical resources available in group therapy are adequate for dealing with projective iden-tification.

Up to this point I have been considering the question of analyzability primarily in terms of the technical problems raised by projective identification. I want to consider now the relationship between violent projective identification and hate, after which, I believe, a broader statement as to what is at issue in analyzability may be possible. I shall begin with a *clinical vignette*:

A 30-year-old man, in his fourth year of analysis, began an

hour by saying he had met a colleague of mine in the street. At least, he assumed the man was a colleague, having seen me with him on occasion at lunch. As they came into my building the patient had walked behind this man, and he stayed behind him on the elevator. For some reason the patient felt very nervous.

He then said he had just come from school. (He is woefully behind in life: at the age of 30 he is taking classes he should have finished at 18.) He had had his usual hang-ups in class: "The damndest, craziest fantasies kept coming into my head," and he couldn't follow the professor's lecture. The fantasies were the same as always—about girls, better careers for himself, etc. He "would so like to understand what the hell it's all about!"

Nothing characterizes this patient more than his wish to understand. He strives mightily to comprehend any interpretation I offer. He has striven this way for years on end, with little change. Yet he remains articulate, gentle, friendly, cooperative: all one could ask for—*in a colleague*! It is precisely by entering into the analyst from *behind* that he becomes such a colleague, his nervousness while standing behind "my colleague" indicating a dim awareness on his part of his intrusive identification.

In the Wolf-Man case, Freud (1918) gives a masterful description of this type of violent projective identification: "The patient with whom I am here concerned remained for a long time unassailably entrenched behind an attitude of obliging apathy. He listened, understood, and remained unapproachable. His unimpeachable intelligence was, as it were, cut off from the instinctual forces which governed his behavior in the few relations of life that remained to him" (p. 11).

It is to be remembered that this patient's first course of treatment with Freud lasted four and a half years. Only at the very end, under the pressure of an imposed termination date, did Freud (1918) obtain "the information which enabled me to understand his infantile neurosis" (p. 11).

I will submit that what appears to be simply an earnest

insistence by my patient to be just like the analyst—understanding and helpful and *analyzed*, etc.—is in fact a manifestation of the hate which Freud speaks of as being older than love. It is a hate that must be conceptualized in ontological terms, rather than instinctual.

This *ontological hate* refers to a negative condition of being set against the sources of life. Put another way, this hate does not allow life to come into being. It positions itself behind life in order to shut off the wellsprings. This hate primordially repudiates any idea of being "behind" someone in the sense of supporting and nourishing and protecting and comforting. On the contrary, to be "behind" someone, as for this patient, means completely to enter into and take over. The patient positions himself behind me, not to be given to by me, but to *become* me. In his becoming me, I become annihilated.

At issue with this patient is not only that he goes into his own *behind*; in addition, he does not remain in front where he can be given to. He digs out his own fantasies rather than listening to the professor up front, or stands behind the analyst rather than lying in front on the analytic lap where he can be held and fed. His "onslaught on the mother" indicates a condition of being, and its description is facilitated by employing an ontological framework. It is this condition which I referred to as *ontological hate*. The *behind* is preferred to the breast, and this preference expresses a negative ontological principal. I suppose one could think of it as the ancient and continuing confrontation between the dark, nether worlds below and the regions of light above.

Unfortunately, ontology isn't of much use in psychology. Nonetheless, it is this sort of "impractical" ontology which I believe Freud was trying to define scientifically with his death-instinct theory. There is a remarkable passage in an article by John Wren-Lewis (1966) in which he says that Freud

had come to the conclusion that the formation of the super-ego, the moral conscience, involved some absolutely basic negative principle which he called the death-wish, a principle far more negative than mere aggression. He went on to try to fit this idea into a materialist metaphysic, by interpreting it as something like the inbuilt urge of all living materials

> to return to the inorganic state; he also toyed with the notion that the interplay of the death-instinct, (Thanatos) and the love-instinct (Eros) might be a manifestation at the human level of the negative and positive forces of electricity. These speculations have brought his whole idea of a death-wish into discredit in subsequent psychoanalytic thought, but in the midst of this metaphysical bath-water, which we can let go happily, there seems to me to be a baby of insight which is of the utmost importance. The metaphysical language points to it, yet at the same time obscures it. The truth is that moral sadism is not a *product* of some occult negative force, but a negative principle in itself, the fundamental turning of the spontaneity of the inner life against itself [pp. 101-102].

Freud clearly recognized the existence of a primal hate. However, in attempting to adapt it to various scientific models, his profound insight became nearly inundated in metaphysics.

I suggest that in addition to ontologic hate, there is another set of motivational forces actuating projective identification. I shall call this set of forces "consuming love," which, like ontological hate, annihilates and destroys the separate existence of the object (cf. Freud's statement quoted earlier: ". . . the phase of incorporating or devouring—a type of love which is consistent with abolishing the object's separate existence"). Nonetheless, as Freud indicates, this consuming is still related to love. It is linked to passion, and it derives from instinctual sources. Ontological hate, however, older than love, annihilates *by choking off the life of the object before it ever comes into being*. It does "not after all stand in any simple relation" to love.

For example, the patient just presented here has said many times that he can't picture me out of the office—"I just can't imagine you in any other place or situation. Only in your office." This sort of comment is frequently heard from patients. It usually indicates a state of violent projective identification and is grounded in ontological hate.

Such a patient absolutely insists that the mother should have no life of her own. Nothing is to live in her; she is to have no intercourse; she is to beget no children; the teeming traffic of sex and babies and milk is not to swirl through and out of her. In the office—where my patient visibly works so hard, is so "cooperative," manifests only the best intentions—nothing comes alive. The mother is locked in with her still-born. His ontological hate denies the fact that she *ever* lived.

Projective identification, which is one of the inalienable rights of the infant—the right to rid itself of unbearable pain—is also a nearly perfect vehicle for ontological hate in its remorseless, alienating attacks on the sources of life itself. On the matter of analyzability the technical issues are similar, whether projective identification is derived from ontological hate or from consuming love. Prognostically, there is a great dissimilarity, depending upon the ratio of one to the other. In dealing with projective identification, it is my experience that hate must have first priority.

Perhaps it is consuming love and ontological hate to which Robert Frost draws attention in his poem, "Fire and Ice."

> Some say the world will end in fire,
> Some say in ice.
> From what I've tasted of desire
> I hold with those who favor fire.
> But if it had to perish twice,
> I think I know enough of hate
> To say that for destruction ice
> Is also great
> And would suffice.

Perishing by love and freezing with hate are clinically evident, I believe, in three consecutive dreams of an acutely suicidal patient, in which one can follow the change from consuming love to ontological hate and, *pari passu*, the patient fixing her thoughts on sleeping pills, graves, and cemeteries.

Mrs. R. is 34 years old, thrice divorced, with two children, Paul, 14, and John, seven. She is in her second year of analysis.

On a Wednesday she brought in the following dream:

"A house is burning and I'm there. I felt I had to save John's baby book. I did and then ran in to get Paul's, too. I was very worried about losing the books. My legs got burned a little, but everybody was safe. I saved the baby books."

I had that week made a time change in her analytic hours, which the patient mentioned after telling the dream. The house in the dream was the one she had lived in at age ten, when her baby sister was born. She had hated this sister "with a passion."

Her passionate hate (house on fire) for her mother's baby (her sister), as well as for the analytic babies whose existence the schedule change made her aware of, is apparent. She also tries to keep safe from the holocaust raging inside her yet another baby—herself—hidden away in her children's baby books. This hate is linked with love. Her consuming love threatens the other babies, but she herself wants the mother. She tries to preserve a hiding place for the needing baby in herself so that the mother can find it. The babies need the mother (unless she comes, they die), and the mother risks her life seeking her infants. Ontological hate is peripherally visible in the emphasis on the inanimate (the books); nevertheless, "everybody was safe."

The next day, Thursday, Mrs. R. brought the second dream:

"I'm at this river back home. It's really lovely. The water is crystal clear. Then there's this tall building by the river, and I can see its reflection in the water. The water is so absolutely clear that I can't tell the difference between the real building and the reflection of it in the water. It's very peaceful."

Mrs. R. then said that back home it wasn't at all like in the dream. Huge chemical plants line the river. "They pour all their crap into it, and it's so polluted you can't believe it."

She had had trouble sleeping the night before and had almost taken some tranquilizers. (She keeps hundreds of pills in her house, enough to kill her many times over.)

The differentiation between mother and baby, clearly maintained in the dream of the day before, is now obscured. The analytic mother who sits up (tall building) is indistinguishable from the soiling and wetting baby (reflection on river below) lying on the couch. The patient's projective identification is massive: the feeding mother and soiling infant are interchangeable. The baby denies that what it produces is crap and urine, insisting that, like the mother, it pours out lovely, life-giving fluids. In point of fact, the patient wants to feed herself pills which twice before nearly killed her.

"Back home"—that is, internally—she sees it is very unlike the dream. She tosses and turns throughout the night, restless and fitful. She is not at all peaceful, not an infant sleeping after a good feed.

Friday she brought the third dream:

"There was this group of people crucifying a baby. They stuck a pin through its heart. I was shocked, but they said it was best for the baby."

She had taken some sleeping pills, had slept fifteen hours, and felt great: "I don't even know why I'm here." The baby having been disposed of, there is no need for the mother. Projective identification is "shockingly" violent.

The hate is ontological. The pin is stuck into the center of life itself, into the heart of the baby. In destroying the baby the mother also ceases to exist ("I don't know why I'm here"). Life at its beginnings is stilled.

Mrs. R. remembered, to her surprise, that she had been thinking of graves and Forest Lawn Cemetery on her way to the session. She then said that she had "again spent the whole morning watering the lawn." She liked "the cool smell of grass and water." Unfortunately (here she giggled), she had flooded the neighbor's yard (her neighbor is a woman of whom she is unaccountably terrified); the gardener warned her that if she didn't stop watering so much, she'd rot both yards.

In wresting from the mother the mother's nurturing and generative capabilities (feeding herself pills and "again" watering the lawn), the infant destroys both itself and the mother (both yards). The "cool smell of grass and water" continues the reversal seen in the river dream: the smell doesn't come from a living conjunction—neighborly neighbors: living infant-mother—but from a common grave under a forest lawn (the entombed stillborn inside the never-to-be mother, pubic hair marking the urine-drowned gravesite).

— 329

This clinical example of "what's best for the baby" embodies, I believe, the ontological hate that Wren-Lewis refers to as the "fundamental turning of the spontaneity of the inner life against itself."

In his article "Hate in the Countertransference," Winnicott (1947) describes a dream he himself had at a time he was doing "bad work" with a psychotic patient. He writes: "In the next phase of the dream I was aware that the people in the stalls were watching a play and I was not related through them to what was going on on the stage. A new kind of anxiety now developed. What I knew was that I had no right side of my body at all. This was not a castration dream. It was a sense of not having that part of the body" (p. 197).

In interpreting this part of the dream, Winnicott says that it "referred to my relation to the psychotic patient. This patient was requiring of me that I should have no relation to her body at all, not even an imaginative one; there was no body that she recognized as hers and if she existed at all she could only feel herself to be a mind. *Any reference to her body produced paranoid anxieties, because to claim that she had a body was to persecute her.* [italics mine] . . . This right side of my body was the side related to this particular patient and was therefore affected by her need to deny absolutely even an imaginative relationship of our bodies. This denial was producing in me this psychotic type of anxiety . . ." (p. 198).

Winnicott describes this dream as marking for him "his arrival at a new stage in emotional development" (p. 197). After working through the dream he was able to take up the analysis of the patient again.

His patient I would think of as in a state of violent projective identification. As a corollary, she *hates* ontologically. She can't stand to have a body, for body means life—breasts and feeding and cleaning and penis and intercourse, etc. For her, being itself persecutes, so to "claim that she had a body was to persecute her."

Winnicott explicitly states that only in working through something in himself could he work with the patient. From his description I think that primarily at issue with his patient is the mechanism of violent projective identification ("What she needed of me was that I should have only a mind speaking to her mind") and ontological hate ("On the evening before the dream I had become irritated and had said that what she was needing of me was little better than hair-splitting" (p. 198). This is much like my last patient saying "I don't even know what I'm doing here."

Now if violent projective identification and ontological hate are part of the analytic process generally and not found only in psychotic patients (which Winnicott's self-analysis would certainly support: he worked out something in himself), then I think that an ego psychological approach to the analytic situation and the matter of analyzability is inadequate. Winnicott's statement that "the analyst must be prepared to bear strain without expecting the patient to know anything about what he is doing"(p. 198) points in a different direction entirely from a statement, for example, by Rangell in his article "The Psycho-analytic Process" (1966). Rangell writes of "the analyst's characteristic and well-known identifying stance, in which he takes up a position equidistant from the interacting intrapsychic structures within the patient. Its corollary sole and primary aim is to detect, to understand, and to interpret to the cooperating rational ego of the patient with which he is in alliance, the network of intrapsychic conflicts operative between these psychic structures" (p. 20).

I think Rangell's description misses an entire dimension of psychic life and has no relevance for ontologic hate. Specifically what I feel is lacking here is the later Freud, with his profound insight of psychic reality, however gropingly stated in his death instinct theory.

Freud was nearly 60 years old when he described the hate which is older than love. He was 64, still at the very height of his powers (*The Ego and the Id* [1923] and *The Problem of Anxiety* [1925] lay several years ahead), when he elaborated the death instinct. Admittedly, the death instinct doesn't parse biologically or metaphysically or metapsychologically.

Nevertheless, I agree with Wren-Lewis that it expresses an insight of the utmost importance.

I think that Melanie Klein made a fundamental contribution, not only in grasping this insight that Freud took most of his lifetime to achieve but also in fathoming its clinical shape, giving it a name, and thereby enabling it to become clinically approachable. Violent projective identification, I submit, is one form in psychic space of ontological hate (death instinct).

Meltzer and his co-workers have further contributed to understanding the spatial aspects of projective identification within the psychic space of the analytic couch, as well as precisely locating it there in time, in its sequential unfolding within the analytic process itself.

Summary

The understanding of projective identification as a major mental mechanism changes the concept of analyzability. Projective identification is an inevitable and ubiquitous phenomenon in the analytic process. Under conditions of projective identification, analyzability depends chiefly on the ego state of the analyst, not of the patient. The concept of a working alliance needs re-evaluation.

Projective identification is actuated by consuming love and ontological hate. Within the framework of projective identification, hate achieves structural status. Hate is older than love. In the analytic process, ontological hate as expressed in projective identification must have priority.

Discussion

R. E. MONEY-KYRLE, PH.D.
London, England

I have read Dr. Kurth's paper with pleasure and interest, and I agree with its main thesis: that a deep understanding of projective identification, particularly of the "ontological" hate which can be expressed in it, does add greatly to the power of analytic therapy. It is, I take it, "ontological" in the sense that Melanie Klein felt it to result from a primal envy of life and creativity, which she linked with the "death instinct." Moreover, she thought it innately present in different degrees in different individuals. But perhaps its commonest clinical manifestation occurs when the mother or analyst does not understand and receive that projective identification of bad feelings which is the baby's "inalienable right"; for then, just as in former days a beleaguered city which did not surrender by a certain time was considered fit only for assault, murder, and rape, so the baby, or patient, in fantasy violently enters to destroy, and may then feel itself imprisoned in a dead mother or analyst and unable to get out.

As to the analyzability of a patient under conditions of violent projective identification depending on the ego state of the analyst and not on the co-operation of a patient who, for the time being, cannot co-operate, I would suppose this to be in part the result of a more general difficulty, namely, that no analyst can be fully successful in dealing with something in a patient with which he is not fully familiar in himself. If so, the awareness of this difficulty is surely a recurring problem each time we begin to see "as through a glass darkly" the next insight we may be about to gain from the infinite depths of the unconscious.

PETER H. KNAPP, M.D.

Boston, Massachusetts

The central points of this paper are clear: First, all individuals have early modes of reacting in which there is faulty differentiation between the self and a key other person and in which dangerous, painful, or otherwise distressing impulses and attitudes are attributed to the outer environment; second, when these primitive modes are mobilized in the psychoanalytic relationship, they must be dealt with, because otherwise they act as premises distorting and largely vitiating all the more mature and rational layers of communication which may coexist with them.

I applaud Dr. Kurth's emphasis on these important principles. I endorse his ideal of making them clear to the patient "with a cartographer's persistence and preciseness," and I support his assertion that to do so requires not only patience but fortitude, for the task places an extraordinary strain on the attitudes and resources of the therapist.

Having said that, let me make some critical remarks. It is ironic, though scarcely paradoxical, that few of those able to grasp the most archaic strata of psychic functioning have a comparable ability to formulate them in language which is precise and unambiguous. Among those few, Greenson, Winnicott, Bertram Lewin pre-eminently, and some of the giants outside of psychoanalysis, such as Piaget and Cassirer, have a place in my personal pantheon. I would have to exclude the present paper, for it leaves me with too many questions.

First of all, it covers a vast terrain. Projective identification, analyzability, and hate include much of the entire realm of pregenital psychology and raise a plethora of questions about technique and about the whole problem of the origins of human destructiveness. Furthermore, "projective identification" and "violent projective identification" are not clearly delineated. Reference to Melzer's work does not provide self-evident clarification. The author implies that projective identification is always present in the early phases of development, and that when hate is involved it is "violent"; but later he quotes Freud among others as indicating the near inseparability of destructive and libidinal currents in early oral developmental phases. Does the predominance of hatred make for a projective solution rather than an introjective one? Or is it just that destructive components early in life impede development diffusely, leaving residual ego defects and faulty self-differentiation?

I'm inclined to agree that "normal" patients frequently use projective identification. Indeed, Pinderhughes has recently clarified the role of this type of mechanism in the widespread social "disease" of racism. However, we must ask what are the cues, going beyond the stereotyped and automatic conventions of ordinary language, which indicate a condition sufficiently pathological to be called projective identification. Is every use of "you know," or even of "you-me" confusion, to be so dignified? Moreover, important questions lurk in Kurth's own linguistic model: adultomorphic metaphors of assault, of expelling part of the self, entering into others, have complex and sometimes contradictory implications.

Finally, I wonder if in pitting ego psychology against primitive introjective-projective fantasies he is not setting up a false dichotomy. Either one can be ridden as a hobbyhorse, and both can be seen as formulations that have been helpful in clarifying disparate aspects of behavior.

The question of analyzability of patients is disposed of by an implicit pun. Kurth reduces it to the doctor's "analyze ability." The burden is thrust upon the analyst. With all due regard for the importance of this reminder, it ignores the fact that there is a wide and still poorly understood spectrum of abilities among patients to go through and gain from the process of analysis. One might as well say that the curability of tumors is a function only of the skill of the surgeon. The author remarks that there is "no point in casting about for alliance with one part or another of the patient's ego, except for the patient finding his way to the consultation room." That alone may be an important exception, if we take it to stand for a persistent attempt at sticking to a difficult therapeutic bargain. We are given here no details about how to deal with the primitive processes under consideration, nor any way of assessing how deeply it is possible to change them. There is a danger of playing conceptual games with the limitations of analysis, like a tailor designing ever more primitive clothes for the Emperor.

As to hate, there is also a danger of decrying Freud's "mythology" only to substitute yet another. The potentially interesting mix of Melanie Klein and existential "ontology" is not developed fully enough here to clarify the obscurities surrounding the origins of hate and the complexities of its dynamic epigenetic and structural organization.

A final critique concerns Kurth's reliance upon Seeley: that what we need in order to advance the future of psychiatry is "clarification of theory" rather than "inventions of practice." True, purely clinical innovations by themselves are of limited value. However, "clarification" must mean more than mere verbal elegance and certainly more than the elaboration of new theories; we have had enough of that in psychoanalysis. I submit that what we need now are systematic ways of observing and recording our observations and ways of testing theory. To paraphrase Kant, concepts without (psychoanalytic) percepts are as empty as percepts without concepts are blind.

Despite all this, however, the paper still has a fascinating, primitive bear by the tail. We must be grateful to Kurth for continuing to work at clarifying these murky levels which contain so many pivotal phenomena. To name only one, I have been struck by what one might call structural reversibility in projective identification: an analysand may bring material susceptible of at least two interpretations, both of them correct.

I think that this type of double version can be discerned in the dream of Kurth's patient about seeing the analyst talking to a strange man. In one version the dreamer portrays himself as the doctor, weak and ingratiating, and in the other as the intruder, powerful and intimidating. By means of such dreams, employing fluid, partially differentiated fantasies, the small child who continues to exist in each dreamer actually plays with both versions and plays both versions of self.

A final caution: for these manifestations of projective manifestation to emerge as a dream there must be a dreamer, aware of dreaming, not a "dreamer performing dreams," to use Jung's description of the schizophrenic. If the dreams are to become assimilated in analysis there must be analytic dreamers, patient and analyst, who can grasp and express these strata, who can enter one another and come back, aware of where they have been. This is why I say ego psychology and alliance are here to stay, along with primitive fantasies.

Much remains to be discovered about these phenomena of dreaming and of empathic communication; we need more research. If Kurth has not laid projective identification, analyzability, and hate to rest, he has kept them thoroughly alive, and for that we can be grateful.

MARK KANZER, M.D.

New York, New York

The differences between the Kleinian and the contemporary Freudian structural schools have been amply discussed elsewhere. To the proponents of the former, the studies of Meltzer on projective identification, here elaborated by Kurth, may offer opportunities for a clarification of theory and practice. For the latter, their basic criticisms of the Kleinian school remain unchanged—i.e., the fixation on a mythology of the infantile mind which is made retroprojectively to harbor the maturer functional capacities and adaptive experiences of the personality. The oversimplified and distorted Kleinian mechanisms constitute a closed system of ideas which confirm each other, exclude alternatives, and are not susceptible to external validation.

I shall illustrate the latter viewpoint by an appraisal of one of Dr. Kurth's cases. We are told that "prismatically" (not structurally!), violent hate-impelled projective identification involves "envy, persecutory anxiety, possessive jealousy, defi-

ciency of trust, intolerance of separation, etc." These tendencies are supposedly present in the mind of the infant and
are sufficiently explained in terms of the instincts and a
"primordial" rejection of the external world. Apparently no
history of individual development is necessary, and we receive
none. The contemporary adjustments of the patient, mentioned in passing, are merely a façade through which the
persistent primordial nucleus may be discerned, and appear to
be the sole determinant of behavior.

Thus there is no need for the differentiation of individual
personality types or neuroses. In introducing us to the patient,
we are assured that the circumstance that he is psychotic may
be considered "irrelevant." No doubt the converse applies in
other cases—in fact, the great merit of the newly promulgated
concept of violent projective identification appears to lie in
the fact that the common remarks of analysands ("I was
thinking about what you said in yesterday's hour"; "I really
wanted to come today," etc.) may be confidently interpreted
as infantile impulses to fuse in violent identifications with the
analyst. The closed system is manifested in the admonition
that "the fact that seemingly intact neurotic patients employ
such a violent psychotic mechanism serves only to make it
more elusive." The equation having been established, any
other interpretative work is regarded as "pointless" until the
patient has yielded to the insistent instruction.

The youth in question had encountered a drug salesman in
the waiting room of the analyst's office. He was upset at the
prospect that time schedules had been mixed up, and fled
from the competitive situation. The dynamics of the episode
were illuminated by a subsequent dream in which the analyst,
at the end of the session, was seen as laughing and joking with
another man who entered. The therapist revealed himself to
be as self-conscious as the patient himself. Such reversals of
identity are common enough in dreams and invite the clinical
surmise in the above instance that the patient, if *he* were the
analyst, would assume a more friendly mien at the end of the
session. He hints that the analyst himself suffers from his own
fault of self-consciousness, a hint which (as Greenson points

out) calls for frank discussion rather than the bland assumption that the patient must be engaging in projection. The leap to an id interpretation about homosexuality obscures these important "surfaces" of contact.

We are told that the patient remained in a confused state on the day following the dream. Dr. Kurth prefers to emphasize the confusion rather than the predominantly successful way in which (so far as I can tell) he pursued most of his activities. Even the "confusion" makes a great deal of sense if the bank teller is seen as a substitute for the analyst and the "confusion" as a parody of the habitual rejection of normal and common-sense elements in the analytic situation. The teller even gives the analyst's habitual geographical interpretation that the patient "really seemed out of it."

Dr. Kurth proceeds to treat the entire occurrence and its narration as inaccessible dreams and asks us to believe that though the analysand "came to the hour [and] brought in a dream and associations to it, [this] does not change the fact that the patient *is not awake*." (I would shift the italics here to the word "fact.") I do not understand the question that follows: "How does one interpret the dream without awakening the dreamer?" Again the closed system—why *not* awaken the dreamer and make the interpretation? That would be safer than to permit him to pursue his somnambulistic course out of the office at the end of the session.

As to the question, "What can an ego psychology contribute to the therapeutic process in the absence of a waking state?", it is difficult for that matter to know what a geographic reorientation can contribute, in the absence of a waking ego. To be sure, even in sleep and hypnosis there is some activity of the waking ego. To deny the existence of a therapeutic alliance, which may be discerned even in a patient's dreams, is to allow for only two states of contiguous narcissism. Thus, when Dr. Kurth rejects the recommendation given not only by Dr. Rangell but also by both Sigmund and Anna Freud that the analyst take a stand between the ego and the id, he seems to have in mind the model of a meeting only in the sphere of the id. The intermediate stand rules out neither id contacts nor the analyst's self-analysis; it does call for the supplementary ego contacts without which there is neither control over nor therapeutic benefits from the mutual regressions.

The neglected normal ego of Dr. Kurth's patient makes another appeal for recognition when a follow-up dream takes as its point of departure an upsetting experience in which the analyst was encountered outside the office. His appearance is contrasted with that inside the office where he gives the impression of a "regular guy—more my age." In the dream, the analysand proceeds to the office and finds the door splintered as if some one had broken in. He enters, but fears he will be trapped. The obvious suggestion of a wish to break through office barriers to the establishment of friendly contacts (just as in the other dream) is given no consideration at all. We are not told how the analyst reacted to the encounter with the patient on the street. We may well suppose that the repeated refusal to recognize the ego's wish for normal and mature contacts with the analyst will build up a state of frustration and latent angry violent projective identifications which need not be attributed solely to infantile rejections of the outer world. Alternative constructions are rigidly excluded in a world in which the therapeutic alliance is rejected by the analyst.

The contrast put forward between those analysts who postulate a therapeutic alliance and others who emphasize the role of early introjective and projective processes is spurious. It applies only if one assumes that there is no element of a normal ego operating to observe and learn about the infantile processes, and thus to control and assimilate them. Without such an assumption, we cannot apply Freud's ideas about conflict, symptom formation, and normality or the potentialities of analytic cure. Dr. Kurth's presentation is of service in clarifying these issues.

MARJORIE BRIERLEY, M.B.B.S.
Cumberland, England

This is a striking and persuasive paper. Clarification of theory always has to be tested by practical experience. Thus Dr. Kurth's theses seem to me to demand evaluation by clinical evidence from as many working psychiatrists as can provide relevant material to corroborate, modify, or offer alternative hypotheses. Although here I can be of little help, my former practice having consisted almost entirely of psychoneurotic and character cases, some of these patients naturally exhibited psychotic traits, e.g., they were obsessionals with persecutory tendencies or anxiety types with schizoid difficulties in maintaining relationships. Some of the latter were inhibited by fear of destroying their objects—Dr. Kurth aptly phrased this "consuming love." But I can recall no instance of the kind of confusion of identity he illustrates.

The obsessionals' persecutors were always felt to be distinct from themselves, enemies with whom they had to contend. Indeed, in 1945, when I discussed the variety of identificatory relationships, I was interested in a more positive aspect that had come to my notice, namely, that projective identification could be the narcissist's route to good object relationships. Hence I suspect that even if this violent projective identification is a very early and universal mechanism, it is chiefly psychotics who succumb to it, though this can only be a surmise on my part.

On general grounds it is well to be wary of suggestions that any one phase of development or any single mechanism is of equal importance in all cases. Pathogenic situations do vary in level of origin from person to person. Certainly the earlier they occur, the more disastrous they are likely to be, since what happens first necessarily affects all that happens later.

The patients Dr. Kurth described were indeed helpless and totally dependent upon his recognition of their condition and his ability to help them; otherwise their analyzability would

— 341

have come to an end. But do not such crises differ in *degree* rather than in *kind* from those that occur in analyses where there is more of a so-called therapeutic alliance? Every patient is dependent on the analyst for aid and support in assimilating whatever he has so far succeeded in keeping out of consciousness. Any persisting blind spot in the analyst can prevent further progress.

Winnicott's dream is a remarkable example of self-help stimulated by a patient. My impression is that less dramatic instances of unconscious response to a perplexing situation are not infrequent. The analytic process affects both participants, and the patient tends to enable the analyst to continue his own analysis while conducting the patient's. Therapeutic alliance or not, the mere presence of the patient indicates at least minimum cooperation, even if he wonders why he is there. Surprise often accompanies new insight, but the "shock" mentioned here is evidently more than mere surprise. It is interesting that the male patient experienced his therapeutic shock through the accidental meeting with his analyst in the street. Probably awakening by persistent interpretation in the consulting room is more gradual?

We are accustomed to think of the capacities for love and hate as inborn potentials, but is it so easy to be quite sure that hate precedes love? True, there is plenty of evidence from dreams, etc., that being born is an unpleasant and frightening process, and that fear can easily be accompanied by feelings of aversion or revulsion, larval prototypes of hate. The first cries of infants that I heard while doing my stint of deliveries appeared to range between thin wails and quite strong protests. We have less reason nowadays to think that intrauterine life is the state of bliss that Ferenczi supposed it to be, but it must surely have phases of contentment as well as unpleasant disturbances. How can we be absolutely certain what the first feeling may have been in any given individual?

As a concept, ontological hate is in many ways preferable to the death instinct, though hate rather implies a definite object and may seem premature when applied to a congenital endowment. We already distinguish quite a number of mental polarities, and there is no logical reason why we should not accept another, analogous to metabolic anabolism and katabolism, *if this is necessary.*

Apart from all the later complications of anxiety, primary fear is self-preservative. The initial fears of the newborn are assuaged by a loving reception and continued care and consideration. Only what Winnicott called "adequate mothering" can provide the feelings of security that are a sound basis for development. When these are lacking, i.e., where mothering is far from adequate, libidinal potentials are not activated, and the infant is left to deal with a frightening world by fighting or by flight. May not unwillingness to live be a flight reaction engendered by a deprivation in infancy of what makes living feel worthwhile? In short, may not these patients be suffering from what Laing called "ontological insecurity" rather than from "ontological hate"?

DONALD MELTZER, M.D.

London, England

While my remarks on Dr. Kurth's paper will be largely critical, I wish to state at the outset that I find the quality of thought and of analytic work implied in it very high indeed. In its structure it seems really to be two papers: one on the experience of one analyst in finding that the conceptualizing of projective identification in the transference has extended the range of his analytic work, and the second on a particular view of hate ("ontological") which is felt to render it more discussible in structural terms. As only the first of these two parts relates very specifically to my own work, I will confine my remarks to it.

In my book *The Psycho-analytical Process* (1967) I have delineated "massive" projective identification from those other operations of the mechanism which occur, in keeping with Melanie Klein's description in her 1946 paper, where the central identity of the self is not involved. In her later paper "On Identification" (1955), using the Julian Green novel *If I*

Were You (1950), she took up this second issue. My own contribution was an exploration, or rather, the beginning of an exploration, of the nature of the confusional states other than altered sense of identity which accompany this "massive" projective identification. I also tried to reserve the problem of the "violence" of the intrusion into the object as a separate issue related to the degree of damage done to the object, the consequent severity of persecution, and the intensity of the depressive pain incipient to any reparative process. In his replacement of "massive" by "violent," Dr. Kurth has undone this distinction and sacrificed a certain clarity in clinical description and differentiation.

Along with this loss, it is discernible that Dr. Kurth has also lost touch with the central significance in my choice of the term "geographical." While I stressed the blurring of boundaries between self and object (the identity problem), I was interested in separating these off from certain phenomena of the consulting room related to the orientation of the patient in time and space. These matters are in fact rather beautifully illustrated by Dr. Kurth's first patient in his feelings about the analyst inside and outside the consulting room as well as in his feeling about himself awake and asleep. Dr. Mason's patient, on the other hand, presents a state of mind which I would see as related to only one of the five areas in the geography of psychic reality, namely the inside of the body of the internal mother when she has been bereft of all internal penises and their delineating functions.

It is precisely the phenomenology of these five areas (internal-external, inside-outside, and the "nowhere" of the delusional system) which I have attempted to circumscribe by the term "geographical." Each of these areas is presided over by different "laws": for instance, "causality" in the outside world, "justice" in the inside world. Each has a distinct type of dimensionality, a unique degree of reversibility, a different meaning for time, death, being. Our understanding of these differences is still rudimentary. As it grows, psychoanalysis should begin to find firm points of contact with philosophy, theology, semantics, aesthetics. Mere borrowing of terms such as "ontological" seems to me to deter rather than advance such rapprochement.

I wish to turn attention now to Dr. Kurth's idea that analyzability depends "rather on the analyst's capacity for dealing with primitive fantasies and the primitive anxieties fueling them." Whether this is a "Kleinian" attitude I cannot say, but my own book is, rather, dedicated to the view that psychoanalysis is a process with a "natural history" which is an emanation from the patient's unconscious, and that the analyst must do his best to "preside" over its evolution and allow it to take place. Theories can block this development.

I do not believe that theories matter in themselves. They are at best a notational system in our overwhelmingly descriptive science. If they help an analyst to take note of his experiences of the patient, to put them into words for himself and the patient, that is sufficient justification for their existence. To say that "unless the projective identification is immediately and continuously interpreted, the analytic process deteriorates rapidly" seems to me a political attitude rather than a statement of individual experience. I am aware that in scolding Dr. Kurth I am evading scolding myself, for I suspect that my book (which I will reread only as a form of punishment) is loaded with similar statements.

In summary then, I find the clinical work described in Dr. Kurth's paper of very high quality and a pleasure to read. The theoretical position I find not in harmony with my own, in that it takes a step backward in losing the distinction between the *disturbances of identity* and of *orientation* related to massive projective identification, confuses the issue of the *violence* and the *degree* to which the mechanism is employed, and relates analyzability to the theoretical equipment of the analyst rather than to the personality structure which may suit him for one patient and not for another. I believe, with Bion, that every analysis and every session of it must be a learning experience for both patient and analyst; otherwise it is likely to fail to benefit either.

I think it is always important to keep the history of psychoanalysis in mind, for it is a science which was founded on

Freud's unusual capacity to work both inductively and deductively. Theory and technique grow together in a spiral fashion as a result, and the main substance is basically descriptive of the phenomenology of the consulting room.

Melanie Klein's delineation of the mechanism of projective identification was a step in the clarification of the area of narcissistic identifications which Freud described through the Schreber and Wolf-Man cases. Nor was hers the first such attempt: consider Helene Deutsch's fine outline of the "as-if personality type." It surely is only one of the basic fantasies which produce narcissistic identification. Bick has defined a skin-to-skin type of mimetic identification. Others will follow as our sensitivity to the phenomena thrown up by the psychoanalytic process increases.

Author's Response

At a recent seminar I made a rather long and somewhat earnest theoretical statement. When I had finished, the leader of the seminar confessed that he did not know what I was talking about; nor, it turned out, did any of the others present. I shall use two German words to describe how I felt at that point: I felt *klein* (small) and without *freude* (joy). I can say that for the space of several moments I experienced being "kleinian" and not "freudian." I mention this experience because, in my judgment, being kleinian or freudian—in the precise sense that I am using these terms—is not compatible with being scientific.

If a fellow-worker's "scolding" makes me kleinian, or his approving makes me freudian, then my usefulness as a scientific worker ceases. I know that I am vulnerable to kleinian and freudian experiences of the sort I just described. I have observed also that I am more vulnerable to such experiences in the context of theoretical statements.

When Dr. Meltzer says that he finds the clinical material in the paper of "high quality," I am assuming that the observations there recorded approximate his own. I assume also, from Dr. Kanzer's discussion, that my observations do not approximate his.

346 —

I observe a patient who is "not awake," even though he comes to my office, steers himself to the couch, uses grammatical syntax, etc. I am not describing somnambulism, obviously. Kanzer, however, does not see what I see, nor hear what I hear. When Kanzer asks, "Why *not* awaken the dreamer and make the interpretation?" I have no doubt that Kanzer does not know what I am talking about. Which is fine! What is now needed, as Dr. Brierley indicates, is a great many more observations.

The congruence of my observations with that of a fellow worker merely sharpens a focus for observations in the future. Eventually they may be accurate enough to allow a useful ordering of the events contacted through our experiences. I believe it was Bronowski who said that the greatest obstacle to scientific work is a premature ordering or systematizing of events that have not been sufficiently observed. I suggest it is more realistic to think of ourselves not as Freudian or Kleinian, but as Babylonian: early gazers at the human firmament.

If someone had observed centuries ago that the planets have parallax, this simple observation would have disproved the immutability of the superlunary sphere. Yet not all observations are so simple. Copernican astronomy disregards common, everyday sense experience, although I understand that all surveyors to this day are practicing Ptolemaians. That my patient is not awake also disregards common-sense experience. In this century, the physicist D. C. Miller obtained a "positive" Michelson-Morley experiment thousands of times over a span of many years, yet these observations had no effect on the acceptance of relativity. It seems evident that we need not only observations, but a better understanding of the nature of observation.

We need also great improvements in language for communicating our observations. In *Second Thoughts* Bion writes, "In psychoanalysis, precision is limited by the fact that communication is of that primitive kind which demands the presence of the object . . . When it is not present intercourse between psychoanalysts will tend to jargon."

— 347

Psychoanalysis needs more observations, so that we're talking about the same things; better language for communicating our observations; and better understanding of the nature of observation—a grasp of the revolution in modern science.

I'm learning that my work is based on a good many presuppositions which need discarding or modifying, such as anachronistic notions of causality or naiveté about the complexity of systems. I have noted a disregard of the link between scientific observation and experience, an unawareness of the centrality of value judgments in scientific enterprise, a belated recognition of the problem of learning as fundamental. At issue, in my opinion, is not whether I'm a credible Freudian or Kleinian, but whether I'm a credible worker in my particular scientific field in the last half of the twentieth century.

In science the criterion for validity is empirical, and I do not believe there is one among us who entertains the notion that psychoanalytic institutes, for example, populated by ex-analysands, are models of scientific enterprise and civilized behavior. And I am not impressed, I must hasten to add, with the results of my work with analysands. I am impressed with the refractoriness of human nature and the incapacity for growth and change in a species which must change if it is to survive.

I remember attending a series of seminars some years back. The analyst presented his work with a patient, I believe at that time in its seventh or eighth year. I felt puzzled at the length of treatment and secretly thought there must be faster ways "to wake the patient up." Since then, my experience has paralleled that analyst's: despite daily work with a patient, continued tirelessly for years, the destructive forces operative in mental life exercise a hegemony that is sobering.

Kanzer states, "The obvious suggestion of a wish to break through office barriers to the establishment of friendly contacts (just as in the other dream) is given no consideration at all." The wish to establish friendly contact was considered many, many times—by the patient. Throughout our work together (now in its seventh year) the patient has acknowledged—intermittently and with the greatest difficulty—that he sees me "as really a good guy." He has made statements like "I'd rather die than let you know I like you or need you." He has wept bitterly because of the hatred he turns on those who love him and offer him kindness and affection.

As for my chance meeting with the patient on the street, I greeted him with warmth and affection.

Meltzer's formulation of the "presiding" function of the analyst in the evolution of a psychoanalysis suggests to me an underlying dualism. I feel the evolution of psychoanalysis is away from dualism and in the direction indicated, for example, in the work of Charles Peirce.

I found Dr. Brierley's statements—their tentativeness, their foundation in her own experience, their general tone of quiet mulling—wonderfully evocative. The priority she assigns to observation cannot be overemphasized. I've discovered for myself that it is one thing for me to philosophize about inductive science and quite another to practice it.

I want to focus on one statement Dr. Brierley makes, for it raises again a most baffling issue, one psychoanalysts have wrestled with since *Beyond the Pleasure Principle*: "Apart from all the later complications of anxiety, primary fear is self-preservative." The hating I observe in my patients—which may be an entirely different aspect of reality from primary fear, although I do not think so—is not self-preservative. This hating attacks life and those that make it possible. In my experience it is not self-aggrandizement gone wrong, it is a "primordial repudiation." If subsequent observations link primary fear with ontological hate and not with self-preservation, how can we account for this in terms of the dynamics of evolution, adaptation, and survival? I submit that the unprecedented destructiveness of the twentieth century gives urgency to the question.

I am not familiar with Laing's work, but if "ontological insecurity" refers to environmental failure, this is not what I am trying to draw attention to with the eminently expendable term "ontological hate."

Dr. Knapp's discussion throws out all kinds of sparks. I

agree with him that we need "systematic ways of observing and recording our observations." I would add that we need also a deeper understanding of systems and the complexity of systems. Garrett Hardin cites the work of Thomas Park, who for ten years has raised two species of flour beetles in a closed, precisely monitored universe. According to the competitive exclusion principle, one species will always win out and survive; this has invariably happened. *But*, Park and his co-workers have not been able to specify which species! The interaction of flour beetles with their environment is so complex that it is, so far, not possible to specify the conditions which give a competitive advantage to one species over the other. Whenever I hear a case history these days, I can't get those damn flour beetles out of my mind!

I feel that an important problem for psychoanalysis is how to delimit a system which can be approached scientifically. I do not believe, for example, that the life history of patients is useful to work with—not because a patient's history isn't important; it is simply too complex and inaccessible to scientific observation. It's a simple and obvious fact that we are in no position to observe scientifically experiences of which we are not a part. Yet we gather our histories and recapitulate entire childhoods, deductively elaborating sweeping conclusions. The issue of history-taking brings to mind Marlowe's words:

> Thou hast committed—
> Fornication? but that was in another Country:
> And, besides, the Wench is dead.

I think being an analysand is a difficult experience. Why an analysand chooses to stick to this "difficult therapeutic bargain" is a mystery to me. Knapp states this felicitously: ". . . poorly understood spectrum of abilities among patients to go through and gain from the process of analysis."

Judging from my experiences of self, family, analysands, community—including the psychoanalytic community—I have little doubt that hate and primitive fantasies are here to stay; whether the same is true of psychoanalysis and cooperative alliances and ego psychology, I am not prepared to say.

I found Dr. Money-Kyrle's discussion, particularly his image of the "beleaguered city," haunting and spacious. Containing the "bad feelings," to use Money-Kyrle's term—for example, through the function of reverie by the mother, as Bion so beautifully describes it—may serve, in my experience, to mobilize ontological hate. If so, the "mother's" ensconcement through the "father's" structuring capabilities presents an intolerable affront to the infantile Pretender, even as "His" containment in flesh is an infinite and unfathomable humiliation.

I wish to thank my colleagues for their extraordinarily lively and stimulating discussions.

REFERENCES

Bibring, E. (1937), Therapeutic results of psychoanalysis. *Internat. J. Psycho-Anal.*, 18:170-189.

Freud, S. (1915), Instincts and their vicissitudes. *Standard Edition*, 14:109-140. London: Hogarth Press, 1957.

—————— (1918), From the history of an infantile neurosis. *Standard Edition*, 17:3-123. London: Hogarth Press, 1955.

Green, J. (1950), *If I were you*. London: Eyre.

Greenson, R. (1968), The "real" relationship between the patient and the psychoanalyst. Unpublished paper presented to Los Angeles Institute for Psychoanalysis, 1968.

Klein, M. (1946), Notes on some schizoid mechanisms. *Internat. J. Psycho-Anal.*, 27:99-110.

Klein, M. et al. (1955), On identification. In: *New Directions in Psychoanalysis*, ed. M. Klein, P. Heiman & R. E. Money-Kyrle. New York: Basic Books, pp. 309-345.

Mason, A. (1968), Analysis of a homosexual man. Unpublished.

Meltzer, D. (1967), *The Psycho-Analytical Process*. London: Heinemann.

Rangell, L. (1966), The psycho-analytic process. *Internat. J. Psycho-Anal.*, 49:19-26.

Rosenfeld, H. (1950), Notes on the psychopathlogy of confusional states in chronic schizophrenias. In: *Psychotic States*. New York: International Universities Press, 1965, pp. 52-62.

Seeley, J. (1967), *The Americanization of the Unconscious*. New York: Lippincott.

Segal, H. (1967), Melanie Klein's technique. *Psychoanalytic Forum*, 2:197-226.

Sterba, R. (1934), The fate of the ego in analytic therapy. *Internat. J. Psycho-Anal.*, 18:117-126.

Winnicott, D. (1947), Hate in the countertransference. *Collected Papers*. New York: Basic Books, 1958.

Wren-Lewis, J. (1966), Love's coming of age. *Psychoanalysis Observed*. New York: Coward-McCann, 1967.

Zetzel, E. (1956), Current concepts of transference. *Internat. J. Psycho-Anal.*, 37:369-376.

Somatic Symptomatology in Phobia:
A Psychoanalytic Study

MELITTA SPERLING, M.D.†

A Charter Member of the Psychoanalytic Association of New York
and of the American Academy of Child Psychiatry, the late Dr.
Sperling was also Clinical Professor of Psychiatry, State University
of New York, Downstate Medical Center, Division of Psychoanalytic
Education; Training and Supervising Analyst in the Faculties for
Adult and for Child Analysis at the Psychoanalytic Institute there;
Chairman of the Post-Graduate Psychoanalytic Study Group on
Psychosomatics; and Consultant, Veterans Administration Hospital,
Northport, N.Y. As former Director of the Department of Child
Psychiatry at the Jewish Hospital of Brooklyn, N.Y. and Member of
the Faculty of the Joint Committee for Postgraduate Education of
the Kings County Medical Association, she initiated the teaching of
psychoanalytic child psychiatry there to the medical profession 30
years ago. Dr. Sperling authored 70 psychoanalytic articles and was
the recipient of the Clinical Essay Prize for Psychoanalysis.

Discussants

JOSE A. INFANTE, M.D.

Formerly Training Analyst at the Psychoanalytic Institute of the Chilean
Psychoanalytic Association and Associate Professor of Psychiatry at the
Catholic University of Chile, Dr. Infante is now practicing in Topeka,
Kansas. He has written many papers on psychiatry and psychoanalysis.

SUSANNA ISAACS, F.R.C.P., F.R.C. PSYCH.

Dr. Isaacs, a Child Analyst, is Physician-in-Charge, Department of Child
Psychiatry, Paddington Green Children's Hospital in London. She is a
Member of the British Psycho-Analytic Society and a Fellow of the Royal
College of Physicians and of the Royal College of Psychiatrists.

JOSEPH WOLPE, M.D.

Dr. Wolpe is Professor of Psychiatry and Director of the Behavior Therapy
Unit at Temple University Medical School and the Eastern Pennsylvania Psychiatric Institute in Philadelphia. He has published over 100 papers and three
books on behavior therapy and related topics, the best-known being *Psychotherapy by Reciprocal Inhibition* and *The Practice of Behavior Therapy*.

MELITTA SPERLING

VICTOR CALEF, M.D.

Dr. Calef is in the private practice of psychoanalysis and is Associate Chief of the Mt. Zion Psychiatric Clinic, Mt. Zion Hospital and Medical Center, San Francisco, and Training Analyst at the San Francisco Psychoanalytic Institute and Society.

GEORGE H. POLLOCK, M.D., PH.D.

Dr. Pollock is Clinical Professor of Psychiatry at the University of Illinois College of Medicine; Director of the Chicago Psychoanalytic Institute; President of the Illinois Psychiatric Society; and President-Elect of the American Psychoanalytic Association. He is involved in teaching, private practice, administration, and research, and has published 62 papers and edited one book.

ALEX BLUMSTEIN, M.D.

Supervising Analyst and Training Analyst Emeritus in the Southern California Psychoanalytic Institute, Dr. Blumstein has taken an active interest in teaching Object Relations Theory there. He is in private practice of psychoanalysis in Los Angeles.

Somatic Symptomatology in Phobia:
A Psychoanalytic Study

MELITTA SPERLING, M.D. †

New York, New York

THE ASSOCIATION OF PHOBIA with somatic symptoms is so frequent, and the ability of phobic patients to rationalize and conceal their phobia with the somatic symptoms so great, that many phobic, and especially agoraphobic, patients are often treated solely for their somatic symptoms by the medical practitioner while the phobia is not recognized and remains untreated. Such is also frequently the case with other neurotic disorders, particularly with certain types of depression, in which somatic symptoms prevail and mask the underlying neurosis (Sperling, 1959a).

I have analyzed a considerable number of patients with multiple phobias and with severe agoraphobia in whom the phobia had not been diagnosed and who came to me for analysis because of their somatic complaints, which had not responded to medical treatment. I have also observed that some psychoanalysts who treat phobic patients for their neurotic behavior tend to refer such patients for medical treatment of their somatic symptoms, especially when these symptoms develop during analysis or are of a very severe nature. In this way, the totality of this neurosis, which can express itself either neurotically or somatically or in a combination of both, is missed, and the somatic expressions of the phobia escape analytic investigation.

I have repeatedly seen patients who came for analysis because of phobia and character problems develop somatic symptoms during the analysis, usually at a time when the phobic mechanisms had been undermined by analysis but the character structure of the patient had not yet been sufficiently modified. On the other hand, some patients who had somatic symptoms preceding or concomitant with their phobia were prone to act out during this phase of analysis after their somatic symptoms and phobia had subsided (Sperling, 1968).

Because such observations suggest that the psychoanalytic investigation of these phenomena could contribute to a fuller understanding of the genesis and dynamics of phobias, I have based this study on extensive and intensive psychoanalytic study of children, adolescents, and adults whom I have analyzed during all phases of phobia, whether apparent as such or manifested in (a variety of) somatic symptoms.

Concerning the study of the genetic factors, I have treated psychoanalytically many phobic mother and child couples, either in simultaneous or successive analysis (Sperling, 1946, 1949a, 1949b, 1949c, 1950a, 1951, 1952a, 1952b, 1955b, 1958, 1959b, 1967). This method enabled me to gain a fuller understanding of the role of the mother-child relationship in this condition and of the factors which determine the choice of the presenting symptoms—whether an overt phobia or one predominantly masked by psychosomatic symptoms—and made it possible to observe the shift from the overtly phobic to the somatic behavior and vice versa, and the conditions in which this occurred.

Fifteen years ago I studied a severe phobia *in statu nascendi* in a two-year-old child (1952a). *Linda* had been referred to me by the hospital where she had been confined twice for attacks of paroxysmal tachycardia for which no organic explanation could be found. In my treatment of the child, these attacks were found to be somatic expressions of anxiety attacks. When the overt phobia appeared the attacks subsided, although all medication and medical treatment had been discontinued.

The pregenital determinants of Linda's severe phobia were clearly observable. Oral- and anal-sadistic impulses and fantasies, focused upon the disappointing mother and rival brother, were intense. Other genetic factors were separation anxiety and depressive feelings that Linda experienced in a disturbed mother-child relationship in which the mother could not accept any overt expression of her daughter's anxiety or manifestly disturbed behavior. Only after the mother had been enabled, through concomitant psychoanalytic treatment, to allow such expressions, did the overt phobic behavior appear.

Linda had been abruptly weaned and prematurely and abruptly toilet-trained. She had had surgery (a tonsillectomy) at the age of one and a half, and she had reacted to the birth of a baby brother when she was two years old with an intensification of oral- and anal-sadistic impulses, and to a further deterioration of her relationship with her mother with an intensification of separation anxiety. For Linda, separation from her mother meant that mother had disappeared and was lost forever. The child's attacks of paroxysmal tachycardia, which usually occurred during the night, were actually a form of sleep disturbance and the equivalent of nocturnal anxiety attacks and, particularly, of separation anxiety.

I considered the formation of a phobia in Linda as a protective device in defense against a psychotic development. I had stressed this function of a phobia at that time (1949b, 1952a, 1958)—that of preventing ego disintegration by localizing and externalizing the destructive energies of pregenital impulses by means of projection, condensation, and displacement; that is, by phobic mechanisms—and this was also recognized by others (Segal, 1954).

A remark in E. Weiss's paper "The Psychodynamic Formulations of Agoraphobia" (1966) is of interest in this connection. He refers to a patient whom Freud was called to treat for agoraphobia. Freud hypnotized her and she lost her phobia. She subsequently developed a psychosis, and when Freud was called to treat her for this, he hypnotized her again and gave her back her phobia.

Because of my special interest in psychosomatic diseases in children, I had an opportunity to analyze a considerable number of children referred to me for a variety of psychosomatic diseases, with or without coexisting overt phobic behavior. I found that in many of these cases the somatic symptoms had camouflaged a severe phobia which had to be brought to the fore and analyzed in order to make possible a permanent resolution of the somatic symptoms.

The most startling finding, however, was the fact that the psychosomatic disease of the child often not only served to conceal the child's phobic tie with the mother, but in some cases also helped to conceal the mother's own severe phobia (1946, 1951, 1963). I have found one psychosomatic syndrome—mucous colitis—occurring especially frequently associated or alternating with or as a substitute for phobia. I have seen this in children, in adolescents, and in adult patients, and I would like to present case material from the analysis of each of three such patients—an adolescent, an adult, and a phobic mother and her child—to illustrate and serve as a basis for my discussion.

Case 1

Lenny, aged 12, was referred to me because of debilitating mucous colitis. I found that he had been suffering from a severe phobia since the age of three or four. He had been an anxious child who clung to his mother and would often plead with her to promise that if he should have to die she would hold his hand and die with him, and that if she should die he could hold her hand and die with her.

Following some traumatic experiences in puberty, when he was involved in a marked masturbation conflict, reactivation of his unresolved oedipal conflict and castration anxiety led to regression to the anal-sadistic phase. It was then that he developed mucous colitis, so intense as to completely immobilize him. He could not attend school (he had a school phobia from the start) nor go anywhere at all, for he always had to be near a toilet and could not leave the house without his mother. My impression was that the onset of the mucous colitis at that time prevented the outbreak of a manifest psychosis.

Analysis revealed that the unresolved preoedipal separation conflict of the anal phase had provided the pathological basis for a particularly intense oedipal conflict. During puberty a combination of traumatic events—among them the death of his grandfather (a paternal image) and, following this, sharing the parental bedroom—reactivated the oedipal and pre-oedipal conflicts.

In Lenny's case, as in most of these cases, the failure of the phobic mechanisms to protect the patient from panic and imminent loss of control mobilized the earlier established psychosomatic response. The somatic symptoms served as emergency outlets for unconscious impulses which threatened to break into consciousness (Sperling, 1955b).[1]

It seems to me that the role of pregenital and, in particular, anal-sadistic conflicts in the genesis of phobia has not received sufficient consideration (Deutsch, 1929; Sperling, 1952b, 1967). I think it is the fixation to the anal-sadistic phase of instinctual development which explains the association, alternation, or substitution of phobia with somatic symptoms in these patients, and I should like to elaborate on this point.

While *separation anxiety* operates from the beginning of life, *separation conflicts* are activated during the anal phase when anal drive and ego deveolpment as well as locomotion make their expression possible. Fixation to the anal-sadistic phase also has implications for the vicissitudes of object relationships. These will remain highly ambivalent, and the narcissistic orientation and magical thinking (fantasy of omnipotence) which are prevalent then lend a sense of urgency and reality to unconscious wishes and fantasies. The ambivalence, omnipotence, and narcissism become associated with the processes of elimination and retention, and thus sphincter control may become the most important vehicle for control of impulses in general.

Conflicts about sphincter control may become equated with control of impulses (internal reality) as well as with control of mother and external objects and situations (external reality). The inordinate need for control over one's self (instinctual impulses) and a simultaneous fear of loss of control then becomes equated with control and simultaneous

[1] For a full account of Lenny's psychoanalysis, see "Mucous Colitis Associated with Phobias in a 12-Year-Old Boy" (Sperling, 1950b).

fear of loss of control of external objects and external situations. Sphincter control may thus become a measure of the ability to control reality and of impulse control.

Such a need for control and the fear of loss of control is a characteristic and dynamically important feature in phobia and is genetically linked to the conflicts of the anal-sadistic phase. The unconscious equation of feces with objects (part and whole objects) makes the anal sphincter and its function singularly fit for the symbolic expression of separation conflicts which the child is not capable of resolving in reality.

In this connection Segal's (1954) and Wangh's (1959) cases are pertinent. Both patients suffered from intermittent diarrhea and hypercathexis of the anal sphincter. Both patients had problems with sphincter control and an inordinate fear of loss of sphincter control. Their identification of people with feces was striking, as was the equation of sphincter control with impulse control and with magical control of external objects and reality.

This extreme need for omnipotent control in phobic patients reveals itself as a wish for control over life and death, and it may be intensified by events which have the meaning of separation or loss—real or imagined—such as illness, surgery, birth of a child or a sibling, death of a parent, etc.

Phobic manifestations as an indication of problems in separating and establishing a necessary degree of age-adequate independent functioning may make their first appearance during the anal phases from one and a half to three years. An acute phobia can be precipitated during this time and at any age thereafter in a person so predisposed to this fixation by an event which represents an acute separation threat and which has the meaning of impending death (Sperling, 1952a, 1967). The proper management of these phases is extremely important for character and symptom formation, especially of psychosomatic and phobic symptoms.

Certain disturbances in bowel function, even certain difficulties in bowel training, can be the first somatic expression of such a struggle for control over and separation from mother (Sperling, 1950b, 1952a, 1952b, 1954, 1955a, 1955b, 1967).

This was the mechanism Lenny employed (he had suffered from episodic diarrhea in prelatency and during latency) in his struggle for control over and separation from mother when his phobic defenses failed and he was threatened with the outbreak of a psychosis.

I have observed this phenomenon—namely, the somatic expression of conflicts over separation and control—in the analysis of adult patients who often alternated between the somatic symptom of diarrhea and overt phobic behavior (1948), as in the following fragments from the analysis of Mrs. A., a patient in whom a severe chronic agoraphobia was covered up by an equally severe chronic mucous colitis. This case seems to lend itself particularly well to (1) illustrating the dynamic factors which account for such a phenomenon and which help us to understand its function and value in the patient's psychic economy; (2) explaining the failure of medical treatment which does not recognize nor take into consideration the underlying neurosis in such a case; and (3) explaining the failure of psychoanalysis in such a case if it does not consider and deal with the somatic symptoms as an integral part of the patient's neurosis.

Case 2

Mrs. A. had suffered a severe, chronic mucous colitis for 14 years when she came to me for analysis. She had been in prior psychoanalytic treatment for three years because of feelings of depression which she and others considered to be a result of the colitis. The colitis symptoms, for which her internist was treating her with diets and medication, had not been dealt with in that analysis.

Now 34 years old, she came to me because of an acute exacerbation of the colitis which did not respond to medical treatment. A series of tests and examinations, undertaken because of her weight loss and the acute increase in symptoms, revealed a spastic colon and hypermotility of the lower gastrointestinal tract.

The patient had developed mucous colitis at the age of 20 and her symptoms had become progressively worse. She had to run to the toilet incessantly before leaving her house, and then would have to return from the doorstep or street. Her radius of mobility spanned only the distance between toilets because she had to be sure of being able to reach one quickly.

She now felt immobilized by her illness, afraid to go out because of lack of sphincter control. Her frequent soiling accidents created embarrassing situations which caused her severe humiliation and intensified her depression. She rationalized her fear of the street, restaurants, theater, gatherings, crowds, traveling, etc., with her colitis.

The distraught woman lived in fear of certain sensations which usually preceded the onset of the diarrhea. First, she would get what she called sensations in her "upper stomach." This was a feeling of discomfort that would turn into nausea. Then the sensations would extend into her "lower stomach." When this happened, "it was too late to do anything," because an explosive and uncontrollable diarrhea followed almost immediately.

My efforts were concentrated on establishing a therapeutic relationship by helping Mrs. A. understand her use of the diarrhea as an expression of her unconscious feelings. In each instance, the connections between her feelings and the resultant symptoms had to be established with the help of dreams and associations. She began to see that the loss of control over her anal sphincter could also be linked to feelings of not being in control of situations and people—that is, of reality—and that the diarrhea in her case was the equivalent of an overt phobia and, like a phobia, served to prevent her from exposing herself to phobic situations. If she dared to so expose herself—to leave the house, go to the theater, a restaurant, or a dinner party—the ensuing loss of sphincter control and explosive diarrhea would force her to leave this situation and return home.

Mrs. A.'s increasing insight into her behavior enabled her to accept some responsibility for her somatic symptoms and thereby to gain control over, instead of feeling at the mercy of, her diarrhea. Concomitant with the improvement of her somatic symptoms, Mrs. A. expressed feelings of being trapped—like "a caged animal," but one that needed to be caged or she would go wild and then could hurt others and herself. To be aware of her repressed impulses was particularly dangerous to her because of the nature of the incorporated parental images. She felt justified in hating her father because she felt that he had rejected her. She thought of him as crazy, cruel, and irresponsible, and because she resembled him physically, she feared that she might have inherited such tendencies from him.

According to the patient, her parents were always fighting; there was a war going on between them and the house was a battlefield, especially at mealtimes. This was her anal-sadistic concept of sexuality as expressed in her colitis. She had craved her mother's approval and love and had overidealized her, becoming very submissive and close to her, and competing with father and other men for her attention. In her analysis bitter feelings emerged that her mother was a narcissistic, egotistical person who had used her and then (shortly before the onset of the mucous colitis) "dropped" her in favor of an aunt to whom she instead became very close.

Mrs. A. felt trapped in her marriage as she had felt trapped with her mother. When she married at 19, she knew she did not love her husband, but she felt that he loved her and— even more pressing—that she was indispensable to him. She could not leave him because "I am his whole life," just as she had not been able to leave the mother who had been *her* whole life. Her wrenching disappointment and the fight that resulted when her mother "dropped" her for the aunt made her decide to move with her family away from her mother's home to their own apartment. It was shortly after this decision, which had the meaning to Mrs. A. of giving up any idea of leaving her husband, that she developed mucous colitis. "If only I could have left him when my child was a baby!" she would often exclaim in her analysis. (Her mother had left her own husband when the patient was a child, though Mrs. A. expressed it as when she was a "baby.")

At the same time Mrs. A. developed the colitis she also developed food phobias: certain foods became "poisonous"

— 363

and had to be eliminated immediately because of their poisonous effect. Some foods had the "ability" to provoke almost instant diarrhea. Sometimes, when it was severe and she was sitting on the toilet and emptying herself "completely," she would feel elated, almost hypomanically so, "like other people feel when they drink champagne." Other foods would stay in her stomach "like a stone" and she would become constipated. At the first signs of constipation, she would give herself an enema and wait in fear of the terrible explosion to come. She was as much in dread of the constipation as of the diarrhea, and, as with the diarrhea, she would then not dare to leave the house. It was found that her feelings about these "poisonous" foods related mainly to her mother, but there were also definite associations with certain of them to her father.

Analysis also revealed that Mrs. A. envied any woman who could divorce her husband, either to live alone or remarry. When she left her mother (whom she then devalued as an object in reality), she transferred that unresolved dependent relationship to her husband and overcompensated for her feelings of dependence and inadequacy by devaluing him and feeling that he could not live without her (nor she without him).

Her hatred and rebellion against her husband and her symbolic freeing herself from him were expressed in her somatic symptoms, especially in the diarrhea. Her illness, of course, only increased her dependence and so further cemented the tie with her husband (mother). The precipitating factor in her decision to move was her severe disappointment in her mother. In the diarrhea which she then developed she was spewing out the worthless mother as well as the mother substitute, her husband, as feces.

Mrs. A. had hitherto been completely unaware of these connections. Now she could see that not only had her colitis been treated as a purely organic disease and not dealt with in her first analysis, but that the severe phobia underlying it had not been recognized and analyzed. She became aware that her feelings of depression, which had been regarded as a reaction to the colitis, belonged to the unresolved separation conflict, and that the colitis had been her unsuccessful attempt to resolve this conflict somatically. She had envied and hated those who could be aggressive and express themselves freely, for in her mind to be aggressive was associated with wildness and uncontrolled sexual behavior. Only in the colitis could she fight or explode openly.

At one point during these growing recognitions she was prone to involve herself in some potentially self-damaging acting out. Fortunately this could now be prevented through analysis, and she was able to utilize the energies and feelings freed from her somatic and phobic symptoms very constructively.

Shortly before the acute exacerbation of the colitis which brought her to me, Mrs. A. had suffered a severe disappointment in her analyst, with whom she had an overly positive relationship. (There may have been some countertransference problems on his part contributing to this unfortunate occurrence.) To the patient, the incident with him unconsciously represented a repetition of the experience with her mother which precipitated both her move from home and the colitis. This could be reconstructed in her analysis on the basis of dreams and associations. Two dreams are of particular interest in this connection.

Dream 1. "I was in Dr. M.'s [her former analyst's] office; there was a fight going on and I ran out of the office. I found myself unable to cross the wide street; it was too dangerous. There were cars coming in both directions."

This dream reflected her situation following the fight with her mother when she physically left her but yet remained fixated to her and unable to make the transition to true heterosexuality. Instead, she had carried over her demands from her mother to her husband—an unsuitable mother-substitute—and developed colitis. In her first analysis she had transferred the unresolved relationship with her mother to her analyst; since this transference had not been analyzed, the patient suffered a repetition of her experience with her mother. She felt betrayed and disappointed, left her analyst suddenly, and had a severe exacerbation of her colitis.

Additionally, this dream indicated Mrs. A.'s conflict and dilemma in her analysis and present life situation. She would have wanted to repeat with me what had happened both with her mother and her first analyst, but I was consistently analyzing the transference and the phobia underlying her colitis. At the time of this dream, she no longer had colitis, which in the past had served her to establish magical control and to deny her phobic dependence. Instead, she had the experience of *agoraphobia in the dream*. This brought her basic problem into analytic focus.

Dream 2. She could not walk and would never be able to walk again. She was being driven around in a car "like a baby in a carriage." She associated that her mother did not drive— her husband does the driving, and he now takes her mother's place—and also that when she had felt betrayed by her mother she determined to leave her, and later repeated the same action with her analyst.

In both instances, what occurred was unconsciously experienced by the patient as an acute separation trauma and as a situation over which she had no control. In reality she behaved as if she were in full control—she had left her mother and she broke off the analysis. This was typical behavior for her, and is typical of such patients who do not appear overtly disturbed. The conflict over separation and the struggle for control were acted out somatically in the acute exacerbation of her symptoms.

Case 3

Particularly instructive for an understanding of the interrelated dynamics of a child's psychosomatic illness and her mother's phobia are the cases of Lisa and her mother, Mrs. L. Lisa was referred to me for the treatment of ulcerative colitis when she was six and a half years old and had been sick for four years. I worked with Mrs. L. in preparatory analysis for nearly a year before starting Lisa's treatment, then intermittently during the three and a half years of Lisa's analysis, and thereafter for another three years.

From adolescence on, Mrs. L. had suffered from various psychosomatic complaints—particularly periodic chest pains, dizziness, headaches, gastrointestinal distress, and constant tension—for which she had been treated medically and with psychotherapy in the past without relief. It was found that, although she had had phobic manifestations during childhood and adolescence, she became severely phobic about the time Lisa got sick with ulcerative colitis.

Analysis revealed that Mrs. L. had at that time begun to feel very insecure in her marriage and had thought of leaving her husband. (She had married very young a man considerably older than herself and had remained in close proximity to her parents.) Also, her closest friend, to whom she was attached in a latent homosexual relationship (an important mother substitute), had just married and moved to a distant place. Mrs. L.'s older child was of school age, and she knew that she would not have any more children. Thus, after the loss of her friend, Mrs. L. became even more dependent upon her mother. At the same time, she resented her mother's increasing domination and was fearful of exposure of her own phobic dependence upon her. She experienced the loss of control over her objects (husband-friend-mother) as an imminent threat to her ability to control herself.

In this crisis, she tried to counter this threat by finding an object whom she could control and who would be completely dependent upon her. It was then that she discharged the nurse who had been with Lisa since her birth and took over the child's care herself. Shortly thereafter Lisa developed ulcerative colitis.

Lisa's illness saved Mrs. L. from a breakdown, it gave her a purpose for living, and it also dispelled thoughts of breaking up the marriage. Since Lisa's illness necessitated that her mother be in full attendance—their relationship became "of necessity" a very close one—it also provided Mrs. L. with a perfect rationalization for her phobia, which was so severe that she could not walk outside the house for even the shortest distance, or drive her car, or go to a store. She became completely tied to her sick child and to her house.

Mrs. L. was afraid of being alone in the house, particularly in the morning, when she had to spend much time on the toilet performing anal rituals. Lisa's ulcerative colitis provided Mrs. L. with an excellent rationalization for the kind of toilet symbiosis in which they spent much time together in the bathroom. Mrs. L. attributed her fear of being alone in the toilet to an experience of fainting there when she was pregnant with Lisa, and to her belief that only by leaving the bathroom door open had she been saved from disaster. She was forever afraid of something horrible happening (she always carried smelling salts and other remedies for quick revival in her handbag), but she could not define what it was she anticipated. Words such as "fear," "death," "control," "insanity" were taboo; she could use them only after she had been in analysis for some time.

Before Mrs. L. became completely house-bound, one anal practice consisted in plugging up her anus with cotton before leaving the house, for she avoided using a toilet other than her own or her mother's. Analysis showed that losing, or not having, control over her anal sphincter meant not having control over people or situations and stood for losing control of herself. Her anality was very marked, in both the erotic (anal stimulation was an important factor in her sexuality) and aggressive spheres. Her anal fixation was an important etiological factor in her phobia, in her somatic symptoms, and in her child's psychosomatic illness.

The subsiding of Lisa's ulcerative colitis and the change in her behavior, especially when she started attending school regularly and became interested in other children and began a life of her own, exerted pressure upon Mrs. L. to face up to and work on her own phobia and problems.

As she did so, she was able to reveal her most essential anal ritual, and then the full extent of her magical thinking and need for omnipotent control were brought into analysis. She had always carried in her handbag a syringe with which she would give herself frequent on-the-spot enemas. (This was the syringe which she had used on Lisa when she was little and in the early phases of her ulcerative colitis.) This ritual served many functions and had many meanings on various levels which cannot be dealt with here. Its most essential function, however, was to establish instant control in any phobic situation when there was a danger of loss of control. It also allowed Mrs. L. to reproduce the infantile situation of receiving enemas from her mother, playing the roles of both mother and child and male and female in one.

Of Mrs. L.'s many childhood memories revolving around sphincter control and sexuality, one seems particularly pertinent as a special link between sphincter control and her phobia: She could not have been more, and probably was less, than three years old, and could see herself at her grandparents' house in her grandfather's bed, where she had been put to nap. She heard her grandfather, whom she feared, say, "What if she wets the bed?" She remembers that she could not sleep then for fear that she might. Mrs. L. did not remember bedwetting, but she doubted her mother's assurance that she never did so.

Shortly after this incident, Mrs. L.'s grandfather took sick and, after a brief illness, died in that same bed. Some years later a close relative, who had not given any prior indication of illness, became suddenly sick during the night and almost immediately died. Mrs. L. was very disturbed about this and inquired why they had not brought him to a hospital. His widow explained that the man had already lost control over his anal sphincter and that this was a definite sign of imminent death. Thus, to Mrs. L., sphincter control came to stand for control over life and death. Because of the anal fixation, her sexuality and sexual excitement also assumed anal characteristics and had to be controlled in the very way she controlled her anal sphincter.

I would like to make brief mention of a 52-year-old patient, Mrs. M., whose case is of interest from several aspects. Mrs. M. suffered from recurrent attacks of paroxysmal tachycardia and from an incapacitating agoraphobia since the age of 22. Neither her paroxysmal tachycardia nor that of my youngest phobic patient, two-year-old Linda, had responded to medical treatment, but both had yielded to psychoanalytic intervention.

Mrs. M. also had a mirrorphobia. On several occasions when looking into the mirror she had seen a wild face with hair hanging over the eyes. Terribly frightened, she thereafter avoided looking into mirrors and kept none in her room. It was found that the wild visage she saw in mirrors was her concept of an insane person, and that she had a fear of going insane.

Analysis also disclosed that she had intense fears of being overwhelmed by uncontrollable impulses. Dreams of wild animals, especially of wild horses, led her to discover her wishes of running wild sexually and of running away, which she had been expressing in the paroxysmal tachycardia—running wild, losing all her inhibitions, and running away like a wild horse from captivity.

Mrs. M.'s agoraphobia became manifest after her marriage, and for many years she had required the constant presence of a companion nurse and often the presence of her personal physician. She was never without smelling salts and various medications. Her anal fixations were marked, and she had many compulsive and obsessional traits. The agoraphobia, which also served to keep her in a frustrating and sexually unsatisfactory marriage, became totally crippling after her youngest child entered school, and she could not go anywhere by herself.

Although the prognosis for a cure or even for considerable improvement of a severe agoraphobia with paroxysmal tachycardia of 30 years duration would be considered poor, Mrs. M. responded surprisingly well to psychoanalytic therapy. I have remained in contact with her for some years since termination of her analysis (and assisted several members of her family with various problems), and she has retained the good therapeutic results.

Discussion

In this paper, I could present only few and fragmentary cases, focusing on those features which I consider essential to my thesis. I had to neglect the oedipal and other aspects of phobia which have been established by Freud (1909) and subsequent investigators of this subject, too numerous to be listed here. Although many of these writers have noted the frequent association of phobia with somatic symptoms, the function and dynamic interrelation of these symptoms with phobia has not been investigated psychoanalytically.

Weiss (1966) especially stressed feelings of being sick and somatic symptoms as belonging to agoraphobia, but he failed to recognize their dynamic significance. H. Deutsch (1929), who considered phobia as a neurosis midway between hysteria and compulsion neurosis, was aware of the importance of anal fixation in phobia. She described in one of her patients the change of phobia into an obsessional neurosis with marked sadistic and murderous aggression against the mother. She observed in another case the shift from phobic to somatic behavior during the analytic session. Deutsch considered the patient's convulsion as hysterical. The patient interpreted it as a "fit of rage" and as her way of discharging destructive impulses and protecting herself from loss of impulse control and dangerous acting out.

The conflict over control and the fear of loss of control is a most prominent feature in phobia. In my opinion, the fixation and regression to the anal-sadistic phase explains and clarifies many problematic issues in phobia. It explains the frequent association of phobia with and substitution of it for somatic symptoms, especially colitis and diarrhea, in situations in which the phobic mechanisms fail to achieve externalization of the instinctual danger and to protect the patient from panic and imminent loss of control. These somatic symptoms are not merely anxiety equivalents; they are pregenital conversions in which specific anal-sadistic impulses and fantasies, particularly those related to separation conflicts and struggles for omnipotent control, are expressed and discharged. Sphincter control becomes equated with impulse control, and the conflicts about sphincter control are reflected in the inordinate need for, and fear of loss of, control in phobia.

The ambivalence, narcissism, and omnipotence of the anal phases color the object relationships and the ego and superego development. Overstimulation and hypercathexis of the anal sphincter lend anal characteristics to sexuality and sexual excitement, which have to be controlled like the anal sphincter. A clearer recognition of the pregenital substructure of phobias might enable us to deal more effectively with this widespread neurosis, which can express itself either neurotically or somatically or in a combination of both.

Discussion

JOSE A. INFANTE, M.D.
Topeka, Kansas

Melitta Sperling's paper presents a number of important observations on phobia, which she documents with rich clinical material. For the purpose of my discussion, I would like to summarize what seem to me her most relevant points: (1) the formation of phobia as a protective device against a psychotic development; (2) the role of pregenital and, in particular, anal-sadistic conflicts in the genesis of phobia; (3) the association, alternation, or substitution of phobia with somatic symptoms, especially mucous colitis; (4) the fear of loss of control as a dynamically important feature in phobia.

Before commenting on these, I want to make explicit that from my point of view there are at least two very different kinds of phobias: the true agoraphobias and the phobias to objects or specific situations (including some cases of street phobia). The first group was characterized by E. Weiss (1966) as an anxiety reaction to a danger which is consciously sensed as internal and which appears when the patient leaves a place of support. Other constant features are the need to be taken care of and the inability to tolerate the sensation of being enclosed. As Dr. Sperling puts it, "They must feel free to leave a place whenever they wish." I think that this distinction is important because there are genetic and dynamic differences between the two groups. I understand that when Sperling is talking about phobias in her paper, she is referring to agoraphobias in the way in which they have been defined here, and I will continue my comments under that assumption.

I fully agree with the idea that the formation of agoraphobia is a protective device against a psychotic development, but I don't think that this is true for other phobias. While Dr. Sperling does not offer an explanation for this fear of ego

— 373

disintegration, she implies that pregenital conflicts, especially fixation and regression to the anal-sadistic phase, are prominent. H. Segal (1954) stressed the importance of the paranoid-schizoid mechanisms in this situation, and said that her phobic patient at the peak of her anxiety felt threatened by madness. Segal's interpretation was that in this situation the patient lost a large part of her ego by projective identification and was overwhelmed by the persecution of bad disintegrated objects. Then she says, "The formation of a phobia averts such catastrophic situations, which she is then able to avoid." Edoardo Weiss's explanation is that when a repressed ego state threatens to replace the adult ego, it loses the sensation of its stability and is weakened because much ego cathexis is invested in the regressed ego state.

In phobias to objects or to specific situations, the classical mechanisms described by Freud—repression, projection, and displacement—are easily identifiable, but this is not the case in agoraphobia. Here the danger is always experienced as something internal, as I said before, and hence we cannot talk of projection or displacement in the classical sense. I think that this internal danger is closely connected with the fear of loss of control that Sperling emphasizes in her paper. The real fear is the loss of control of the mind, which is not only expressed as fear of loss of control of the anal sphincter but also, in other patients, as the fear of loss of control of the urethral sphincter or of motility. Impotence and frigidity are very common also, because of the fear of "losing control" during the orgastic experience.

We can now redefine agoraphobia and claustrophobia as particular aspects of a fear of ego disintegration. I have seen this in all my agoraphobic patients and it seems to me very clear in the examples presented by Sperling. The question is, Why is this fear so intense in these two specific situations? I suggest that the answer lies in the way in which these patients use the *primitive* mechanism of projection to get rid of their bad internal objects. My hypothesis, which I cannot develop here, is that open space is a stimulus for excessive primitive projection leading to ego disintegration, just as enclosed space evokes the fear of being stuck with all the bad objects without the means to dispose of them. The translation of these mechanisms into somatic symptoms is well illustrated in Dr. Sperling's second and third cases. Mrs. A. "was as much in dread of the constipation as of the diarrhea," and Mrs. L. plugged up her anus with cotton before leaving the house, while at the same time "she always carried in her handbag a syringe with which she would give herself frequent on-the-spot enemas."

The main point that I have tried to stress here and that I think is consistent with Sperling's observations is that there are two kinds of phobias: (1) phobias to specific situations and objects belonging to the oedipal phase, whose mechanisms are repression, projection, and displacement, and (2) agoraphobia and claustrophobia, originating in the pregenital phase, and whose main mechanism is primitive projection. While castration anxiety is predominant in the first group, fear of ego disintegration is present in the second.

SUSANNA ISAACS, F.R.C.P., F.R.C. PSYCH.

London, England

Melitta Sperling's paper aroused my interest and admiration. It also stirred hope that psychoanalytic work with children will further encourage a resolution of the unscientific squabbles which have beset our profession. For it is an observable fact that in babies and young children emotional expression and body function are intimately, indeed inextricably, interrelated. The two-year-old with paroxysmal tachycardia, described by Dr. Sperling, provides an unusually vivid demonstration of how dangerous it can be to ignore what has come to be regarded as a truism.

Truisms about psychosomatic disease and the psychogenic aspects of organic disease do now abound. It has become a sign of the up-to-date physician or pediatrician to give evidence of an interest in the interaction of mind and body. Unfortunately, truisms tend to be used to express interest while ensuring that no further enquiry shall be made. It is therefore salutary that Dr. Sperling should remind all of us psychoanalysts, and I hope our more physically orientated colleagues too, that mind and body can be simultaneously disordered and that the body's weaknesses can be exploited as a defense against self-awareness.

But I am not so content with Dr. Sperling's use of the word "phobia" to denote intense persecutory anxiety, even though this widening of the use of the word from its classical Freudian meaning has the advantage of drawing attention to the psychotic element underlying even the most ordinary phobias of everyday life.

As I have already indicated, one of my responses to this paper was to hope that work on tiny children, who are chronologically very close to the emotional roots of their mental and physical life, would diminish the misunderstanding between the various groups of Freudian psychoanalysts and thus open the way to further discovery.

An area of interest to me as a psychoanalyst trained in the Kleinian method is the role of projective identification in normal and abnormal development. The concept of an individual experiencing him or herself as capable of concretely projecting aspects of the self *into* the object seems to me invaluable in reaching toward understanding of the type of mother-child interrelated, psychosomatic illness which Dr. Sperling describes. For the object experienced as containing or being taken over by the projections is, of course, introjected.

The normal use of projective identification is as a method enabling the object constructively to modify the experience received and convey this capacity to the originator of the projection. This mechanism is the basis of preverbal communication and thus extensively used by all infants. But it is not a method exclusive to infants and abnormal adults. When resorted to with excessive hate or intrusiveness the object is experienced as disintegrated and is thus incorporated in a dangerous form. A maternal object unable to tolerate the normal, let alone the abnormal, use of projective identification leads to a distortion of development at the stage when concrete thinking is inevitable and appropriate.

Of course, a mother who herself is in a state of disordered and excessive projective identification with her baby cannot deal normally with its efforts at communication. Such a situation appears to me to underlie the type of relationship in which the mother develops manifest illness as the child improves.

This description does not of course account for the occurrence of psychosomatic illness rather than psychosis or an attempt at containing the appalling anxiety in a specific phobia. A part is played by all these and more: innate factors of organ sensitivity, the greater vulnerability of the environment to disturbance in some areas of function than others, the ego's capacity to use splitting as a defense against confusion and in the service of developing an idealized object as a normal stage of development and the innate strength of the infant's narcissistic omnipotence and envy.

The concept of projective identification with the individual's own body, viewed as external to the self, is also in need of investigation and elaboration.

Dr. Sperling's technique of concomitantly or consecutively analyzing both mother and child may be one factor in her apparent lack of awareness of projective identification in the cases she describes. The subtleties of the transference are not easily perceived, and as clear a field as can be obtained is essential. When two members of one family are in analysis with one psychoanalyst, the recognition of transference complications even at a relatively superficial level is difficult; indeed, in any but the most skilled and experienced hands it is impossible. Thus in my view it is a method to be avoided when possible. Indeed, I favor a situation in which even parental counseling is provided by someone other than the child's analyst. Otherwise greed, envy, and jealousy are avoidably increased and the role they play in the preverbal communications of child and therapist is distorted.

JOSEPH WOLPE, M.D.

Philadelphia, Pennsylvania

To a behavior therapist, what Dr. Sperling's article most strikingly reveals is how little the strict psychoanalyst gets to know about his patient as a present-day living person. This deficiency of information seems to be a natural consequence of the rules of free association. Since direct exploration of the patient's complaints is precluded or pre-empted, details about them or their relation to other events are gleaned, if at all, only indirectly or incidentally.

Dr. Sperling's discovery that somatic symptoms are frequently related to phobias and other forms of anxiety is no news at all to behavioristically-oriented therapists, who routinely probe the day-to-day reactions of their patients, relating them to each other and to their causal antecedents—a process known as "behavior analysis." The antecedents of any reaction (normal or neurotic) consist of various combinations of external stimuli and intraorgasmic events (notably images and autonomic responses). In behavior therapy the function of the analysis is to obtain the clearest possible specification of the patterns and chains of antecedents of a neurotic reaction. These analyses have consistently shown that neurotic somatic symptoms have anxiety responses as antecedents (see, for example, Wolpe, 1958, p. 148).

What comes into focus here is the basic issue of the validity of the psychoanalytic theory of neurosis. Although this is unquestioningly accepted by Dr. Sperling, it is a fact that the theory has not to date been shown to stand up to scientific testing. It is very often impossible even to put psychoanalytic propositions to the test because of the lack of clear definition of terms, but in at least one instance a test has been carried out (Wolpe, 1961). Psychoanalytic theory holds that when neurotic symptoms have been removed, no lasting recovery can be expected as long as the putative repressed complexes remain repressed. Otherwise, it is said, there will sooner or later be relapse or symptom substitution. Follow-ups of several years' duration on neurotic cases successfully treated by behavior therapy (e.g. Wolpe, 1958) do not reveal relapses and symptom substitutions. This finding makes the assumed causal role of the repressed complexes very dubious indeed.

The frequent failure of even the most skillful psychoanalytic interventions to produce clinical change points to the same conclusion. A case in point is surely Dr. Sperling's Mrs. A. Her lengthy analysis was clearly conducted with the utmost dedication and accomplishment, yet when she broke it off there was not, it appears, any significant change. The relevance of the analysis to the illness was not upheld by the course of the case. It is perhaps because this happens so commonly that most psychoanalytic case reports say little or nothing about outcome, and tend to concentrate on elaborations of "dynamics."

VICTOR CALEF, M.D.

San Francisco, California

The alternation of psychological symptoms with psychosomatic ones has long and frequently been noted. However, as Dr. Sperling suggests, little has been done to detail the metapsychological determinants which permit the symptoms to substitute for one another under certain circumstances and to coexist under others. The commonly accepted idea that each may serve as a defense or screen to hide the other is a generalization which is descriptively and clinically valid but which has limited, if any, theoretical or pragmatic value. It may perhaps be more misleading than correct.

Dr. Sperling calls on her clinical experience in the analysis of psychosomatic symptoms and phobias, noting the alternation of symptoms, their apparent substitutive, defensive functions, and their occasional coexistence, and she finds an explanation in the pregenital fixations of patients who have hidden "phobias" screened by somatic symptoms (for example, colitis). Traumata in the anal-sadistic phase of development, Dr. Sperling believes, account for both the somatic symptoms and the "phobias." She finds similar (unconscious) meaning in both sets of symptoms, and implies that both are resolved by interpretation.

It is significant when a clinician of Dr. Sperling's experience and competence describes and explains a certain group of clinical occurrences. In this instance in particular it is not only a matter of the clinical phenomena of certain disease processes and their explanation; Dr. Sperling also clearly implies that patients with severe somatic ills respond favorably with remarkable consistency to analytic interpretation by a competent analyst. Many of the patients Dr. Sperling refers to are not only severely ill, but have also failed to respond to the previous administrations of other physicians (including other analysts). One of the inferences which I draw from my reading of Dr. Sperling's paper is that if the psychoanalytic practitioner would apply his tool properly he would be rewarded by equally excellent therapeutic results and find the same psychodynamic explanations as does Dr. Sperling.

Would that it were so simple. Though I have no statistical data available, I have the impression that few analysts have duplicated or can duplicate Dr. Sperling's therapeutic successes with the kinds of cases she describes. I say this not to cast doubt on Dr. Sperling's therapeutic triumphs or upon her theoretical explanations. (I have said that it is significant when an experienced analyst reports certain experiences, by which I mean to imply that there probably is a high degree of validity to her report.) Rather, I bemoan the fact that from the report of these remarkable experiences so little can be learned by those of us who cannot claim the same success with the analysis of psychosomatic states. The reason for this, in my opinion, is simply the way the report has been rendered. To describe the case histories and the therapeutic work with patients in the language of metapsychological deductions (which simultaneously announces the unconscious meaning of the symptomatology) does not help to clarify our understanding of the case material or the technique of therapy. Dr. Sperling's accounts seem to be composed of just such a psychoanalytic shorthand, which simply fails to illustrate the therapeutic technique and the unveiling of the explanatory reconstructions. The reader therefore has to supply his own clinical experiences and theoretical explanations in order to evaluate the work reported. This exercise, however, has produced some thoughts, which I would like to discuss briefly.

There is first of all a diagnostic issue which cannot be avoided because it is a crucial one, though it may appear to be quibbling. There is considerable doubt whether "phobia" is a correct designation for many of the symptoms which Dr. Sperling designates as such. Many analytic authors (including the first one) recognized that certain symptoms, although expressed by patients as fears or "phobias," were not directly and dynamically related to the hysterical fears which are usually called phobias. The former fears were recognized as belonging to the obsessional neuroses, since they had their genetic origin in the anal-sadistic phase of development and were constructed out of dynamic forces similar to obsessional ideas. A close look at the symptoms reported by Dr. Sperling suggests that many of them are obsessional ideas rather than hysterical phobias, and that some of them border on food fetish and/or somatic delusion. If this be so, and I suggest that it is, then it is no great surprise that Dr. Sperling found in her cases so many pregenital components in the psychosomatic states. They are not, correctly speaking, hysterical phobias in the classical sense.

From a purely clinical point of view there is little doubt, nevertheless, that Dr. Sperling is correct about a number of things, including the alternation and coexistence of sets of symptoms. For example, there is little doubt that the clinical pictures she describes derive from certain pregenital fixations which give the symptoms their specific coloration. There is also little doubt, I think, that a central issue in psychosomatic ills is the need to "control," manifested in numerous and interesting ways. However, a comparison of my own experiences with those reported by Dr. Sperling suggests that the issues are more complex. The patients I have known who have suffered from psychosomatic symptoms have demonstrated what I sometimes believed to be an illusion of control which bordered on delusion. The "delusion" was not simply that of believing in and wishing for control, or acting as if in control of themselves, their sphincters, and other people; some seemed to have the magical belief (unconscious, to be sure) that they could control somatic processes which are under the control of the autonomic nervous system. Moreover, my patients seemed to develop their somatic responses at those times when the magical illusion of control was shattered by events beyond their control. Their symptoms did not seem to respond to interpretations. At times there did appear a recession of the symptoms when, by magical means, their illusion of control was restored through some internal or external event—sometimes from the belief that the therapist could and would restore the controls for them. It is just such impressions, arising out of a few experiences and very difficult to record and substantiate, which compel me to express the wish that Dr. Sperling could have described her therapeutic work with the patients in greater detail, rather than simply telling us that "phobias" have pregenital determinants.

From a purely theoretical point of view we should no longer be surprised to find pregenital and genital meaning in symptomatology; we have many explanatory concepts for this phenomenon. It is not simply the concept of multiple determination which makes us comfortable with the coexistence of preoedipal and oedipal determinants of clinical symptoms. Freud's last concept of anxiety as a continuum (from birth) should make the dichotomy of pregenital versus genital in symptom formation unnecessary. Moreover, clinically we see symptoms whose meaning vacillates, since at times they reflect elements from the point of arrest and at times from the point of fixation (though it is also true that some symptoms will contain elements of both). The issue then is not whether a symptom is determined by genital or pregenital traumata, or even whether symptoms have pregenital components, but rather whether the pregenital components offer an explanation for the phenomena under consideration. I would like to suggest that they do not, and that we need rather to look for an explanation in the fact that some egos seem to tolerate several stages of regression and various states of consciousness simultaneously, while other egos tolerate only limited regressions and abhor alterations in the state of consciousness. When we discover what the differences are between such egos we will be closer to a discovery of why certain symptoms alternate in some people and sometimes coexist in others. I think the issue remains unresolved.

GEORGE H. POLLOCK, M.D., PH.D.
Chicago, Illinois

Dr. Melitta Sperling, a pioneer in the psychoanalytic study of somatic dysfunctions, raises questions in her presentation that are of great significance. Since a discussion that is only laudatory is not necessarily useful, my comments will deal with questions and issues that may be profitably elaborated in her response.

Dr. Sperling again presents a theoretical thesis with clinical material to demonstrate its validity. Essentially, her study is broadly related to the mind-body problem. Even when we consider the many possible multiple determinants we are still grappling with the "black box" problem—we can discover significant antecedents; we can effect change through psychoanalytic means; we can determine outcome; but we do not as yet know what has gone on in the intermediate stage to produce the clinical result.

Many levels may contribute to the resultant phobia. Dr. Sperling asserts that somatic symptoms may camouflage a severe phobia, but the somatic symptoms may be more than defensive manifestations: they may be expressions of a severely regressed state, they may be manifestations of a fragmented self-organization, or they may be independent though concomitant features of the phobic state.

Dr. Sperling's patients present severe psychopathology. Their fixation points may reflect pathogenic traumatic resultants stemming from early difficulties in the self-system, in impulse control, and in object relations. In some of her clinical data, there is a suggestion of pathological persistent symbiosis, and this may relate to the severe separation anxiety seen in the cases described.

There are different meanings to phobias, just as phobias may be expressive of intrapsychic pathology stemming from different developmental levels of fixation and arrest of development, e.g., the circumscribed phobia of Little Hans differs from the more massive agoraphobia. Phobia is but a descriptive term applied to the patient's difficulty; in and of itself it is not an indication of a specific lesion. Only through analytic work do we discover the true pathology and the underlying meanings of the overt manifestations of the illness. The patients described by Dr. Sperling are more severely disturbed than those whose personality structure is more integrated and cohesive; I would therefore question the universality of her formulation that "the conflict over control and the fear of loss of control is a most prominent feature in phobia. . . . The fixation and regression to the anal-sadistic phase explains and clarifies many problematic issues in phobia." I agree, but would add the modifier "in some phobias."

What do somatic symptoms mean? Can they not refer to different conflicts, different levels of regression and expression, or manifestations of hypochondriasis, conversion, fragmentation of self or body ego, or even secondary gain? Why should some phobias have accompanying somatic manifestations, while others do not? Is it not true that many events occur in the so-called anal stage—sphincter control, acquisition of verbal ability, locomotor control, ideation, fantasy, perceptual differentiation, to name a few? Which variables are crucial, which are correlational but without the same importance as others? These and many other questions follow from Dr. Sperling's significant paper.

There are phobias and phobias—some may be manifestations of severe psychopathology, whereas others may accompany "healthier pathology." Perhaps at our present stage of knowledge and experience we must present only tentative or provisional formulations. Searching for global theory may do a disservice to the discoverer whose contributions may be valid, though less than universal, explanations.

ALEX BLUMSTEIN, M.D.

Los Angeles, California

Dr. Sperling offers us her extensive and rich clinical observations as a basis for her dynamic formulations with regard to somatic symptomatology in phobia.

She states that fixation to the anal-sadistic phase also has implications for the vicissitudes of object relations in her cases. My attention is drawn to the comment about vicissitudes of object relationships, since I believe this may be fundamental to understanding her excellent therapeutic results.

Mahler (1972) states as a "Freudian tenet . . . that object relationship" is the most reliable single factor by which we are able to determine the level of mental health on one hand and, on the other, the extent of the therapeutic potential.

Dr. Sperling seems to establish increased awareness of self- and object representation, particularly when she works with mother and child. She writes of a "fuller understanding" in the mother-child relationship. I would assume that Dr. Sperling's own clear image in the transference is basic to that understanding.

It may well be that adequate sphincter control is related to separation of self- and object-images on a relatively constant, objective level. For example, Lisa's ulcerative colitis subsided when she became interested in other children and developed a life of her own.

A brief account of a patient with symptoms and phobias (agoraphobia and claustrophobia) might offer some basis for discussing one of the therapeutic aspects of Dr. Sperling's paper. The case is that of a young woman who lived with her mother and who could rarely leave her home or travel even a short distance. She feared losing bowel control before she got to a "safe" toilet. In the first part of her analysis she concentrated on her gastrointestinal distress and rarely spoke of her phobias. As the analysis progressed she had fantasies of losing her abdominal contents and replacing them with part objects of her mother and of me. These fantasies were related to another fantasy of being alone, as a small child, helpless in a forest. The forest was seen in dreams and associations as a symbol for her mother and later for her analytic work with me. She was profoundly fused with her mother, and at times she would look in a mirror and see her mother's face, rather than her own. This neither shocked, confused, nor comforted her in her conscious processes. In the transference she struggled to see herself as separate from me. After establishing her separate self-image, and after working through some of her symbiotic structuring, she began to express affects related to her psychosexual drives in the transference. Her gastrointestinal symptoms subsided and her agoraphobia and claustrophobia were reduced sufficiently so that she could go on an ocean voyage. She suffered some discomfort, which diminished on subsequent trips. Her fear of losing bowel control did not recur.

It seemed that her self-image became linked to the neutralized energy of her ego, and so to her own sphincter control. Previously there had been an unconscious confusion as to who was in control of her anal sphincter.

Dr. Hanna Segal (1954) states that the formation of a phobia averts catastrophic situations. The patient projects her fantasies (including objects) and finds them in definite external situations which she is then able to avoid.

Dr. Wangh (1959), in discussing the structure of phobias, lists as one decisive element in his patient the impairment of the ego function over drives because of the patient's failure to solve the earliest ambivalence conflict by means of a stable identification. I assume that "stable identification" would include neutralized energy and relatively constant self- and object-images which would contribute to sphincter control.

It would be valuable to know Dr. Sperling's views on the need for separating self- and object-images in the transference as a factor in the establishing of sphincter control in various parts of the body, and what relationship, if any, this has to alternations between somatic symptoms and phobias.

Author's Response

Editor's Note: We received the following letter dated September 23, 1973 from Dr. Otto E. Sperling: "My wife read the discussions with great interest and was glad to see there was so much agreement with her point of view. But to do justice to the discussants by answering individually would be impossible for her because she is very ill and in the hospital. Please thank the discussants for their valuable contributions. . . ."

REFERENCES

Abraham, K. (1913), On the psychogenesis of agoraphobia in children. *Clinical Papers and Essays on Psycho-Analysis*. New York: Basic Books, 1955.

Deutsch, H. (1929), The genesis of agoraphobia. *Internat. J. Psycho-Anal.*, 10:51-69.

Freud, S. (1909), Analysis of a phobia of a five-year-old boy. *Standard Edition*, 10:5-149. London: Hogarth Press, 1955.

Mahler, M. (1972), On the first three subphases of the separation-individuation process. *Internat. J. Psycho-Anal.*, 53:333-338.

Segal, H. (1954), A note on schizoid mechanisms underlying phobia formation. *Internat. J. Psycho-Anal.*, 35:238-241.

Sperling, M. (1946), Psychoanalytic study of ulcerative colitis in children. *Psychoanal. Quart.*, 15:302-329.

———— (1948), Diarrhea: A specific somatic equivalent of an unconscious emotional conflict. *Psychosom. Med.*, 10:331.

———— (1949a), Analysis of a case of recurrent ulcer of the leg. *The Psychoanalytic Study of the Child*, 34:391-408. New York: International Universities Press.

———— (1949b), Neurotic sleep disturbances in children. *Nerv. Child*, 8:28-46.

———— (1949c), The role of the mother in psychosomatic disorders in children. *Psychosom. Med.*, 11:377.

———— (1950a), Children's interpretation and reaction to the unconscious of their mothers. *Internat. J. Psycho-Anal.*, 31:1-6.

———— (1950b), Mucous colitis associated with phobias. *Psychoanal. Quart.*, 19:318-326.

———— (1951), The neurotic child and his mother. *Amer. J. Orthopsychiat.*, 21:351-364.

———— (1952a), Animal phobias in a two-year-old child. *The Psychoanalytic Study of the Child*, 7:115-125. New York: International Universities Press.

———— (1952b), Psychogenic diarrhea and phobia in a six-and-a-half-year-old girl. *Amer. J. Orthopsychiat.*, 22:838-848.

———— (1954), Psychosomatic medicine and pediatrics. In: *Recent Developments in Psychosomatic Medicine*, ed. R. Cleghorn and E. Wittkower. London: Pitman, pp. 381-396.

———— (1955a), Observations from the treatment of children suffering from nonbloody diarrhea or mucous colitis. *J. Hillside Hosp.*, 4:25-31.

———— (1955b), Psychosis and psychosomatic illness. *Internat. J. Psycho-Anal.*, 36:1-8.

———— (1958), Pavor Nocturnus. *J. Amer. Psychoanal. Assn.*, 6:79-94.

———— (1959a), Equivalents of depression in children. *J. Hillside Hosp.*, 8:138-148.

———— (1959b), A study of deviate sexual behavior in children by the method of simultaneous analysis of mother and child. In: *Dynamic Psychopathology in Childhood*, ed. L. Jessner & E. Pavenstedt. New York: Grune & Stratton, pp. 221-242.

———— (1961), Analytic first aid in school phobias. *Psychoanal. Quart.*, 30:504-518.

——— (1963), A psychoanalytic study of bronchial asthma in children. In: *The Asthmatic Child*, ed. H. I. Schneer. New York: Harper & Row, pp. 138-165.

——— (1967), School phobias: classification, dynamics and treatment. *The Psychoanalytic Study of the Child*, 2:375-401. New York: International Universities Press.

——— (1968), Acting out behaviour and psychosomatic symptoms: Clinical and theoretical aspects. *Internat. J. Psycho-Anal.*, 49:250-253.

Wangh, M. (1959), Structural determinants of phobia. *J. Amer. Psychoanal. Assn.*, 7:675-695.

Weiss, E. (1966), The psychodynamic formulation of agoraphobia. *The Psychoanalytic Forum*, 1:378-386. New York: International Universities Press.

Wolpe, J. (1958), *Psychotherapy by Reciprocal Inhibition*. Stanford: Stanford University Press.

——— (1961), The prognosis in unpsychoanalysed recovery from neurosis. *Amer. J. Psychiat.*, 118:35-39.

Delusion and Artistic Creativity: Some Reflections on Reading William Golding's The Spire

HANNA SEGAL, M.B., CH.B., F.R.C. PSYCH.

Dr. Segal is a Member of the British Psychoanalytic Society. She is the author of *Introduction to the Work of Melanie Klein*, as well as of numerous papers on the theory and technique of psychoanalysis. Her two main papers on applied analysis are "A Psychoanalytic Contribution to Aesthetics" and "Notes on Symbol Formation," both of which appeared in the *International Journal of Psycho-Analysis*.

Discussants

JOHN A. LINDON, M.D.

Dr. Lindon is Supervising and Training Analyst, Southern California Psychoanalytic Institute; Associate Clinical Professor of Psychiatry, University of California, Los Angeles; and President, the Psychiatric Research Foundation. For many years he has done research in, lectured on, and written about unconscious sources of creativity. Dr. Lindon has been Editor of *The Psychoanalytic Forum* since its inception.

JOHN A. P. MILLET, M.D.

Son of the well-known American artist, Dr. Millet's practice has been especially concerned with the problems of artists and musicians. For his graduation thesis from the New York Psychoanalytic Institute in 1935, he reported a dream forecasting the impending death of a brilliant artist. He has contributed to psychoanalytic therapy in his study of "unconscious paintings," and for the past several years has directed the Ruth M. Knight Counseling Service for students of the Manhattan School of Music in New York City. Dr. Millet is Honorary Consultant, Columbia Psychoanalytic Clinic for Training and Research.

MEYER A. ZELIGS, M.D.

A practicing analyst in San Francisco, Dr. Zeligs is the author of *Friendship and Fratricide: An Analysis of Whittaker Chambers and Alger Hiss*. During the past decade he has been an active participant in interdisciplinary colloquia dealing with the relation of psychoanalysis to history, drama, and jurisprudence.

First appeared in *Internat. Rev. Psychoanal.*, Vol. I. Published here with permission of the editor.

He recently participated in a panel on "The Methodology of Psychoanalytic Biography."

JAMES S. GROTSTEIN, M.D.

Assistant Clinical Professor of Psychiatry, University of California, Los Angeles, Dr. Grotstein is also Senior Instructor, Analyzing Instructor, and Supervising Instructor in the Los Angeles Psychoanalytic Institute, and Consultant on Schizophrenia for the National Institute of Mental Health. His primary professional interest is the psychoanalysis of psychosis.

JULIO ARAY, M.D.

Dr. Aray is a Direct Member of the International Psychoanalytic Association, a Founder Member of the Venezuelan Psychoanalytic Association, and Professor of the Venezuelan Institute of Psychoanalysis and of the The Instituto Psiquiatrico del Estel (El Peñón.) He is the author of the book *Abortion: A Psychoanalytic Study*, and as a correspondent member of many psychoanalytic and psychiatric journals has written extensively about mania, phobia, and other creative themes.

Delusion and Artistic Creativity: Some Reflections on Reading William Golding's The Spire

HANNA SEGAL, M.B., CH.B.

London, England

WHAT I AM GOING TO PRESENT has no pretensions to literary criticism, nor is it an attempt to "psychoanalyze" a book. Nor, through the book, its author. What I want to offer are some reflections which were stimulated by reading William Golding's book on a theme which has always fascinated me—the origin and nature of artistic endeavor.

The Spire is the story of the endeavor of Jocelin, Dean of the Cathedral, to build a 400-foot spire, as he had heard had been achieved overseas in France. Against the opposition of his Chapter, and in spite of many arguments that such a spire cannot be built because the church has no foundations and the structure no strength, he is certain that he will translate his vision into reality. He had been vouchsafed a vision which convinced him that he was chosen by God for this task, a conviction which is also nourished by the fact that he has had a miraculously rapid promotion in the church up to his present position. He is supported in his endeavors by an angel who "warms his back." Roger Mason is the only man capable of building such a spire, but he begins with doubt, and later becomes completely opposed to the plan. Jocelin must compel him to do the building.

Apart from Jocelin, there are four protagonists: Roger Mason; his wife, Rachel; Pangall, an old servant of the cathedral; and his beautiful young wife, Goody. Jocelin compares them to the four pillars of the cathedral: "My spire will stand on them as on the four pillars." Pangall is old and crippled,

Goody young and beautiful, and Jocelin's favorite—his "golden child." He had arranged her marriage to Pangall, but the marriage is sterile because, as becomes clear later, of Pangall's impotence. Roger Mason is the powerful builder, Rachel his earthy counterpart; but that marriage, too, is sterile, as Rachel later confesses to Jocelin, because she always laughs at the crucial moment.

When the novel opens, we are carried along by Jocelin's exultation: he is full of power and conviction about his mission; he radiates a godlike patronizing love, which includes his enemies as well as his friends. But right from the start one can feel the underlying anxiety and tension, and Jocelin's mood very quickly becomes irritable as his plans are opposed or his authority seems flouted.

He exults in his imagination of his cathedral. He contemplates the model:

> The model was like a man lying on his back. The nave was his legs placed together, the transepts on either side were his arms outspread. The choir was his body; and the Lady Chapel where now the services would be held, was his head. And now also, springing, projecting, bursting, erupting from the heart of the building, there was its crown and majesty, the new spire. They don't know, he thought, they can't know until I tell them of my vision!

Four portraits of Jocelin are to adorn the four faces of the spire.

From the beginning of the book, he meets with opposition from his Chapter, from Pangall, and from Roger Mason. Pangall accuses him of ruining and defiling the cathedral, built by Pangall's father and forefathers, and he also complains of the workmen's desecration of the cathedral and mockery of himself. Mason opposes the building of such a tall tower because, in his expert opinion, the structure of the cathedral has no strength to support it. But Jocelin ignores the Chapter's and Pangall's complaints, as well as Mason's realistic warnings. He has noticed Mason's interest in Goody and realizes that this gives him power to hold the man. Guiltily but exultantly, Jocelin thinks, "I've got him in a net."

The story of the building and final collapse of the spire is

marked by several climaxes which make the underlying symbolism of the story clearer. The first climax comes when
Roger Mason, having decided to dig to the foundation of the
cathedral to gauge its strength, opens up a pit; and slowly the
cathedral starts filling with the stench of the dead. There is no
foundation, and when the floors are removed the waters start
moving. And the earth creeps.

There is a dramatic moment when the foundations begin to
collapse. Pangall, as always, complains that he is the butt of
the workmen's mockery. Just before the waters start moving,
Jocelin gets a glimpse of the workmen chasing Pangall, one of
them holding the model of the cathedral between his legs,
with the spire "sticking out obscenely." He half-sees Pangall
being pushed about and later disappearing into the pit, and
also catches a glimpse of Goody, part naked, covered by her
flaming red hair. But he immediately represses the sight, is
unclear about what he has seen, and becomes confused. After
the opening of the pit Pangall disappears and Roger again
begs to be let go. But Jocelin is more convinced than ever of
his mission: if the cathedral has no foundations, that but
further confirms its miraculousness. He also realizes that with
Pangall's disappearance Roger is finally caught in the net. He
sees Roger and Goody "as in a tent."

From the moment of the opening of the pit, Jocelin's folly
becomes more apparent. His confusion increases. He spends
more and more time up on the tower, watching the building
of the spire. Somewhere on the tower Roger has his "swal-
low's nest," in which Goody visits him. Another climactic
moment occurs when Jocelin overhears their intercourse and
becomes acutely aware of his jealousy and his guilt.

Parallel to his angel, Jocelin has also his devil, and this
devil, which torments him with sexual feelings, attains more
power. He has a masturbatory fantasy in a state of semi-sleep,
waking up from which he realizes with horror his sexual
feelings toward Goody, as well as his homosexual feelings
toward the young sculptor who is engaged on his portrait. By
recurring and increasing hotness in his back he feels his angel
beginning to exhaust him, and at times the angel becomes

indistinguishable from the devil. He is occasionally threatened by the emergence of the memory of what he saw at the pit, but inevitably he represses it again and becomes more confused. The structure of the spire begins to collapse, and yet another climax is reached when Jocelin finds Goody in the throes of childbirth, her red hair and red blood fusing in his mind—a dramatic childbirth which leads to the death of Goody and the child. His guilt at what he has done to Goody and Roger begins to break through, but more than ever it is important to finish the spire, to justify such sacrifice: "This I have done for Him through love."

Roger, having nowhere else to go, now works gloomily on the spire, but things progressively deteriorate: the cathedral is deserted, the workmen take part in devil-worship, the countryside is desolate, and the pillars of the cathedral begin to sing. Jocelin pins his hopes on the Nail from the Cross that was promised to him by the bishop, but when the bishop comes and offers him the Nail, it is only incidental to his main business there—a Court of Enquiry into Jocelin's fitness to continue as Dean.

Simultaneously, Jocelin receives a visit from his aunt. She had been the mistress of the king, and it was largely her money that provided for the building of the spire. In exchange, she wanted to be buried in the cathedral. Jocelin manipulates for the money but refuses her request, as to him it would be defiling the cathedral. Now, however, she comes alarmed by reports about his health. The crucial moment in their conversation occurs when he says, "after I was chosen by God. . . ." And she laughs, saying, "Who chose you—God? *I* chose you," and she describes how, after a particularly happy love-making, because they were happy and wanted to spread their happiness, she and the king decided to elevate Jocelin to his post.

At that moment the basis of Jocelin's conviction is shaken: he has not been chosen by God but by this sinful, despised couple. A complete collapse now sets in: his doubts and guilt break through and illness breaks his spine. Crippled by illness, he crawls on all fours to Roger Mason to beg his forgiveness, but Roger, lying drunk and despairing in his digs, only curses him. In a semi-confused state, but with an awful clarity, Jocelin confesses that the pit, the cellarage, knew it all; it knew that he had made Goody marry Pangall because he knew of the man's impotence. He also knew of Pangall's murder at the pit.

Jocelin is brought home and nursed physically and mentally by Father Adam, whom he always called "Father Anonymous" because of his striking humility. And it is only then that he describes the details of his vision, in which the spire represented his prayer reaching Heaven; to which Father Anonymous replies sadly, horrified, "They never taught you to pray."

A synopsis is always very unsatisfactory. For those of you who know the book, it must seem a very thin account of the real thing. To those of you who have not read *The Spire*, it does not nearly convey the richness and complexity of the themes.

I have chosen only such elements of the narrative as will illustrate my own views of it. The cathedral obviously represents Jocelin himself. This is clear from his first seeing the model of the cathedral as a human body; and it is his own face that will adorn the spire. That the erect spire represents the penis and potency comes even clearer when the workman pursuing Pangall sticks the spire "obscenely between his legs."

The sexual fantasies involved in the building of the spire are both clear and complex. Heterosexually, the spire-penis is meant to reach Heaven-mother (after Goody's death, Jocelin has a fantasy of the spire reaching Goody in Heaven, and she is confused in his mind with the Virgin Mary). Seen homosexually, the spire is an offering to God the Father. Jocelin's relationship with God is experienced in quite physical terms. The angel that warms his back and later becomes indistinguishable from the devil is felt as a sexual penetration by God. Toward the end, when the angel and devil fuse, he feels that the angel "kicks him in the arse."

There is also a homosexual relation in which Jocelin does not submit to God or the angel, but *is* God to another man.

The sculptor who sculpts his face and follows him around is a dumb young man with a permanently open and humming mouth, and it is his face and mouth that get confused with Goody's genitals in Jocelin's masturbation fantasy. The spire, however, represents not only his potency, but his omnipotence. He represents it to himself as an offering to God, but it is clear throughout that it is his own penis-spire that is to dominate the landscape, reach Heaven, and stand forever an object of universal admiration.

This building—of his own self and his omnipotent potency—is done on the basis of the total destruction of his parents. He says himself, with anguish, "How many people at the moment are built into this cathedral!" His parents are represented by the two sterile couples, Pangall and Goody, Roger and Rachel; in the one couple the man is impotent; in the other, the woman.

As his plan develops he further destroys those couples, allowing for the murder of Pangall and Roger's unfaithfulness. As Roger tells him, the four pillars are hollow: they cannot support his spire. The hollow pillars are the hollow, sterile marriages, representing his fantasy of his parents' sexuality. But to build this spire he needs Roger's strength: to build his own potency he must reconstruct in his internal world a potent father and marriage; thus, he brings Roger and Goody together to form a couple.

This bringing together of the sexual parents is done, however, entirely under his control. They are in his "tent." He overcomes his extreme jealousy by acquiring control over their sexuality and gratifying his own desires by identification with them—by what is called, in psychoanalytical theory, projective identification. He puts his heterosexual feelings into Roger and uses him to possess Goody, and his feminine feelings into Goody, through whom he imprisons and entraps Roger. He gets his own sexual satisfaction, like a voyeur, through watching them, controlling them, and identifying with them. Their union results in a baby, but this is not allowed: the baby dies, killing Goody in the process, and Jocelin thinks that it is his sudden appearance in Goody's room which brought about that death. The sexual parents, manipulated by Jocelin, are not allowed to build a baby: they are only allowed to build Jocelin's spire.

Jocelin's building of the spire is the building of a delusion—the delusion that the parents never had potency or creativity. (The cellarage, as he calls it, of the cathedral contains nothing but dead bodies.) If the cathedral is Jocelin, the cellarage is his unconscious, containing nothing but a fantasy of dead bodies.

Wherever the signs of sexual potency are found they are destroyed anew, like Roger's and Goody's baby. Jocelin's aim is to be the only partner of both father and mother, and only his spire is allowed intercourse with either. It pretends to be an offering to God, but it is only an offering to his own power. I said that the cathedral represented Jocelin himself, but this is only partly true. In fact, the cathedral was there before him, as Pangall bitterly reminds him; it represents also the body of his mother and the potency of his father, which he ruthlessly destroys to create his own spire. The spire is supposed to be a completion of the cathedral, but in fact the cathedral is sacrificed to it. It represents a fantasy of taking over his mother's body and the sexual powers of his father to use them for his own needs, as he uses Roger and Goody.

This structure cannot be maintained, for reasons of guilt and of psychic and external reality. The basis of his structure is that there was no sex between the parents. When his aunt tells him how she and the king had chosen him, it represents to him the statement that he was not chosen by God but was born out of ordinary happy love-making between the sexual parents, as represented by the king and the aunt whom he condemns and despises. Confronted with this knowledge, he realizes that the whole foundation of his inner world, represented by the cathedral, was false. He has to admit that the sexual parents existed and that it is he in his own mind who has murdered them. The spire sways and threatens to collapse. Despair sets in, and the collapse of his omnipotent fantasy becomes the collapse of himself, as he had developed no other relation to his internal parents that he could turn to. "They never taught him to pray."

Described in that way, one could see the book as a case history of a manic delusion and its collapse. But, of course, a good novel is never merely a case history; it presents universal problems that can be seen from many angles. I think that in the author's mind the book was meant to illustrate problems of true and false faith, as exemplified by Jocelin and Father Anonymous. But it can also be seen as exposing the common roots of delusion and artistic creativity and the difference between them. Why was Jocelin's spire a delusion and not a great artistic creation? Is it accidental that it is going to collapse? What did Jocelin have in common with the artist, and in what way did he differ? Jocelin exclaims at one point, "There is no innocent work." Is the artist's work different from Jocelin's? I agree with Jocelin that there is no innocent work, and that the artist's work in particular has one of its roots in destructiveness.

Adrian Stokes, in his book, *The Invitation in Art*, emphasizes that at the beginning of every artistic creation is an act of aggression: the sculptor has to break and chip the stone, the painter and the writer feel that they defile the white canvas or paper with the first stroke of the brush or pen—and from that moment they feel committed to the restoration represented by completing the work of art.

In 1950, in a paper called "A Psychoanalytic Contribution to Aesthetics," I put forward the thesis that the artist's work is a way of working through the depressive position. The depressive position is a concept brought into psychoanalytical theory by Melanie Klein. According to her, at a certain time in its development the infant begins to relate to his mother and then to other people in his environment as to whole and separate persons, in contrast with an earlier stage wherein no such clear perception exists. Confronted with the wholeness and separateness of the parents, the infant, and later the child, experiences the impact of his own ambivalence toward them, in that he experiences separation, jealousy, and envy; he

— 399

hates them and in his mind attacks them. As at that early stage of development the infant feels his wishes and fantasies to be omnipotent, he feels that the parents thus attacked become fragmented and destroyed, and he introjects them as such into his internal world. This is one aspect of the infant's cellarage. But in that he also loves his parents and needs them, this destruction brings about feelings of mourning, loss, guilt, and a longing to undo the damage done and to restore in his mind the parents to their original state, a process which we call reparation. When the child becomes aware of parental intercourse and fertility, the reparation involves restoring to them in his mind their full sexual potency and fertility. It is in this situation, in the "cellarage," that the creative urges are rooted.

The artist in particular is concerned with the task of creating a whole new world as a means of symbolic restoration of his internal world and his internal parents. It is clear that the artist and the creator of the delusion are close to one another in the vividness of their experiencing the destruction of their whole inner world and of their need to create a complete world anew. The artist's compulsion to create may at times be as overriding and ruthless as Jocelin's. There is a beautiful description of this aspect of creativity in Patrick White's *The Vivisector*, in which the young painter's mother says to him: "You were born with a knife in your hand, or rather in your eyes."

The artist in his work, whatever his medium, creates an illusion, but at times it comes close to a delusion: his created world becomes very real to him, as in the famous story about Dumas, who rushed out of a room sobbing, "I have killed my Porthos," when he was describing the death of his hero. So both the artist and the person suffering from a delusion start with a common cellarage—the destruction of the parental couple in their fantasy and their internal world—and both have the overriding need to re-create a destroyed and lost structure.

Here, however, the similarity ends. Jocelin does not aim in his creation at restoring any objects: what he is creating is his picture of himself, including an omnipotent potency, at the expense of the parental figures. He seems to be serving God, but it is his spire, standing for a part of his own body, which is to reach heaven omnipotently. The artist, on the other hand, is concerned primarily with the restoration of his objects. Proust, for instance, says that the book, like memory, is "a vast graveyard where on most of the tombstones one can read no more the faded names." To him, writing the book is bringing this lost world of loved objects back to life: "I had to recapture from the shade that which I had felt, to re-convert it into its psychic equivalent, but the way to do it, the only one I could see, what was it but to create a work of art."

Jocelin has some awareness of where he went wrong in his creation when, toward the end of the book, he says, "But what is heaven if I can't reach it, holding them each by the hand?" He refers to Roger and Goody, destroyed by him and standing for his sexual parents, whom he had never restored in his internal reality. From this difference—restoring the object rather than the self—follow the crucial differences between the artist's and the psychotic's relation to his creation and the means which he employs. To begin with, the creative artistic process lessens the guilt of the original destructiveness by real creation. When the artist in Patrick White's book is asked why he painted a cruel portrait of his crippled sister, he answers: "I had my painterly reasons: these come first, of course. Then I think I wanted to make amends—in the only way I ever knew—for some of my enormities." This answer expresses both the original attack and the amends, as does the picture itself in its cruelty and its beauty. This aspect of attack and amends recurs constantly in *The Vivisector*. For instance, the painter's mistress dies in an accident, probably due to his cruelty, and for years after her features reappear in various forms in his work.

The delusion formation, on the other hand, perpetuates the guilt by repeating the crime—in Jocelin's case, in his repetitive destruction of the couple representing the sexual parents and the destruction of their child.

Also, in that the work of art primarily represents the object

—401

and not the self, the artist can visualize a separation between himself and the completed work. He can finish it and move on to the next one. Allowing the object to be separate once again is an important part of overcoming the depressive anxieties and completing the reparation. It enables the artist to have a certain objective detachment from his work and a critical attitude to it. He is never completely identified with it.

Very important consequences follow from this. Unlike Jocelin, the artist does not become confused: in allowing the object to become separate, he allows differentiation between his internal world and the external world, and he is therefore aware of what is fantasy and what is reality. In that way his work is not only not confused with him, it is also not identified nor confused with his fantasy objects. He can see it as a symbol, and as a symbol it can be used for communication.

To Jocelin, the cathedral and the spire are himself. The artist is aware that his creations symbolize aspects of his internal world: they are neither himself nor his internal objects. This awareness also enables the artist to have a reality sense. If the artist succeeds and Jocelin fails, it is because the artist, as we know, is a supreme artisan; he does not confuse his wishes and his fantasies with realities but has a realistic appreciation of his material, which Jocelin completely lacks. Where Jocelin relies on infantile omnipotence and magic, on the holy Nail from the Cross, the artist relies on his reality sense—and by that I mean reality sense in relation to his own psychic world. Where Jocelin aims at maintaining an unconscious delusion that he is the source of omnipotence, the artist seeks to restore an internal truth.

For example: Jocelin, in his view of himself as chosen by God, is as blind to his own nature and his inner realities as he is to the material realities of the cathedral. When he feels threatened by the emergence from repression of the memory of what happened at the pit, the murder of Pangall, he flees up the tower, where he recovers peace. His creation is an escape from realities, external and internal. The artist, on the other hand, is always in search of the psychic truth: he explores the world externally and, even more, internally, searching for the understanding of the cellarage, as Golding is doing in his book.

What is the difference between Jocelin and William Golding, who wrote *The Spire*? Jocelin must represent something of the author, in the sense in which Flaubert said, "*Madame Bovary, c'est moi.*" The cellarage, which represents Jocelin's unconscious, must be well known to the author, who can describe it with such feeling and depth. Yet Jocelin is clearly not all there is to his author: the author must have encompassed and overcome that part of himself represented by Jocelin and seen it fully related to all his objects, past and present. Jocelin is but one part of Golding—the cathedral as a whole and the novel as a whole, which represent the author's internal world and its conflicts. Mason, the artisan and potent man, in particular represents both a potent internal father and the potent part of the artist in the artisan. Father Anonymous represents the humility with which the artist views himself in relation to his task. Jocelin is wholly narcissistic; his creator is obviously aware of the reality of human relationships and capable of reintegrating what has been split and destroyed by the act of writing his book.

Where Jocelin's spire will soon collapse, William Golding's cathedral and spire stand complete, containing and bringing to life a whole new world in which we can become engrossed. But the theme which William Golding chose is itself significant: the collapse of a work of art is always a threat of which the artist is aware. And here Golding describes a particular threat which must be experienced by every artist. Artists are often accused of being narcissistic, which is a great misconception; but the particular kind of omnipotent narcissism represented by Jocelin must be a temptation that they probably always have to struggle with and overcome.

HANNA SEGAL

Discussion

JOHN A. LINDON, M.D.
Los Angeles, California

With the clarity we have come to expect of her, Dr. Segal has brilliantly summarized Golding's book *The Spire*, examined those elements which help demonstrate her psychoanalytic views, and considered the concepts of delusion versus artistic creativity.

In addition to what she has done in her paper, she has stimulated me to think and ponder *beyond* it; to wonder most seriously, Why does the artist *continue* to create? I will raise that question after I have commented on Dr. Segal's synopsis and interpretation, mainly limiting my discussion to points where I differ with her.

Near the end of her synopsis, after describing the death of Goody and the child, Dr. Segal says, "Roger, having nowhere else to go, now works gloomily on the spire. . . ." I wondered whether this did not represent Jocelin's omnipotent control over Roger through projective identification. Subsequently, as I read the book, I increasingly wondered, Why did this master builder go on—and on, and on—against his professional judgment, though it became evident and inevitable that disaster would follow? The more I asked these questions, the more the explanations given failed to satisfy. I will come back to this point.

Later in her synopsis, Dr. Segal describes how Jocelin's conviction is shaken, and how, crippled by illness, "he crawls on all fours to Roger Mason to beg his forgiveness. . . ."

I don't believe Jocelin goes to Roger Mason to genuinely beg his forgiveness; I think that Golding, with his novelist's intuition, intends a deeper meaning, in that the illness that breaks Jocelin's spine is "consumption," and in that Golding has Jocelin say to Roger Mason, the master builder he has destroyed:

404 —

> Once you said I was the devil himself. It isn't true, I am a fool. Also, I think—I'm a building with a vast cellarage where the rats live; there is some kind of blight on my hands. I injure everyone I touch, particularly those I love. Now I have come in pain and in shame, to ask you to forgive me.

A brilliant description of a consuming envy.

But a moment later, Jocelin tells Mason that there is still something Mason can do. Mason, hoarse with anger, replies, "That was what you came for, wasn't it Jocelin? An eye for an eye, a tooth for a tooth. If I don't—you'll tell" (about Mason's affair with Goody). Jocelin is genuinely horrified and tries to retract what he said. In terror he reports, "Something made me say it, something out of my control." Even his attempt to ask forgiveness breaks down, and the delusional attempt to control and manipulate seizes power.

Another quote from the book to show Golding's deep insights, which I believe call for a different emphasis than Dr. Segal's: After Jocelin has described the details of his vision in which the spire represented his prayer reaching heaven, Father Adam asks in astonishment, "But was this all?"

> More light came from the window, as Father Adam moved away **from** it. Now he was close and his next question made no sense, "When you hear things do you see them?"

Obviously Adam suspects that Jocelin is hallucinating. Jocelin then answers, "What does it matter," and Father Adam replies, "They taught you nothing? All those years ago?"

Then follows a conspicuous and creative ambiguity; I must have read this passage a dozen times before I understood that the ambiguity was intentional: Adam or Jocelin—we don't know which—says "You heard her. You know how it was." The other replies, "It were better a millstone were tied about their necks."

This blaming the aunt and the king leads to an important insight: "Oh no, he thought. That's too simple, like every other explanation. That gets nowhere near the root." And still the reader is not sure whose insight it is. Golding leads us to hope it is Jocelin's, because the next quote has Father Adam speaking now in open astonishment: "They never taught you to pray!"

I believe that a profound working through is occurring here in the dying Jocelin, and that the author deliberately leaves it ambiguous so as to stir this hope in us: to say "they never taught you to pray!" is yet projecting one's own responsibility onto the "*they*," but Jocelin does not give in to this; instead he accepts the responsibility for his actions.

Then for the first time Jocelin gives up his omnipotence and cries out to Adam, "Help me!" And with this cry Jocelin is able to come in touch with his grief.

Then Adam says: ". . . once you knew about prayer and all its stages; but you have forgotten. . . ." Here Adam—and the readers—recognize what Jocelin has worked through: it was not that "*they*" had failed to teach Jocelin, but that it was Jocelin the priest who in his sinful hubris had discarded prayer.

Now I wish to examine the second part of Dr. Segal's paper, again keeping in mind (1) the origin and nature of the artistic endeavor, and (2) the question, why does the artist *continue* to create?

Dr. Segal says, "but to build this spire he needs Roger's strength: to build his own potency he must reconstruct in his internal world a potent father and marriage; thus, he brings Roger and Goody together to form a couple. . . ." I question this interpretation. I think Jocelin's aim is still *not* to have a potent father and marriage, *nor* a couple, but to use Goody as a means of controlling Roger; i.e., there is no real attempt to reconstruct a potent father and marriage but rather that it is further delusional omnipotent control.

Another point: Dr. Segal says, "The sexual parents, manipulated by Jocelin, are not allowed to build a baby: they are only allowed to build Jocelin's spire," and "Jocelin's aim is to be the only partner of both father and mother. . . ." But is this his aim? Wouldn't this be a healthier thing than what seems to be the case: that Jocelin cannot acknowledge either father or mother as good objects, for his envy is stirred and he destroys them.

Dr. Segal says, "The spire is supposed to be a completion of the cathedral, but in fact the cathedral is sacrificed to it. It represents a fantasy of taking over his mother's body and the sexual powers of his father to use them for his own needs, as he uses Roger and Goody." But isn't Jocelin even more pathological than this? Isn't it that he is driven to destroy what he wants, that the very act of acknowledging that he wants mother's body and wants father's sexual powers, those very desires stir the mad envy in the poor man?

Dr. Segal interprets: "When his aunt tells him how she and the king had chosen him, it represents to him the statement that he was not chosen by God but was born out of ordinary, happy love-making between the sexual parents, as represented by the king and the aunt whom he condemns and despises." In my opinion, the case is stronger than that. Let me quote from Golding, who has the aunt report to Jocelin that *she* chose him out of generosity when the king wanted to give her a gift. She tells how she and the king thought it such a joke to play on a novice. Golding has the aunt say to Jocelin, "Mind, I'll admit it wasn't just generosity." Then talking of her sister, Jocelin's mother, she says, "She was so, *so pious*, so dreary and she'd always—well it was *half* generosity, call it that, because she was like you, in a way, stubborn, insulting. . . ." Then the aunt thinks aloud, "I wonder if I was triumphing a little?"

I think this brings on Jocelin's complete collapse, for the despised aunt whom he treated with such contempt, control, and manic triumph turns out to have triumphed over him all along. His manic defenses crumble. The dread that the omnipotently controlled object will break free of the control and will retaliate had come true with its nightmarish terrors for Jocelin.

Now to the last part of Dr. Segal's paper, where she raises questions about the common roots of delusion and artistic creativity and the differences between them: "What did Jocelin have in common with the artist, and in what way did he differ?"

Quoting Adrian Stokes, she says, ". . . at the beginning of every artistic creation is an act of aggression . . . the painter and the writer feel that they defile the white canvas or paper with the first stroke of the brush or pen—and from that moment they feel committed to the restoration represented by completing the work of art."

I do not agree that just restoration is the aim of the creative artist. I don't think Dr. Segal does, either. If it were just a restoration, are not the painter and writer paralyzed artistically? Artists must do more than restore their objects, they must make more with their creativity than they had been before; otherwise there would be a clean sheet of paper which they would never touch. I agree with Dr. Segal that the artist in particular is concerned with the task of creating a whole new world as a means of symbolic restoration of his internal world and his internal parents, but in my view it is more than just restoring them: it is making them better.

I agree with Dr. Segal that "To begin with, the creative artistic process lessens the guilt of the original destructiveness by *real creation*." So much depends on whom the artist is dependent for the definition of what is a "real creation." The mature artist depends primarily on his own unconscious approval.

Contrasting Jocelin with the artist, Segal states: "The delusion formation, on the other hand, perpetuates the guilt by repeating the crime—in Jocelin's case, in his repetitive destruction of the couple representing the sexual parents and the destruction of their child." But is there that distinct a difference?

She continues: "Also, in that the work of art primarily represents the object and not the self, the artist can visualize a separation between himself and the completed work. He can finish it and move on to the next one." But *why* is there a next one?

In the last page of Dr. Segal's paper we come to some points which I hope will answer this and other questions I have raised. Segal asks what is the difference between Jocelin and William Golding, who wrote the book? She goes on to say how Jocelin must represent something of the author: "Jocelin is but one part of Golding—the cathedral as a whole and the novel as a whole, which represent the author's internal world and its conflicts. Mason, the artisan and potent man, in particular represents both a potent internal father and the potent part of the artist in the artisan."

Perhaps here we may find a clue as to why the artist continues to create, and to the question of whether there is much difference between delusion and artistic creativity. For the author of this book—and I am raising this as a question about all creative artists—in allowing Jocelin omnipotently to control, possess, use, and destroy Roger Mason, the master builder, acts out his own repetition compulsion—hopefully in an artistic way—of one of his own original destructive fantasies toward the good father.

Why is Roger Mason so helpless in Jocelin's hands? For example, why is he so consumed with guilt at his sexual intercourse with Goody, who is a beautiful widow and who, unlike Roger's wife, doesn't laugh at the wrong time? I think one can see here the repetition compulsion of attacking the parents for their sexual potency—near the end of the book Jocelin is even spoken of disparagingly as always being like an adolescent girl; the parental potency would thus arouse envy—but I believe the envy is more of their goodness and their creativity, as evidenced also in destroying their child.

Golding uses the term "master builder" with conspicuous frequency. In Ibsen's play *The Master Builder* the hero rises to high position by omnipotently exploiting everyone, particularly the good sons. He, too, has defied God. He, too, feels mysteriously driven to build a high tower which is the death of him.

The Spire can be seen as the impotent son (ironically called Father because of his priesthood) who omnipotently destroys the good father. For Dr. Segal to have compared the two works of art would have distracted from her main theme, but knowing her thoroughness I wonder if she didn't feel that Golding was artistically calling our attention to his tribute to Ibsen.

—409

In this context of creativity Golding himself achieves an artistic creation in *The Spire* which had the power to sweep me up in it, even though I came to it merely to study it. I think this book is an artistic creation, for, as in an absorbing performance of *Hamlet*, where we the audience are allowed a further working through in a carefully structured arena similar to a successful dream, Golding as a creative artist takes the responsibility for the bad parts of us. In a sense he is saying: "Trust me, it will be my dream; I'll bear the responsibility. And I'll do it in such a way that I won't make you feel *unduly* anxious or guilty or responsible."

Why then, if a work is done in such a way, with sufficient artistic creativity to meet with audience approval, and if the author knows he has done something good—why then isn't he happy? Or content? Why is it that almost every major writer in this country is a heavy drinker? (Putting aside all the other use of psychoactive drugs.) Why is it that no matter how wealthy he has become, how many honors he has received, the creative writer is *driven* to write more?

I believe it is because no matter what we the readers say, no matter how much *we* approve, the artist's unconscious knowledge that he has once again, in fantasy, destroyed the goodness and the true creativity of such fathers as Roger Mason drives him to further creative strivings.

Let me close with one last speculation: that the truly creative writer is engaged in an egodystonic occupation in his attempts to work through his unconscious conflicts. In other words, if he is successful in having it accepted as a creative work, the author has slipped it by his unconscious censor—for the moment. *But* unconsciously he *still* knows that he, the author, not his character, Jocelin, destroyed Roger Mason, the master builder. This stirs more unconscious guilt, which drives him to create again. His artistic creativity is both his gift and his curse. We lesser mortals, not having the gifts, are spared the curse.

JOHN A. P. MILLET, M.D.
New York, New York

In attempting a review of Hanna Segal's imaginative reflections I wish first to congratulate her on the title she chose. They are indeed reflections and not much more, except insofar as they reveal a certain orientation toward psychoanalytic theory that suggests a background of study in the tent of Melanie Klein.

While several analysts with literary interests, beginning with Freud himself, have attempted to psychoanalyze an author in absentia, the exercise cannot be said to contribute much to the development of an empirical science, even though it offers the literate analyst a delightful exercise in imaginative interpretations of the author's creations and personality.

Since I have not read the whole book I shall not attempt a sally into an untried field. Leaning upon the author's own abstract of the book, and fortified to some extent by selected readings in the original text, I find it hard to agree with Dr. Segal's basic thesis that the building of the spire symbolically represents the delusion that the parents never enjoyed sexual potency, and that in his plotting of the two couples Golding is reconstructing their images as devoid of the capacity for reproductive creativity. I am inclined to think that the author might consider these assumptions an assault on his artistic integrity. I would further surmise that the author himself has an intimate connection with those inner sources of literary creativity which supply him with the archetypal images of the characters in his book.

To me the psychological core of the book is Jocelin's delusional belief that he is charged with a task that he of all men has been chosen by God to perform—in other words, that Jocelin's original "infantile omnipotence" has maintained such a hold on him that the only way it could survive would be by direct command of the Almighty. In this way he

—411

could escape all assaults of the World, the Flesh, and the Devil. Discovery that his assignment to the task came from a source which ran counter to the requirements of his narcissistic hypothesis spelled the beginning of the inevitable end. There is in this story, laden as it is with all sorts of sexual symbolism, something of the quality of a Greek tragedy in which the hubris of the tragic hero sows the seeds of his ultimate destruction.

The writing is superb. Though knowing nothing of the author's personal history, one is tempted to assume that he is not a stranger to the contradictory passions which find their origin in the dynamic swell of creative force. The image of "the waters beginning to move" heralds the impending collapse of the delusional structure.

The "reality" of the artist is different in quality from that of the less sensitively organized members of the human family. His creations are unique to his particular imaginative perceptions. This is what makes the artist a source of wonder and awe to others in every age. His moral system, like his artistic creations, finds validity within the unique self-system, as does his orientation to those passions which lay claim to him. Small wonder then that what seems to the general public to savor of irrationality and illusions can only find empathy and acceptance within the artistic community.

Delusions as such can be the unhappy lot of artists and nonartists alike, and have little or no relationship to creative powers. So far as I can see, psychoanalytic interpretations of an artist's productions yield nothing to the enjoyment of the production itself, and can in no way be considered to have scientific value in the same sense as evidence supplied by direct communications with the artist himself.

MEYER A. ZELIGS, M.D.

San Francisco, California

As a preface to my discussion of Dr. Segal's reflections on *The Spire,* I should like first to make a few cautionary remarks on the methodological hazards of such endeavors. Literary criticism, in its many forms and intents, is beset with pitfalls, even deadfalls. Dr. Segal has presented her views with forthrightness and vigor. The ready use, however, of psychoanalytic concepts and interpretations and the ease with which such dialectical formulations find their way in our approaches to the study of creativity should be a matter of concern to psychoanalysts and literary critics alike. The prevalent use of neologisms such as "psychohistory," "psychobiography," "psychodrama," "psychosocial," "psychosexual," "psychopolitical," et al. attests to how widespread "psycho" jargon has become. Signals which formerly slowed scholars as they approached the conceptually hazardous interdisciplinary crossroads have given way to fast freeways connecting the unconscious way stations with all levels and forms of human endeavor, from artistic to political.

In a recent paper on methodological problems of applied psychoanalysis, the late Dr. Schmidl recalled how Freud first applied psychoanalytic concepts to problems lying outside the field of psychoanalysis proper. He cited Freud's restraint and modesty in such undertakings, in contrast to the boldness of his clinical interpretations. Indeed, Freud maintained a remarkable humility and humor about his contributions in this area. In one of his later prefaces to *Moses and Monotheism* he commented, "To my critical sense . . . this book appears like a dancer balancing on the tip of one toe."

Psychoanalytic interpretations or "reflections," no matter how brilliantly conceived, will remain mere speculations unless they are based on hard facts. Even "reflections" on a fictional work must be supported by an understanding of the mores and beliefs prevalent at the time in which the literary work was set. This is especially so in the case of Golding's narrative. *The Spire* is a classic "period piece" in which familiarity with the social, religious, and architectural setting is essential to understanding it. On the basis of these self-imposed criteria, I had no choice but to disqualify myself as a discussant of *The Spire*, since my own knowledge of fourteenth-century Catholicism in England was indeed sparse, and I knew even less about cathedrals or Gothic architecture during that period. And it came as no surprise to me that my first reading of *The Spire* was laborious and unrewarding. I had read *Lord of the Flies* years ago, but knew little else of Golding as person or author. *Lord of the Flies* was a thrilling story; I was eager now to read *The Spire*, but it proved too complex, too demanding, too difficult to comprehend on the first reading. It is a book which simply cannot be read cold. However, I had committed myself to the Editor of the *Psychoanalytic Forum* to write a brief discussion of Dr. Segal's paper. I settled down once again to Golding's condensed language. Despite its precision, beauty, and mastery of form, it was still not reducible to simple fact. Golding has been justly described as a "fiercely intelligent" novelist, who brings all his intellectual powers to bear in his fictional conceptions. I was saved by my wife's extensive knowledge of medieval English history and religion. She happily read through "The Spire" in two sittings, and our subsequent discussion of the book mobilized further readings and research on my part, after which I returned to Dr. Segal's "reflections."

In her opening statement, Dr. Segal emphasizes that her presentation is not an attempt to "psychoanalyze a book." The need to forewarn her readers at the outset with such a disclaimer was, I thought, rather paradoxical, for, after a short synopsis of the plot, she proceeded to deploy the heaviest psychoanalytic (Kleinian) artillery. Not unlike other clinicians who engage in literary criticism, Dr. Segal observed Jocelin, the book's main character, as though he were a patient under Kleinian analysis. Her statement that she chose "only such elements of the narrative as illustrate my own views of it" was tantamount to saying that her formulations of the psychodynamics of the story, especially of Jocelin's disturbed religiosity, lent themselves nicely to Kleinian interpretation. Dr. Segal, of course, has every right to select whatever material she sees fit and interpret it accordingly; I do not take issue with her on that score. Moreover, she is on firm ground in equating the cathedral with Jocelin himself, for this follows the author's description exactly. In *The Spire*, Jocelin views the model of the cathedral and the proposed spire as a human body and plans to have stone heads sculpted in his own image to adorn the completed spire. Golding's metaphoric use of the spire as the central theme in the novel is, obviously, not an original one; analogues ranging from the Bible's Tower of Babel to Melville's *The Bell Tower* and T. S. Eliot's church-building play, *The Rock,* are but a few examples, including of course the obvious influence of Ibsen's *The Master Builder.* Dr. Segal's reflections, though closely reasoned, lack an historical perspective and a literary frame of reference. She did not take cognizance of the author's own life and experiences or of documented sources which would have shed some interesting light on Golding's narrative. *The Spire* is a direct fictional representation of the Salisbury Cathedral, built in England in the fourteenth century. The edifice with its four-hundred-foot spire still stands, a wonder to behold in the eyes of tourists, for it leans twenty-three degrees from the perpendicular and, unlike Golding's mythical structure, is not expected to fall. According to one tradition, the first Bishop of Salisbury Cathedral chose, after the Virgin Mary appeared to him in a vision with appropriate instructions, a soggy meadow as the site for the construction. In *The Spire,* Dean Jocelin receives the inspiration for his spire in a vision from God. Furthermore, if a diagram were pieced together from the descriptive material in the novel, it would closely overlay a plan of the Salisbury Cathedral. It is a known fact that the author lived in Salisbury for twenty years, and that were it not for his seventeen years as a master in Bishop Wordsworth's school, under the shadow of the great spire in Salisbury, and the cathedral's carefully recorded and preserved chronicles, *there would be no novel.*[1]

Peremptorily, Dr. Segal extrapolates and highlights those elements in the narrative which depict sexuality, such as the "penis-spire" as representing Jocelin's potency and omnipotence. Dr. Segal celebrates and escalates the theme of phallic potency. With true Kleinian grit she goes on to elaborate

[1] I am indebted to Professors Oldsey and Weintraub, *The Art of William Golding,* for the above historical and biographical facts.

". . . this building of his own self and his omnipotent potency (sic!) . . . is done on the basis of the total destruction of his parents." These patricidal and matricidal fantasies about Jocelin's parents, to whom there is no reference in the story, were somehow extrapolated from Golding's lament, "How many people, at the moment, are built into this cathedral." Dr. Segal's interpretive spiral goes into still higher orbit as she divines that Jocelin, having murdered his "sexual parents," must make reparation by reconstructing a potent father and a marriage. And it is for this reason, continues Dr. Segal, that "he [Golding] brings Roger and Goody together to form a couple." Surely this must be an exploitation of the author's literary intent. Does Golding's having shaped the story so that its main object, the spire, was portrayed both as a physical fact in the external world and as a presence within the mind of the protagonist himself license such liberties?

In the title of her paper, "Delusion and Artistic Creativity," Dr. Segal leaves the reader confused about the relationship between Golding's motivation as an artist and Jocelin's, *not Golding's*, delusional anxiety. Though Jocelin's need was indeed to erect a spire, he, himself, was portrayed neither as an artistic nor a creative character. He was a not unusual fourteenth century clergyman, guilt-ridden by instinctual drives, deluded by his own fantasies of omnipotence and impelled to "get closer to heaven." Such a desire, not unusual in medieval religious characters, was one of the forces which shaped their religious architecture and was evident in their prayers. But what of Golding's artistic creativity? How does the spire reflect the author's own fantasies, and how does his mastery enable him, as a writer, to create such a deluded and agonized Jocelin? How, through the synthesis of such a character, does Golding sublimate his own inner conflicts? We simply do not have enough facts at hand about Golding's life to answer properly. Dr. Segal has properly distinguished between Golding's clarity as an author and Jocelin's confusion as a fictional character. She points out that the author thereby differentiates between fantasy and reality, that is, between his internal world and the external world. But how does this help

us to understand the dynamic relationship between Golding's creativity and Jocelin's delusions unless we know something *factual* about Golding's own life? And how can Dr. Segal summarily state that Jocelin is "one part of Golding" (what part?), "Mason . . . represents [Jocelin's] . . . potent internal father," when we know nothing about Golding's father? Dr. Segal nonetheless, under the banner of preconceived Kleinian assumptions, turns these reflections into convictions.

What I have said may seem a gratuitous polemic on Freudian and Kleinian psychoanalysis. This is certainly not the main purpose of these brief remarks. As scientific investigators, we continue our search for new data, and seek to refine our working models. Psychoanalytic assumption, clinical or applied, must be predicated on sufficiently hard fact to make it valid. The most common methodological failing in the exploration of artistic creativity is the overemphasis on process and psychodynamics at the expense of the aesthetic. This enshadows the "beautiful ambiguity" (Ernst Kris) of artistic creativity.

JAMES S. GROTSTEIN
Beverly Hills, California

In her paper, Dr. Segal discusses the conflict between artistic creativity and the delusional forces which oppose it as an illustration of the depressive position and the manic defenses which oppose and block its attainment. In her analysis of William Golding's *The Spire*, Dr. Segal makes interesting use of a highly compressed, updated morality play—a latter-day Pilgrim's Progress—which not only demonstrates her theme of the parallels between artistic creativity and reparation, but also illustrates the relationship of creativity to destructiveness.

I should like to emphasize first of all in support of Dr. Segal's theme, some technical considerations of Kleinian psychology which can be thought of as the ego psychology which emerges in the depressive position. I should like to discuss this

as a necessary prelude to a further elaboration of some thoughts on creativity which Dr. Segal's paper inspired in me.

The Kleinian emphasis on the importance of the sense of guilt is central to the attainment of the depressive position—which is another way of saying it is central to the achievement of the sense of ego integration, identity, separateness, and a permanent division between reality and fantasy. It is only through awareness and acceptance of one's sense of guilt in internal reality for fantasied damage to one's objects that one can achieve not only redemption in the moral sense, but also individuality and ego growth. This emphasis of the acceptance of guilt is in contrast to classical Freudian tendencies to analyze guilt in order to reduce it, as if guilt itself were abnormal and must be eliminated. But why is this true, that acceptance of guilt, rather than reduction of it, and ego integration are two sides of one coin? Let me attempt to explain.

Jocelin represents a latter-day Everyman who seeks to deny dependency on objects but is, rather, his own object and attempts to monumentalize his omnipotent self-worship by erecting the spire. The spire can be seen symbolically in a number of ways: as a manifestation of his potency, delusionally aggrandized; as a phallic object fused with the maternal cathedral; or as an omnipotent voyeur in infantile fantasy, thus obstructing parental intercourse; it can also represent the sterile and insane ambition to merge with the maternal and the paternal godhead, as amply shown in the story. It is delusional dogma masquerading as true faith.

In order to achieve this insane ambition, relationships are obliterated. The delusion of parthenogenesis omnipotently removes sex and causality from the parental prerogative and reality, and creates the self and its parents by its own ex cathedra will. Joselin's objects exist only to fulfill his own ambitions; they have no independent lives or enjoyment. In short, his hostile, contemptuous, manipulating, and controlling treatment of objects causes them to be internalized as spoiled, damaged, and apparently destroyed objects, thus filling his inner world (cellarage) with dead bodies.

What I wish to emphasize, however, in this part of my discussion is that these internalized dead bodies are of very great and decisive importance for the destiny of the ego. Not only do they menacingly haunt and undermine the ego's foundations with deadly identifications and, in turn, set up retaliating persecutory objects which further attack the ego and result in still more manic defenses to attack the attacking objects in turn, but they also imprison parts of the ego. This is the point of creativity which I wish to stress. The "dead bodies" are not merely former objects which have been damaged or destroyed by Jocelin's fantasied attacks prior to internalization; they are also the constellating, caretaking objects who contain the truth about reality. That aspect of Jocelyn which denies psychic reality has eliminated the awareness of reality relationships in his own psyche; in short, he has projected them into the objects outside his awareness, and has to keep attacking them there. He has to attack these objects because they know too much and because his *own painful self-awareness* is contained in them as well. They know he is a little baby who needs a mother and a father, and they in turn love him but do not need him; they need only each other, and they know moreover that he was the creation of their need for one another. These are all facts he cannot bear.

In other words, parts of the psyche appear to be lost through hostile projective identification into the parental objects, identified and fused with them, attacked, and then internalized as apparently dead bodies. And here I wish to emphasize that the acceptance and acknowledgment of guilt, with the resulting restoration of the objects through reparation, is of great importance, not only in restoring objects which can then be more beneficially identified with, but also in rescuing these lost parts of ego which have been buried as hostages in the objects and which are unavailable to the individual until they are rescued through reparation and restoration. I am stressing the *reparation via introjective recall of the projected identifications of the ego,* not just the restoration of the objects themselves, which are to be identified with now in a better way. Thus the acceptance of guilt means ego

—419

reclamation as well as the reinventorying of good objects for identification and mitigation of a persecutory superego.

I am reminded of having seen in Florence Michelangelo's *Captives*, those creations which had not yet been freed from the stone. I had a most uncanny feeling when I looked at the sculpture and simultaneously recalled learning how Michelangelo perceived his forms lying in wait within the marble and chipped away until he released them. I felt I could actually experience the undelivered, trapped torment of the captives forever imprisoned in marble, longing for release. It gave me a feeling of awe, not for the creative urge alone, but also for the sense of unborn purposeful form waiting to be discovered and experienced. As in Wordsworth's "Intimations of Immortality," it is as if there are infinitudes of unborn babies awaiting earthly assignment to be allowed to experience life. Thus the pain of creativity is parallel to the pain of potential creativity congested, withheld, and unreleased.

The sorting out and "reclamation" which takes place during the depressive position is analogous to the work of analysis as well as of artistic creativity. I think Dr. Segal is correct in asserting the importance of the destructive aspects of creativity via aggression. The momentum of the creative urge leads to the impact of one body against another. Pain is inevitable as the creative urge emerges from its mysterious haunts and dares to *be*, announcing to an unknown world, "I am." It is as if each creation must justify its existence to imagined opposition, and as if the creative artist serves as its advocate and sponsor. Here I can only allude to the phenomena of envy and the envious superego which *attack* the creativity of both creation and creator—and I am including the concept of internalized attacking parents. I am also emphasizing, at the same time, the concept of creativity as *separate* from the creator, something which is experienced as having an independent life, and which almost inadvertently descends upon him. The Greeks understood this very well and believed talents to be independent animating forces, as in the concept of the muses. It is as if the artist contains a gift. I feel this gift is a phenomenon beyond reparation, but attainable only through

reparation. We use the restored objects in order to transcend ourselves creatively. I can only mention here Bion's concept of the importance of separating the container and the contained.

Creativity is the ability to progress from infantile projective identification to externalization (Fairbairn), the former being magical, manipulative, possessive, and the latter being free and given over. In order to make this progression, the patient and/or the artist or the mother must hurdle the obstacle of ambivalence which guards the entrance to creativity. He can foster change and allow his creation to be separate and can release connection and let it be free and clear of all encumbrances. He can mourn.

Perhaps the greatest pain of creation is mourning, but there is a stage of creativity before actual creative delivery which mourning brings to mind: the reconstruction of the lost object and/or of the lost self in identification with it. It is a unique mystery how the apparently dead object becomes resurrected through reparative memory and through "naming" and assembling, not with photographic exactness, but with highlighted details of etched poignancy. I am reminded of the brilliant treatise by Ella Freeman Sharp in which she discussed the creativity of dream work, which must be mentioned at this point, if only, unfortunately, in passing.

The dream work is a rare artist, she stated. We restore our objects and selves in that special way which emphasizes a reclaimed and restored uniqueness beyond the power of the finest Ektachrome to reproduce. The ability to re-create the object involves more than just reparation of objects and resolution of splitting in the technical sense. I believe it involves also another important phenomenon, the capacity to symbolize, which Dr. Segal has brilliantly written about. The ability to symbolize an object is a way of allowing the external object its creative freedom while possessing a representation which can stand for it on the inside. This currency of memory, otherwise known as symbolization, is unique, and I feel not enough justice has been done to it in the literature.

—421

Symbolization, along with fantasy, as in dream work, makes use of the whole inventory of experiences with the object, with all the feelings and wishes and the like, and thus re-assembles and re-creates a very special symbol of that object which is sturdy and impervious in a way that words cannot do justice to. On the other hand, when externalized this symbol becomes the artistic creation. Finally, after the objects them-selves have been reclaimed and reforged in the smithy of reconstruction, they can be externalized in the form of artistic creation or mysteriously reassigned to a more benign amnesia and enter into the alchemic change of ego merging. Now they can be forgotten, or resurrected, the urgency and compulsion gone.

Kleinian analysis, from the standpoint of creativity, can be seen as a morality play characterized by a pageant of memory of unborn selves trapped inside the damaged objects, seeking both to be released and redressed, and opposed by the forces previously brought into play—known as the manic defenses, or the human condition gone awry.

I wish to thank Dr. Segal for her creative investigations of the subject and to ask her to accept my comments as appreci-ation of her work, trusting she knows my own spire owes a lot to her cathedral.

JULIO ARAY, M.D.

Caracas, Venezuela

I will focus my observations on one point that seems to me to be the key of the paper: the primal scene and its possible relationship to the creative processes.

Dr. Segal shows very clearly that Jocelin moves in a very primitive stage and that his Oedipus complex is obviously a pregenital one which corresponds to the Kleinian description of an early Oedipus complex with oral characteristics. Conse-quently, the primal scene, described in various ways by the author, is very primitive and traumatic. We can infer the transcendency of this persecutory conception in the omnipotent project of building up the spire, and also in the sterile couples.

Since the Wolf Man, the characteristics and varying contents of the primal scene have become familiar. One is the fantasy of being inside the womb, in order to contemplate the primal scene from there. This paper shows that Jocelin has a primal scene that makes him oscillate between an intrauterine regression (the cathedral's interior as the mother's interior) and a very persecutory postnatal situation corresponding to the paranoid-schizoid position of the Kleinian School.

Dr. Segal suggests that the creative processes could have arisen from the existence in the unconscious of a parental couple loving each other; and that the child, future adult creator, or artist identifies himself with a creative primal scene wherein the internal parents, instead of destroying babies, make happy babies or repair those who have been destroyed.

The existence in Jocelin's inner reality of a traumatic primal scene could explain his castration anxieties as resulting from his exposure to its violence. The infertility of both couples could also represent a parental couple with whom Jocelin lives a life that sterilizes him and his creative processes. In this case, Goody and her son's death represent the primal mortal scene displaced to a mortal childbirth in which the internal parents kill the creative. The dead baby could be a personification of Jocelin's penis and of one of the maternal babies.

Roger's malediction, as interpreted by Dr. Segal, reminds us of Pelope's tirade against Laius (Oedipus' father): "I wish that you will never have a son, and if you happen to have one, I hope that he be his father's murderer and his mother's lover." As we know, Laius and Jocasta were sterile for many years before they conceived Oedipus, and this fact could throw some light on psychogenetic sterility as a psychosomatic disease and the sterility of the artistic process. So a new possibility of interpretation arises when, in Jocelin's Oedipus triangle, Father Anonymous appears as a repressed part. Is it possible that Anonymous represents an absent father? We have a striking example in Leonardo Da Vinci, who was an illegitimate son and who tended always not to finish his paintings. So the Anonymous Father, absent, could represent a castrated father who induces in Jocelin a castrated identification. Therefore, the small Jocelin's penis becomes, in the omnipotent fantasy, a tremendous penis, reappearing when the spire falls. Dr. Segal convincingly expresses the idea that the great penis, which will be admired by all, is a manic defense to conceal the psychotic breakdown, and that it is a psychotic idealization of the self.

In his regressive level, Jocelin is very confused (identified) because of the sterile parents. In his fantasy he sterilizes them in order to defend himself from a traumatic primal scene, and the inmost part of himself related to these internal objects. He *is* those sterile parents. In the manifest content, he feels that hate destroys the parents of the primal scene, but in his innermost self he is destroyed by the combined couple and loses the good internal objects (good parents—good breast). When he loses these objects he cannot transform this destruction and delirious incoherence into a creative artistic coherence. Thus, he presents himself in a final breakdown as an old, castrated person or as an impotent child, dead like Goody's baby. This dead child could be the result of a brutal primal scene where the penis is used as a lethal instrument against the mother's babies. Here Dr. Segal's paper reminds us of Joan Rivière's investigations into the negative therapeutic reaction in which the patients feel that their unconscious contains a cemetery full of corpses.

The theme of the mother's internal babies introduces us to Jocelin's jealous-envious attack. Why does he attack these brothers so violently? The existence of sexuality between the parents produces in Jocelin the vision of a brutal primal scene. If in the fantasy the parents are sterile and old, we would find a variant from the fixedness of the Wolf Man. That immobility represented the contrary; in the same way, we could think that the parental sterility is a powerful denial of intercourse, which is very threatening to the self because it can produce new children who displace the first child and tend to deprive him of parental protection.

424 —

I agree that artistic work is a way of working through the depressive position described by Melanie Klein. However, there are blind spots about this subject, as there are also about sublimation. We all know about the artistic creations of psychotics: some of them resemble works of genius. The investigations of the Kleinian School show that a psychotic is someone who has not overcome the depressive position and consequently moves in a very particular paranoid-schizoid position with specific defenses and anxieties. Probably we will need further investigation in order to understand fully these characteristics of psychotic artists. If Jocelin were a real person rather than a fictional one, we would ask: Why does Jocelin's omnipotent creative fantasy break down? I suggest that it is because Jocelin did not have good parents to help him overcome the paranoid-schizoid position and because the internalizations of these parents, especially the good breast of the mother, have been very persecutory. These parents would fail as Jocelin's auxiliary self; consequently, they would lead to only partial achievements or to breakdowns of the existent.

In summary, there are at least two types of primal scene, one destructive and one creative. The creative process could result from the existence of fertile internal parents. With this internal parental couple in a primary creative scene, the person would identify with the creative process. Initially, the creative process is manic-omnipotent. If more evolved aspects of the self contributed to it, the creation would emerge as a well-conceived child. Jocelin seems to remain in the initial manic process without later accomplishment. The ruin of a creative, artistic work could come about through a brutal primal scene—traumatic, sterilizing, and confusing. In this primal scene, the internal parents destroy one another and they also destroy the son, as Goody and the baby were destroyed, or as Jocelin is in his psychotic breakdown.

Author's Response

I was gratified and stimulated by the varied comments that the contributors made about my essay. I cannot, of course, answer all the points in detail, and shall confine myself to a few which struck me most.

Dr. Zeligs's approach to the subject, as he is well aware, is very different from mine. He accuses me of not taking into consideration "hard facts." Indeed to my surprise he confesses himself unable to derive aesthetic enjoyment from *The Spire* because of his lack of background knowledge. He assumes that "extensive knowledge of medieval English history and religion" is a prerequisite for such enjoyment. If this indeed were so, our aesthetic experience would be very impoverished indeed. We could not read Proust without knowing that it is a *roman à clef* and the details of French social life at the turn of the century. Nor could we be moved by Goya's "The Second of May" without having first studied the Napoleonic wars. I think Dr. Zeligs and I have different views on the very nature of aesthetic experience. Dr. Zeligs also misunderstands the kind of essay I proposed to write. If it were my intention to produce a piece of literary criticism, the derivation and recorded historical background of the book would no doubt have been very important. He also accuses me of not taking into account the autobiographical facts about Golding. Here again he mistakes my intention; if it had been to describe Mr. Golding's personal problems, no doubt autobiographical data would be of the utmost interest and I could have started, say, with his essay "The Ladder and the Tree," which is very relevant to the theme of *The Spire*. However, I do not find this approach very useful, and I think the autobiographical "hard facts" are usually not nearly hard enough, except in the case of a patient on the couch. What I aimed at is something quite different. It is my thesis—as I expounded it in my paper "A Psychoanalytic Contribution to Aesthetics"—that the work of art carries within it symbolically the story of its own creation and that the study of works of art, and perhaps in particular those concerned with the problems of creativity, such as *The Spire*, can throw some light on the process of creation. The "hard fact" I am studying is the book itself. Dr. Zeligs himself says that the spire in the book represents also "the spire in his mind," and this is the subject of my study.

Dr. Millet similarly has little use for my essay. He accuses me of treating Jocelin as though he were a patient on the couch. I do not think this is so, since in fact I treat Jocelin as *one aspect* of his creator's mind. Dr. Millet says that Jocelin is characterized by infantile omnipotence. I agree, but I examined this omnipotence in greater detail, for instance the particular delusional form it takes in relation to parental intercourse. Dr. Millet says that the study of the book can throw no light on the mind of the author, yet he admits that a writer who depicts a problem with such depth of feeling "is not a stranger" to it.

I regret that neither Dr. Zeligs nor Dr. Millet found anything of value in my approach, and shall turn now to the three other contributors, who implicitly share my view that the endeavor is at least worthwhile. Dr. Aray sees Jocelin as regressing to an intra-uterine situation; I prefer to see it as a massive projective identification into the mother's body. I think Jocelin's taking possession of the cathedral is much too violent, destructive, and sexual to be seen as a regression to a blissful intra-uterine state. Dr. Aray also sees Jocelin's dilemma in terms of the primal scene. I would agree with that if by primal scene he means the total relation to parental sexuality rather than a single incident. Dr. Aray speaks of creativity as resulting from an identification with the good, sexual, and fertile internal parents. I am not sure that I agree; put that way, it sounds too bland and conflict-free. I think it is more a knife-edge situation in which the parental figures are being destroyed and a constant battle is waged to restore them to a pristine state, the identification with the fertile parents being achieved only at moments of resolution in this gigantic conflict. This is perhaps a partial answer to the question of the art of the psychotic or of artists like Van Gogh who are intermittently psychotic. I think that the artist, through the work, temporarily emerges from the psychosis, and must achieve enough depressive organization to be able to encompass, organize, and finally externalize the psychotic internal situation in a work of art; at other times, he may sink back into the psychosis.

—427

Dr. Grotstein emphasizes the importance of the introjective recall of projective identifications. I agree with him completely, and find his reference to the Slaves of Michaelangelo very moving. Here it is not only the object that has to be freed from its imprisonment, but also parts of the self trapped in the object. Jocelin, for example, has no sex life of his own; in his voyeurism he is as much a prisoner of Goody and Roger as they are of him. Dr. Grotstein introduces another very important aspect of the problem when he speaks of the feeling that creativity goes beyond the self, that there is something that can only be reached through reparation but that transcends reparation. This is confirmed by artists' views of themselves as vessels of inspiration or as servants of the Muse. I think this feeling has to do with very important pre-depressive roots of creativity, with some perception of an ideal internal object. This can be regained only through regression but goes beyond it in the sense in which the internal object, liberated from projective identification, is not only the "whole object" of the depressive position, but also the regained ideal object. This is a point beautifully elaborated by Adrian Stokes in his book, *The Invitation in Art*.

It is Dr. Lindon's contribution that I find most challenging, because he shares most of my premises but comes to an almost opposite conclusion. To begin with, I do agree with Dr. Lindon that I seem to underplay envy in my description of Jocelin. He is right in contending that Jocelin does not ever want to bring his parents together except in order to destroy them. I also agree with him about the element of triumph and persecution emanating from the parents as represented by the aunt; the persecution by attacked internal objects is an unavoidable part of the collapse of the manic defenses. My thesis briefly is that Golding the author, unlike Jocelin, faces and overcomes his envy through the process of writing the book. Dr. Lindon contends that on the contrary the creation of a work of art may be the fulfillment of envy. He adduces basically two arguments: one, that the artist obviously does not merely re-create but always creates something "new and better"; and two, that artists experience mental anguish in relation to their work and feel compelled to go on creating as though each new act of creation evoked more gulit and hence more need to create. This is a tempting view, but I do not think I can agree with it. To take first the point of the artist creating something new, I think this is true of every act of internal reparation: an internal reality is re-created which bears little resemblance to any actual external situation, and in that sense is new. It is also new in that internal objects are given new life, thereby becoming not only restored past objects but new creations. There is also an element of identification with the internal creative parent making a new baby, so that restoring those internal parents and identifying with them does give rise to new "artistic babies." Dr. Lindon says "new and better"; that they are better I think is more doubtful. Often the artist experiences the standard he compares himself to—some internal view of the parental perfection—as one that he strives toward but never achieves. But why, Dr. Lindon asks, does the artist go on creating, and why is he such a mental wreck? To begin with, I do not completely subscribe to the "mental wreck" idea. One can think of such giants as Goethe, Cezanne, Renoir, Henry Moore, and many others who, far from burning themselves out in alcohol, drugs, or neurosis, continued growing and maturing until a very advanced age. I think the "mental wreck" artist is more likely to be found among those who founder at the mid-life crisis (as described by E. Jaques in his paper, "Death and the Mid-Life Crisis"). There is, however, no doubt that the artist does experience great mental conflict which I think he tries to answer and resolve in his work. "But why does he have to go on," Dr. Lindon asks. His answer is that the work of art represents envy triumphant, and therefore guilt, but many other answers are possible, one of them being that conflicts will continue and no resolution is ever final. Also, that the artist's aim may be unattainable. No work of art fulfills all that it is asked to fulfill; more always remains to be done. Picasso put it very simply: "No painting is ever finished, one must just know when to stop and then start a new one."

I have no doubt that artistic creation involves a great deal

—429

of rivalry and triumph which can also lead to guilt, but I think that the distinction has to be made between rivalry, which aims at making something "new and better," and envy, the aim of which is destruction and which destroys not only one's object but also one's own creativity.

Index